About this book

This unique collection of largely unpublished, in-depth case studies drawn from Latin America, Asia, Africa, Europe and North America aims to increase our understanding of the importance of women and gender relations in plant biodiversity management and conservation. It intends to provide a state-of-the-art overview of the concepts, relationships and contexts that help to explain the relatively hidden gender dimensions of people–plant relations.

The contributors come from a rich range of disciplines including ethnobotany, geography, agronomy, anthropology, plant breeding, nutrition, development economics and women's studies. They demonstrate how crucial women are to plant genetic resource management and conservation at household, village, and community levels; and how gender relations have a strong influence on the ways in which local people understand, manage, and conserve biodiversity. Continued access to plant biodiversity is crucial to rural women's status and welfare, and their motivations therefore are a principal driving force countering processes of genetic erosion.

The volume covers the following broad areas:

- Women, the domestic arena and plant conservation
- Gender relations, women's rights and plant management
- Gendered plant knowledge in science and society
- Plants, women's status and welfare
- Gender, biodiversity loss, and conservation.

The contributors highlight the gender biases evident in much contemporary scientific research, policy and development practice relating to biodiversity management. And they seek to contribute to a number of important debates, including the determinants of genetic erosion, the significance of gender in ethnobotanical knowledge systems, traditional intellectual property rights systems and women's entitlements therein, and ecofeminist and other debates about the nature of gender–environment relations.

Women & Plants

Gender Relations in
Biodiversity Management and Conservation

Edited by
Patricia L. Howard

Zed Books
LONDON & NEW YORK

in association with

**Deutsche Gesellschaft für
Technische Zusammenarbeit**

International Development
Research Centre

Centre de recherches pour le
développement international

Women and Plants was first published in 2003 by
Zed Books Ltd, 7 Cynthia Street, London N1 9JF, UK and
Room 400, 175 Fifth Avenue, New York, NY 10010, USA
www.zedbooks.demon.co.uk

in association with

Deutsche Gesellschaft für Technische Zusammenarbeit (GTZ),
P.O. Box 5180, D-65726 Eschborn, Germany

and

International Development and Research Centre (IDRC),
P. O. Box 8500, Ottawa, Ontario K1G 3H9, Canada

Cover designed by Lee Robinson/Ad Lib designs
Designed and set in 10/12 pt Berkeley Book
by Long House, Cumbria, UK
Printed and bound in Malaysia by Forum

Distributed in the USA exclusively by Palgrave, a division
of St. Martin's Press, LLC, 175 Fifth Avenue, New York 10010

A catalogue record for this book is available from the British Library
US CIP data is available from the Library of Congress

ISBN 1 84277 156 6 cased
ISBN 1 84277 157 4 limp

Contents

Tables

Figures

About the Contributors

Patricia L. Howard is a rural sociologist and Professor in Gender Studies in Agriculture and Rural Development at Wageningen University who has developed a knowledge base on gender and local plant genetic resource management worldwide.
CONTACT ADDRESS: Hollandseweg 1, 6706 KN Wageningen, the Netherlands. Email: <genag@telekabel.nl>

Linda Dick Bissonnette is an anthropologist and the Heritage Resources Associate for the California Department of Parks and Recreation in the Sierra Nevada foothills. Her career has included teaching, museum curation and cultural resources management.
CONTACT ADDRESS: PO Box 2014, Columbia, CA 95310, USA.

Ephrosine Daniggelis is an anthropologist and nutritionist working as an independent consultant in the area of humanitarian relief and community development. She has worked in the Himalayas (Nepal, Tibet), Indonesia, Western Samoa, Tajikistan and recently in Afghanistan.
CONTACT ADDRESS: PO Box 61201, Honolulu, HI 96839, USA.

Füsun Ertuğ is an ethno-archaeologist and ethnobotanist with a focus on useful plants of Turkey. She is a founding member of the Women's Library in Istanbul, and a member of several scientific institutions and NGOs.
CONTACT ADDRESS: Ridvan Pasa Sok. Refik Bey Apt. 13/14 Goztepe, Istanbul 81080, Turkey.

Allison Goebel is a sociologist and Assistant Professor in Women's Studies and Environmental Studies at Queen's University, whose research focuses on gender and land, agriculture and woodlands in Southern Africa.
CONTACT ADDRESS: Mackintosh-Corry Hall, Room D504, Queen's University, Kingston, Ontario, Canada K7L 3N6.

Laurie S. Z. Greenberg is a geographer specializing in research, business development and educational outreach in sustainable agriculture and food systems in Latin America and in the US.
CONTACT ADDRESS: 1225 Vilas Avenue, Madison, Wisconsin 53715, USA.

Shirley Hoffmann is a geographer specializing in indigenous peoples, Latin America and agriculture. She is a foreign service officer working in programme and project development for the US Agency for International Development, posted in Lima, Peru.
CONTACT ADDRESS: American Embassy-Lima, Unit 3760, APO AA 34031.
Email: <shoffmann@usaid.gov>

Janice Jiggins is an independent consultant and researcher, Gender Representative for the CGIAR Participatory Research and Gender Analysis Programme, and on the Board of the International Farming Systems Association. She has published widely on agricultural R&D, extension and farming systems research, and gender and development.
Email: <janice.jiggins@inter.nl.nt>

Brij Kothari is a specialist in education and Associate Professor at the Indian Institute of Management, Ahmedabad, India. He works on participatory approaches to local knowledge conservation and dissemination and, more recently, literacy, primary education, media and popular culture.
Email: <brij@iimahd.ernet.in>

Millicent Malaza is a sociologist who worked for the Ministry of Agriculture and Cooperatives in Swaziland for fourteen years. She is now a behavioural change consultant in HIV/AIDS and other health interventions in African societies.
CONTACT ADDRESS: 5425 85th Avenue #02, Lanham, Maryland 20706 USA.

Andrea Pieroni is an ethnobotanist and post-doctoral research assistant at the Centre for Pharmacognosy and Phytotherapy at the School of Pharmacy, University of London, UK. His research focuses on traditionally gathered wild food and medicinal plants in the Mediterranean.
Email: <andrea.pieroni@ulsop.ac.uk>

Lisa Leimar Price is an anthropologist and Associate Professor of Gender Studies at Wageningen University. She has conducted research throughout South-east Asia, specializing in biodiversity, natural resource management and ethno-ecology. She has done extensive research on wild plant foods among agriculturalists.
Email: <Lisa.Price@wur.nl>

Paul Sillitoe is an agricultural scientist and anthropologist and Head of the Anthropology Department at the University of Durham whose research focuses on

natural resources management, technology and development, particularly in the Pacific.
CONTACT ADDRESS: Anthropology Dept, 43 Old Elvet, Durham, DH1 3HN, UK.

Yiching Song is a specialist in Communications and Innovation Studies and currently a research fellow at the Centre of Chinese Agricultural Policy of the Chinese Academy of Science working on agricultural technology and sustainable development.
Email: <Yiching.Song@wur.nl> or <yiching@163bj.com>

Nancy Turner is an ethnobotanist and faculty member in the School of Environmental Studies, University of Victoria, British Colombia, Canada, whose research focuses on the ethnobotanical and environmental knowledge of the indigenous peoples of British Columbia.
CONTACT ADDRESS: PO Box 1700, University of Victoria, Victoria, British Columbia, Canada V8W 2Y2.

Margot Wilson is an anthropologist and Associate Professor in the Department of Anthropology at the University of Victoria. She researches medical anthropology, gender issues, culture change, modernization and development, women's work, student field schools and group dynamics.
CONTACT ADDRESS: PO Box 3050, Victoria, BC Canada V8W 3P5.

Stephen Wooten is an anthropologist and Assistant Professor of Anthropology and International Studies at the University of Oregon, whose research interests include agrarian change, political economy/ecology, social organization and expressive culture.
CONTACT ADDRESS: Department of Anthropology, University of Oregon, Eugene, Oregon 97403-1218 USA.

 # Preface

In the foreword to her seminal work *Women's Role in Economic Development* (1970), Esther Boserup announced her intention to show that there had been serious omissions when it came to understanding women's significance to 'development' and the effects of 'development' on women. *Women and Plants* has a similar purpose. It contains the first fruits of a multi-year effort to begin to answer a question posed to me in 1994 by José Esquinas Alcázar, the Secretary of the Commission on Genetic Resources of the Food and Agriculture Organization of the United Nations (FAO), when I worked at the FAO in Rome. He asked me what could be done to show just how important women are to plant biodiversity management and conservation world-wide. He was concerned that debates around 'Farmers Rights' to plant genetic resources were of great importance to women, and yet gender issues weren't being explicitly addressed. He recognized that historically women were the world's first farmers and plant domesticators and yet, in spite of Boserup's work and that of thousands of others who had generated evidence of women's primary role in farming and food production, they were still often not seen as farmers and plant domesticators in their own right.

It didn't take long to learn that it wasn't an easy task to demonstrate women's importance in plant biodiversity management and conservation, since the literature dealing with this topic is highly dispersed and fragmented. Women's management of plant biodiversity is often not broached in the 'women and agriculture' literature, and in any case goes far beyond the boundaries of agricultural production. The world's first compilation of papers on women and gender relations in biodiversity management was based on the proceedings of a conference held at Harvard University only in 1991, the year before the Earth Summit (Borkenhagen and Abramovitz 1991), and even then many of the papers didn't directly deal with biodiversity, reflecting the lacunae existing at that time.

Clearly there is a need to search out, compile and review existing research, and to assess the empirical and theoretical significance of women and gender relations for local plant biodiversity management and conservation systems across the globe, an agenda that I have been pursuing since joining Wageningen University in the Netherlands in 1995. The global purpose of the ongoing review is to provide a robust empirical basis and conceptual frameworks for researchers, policy makers, development practitioners and activists working in fields such as indigenous knowledge, plant biodiversity management and conservation, women and environment, and women and development. The review is helping to demonstrate that, to be effective, plant biodiversity research and conservation efforts must take into account women, gender relations, and the entire range of issues that come to the fore when the fullest possible account of human activity and culture is considered; and that such inclusivity becomes possible only when a gender perspective is explicitly incorporated.

This work is far from complete, but happily it is advanced enough to permit the publication of a range of case studies from across the globe that are based upon in-depth field research. This collection is the immediate successor to the first book to earnestly attempt to deal with the topic. *Gender Dimensions in Biodiversity Management*, edited by M.S. Swaminathan of the M.S. Swaminathan Foundation (1998), is based on case studies from India. Both books reflect the current need to provide a conceptual overview of the heretofore relatively hidden and unexplored gender dimensions of people-plant relations affecting use, rights, knowledge, management, conservation and erosion of plant biodiversity, as well as the significance of plant biodiversity management for women.

Some people might assume from our main title, *Women and Plants*, that this book focuses only on women and is therefore biased. But the secondary title, *Gender Relations in Biodiversity Management and Conservation*, clearly suggests to those who are familiar with the concept of 'gender relations' that men also figure prominently. This is because the relations that men and women establish between themselves everywhere determine what women in particular do with plants, how they do it, why, for whom, and with what consequences for their status and welfare. Further, men and women are two sides of the same coin, and gender relations determine as much how men relate to plants as how women relate to them. It is part of the task of this book to show how misconceptions about men and women, and about the importance of gender relations, have led to the relative invisibility of women in people–plant relationships; this is our justification for focusing on women, and women's work and knowledge. Of course, men and women's plant knowledge, management, and use aren't influenced *only* by gender relationships. People–plant relationships are dependent upon factors related to the local and global environment, ethnicity, culture, economy, history, class or caste position, and family and personal aptitudes, preferences and circumstances. Much of the best-known research (often carried out within the fields of ethnobotany, ethnobiology and ethnoecology, but as well broached by many other disciplines) intertwines this multitude of factors in order to understand people's relations with the plant world in specific contexts. What is often still missing in this work, however, is explicit attention to women or to gender relations.

A narrower although impressive and rapidly growing body of literature about people and plants can be termed 'gender aware' or 'gender sensitive' – it is mainly this literature that is under review. Some of it arises from gender or women's studies, and several of the case studies in this book are drawn from it (Dick Bissonnette, Goebel, Jiggins, Malaza, Price, Wilson and Wooten). These contributors explicitly set out to research women and gender relations, and the ways in which these influence people's relationships with plants, or the ways in which women's relations with plants influence their lives. Another body of 'gender sensitive' research stems from the work of scientists (especially ethnobotanists) who are primarily interested in people–plant relations, and who have discovered through their own experience that women are highly important, if not *the* most important, actors in these relationships. They repeatedly encounter women in the field and consider this fact to be important in itself for various reasons that they explore according to their field of expertise, research goals and personal perceptions (Daniggelis, Ertuğ, Greenberg, Hoffmann, Song, Sillitoe, Turner, Kothari and Pieroni). Dissatisfaction with the conceptual frameworks that guided their research at the outset led Kothari and Pieroni to generate critiques of gender bias in people–plant research, to which Turner has added her own concerns about bias in ethnobotanical and ethnographic research on indigenous peoples in her region.

The significance of the case studies presented in this volume goes beyond the illumination of gender relationships and the importance of women. The 'fullest possible account of human activity and culture' entails opening up the 'black box' of the household. Highlighting normative value and belief systems, and the domestic relationships and the non-monetary sphere of life that are entrusted mainly to women, brings to the fore certain dimensions of people–plant relationships that have received far too little attention to date. This includes, for example, the importance for people–plant relationships of:

- knowledge and production within the domestic sphere;
- household labour availability, use and organization;
- intra-household knowledge divisions and transmission;
- concepts of masculinity and feminity in cosmologies and value and belief systems;
- the social organization of indigenous systems of rights to and knowledge about plants; and
- the relationship between plant biodiversity, power and status within households and communities.

Access to a global body of knowledge on gender and plant biodiversity management and conservation is also essential in order to define parameters for policies and interventions. The relative importance of women as plant managers in different contexts has gone largely unrecognized, and the importance of gender relations in biodiversity management has been inadequately conceptualized and empirically substantiated. Further, the significance of gender relations in plant biodiversity management has cross-sectoral implications that need to be taken up not only in research and practice concerned with biodiversity conservation, but as well with regard to essential problems such as food security, health, poverty, agriculture, trade and technology development. Hamdallah Zedan, the Secretary to the Convention on Biological Diversity, recently highlighted the need to implement the Convention across all sectors (personal communication 2002). This book serves to emphasize and analyse some of the most important interconnections that must be dealt with in these many different spheres of development policy and intervention.

The major world forums and stakeholder organizations dealing with biodiversity conservation have begun to make statements that recognize the importance of women and gender relations to their endeavours, but these often lack sufficient substance to permit implementation. For example, the only specific reference to women in the Convention on Biological Diversity appears in the

Preamble, which recognizes 'the vital role that women play in the conservation and sustainable use of biological diversity and affirm[s] the need for the full participation of women at all levels of policy-making and implementation for biological diversity conservation' (CBD 1992). In the end, we hope that the knowledge presented in this book will help to empower those who want and need to know more.

Acknowledgements are clearly in order. The first should go to all of those who are making concerted efforts to bring the topic of 'gender and biodiversity' to public attention. No one can fail to acknowledge the work of leading feminist pioneers and scholars like Bina Agarwal, Melissa Leach, Dianne Rocheleau, Vandana Shiva and many others too numerous to mention but no less important. Others who work, most often anonymously, within development agencies and NGOs to develop and implement plans of action on women and biodiversity and guidelines for gender-sensitive planning, also deserve recognition for their equally pioneering efforts, particularly Pablo Eyzaguirre at the International Board for Plant Genetic Resources (IPGRI), who has encouraged this work and who has inspired me and many others with his own dedication. IPGRI and the FAO have invested in the development of annotated bibliographies dealing with this topic, and their efforts have been built upon and deserve acknowledgement herein.[1] Biodiversity support programmes at IDRC Canada and GTZ Germany have not only provided sponsorship for the diffusion of this book in the South; they have also paved the way by authoring some of the first publications providing guidance on how to incorporate gender issues into biodiversity research and conservation efforts (IDRC 1998; GTZ 2002).

All of the contributors to this book have stressed that many people and institutions should be acknowledged for their financial, moral and often physical support. However, the most important acknowledgements of all must go to those people, and particularly to those women, whose knowledge and skills are represented here. These include: the men and women of Niamakoroni, Mali (*Aw ni ci!*); the Rai and Sherpa women forager-farmers of the Arun Valley of Nepal; the villagers of Kızılkaya, Turkey; the indigenous people of British Columbia and particularly Dr. Mary Thomas, Nellie Taylor, Ida Matthew (Secwepemc), Ida Jones (Ditidaht), Elsie Claxton (Saanich), Annie York, Mabel Joe (Nlaka'pamux), Florence Davidson (Haida), Helen Clifton (Gitga'at Tsimshian), Chief Adam Dick (Kwakwaka'wakw), Stanley Sam and Katherine Fraser (Nuu-Chah-Nulth); the women and men of Ginestra, Maschito and Barile, Italy; the women and men of La Esperanza, Ecuador; the villagers of Kalasin Province, north-east Thailand; the women and men from rural and urban communities in Swaziland; the Native California Indian peoples of the central California interior including the Yokuts (Yokoch), Mono (Nim), and the Sierra Miwok (Mewuk); the villagers of Jalsha, Kalampur and Chuchuli, Bangladesh, and especially Norindra Nath Borman; the women farmers, local extensionists and maize breeders of Guangxi Province, south-western China, especially Ms Pan Peiyin, Ms Shi Xouxiang, Ms Pan Junyin and Mr Yang Huajun; the people of Haelaelinja community, Was Valley, Nipa District, Southern Highlands Province, Papua New Guinea; and the Arawakan women of the Guainia-Negro region of south-western Venezuela.

I and the other contributors also wish to extend our thanks to the many reviewers and critics who contributed their time and mental energies to this book, including our fellow contributors and Sheila Cosminsky, Carole Counihan, James Fairhead, Christine Hastorf, Eugene Hunn, Clarissa Kimber, Janet Momsen, John Portier and Richard Schroeder.

Patricia Howard, Wageningen, the Netherlands
April 2003

Note

1 See Fernandez *et al.* 2000; IDRC 1998; IPGRI and FAO 1996, n.d.; Biodiversity Support Program 1997; and for the bibliographies see Quiroz n.d., Myer n.d., Nazarea and Sunita n.d., Koda 2000.

References

Biodiversity Support Program (1997) *Beyond Fences: Seeking Social Sustainability in Conservation,* Volumes I and II, Reference No. 14, Gland, Switzerland: IUCN.

Borkenhagen, L., and J. Abramovitz (eds.) (1991) *Proceedings of the International Conference on Women and Biodiversity*, Kennedy School of Government, Harvard University, 4–6 October 1991, Committee on Women and Biodiversity, Harvard University, Cambridge, October.

Boserup, E. (1970), *Women's Role in Economic Development,* New York: St. Martin's and George Allen and Unwin.

CBD (Convention on Biological Diversity) Secretariat (1992) *Convention on Biological Diversity*, Montreal: CBD Secretariat, http://www.biodiv.org.

Fernandez, M., P. Shrestha, and P. Eyzaguirre (2000) 'Integrating gender analysis for participatory genetic resources management: technical relevance, equity and impact', in E. Friis-Hansen and B. Sthapit (eds.), *Participatory Approaches to the Conservation and Use of Plant Genetic Resources*, International Plant Genetic Resources Institute (IPGRI), Rome, Italy, pp. 44–53.

GTZ (Deutsche Gesellschaft für Technische Zusammenarbeit GmbH) (2002) *The Convention on Biological Diversity: Ensuring Gender-Sensitive Implementation*, Eschborn, Germany: GTZ.

IDRC (International Development and Research Centre) (1998) *Guidelines for Integrating Gender Analysis into Biodiversity Research: Sustainable Use of Biodiversity Program Initiative*, Ottawa: IDRC.

IPGRI (International Board for Plant Genetic Resources) and FAO (Food and Agriculture Organization of the United Nations) (1996) 'Incorporating gender-sensitive approaches into plant genetic resources conservation and use', IPGRI/FAO Working Group Meeting, 1–4 October, Rome: IPGRI.

IPGRI (International Board for Plant Genetic Resources) and FAO (Food and Agriculture Organization of the United Nations) (n.d.) 'Strategy for implementing the gender focus of the Global Plan of Action for Genetic Resources in Food and Agriculture', Rome: IPGRI and FAO.

Koda, B. (2000) 'Bibliography on gender, biodiversity and local knowledge in Tanzania', LinKS Working Document No. 2, Review version, 31 March, FAO.

Myer, L. (n.d.) 'Incorporating gender sensitive approaches into plant genetic resources conservation and use: selected bibliography', Unpublished manuscript, Rome: IPGRI.

Nazarea, V., and S. George (n.d.) 'Diversity in the shadows (or why gender and local knowledge are relevant to diversity). A state of the art review and annotated bibliography', unpublished manuscript, Ethnoecology/Biodiversity Laboratory, Department of Anthropology, University of Georgia.

Quiroz, C. (n.d.) 'Literature review', collaborative project (IPGRI–FAO–UGA), 'Incorporating gender-sensitive approaches into plant genetic resources conservation and use: developing a conceptual framework and guidelines', unpublished manuscript, IPGRI/FAO, Rome.

Swaminathan, M. S. (ed.) (1998) *Gender Dimensions in Biodiversity Management*, Delhi: Konark Publishers Pvt. Ltd.

Zedan, Hamdallah (2002) Personal communication, 14 June.

CHAPTER 1
Women and the Plant World: An Exploration

Patricia L. Howard

An account of Mapuche women's efforts to preserve plant biodiversity appeared in 2001 in an unusual story published in *El Mercurio*, a Chilean daily.

> In the forests of the Araucanía range in southern Chile, there is an infinity of medicinal and aromatic herbs that are collected and used by Mapuche shamans (*Machi*). María del Carmen Huenchunao, a veteran *Machi*, said that spirits own all of these plants. The *Machi* learn through their dreams and experience to say prayers before entering the forests, giving thanks to the spirits for the plants that they will take in order to heal people. María speaks Mapudungun, the language of the Mapuche, which she uses to teach Mapuche school children traditional cooking. She says that the people have forgotten to eat traditional foods. 'Now everything is purchased. Rice, noodles: it's the only thing they eat. Because of this, when I began to cook in the school, the children ate little. It wasn't that they didn't like it, but that they didn't know it.' María cooks with the same herbs that she uses to cure people's illnesses. Rather than thickening soups with rice or noodles, she uses *kinwa*, the Mapuche version of the quinoa of the high plains. She also shows the children how *mudai*, the Mapuche drink, is prepared using *kinwa*. 'They watch and they learn. Now they wait for me, and when I arrive at the school they ask: "What are you going to make today, auntie?" "Crazy people's food," I tell them, "food of the Mapuches."'
>
> This 'crazy people's food' will soon be featured on the menus of the most refined restaurants in Chile, offered by chefs who are members of the international 'top chefs' society, Les Toques Blanches. These chefs, interested in rescuing the culinary heritage of their country, made contact with an environmental NGO, the Center for Research and Technology (CET), which supports women who cultivate autochthonous seeds in Araucanía. The chefs met with fifteen indigenous and peasant women who prepared for them the recipes that they conserve in their families. Next, the chefs will share with the women the new concoctions that they create for their restaurants, inspired by the Mapuche recipes and their autochthonous ingredients.
>
> The Mapuche women not only prepare the food: they also cultivate the ingredients used in their recipes. The NGO calls them *curadoras* or 'seed curators': those who, in each community, are responsible for collecting samples of autochthonous seeds and storing and cultivating them at the appropriate time. Neighbours come to these women when they need seed, but the seeds are shared only with those who are able to care for them. Most are legume seeds, and many are unknown to outsiders: *poroto treiler, habas libro, arveja*

vitrillo, poroto coyunda blanco, arvejón blanco, arveja chícharo ... big reds, browns, yellows, greens, maroons and speckled, in addition to the whites and blacks that can be found in any supermarket. The diversity is still greater among the herbs: those used for cooking include *romaza* [Smartweed – *Rumex patientia*], *vinagrillo* [Yellow wood sorrel – *Oxalis corniculata*], and *mastuerzo* [Lesser swinecress – *Coronopus didymus*]. Women cultivate wild species in their gardens to keep them from disappearing. For example, Cecilia Ailio managed to cultivate aquatic herbs at home that, according to her, can cure various diseases. Cecilia's dream is to become a 'doctor', just like her mother. She cultivates *contrayerba* [Breadroot – *Psoralea esculenta*], used to relax the nerves and help people who have been on drugs to return to their normal state; *pichenlahuén*, which acts as a purge and sobers drunks, and *paco de vega*, which alleviates pains in the heart.

The *curadoras*, as true collectors, are proud of the variety of species that they maintain and exhibit them in gardens and especially at the table. Their culture is more concerned with sharing than with hoarding. Since many women don't have the means to store what they produce, they are obliged to cook what the season brings. Such is the case with *digüeñes*, a wild mushroom with a spongy texture that makes conservation difficult and that grows among oaks only in September and October.

The chefs seek to complement the recipes of the Mapuche women without losing their essence; for example by using mashed *porotos* to accompany meats. One chef explains that the greatest difficulty lies in obtaining the Mapuche ingredients, which are brought to the capital in small quantities only when there are cultural festivals. The steady provision of legumes and herbs from Araucanía is required to permit the new style of cooking to take off. The chef thinks that, if enough demand is created, the peasant women will have to find the means to preserve and distribute the foods. He assumes that a free market for these goods will make everyone happy: the gourmets who eat well and María del Carmen Huenchunao, who will become a small entrepreneur. But [the article concludes] this remains to be seen. (Adapted and freely translated from Aguilar 2001.)

The case of the Mapuche women *curadoras* illustrates much of what is explored in this book. It shows that indigenous women have a pre-eminent role in the management of plant biodiversity. They make efforts to preserve this biodiversity in homegardens and by collecting, managing and exchanging 'folk' plant varieties, those that they have developed over millennia or have brought informally from outside their regions and naturalized in their environments. It shows the importance of culinary traditions as well as other domestic arts and skills for the preservation of their culture and of their plant biodiversity, both of which are quickly eroding. It reveals the interrelationship between the Mapuche's spiritual belief system, plant management, and biodiversity conservation. It indicates that there is a relationship between women's specialized knowledge and skills in relation to plants, their contribution to subsistence, and their social position and status within their communities.

It also reveals the gendered nature of knowledge and the importance of women's intergenerational knowledge transmission for the maintenance of biological and cultural diversity. It illustrates the erosion of indigenous knowledge, cultures, and biodiversity, as well as indigenous women's drive to counter this erosion. It shows that outsiders who seek to conserve biodiversity are able to recognize women's knowledge and work, and to promote indigenous cultures and women's status and welfare while at the same time conserving the biodiversity that constitutes their wealth. But it also hints that there is a doubt as to whether creating markets for their plant biodiversity is the means to ensure these ends.

The story of the Mapuche provides a means to explore many of the driving forces behind the large-scale erosion of the world's biological and cultural diversity. It is replete with an indigenous people's intense struggle over hundreds of years to maintain their livelihoods, cultural integrity and autonomy in territories historically and currently overrun and over-exploited by outsiders for economic gain and cultural and political domination.[1] The entire history of the Mapuche, who have inhabited southern Chile and northern Argentina since prehistory, shows that much of their plant biodiversity (or agrobiodiversity)[2] exists because they have 'disturbed' their local natural environments and have shaped those environments to provide all the elements necessary to their well-being. These environments have in turn shaped their culture: that is, nature and culture have co-evolved. Once this co-evolution is made explicit, it becomes axiomatic that the preservation of global plant biodiversity requires the preservation of local cultural diversity. Culture dictates what is sacred, what is desirable, what is taboo, what is beautiful, what is wealth and what is poverty in a world that is biologically bountiful. A world that is culturally poor is likely to be biologically poor, and the reverse is likely to be just as true.

A corollary to the above that is made explicit in the Convention on Biological Diversity (CBD), particularly in Article 8(j),[3] is that the major custodians of the world's biodiversity are those people who directly depend upon it for their livelihoods and cultural integrity. This in turn implies that the preservation of biological diversity must be instrumental to achieving human welfare, where 'human welfare' is defined not only according to biophysical absolutes but according to cultural values as well. In order to preserve much of the world's biological diversity, then, the benefits of such conservation should accrue principally to those who help to create and sustain it. Conservation efforts should focus on maintaining the integrity of local cultural and agro-ecological (ethno-ecological) systems, not only to preserve existing biodiversity, but also to ensure its continual evolution *in situ*. This must not, however, be taken to imply that 'poor' indigenous farmers and rural forest dwellers should be cordoned off in culture–nature reserves and expected to maintain biodiversity for the benefit of humankind and of the plant and animal kingdom, while the rest of the globe enjoys the genetic and aesthetic by-products of their knowledge and labour. Rather, it is the forces that are driving the loss of biological diversity as well as eroding the majority of human cultures that must be addressed, which will not only affect areas that are 'monetarily poor' and 'biologically rich'. Below, some of these driving forces are the subject of an initial exploration, particularly with respect to the ways in which they are related to women, plants, and gender relations.

Cultural Diversity, Biological Diversity and Contemporary Archetypes

Plant biodiversity has been drastically reduced over much of the 'industrialized' world. Most land is in urban areas or under intensive agriculture, and 'nature' has been set apart from production and sequestered on a site-by-site, species-by-species basis in parks and 'reserves' (Tilzey 2000). Few people have a direct productive relationship with nature outside of agriculture. The contemporary definition of agriculture itself has been reduced to monoculture field cropping and specialized livestock production that is based upon chemical inputs and an extremely reduced genetic base. This 'productivist agriculture' archetype is fast replacing cognisance of those ethno-ecosystems that are co-produced by local cultures and nature, where domesticated and wild blur along a continuum that is only distinguishable at its extremes. In these landscapes, which persist in so-called 'marginal' areas of the North and across much of the global South, fields represent amalgams of a wide range of species, from wild to domesticated. This diversity provides much protection against pests and disease, climatic vagaries and seasonal food shortages. Plant growth depends not upon chemical fertilizers, but rather upon mulch gleaned from brush, forests and coastlines, and the dung from animals that are grazed and fed fodder that is gathered in 'wild' areas. These, in turn, sustain a high diversity of animal life. Such biodiverse field production is difficult to conceive without its homologue and counterpart, the homegarden, that in many world regions acts as an indigenous experimental station and gene bank. It contains many semi-domesticates transplanted from the wild and from interstices of fields, and provides a large number of other plant products that are required for life in smaller quantities throughout the year. Nor are the boundaries of 'agriculture' to be seen at the hedgerow or living fence. Beyond this, in 'wild' areas, plant management goes on, gathering plots are marked out and roots are cultivated. The encouragement of growth and selective harvesting ensure, generation after generation, the wild foods and medicinal plants for humans and animals, and the fibres, fuel and other plant resources that meet both material and cultural needs. These 'wild' areas, together with fields and borders and pastures and homegardens, constitute the productive basis and cultural heritage of myriad human lives, as well as the habitats of a multitude of animal and insect species. If we added together all of the world's scientific knowledge about how to live in and with the natural world, both past and present, would it begin to approach the magnitude of human knowledge and experience that these landscapes and these lives still embody today? These landscapes and lives, and their deep reservoirs of knowledge and natural and cultural diversity, are rapidly being lost. Who holds this knowledge? What do these landscapes and lifestyles mean to them? What scope is there to retain them for all generations to come?

On a global scale, and particularly in regions rich in biodiversity – in villages, on farms, in homegardens, forests, common pasturelands, fields and boundary lands – it is mainly women who manage the biodiversity of plant species and varieties. They do so largely within what is often socially defined as the 'domestic' realm. The 'domestic' realm is largely non-monetized, and the women–plant relationships within it are largely invisible to outsiders. The 'domestic' realm is portrayed in contemporary theory as a 'reproductive' sphere where women, as principal agents and managers, carry out unpaid, home-based activities that ensure the maintenance and functioning of people within households. The household, in turn, is characterized as the principal site of collective consumption. In Western cultures, this 'reproductive domestic' archetype is strongly embedded in what historians refer to as the 'cult of domesticity' that prevailed in Europe and its colonies from the eighteenth to the twentieth century. Its influence on the development of the sciences – especially those relating to human evolution and to botany – have much to do with the contemporary failure to recognize and valorize women's relations to subsistence and to the plant world. Just as is the case with the 'productivist agriculture' archetype, the 'cult of domesticity' and its corollary, the 'reproductive domestic' archetype, is a feature of a powerful system of ideas that serves to obscure rather than to illuminate those fundamental aspects of contemporary human–nature relations that are the source of social and environmental instability and crisis.

While the relationship between the 'cult of domesticity', botany and ethnobotany is discussed further on, it is important in this context to give some attention to gender bias in the sciences dealing with human evolution. For centuries this obscured the longest-standing and most important relationship that women have had with plants and with human subsistence. Up until at least the 1980s, Western sciences concerned with human evolution were dominated by a 'Man the Hunter' model. This portrayed women's contributions to subsistence through plant gathering as part of the 'domestic' realm and as insignificant relative to men's subsistence contributions:

> The picture of human sex roles that emerges from the ['Man the Hunter' models] ... is little changed in essence from that drawn by Darwin ... Men are still seen as actively and aggressively engaged in procuring food and defending their families, whereas women are seen as dependants, who remain close to home to trade their sexual and reproductive capacities for protection and provisioning ... [These models] effectively omitted the female half of the human species from any consideration whatsoever. (Fedigan 1986: 33)

It was at an important conference entitled 'Man the Hunter', held in 1966, that those attending began to recognize that the bulk of foodstuffs in hunting-gathering societies is provided by plant food that is gathered primarily by women. The conference spurred further reflection and, in 1968, Richard Lee published his survey of 58 foraging societies demonstrating that hunted foods contributed only an average of 35 per cent of total food supply, except in the Arctic, where meat is of primary importance (*ibid.*: 47). Further reviews of a larger number of hunting-gathering subsistence-based societies revealed that the 'Man the Hunter' model prevailing since Darwin simply had no empirical foundation.

Yet other ideas closely associated with the 'Man the Hunter' model had great influence. Owing to their reproductive status, it was considered that women carried out lighter work and were tied to 'basecamp'. These assumptions were also refuted on the basis of empirical evidence:

> It is clear that in most parts of the world foraging women are assigned the tasks of carrying heavy burdens: food, children, water, and firewood. Sedentary women simply do not exist in hunter-gatherer societies. Where quantitative data have been collected, it has been found that women are away from basecamp for equivalent amounts of time and walk equivalent distances, carrying infants and heavier burdens than do the men. (*Ibid.*: 49)

The 'cult of domesticity' inextricably linked women's contributions to subsistence through plant procurement to the home and to the 'reproductive' domestic sphere. In spite of the evidence that has accumulated and the feminist theoretical contributions (including the emergence of a 'Woman the Gatherer' model of human evolution), the old assumptions continue to hold sway both among scientists and within society: 'when Man the Hunter becomes Man the Provider, it is clear that powerful cultural sex role expectations inform these reconstructions' (*ibid.*: 61).

Western society is still to a great degree steeped in the 'cult of domesticity' that was so deliberately crafted as a handmaiden to patriarchy in the Victorian era. What is ironic is that the art and science of the 'domestic', and its relation to the preservation of the biological world that it has in part created and valorized, seems destined to remain in the penumbra of formal Western science and indeed perhaps of the 'modern' conscience. Even the domestic sciences ('household economics') mainly overlook women's indigenous plant and environmental knowledge and their co-productive relationships with nature. But it is not only in the West that women's subsistence work and 'domestic' work are virtually equated: this appears to be a feature of many of the world's patriarchal social orders.

In all but the most highly industrialized regions of the world, what is characterized as the 'reproductive' domestic sphere is in reality a tremendously *productive*, albeit largely invisible realm. It contributes the majority of subsistence resources in many rural areas. It involves a highly demanding and holistic level of technical environmental knowledge and skills related to plants that can require at least a third of a lifetime to accrue, as well as frequent innovation. The phenomena that give rise to a systematic blindness to the productive, technical and folk-scientific dimensions of women–plant relations in the 'domestic' sphere are due neither solely to scientific bias nor to a neo-classical economic orthodoxy that largely refuses to address women's non-market production. As Margot Wilson argues in Chapter 12, it is clearly patriarchal norms that largely confine women to the sphere of consumption and make their productive work invisible. In her case study in Bangladesh, she shows that the norms that seclude women within the homestead explain much about why it is women rather than men who manage indigenous biodiversity in homegardens. Women's subsistence work related to plants is *intended* to remain in the shadows.

Out of the Penumbra: Reconceptualizing Women and Plants

The case studies in this book systematically explore and illustrate why it is that women's daily activities, in comparison to men's, require greater use of a more diverse range of plant species. The book represents the first major harvest of an ongoing exploration of the literature on local management of plant biodiversity. Thus far, this review (Howard-Borjas 2002)[4] shows that, over much of the world, it is mainly women who are wild plant gatherers and managers, homegardeners and plant domesticators, herbalists and healers, as well as seed custodians. In several world regions and cultures, women are also the principal farmers and informal plant breeders, particularly of indigenous crops. These multiple domains of work are represented in this book by case studies: wild plant gathering (chapters 3, 4, 5, 6, 7, 10, 11, 13 and 14), homegardening (chapters 2, 12, 13 and 15), herbalism and healing (Chapter 8), and farming, seed management, domestication and informal plant breeding (chapters 9, 15 and 16).

The case studies have been compiled to explore and illustrate the importance of women's plant management for biodiversity conservation and the importance of plants for women's status and human welfare. But further, they demonstrate that these are crucial not only for poor countries and tropical regions that are rich in biodiversity, but also for biodiversity conservation in all world regions. African case studies include Zimbabwe, Mali and Swaziland. Asia and the Pacific are represented by cases in Nepal, Thailand, Papua New Guinea, Bangladesh and China. Case studies on Latin America include Mexico, Ecuador and Venezuela. North America is represented by the Pacific North-west and California, while case studies from Europe include Italy and Turkey. A wide range of subsistence bases is also represented, demonstrating that the importance of plant biodiversity and women–plant relationships is not confined to 'hunting-gathering' societies. These subsistence bases include farming–foraging (chapters 5, 6 and 9), farming–pastoralism–foraging (chapters 4 and 10), farming–gardening (chapters 12 and 13), farming (Chapter 16), farming–wage labour (chapters 3 and 15), and wage labour–gardening (Chapter 2). While women are clearly the predominant plant managers in the hunting and gathering societies presented (chapters 7 and 11), they are also the principal wild plant gatherers in all the cases that deal with these resources (chapters 3, 5, 6, 10 and 13) with one exception (Chapter 4). In several of the cases, it is made explicit that women are also those who principally or nearly exclusively manage agricultural production (chapters 9, 15 and 16). While several case studies are focused on minority, tribal, or aboriginal peoples, some deal with dominant cultures or populations that are culturally more diverse, which goes some way towards demonstrating that people–plant relations are gendered and that gender relations are highly significant in the full range of human cultures. While there is only one case study on urban dwellers (Chapter 2), there are several that deal with rural–urban dynamics (chapters 2, 13, 14 and 15).

As well as presenting the results of in-depth research that demonstrate women's predominance in plant biodiversity management in various societies, this book goes much further in that it seeks to explain *how* gender relations influence men's and women's involvement with plants and, in several cases, *why* women predominate – particularly in the management of local plant biodiversity. This is then related to the question of how gender relations affect the social distribution, maintenance and transmission of local ethnobotanical, cultural and environmental knowledge, and how they affect the responsibilities for, and benefits of, the *in situ* conservation and management of plant biodiversity. While there is no attempt made here to develop a new conceptual framework for understanding ethno-ecosystems and, within them, gender relations in the local management of plant biodiversity, the chapters in this book do provide access to a range of theoretical perspectives and concepts that have recently been developed to better define and understand people–plant relationships . These various approaches have focused on certain questions: the contextual and behavioural determinants of these relationships; how relevant indigenous knowledge systems are developed and function; the nature of exogenous and endogenous factors leading to the erosion or conservation of these resources; and the significance of different social groups and their interrelations for plant biodiversity management and use.

The book is organized into five parts, each of which is presented and discussed in what remains of this overview chapter. Each part presents a theme that is essential to the analysis of women and gender relations in people–plant relationships. None of these themes have been broached systematically in any single body of literature to date, nor can it be said that any single chapter within the themes represents comprehensive research on the theme. Rather, each case study highlights or analyses certain key dimensions and, together, the chapters begin to cover the multiple interrelationships entailed and to illustrate their consequences empirically. Moreover, most chapters represent contributions to more than one theme. Together, they demonstrate the need for a more comprehensive and robust conceptual and theoretical framework for analysing people–plant relationships and for promoting conservation efforts that benefit women as well as men.

Part I: Culture, Kitchen, and Conservation

Only rarely is it considered that women's work in the kitchen is essential to biodiversity conservation. However, culinary traditions are a highly important aspect of cultural identity and are usually based upon locally available plant and animal resources. The link between culinary traditions and biodiversity conservation should therefore be self-evident, as it is to CET-Sur, the Chilean environmental group working with the Mapuche *curadoras*.

A large body of research shows that foods are valued not only for their nutritional content, but also for their emotional, ritualistic, spiritual and medicinal traits. Food is, in most cultures, also a fundamental constituent of exchange and hospitality, which are basic organizing principles of many traditional societies. While the idea of what constitutes an adequate meal or dish may be influenced by men (McIntosh and Zey 1998), women are generally considered to be the 'gatekeepers' of food flows in and out of the domestic sphere. Culinary traditions are perpetuated by the careful transmission of knowledge and skills, particularly from mother to daughter (Douglas 1984; Counihan and Kaplan 1998). Most important, culinary traditions and preferences, as well as the culinary arts required to provide edible and culturally acceptable food, have a marked influence on the knowledge, selection, use and conservation of plant biodiversity.

Which plants women select for food depends on a wide range of criteria related to palatability, culinary qualities and beliefs about health and nutrition. But plant varietal selection for food entails more than a concern for culinary qualities and the transmission of ethnobotanical and culinary knowledge and skills: it also relates to plants' biochemical composition, which influences processing characteristics, storability and preservation methods. These are in turn related to the available technology and to environmental factors such as temperature, humidity and the incidence of pests and diseases, as well as to local knowledge, labour and fuel availability. Processing, selection, preservation and storage tasks are interrelated in terms of labour, timing and techniques. These tasks are also often indivisible: the same person selects, separates, processes and stores plant products simultaneously for the next crop, for home consumption, and for sale. The technical environmental knowledge and skills required to develop, maintain and innovate in this post-harvest food chain are complex, dynamic and vital.[5] While much research investigates the ways in which plants are consumed as foodstuffs, relatively little investigates the specialized ethnobotanical knowledge and related skills underpinning domestic post-harvest and culinary practices, how these are transmitted, why and how they change, and how these changes affect biodiversity conservation, food security, nutrition and women's status.

The interrelationship between plant biodiversity and culinary knowledge and tradition is illustrated by the case of the Andes, the cradle of the world's potato diversity. Many researchers have sought to understand why it is that farmers maintain a tremendous number of potato and maize varieties on their farms, and have sought the answer principally in the need that farmers have to adapt plants to fit diverse environments and agronomic conditions. Zimmerer's seminal research demonstrated that these factors alone cannot explain the great diversity of potato and maize varieties produced. Rather, specific varieties are cultivated in order to meet precise culinary requirements: 'groups of species correspond to different uses, such as freeze-drying, soup-making, and boiling' (1991: 301–2). This is also true of the large number of maize varieties that are maintained: 'different preparations rely on groups of cultivars. Agriculturists utilize culinary distinctions as the basis for planting separate fields in different ecological habitats' (ibid., see also Nicholson 1960).

Another riddle that researchers have tried to solve for decades is why so many people across the tropics prefer to grow so-called 'bitter' cassava (Manihot esculenta) varieties rather than 'sweet' varieties, since the former are toxic whereas the latter are not. A very substantial amount of labour is required to remove the cyanide from the bitter varieties, most of which could be avoided if only sweet varieties were grown (see also Hoffmann, this volume). Wilson sought to shed light on this problem when he researched the Tukanoan peoples of the Colombian Amazon. As is the case with many Amazonian and African indigenous populations, only women produce cassava, which is the principal staple crop.[6] Wilson researched cassava crop performance and women's varietal preferences in order to learn why women plant more 'bitter' (toxic) varieties. He concluded that:

> It was expected that interviews would demonstrate that yield and/or resistance to environmental stressors is the most important consideration a Tukanoan woman makes when selecting cultivars for her garden. The results, however, indicate that while yield and damage suffered by the plant may be factors which influence cultivar selection, it is the foods which can be made from each cultivar which is the most important consideration. (1997: 152)

While both men and women are involved in crop selection, have highly specific knowledge and use a variety of criteria, these differ substantially between them, and women's criteria and knowledge are often overlooked by those who research plant varietal selection and conservation. Women very often have a broader set of selection criteria in comparison with men. Where women are the main crop producers, they consciously select varieties that meet a broad range of criteria related to production, processing, storage and preservation characteristics as well as culinary qualities. When men are the main producers, they depend upon female family members to advise them with respect to characteristics unrelated to field crop production, particularly those related to post-harvest processing and culinary uses.

Kitch et al. (1998) used a participatory approach to plant breeding in Cameroon where farmers' selection criteria for cowpea (Vigna unguiculata) were identified. These were related to yield, large seeds, white seeds, long and large pods, quality, and labour inputs. Although male and female farmers ranked varieties about the same with respect to yield and labour requirements, male farmers found quality-related criteria significantly less important than female farmers. This difference was mainly related to the quality of leaves for human consumption, a criterion that women farmers used much more frequently. In Southern Mali, participatory methods were used to identify men's and women's varietal preferences in order to improve cereal varieties. Defoer et al. (1996) noted that women observed eight different processing characteristics, while men observed only three. Bran, flour content and ease of pounding were mentioned by both sexes, and characteristics specifically observed by women were ease of dehulling, humidification, cooking, milling and a low level of broken grains. In Rwanda, the immense diversity of beans (Phaseolus vulgaris) is the greatest in the world, and beans are considered to be a 'woman's crop'. Women farmers manage over 600 varieties, which is the result not only of natural selection, but also of careful selection by generations of women farmers. Shellie (1990), a plant breeder, carried out research on food quality and fuelwood conservation characteristics of bean cultivars and landraces with the purpose of identifying means to reduce bean cooking time and conserve fuelwood. She discovered that, over time, farmers had successfully selected against hard seed coatings which increase cooking time, evident in the low amount of genetic variability for this trait. Further, 'the range in cooking time among landraces ... suggested that some farmers had selected cultivars based upon their cooking performance and were developing fast cooking landraces' (ibid.: 80). Much other research on women's criteria for plant varietal selection demonstrates the same link between genetic selection and diversity and the processing and culinary spheres.[7]

The interrelationships between women, the maintenance of culinary traditions, cultural identity and biological diversity are also made very evident in the exchange and movement of plant genetic resources through migration (Niñez 1987). Laurie Greenberg (Chapter 2) studied the homegardens of women who migrated from a subsistence agricultural economy in the Yucatan Peninsula to a wage-labour, cash economy in Quintana Roo, Mexico. She explores the relationship between the maintenance of culinary traditions, homegardening, biodiversity conservation and the cultural continuity and welfare of an indigenous people. Yucatec Mayan women immigrants' homegardens are sites of in situ conservation, not only of traditional Yucatec crops, but also of elements of traditional Yucatec cuisine, which helps to preserve the cultural identity of immigrants in their new environment. A total of 140 plant species were identified in the 33 immigrant house lots that were studied. The most common use was for food (49 species), including fruits, vegetables and condiments. Immigrant gardens are conservation sites for traditional crop species and varieties outside of the Yucatan Peninsula and provide the only source of many traditional foods in the new settlement area. Women maintain their homegardening and culinary traditions even when agriculture is no longer an option, and men and women alike turn to wage labour to meet subsistence needs.

It is in such a manner that migrants who confront new cultures, culinary traditions and languages may maintain their own traditions even over centuries. Andrea Pieroni's study (Chapter 3) investigates technical environmental knowledge among women within three Arbëresh communities in southern Italy. The Arbëreshë are descendants of southern Tosk Albanians who emigrated during the fifteenth and sixteenth centuries to diverse isolated areas within southern Italy. Traditions related to wild plant gathering and cooking are very popular and are maintained exclusively by women. Arbëresh women use more than 110 botanical taxa as food in their local gastronomy, including about 50 wild species. They have retained their traditional knowledge about the uses of wild food plants for many generations, but today this transmission is seriously endangered as young women move away from agriculture and into the wage labour force, and the Arbëreshë feel the pressure of ethnic discrimination. The heritage of knowledge related to wild herbs is decreasing. More knowledge remains about botanicals utilized in special food preparations that have a strong 'ritual' character in local cuisine, and where the role of women's 'know-how' is still central.

Plant biodiversity not only contributes to culinary and cultural identity and continuity: it is also essential to food security and nutrition, providing the seasonal dietary variety and necessary nutritional elements that make eating both desirable and productive. But researchers and other outsiders often overlook wild food plants and indigenous vegetables and fruits, since the number of species is large, many are very localized (grown or collected in small patches in homegardens, boundary lands, or between crops), and they are mainly managed by women (Akoroda 1990: 31, Chweya and Eyzaguirre 1999, Howard-Borjas 2002). Conceptual frameworks and research on household food security in fact often fail to mention the contribution of homegardening or wild plant gathering and management, much less the importance of women's indigenous knowledge in food processing, storage and preservation.

Across the African continent, local plant biodiversity not only provides food in times of shortage and famine: African culinary traditions include the use of wild plants and a large number of domesticated indigenous species to provide the sauces, relishes and soups that make the bland carbohydrate staples consumed in the region palatable and the diet nutritious. Millicent Malaza's study on Swaziland (Chapter 14) shows that these preparations involve a great diversity of plant species, both wild and cultivated, including many 'indigenous vegetables' that must be produced or gathered on a very substantial scale. It is usually women's task not only to prepare these accompaniments, but also to produce or procure the plants that go into them. Another good example is provided by *Telfairia occidentalis* (Cucurbitaceae), a fluted pumpkin consumed as a 'relish' or soup ingredient accompanying yams, cassava or cocoyam among the Igbos in Nigeria (Akoroda 1990). Used by 30–35 million people, it is a leaf, shoots and seed vegetable that women are culturally obliged to produce or procure for their households. The nutritional content of these staple accompaniments is essential and is often superior to exotic fruit and vegetables, and they are also often less expensive. However, these 'accompaniments' 'are hardly considered food. At best, they are prepared and accepted as a relish or a flavouring agent … it is the basic staple which is considered "food"' (Akoroda 1990: 30, citing Sai 1965).

Ephrosine Daniggelis's research (Chapter 4) confirms the foregoing in relation to Rai and Sherpa women living in remote communities in eastern Nepal. She strove to understand the importance of wild foods and women's technical knowledge in food preparation and nutrition for household food security in a region where food scarcity is a reoccurring phenomenon. Cultivated food is particularly scarce during the pre-monsoon period, but this coincides with the period in which wild foods are abundant. The 'wild' environment, referred to as the *jangal*, lies outside village land and cultivated fields, and is a vast repository of plant biodiversity. Nutritional, ethnobotanical, and ethnographic research helped to portray a holistic picture of women's indigenous knowledge, use and management of *jangal* resources. The 'wild' plant foods that Rai and Sherpa women forager-farmers prepare for their families are important sources of plant protein, vitamins C and A, iron, calcium and fat, and are richer sources of several nutrients than are cultivated vegetables. *Jangal* ingestibles are 'hidden' because they are perceived to be weeds by external actors even though the women view them as the key to survival in an unpredictable environment.

Daniggelis's findings also highlight the importance of women's technical environmental knowledge — specifically, their ethnobotanical knowledge – in the range of post-harvest tasks that are required to make plants edible and nutritious (see also Madge 1994). Several of the wild plants that Rai and Sherpa women gather must be made edible through detoxification, which requires in-depth knowledge of plant characteristics. Wild and domesticated plants are fermented both to extend their availability and to provide a traditional relish. Füsun Ertuğ (Chapter 10) also reports that women in central Anatolia, Turkey, detoxify several species of wild plant foods and preserve and store them for winter.

The integrity of these processes is essential to health and household well-being: not only do culinary traditions and technical environmental knowledge directly affect household nutrition but, as Daniggelis points out, storage, and preservation also considerably lengthen the 'shelf life' of both gathered and cultivated food, and are therefore essential to ensuring food security. Historical research carried out on indigenous women belonging to a hunting-gathering society in the north-west Pacific coast of the United States showed that most wild plant resources were seasoned and stored using special techniques (Norton 1985). Wild plant foods provided requisite nutrition for the Coastal people and, when harvested and stored in quantity, were dependable, all-season staples:

> The edible portions of plants have a truly limited season of harvest and without processing and storage vegetable foods would have been unavailable during a large part of the year.... The primary relevance of plant foods (whether staple or supplemental) to Native peoples lay not in their environmental distribution patterns but in their ability to meet quantitative and qualitative nutritional requirements year-round. (*Ibid.*: 112)

What is made clear from the foregoing is that the kitchen is quite possibly the most undervalued site of plant biodiversity conservation. When women's food processing, preparation and storage knowledge and practices are lost or traditional culinary habits change (see my discussion of Part V on page 31), this can lead to the erosion of plant biodiversity as well as to a decrease in nutritional status, and a loss of status for women in what has heretofore been a dynamic and creative domestic sphere.

Part II: Gender Relations, Women's Rights and Plant Management

Like land and water, plants are vital productive resources. While plants are, in theory, renewable resources, in the absence of particular ecological conditions that help maintain plant population densities, and of social control systems that protect and manage ecosystems and specific varieties, they can be lost. Social controls include systems of management and of access and control rights that are also clearly interrelated. Rights and obligations are often conferred upon individuals or groups who manage, use, conserve or have knowledge about specific types of plants.[8]

An assumption is often made that plant 'ownership' is automatically derived from land tenure – so that, for example, private property owners *ipso facto* hold exclusive rights to plants growing or produced on their land. Another common assumption is that plants growing upon land that is communally held are also communal property. Further, it may be assumed that 'ownership' of a plant is exclusive and permits the owner to dispose of the plant as she or he prefers. However, rights regimes relating to plant genetic resources are often not nearly so simple.

Systems of rights and duties are nearly universally differentiated according to sex, and rights systems relating to plants present no exception. Both are well illustrated by the case of *Telfairia occidentalis* cited earlier. Women cannot cut (kill) *Telfairia* plants belonging to others – to do so desecrates the other's field and, to atone, the earth goddess must be appeased: 'a woman who harvests *Telfairia* from the farm of an absent neighbour without permission has done a great evil.... It is considered a serious affair.... After proper sacrifices, they pray: "Let us not again witness more of such acts in our lifetimes"' (Akoroda 1990: 37). This implies that, to have access to *Telfaria*, each adult female is obliged to plant her own field.

Nor are rights confined to domesticated plants: wild subsistence resources are also generally protected. In British Columbia, Canada, berry gathering was an important female subsistence activity: 'the first real prerogative given to an Oweekeno girl was the hereditary right to use specific, owned berry patches, a right that passed from mother to daughter. Berrying parties were organized by the female owner of the grounds to be visited' (Compton 1993: 371). Norton's histori- cal research on wild plant gathering and management by native US north-west coast women indicated that individual or group ownership and marking of

> terrestrial and maritime harvest sites was often controlled or inherited through the maternal line.... [Women] controlled access to halibut and codfish banks, cedar groves, and berrying grounds as well as claiming beach rights for stranded sea mammals. Nootkan women brought rights to fishing and hunting grounds to their marriages and if a separation occurred the rights reverted to the sole use of the woman. Inter-tribal trade women inherited plots from their mothers on the southern Coast, where several varieties of lilies and other roots were important elements of the diet. (Norton 1985: 132)

Lisa Price's highly innovative research (Chapter 5) specifically focuses on a local, gendered system of gathering rights to wild plant foods, where gathering and management are examined in relation to dynamic entitlements and shifting property rights. Wild plant foods in north-east Thailand are traditionally the domain of women. Many of these wild plant foods are actively managed through protection, selective harvesting and transplanting. Access to these foods for domestic consumption and market sale carries different restrictions at the species level, which are linked to perceptions of market value, taste and species rarity. Price examines in detail how rights to collect these plant foods on what is acknowledged as private property are linked to the system of matrilocal residence, female kinship networks and matrilineal inheritance of farm land. The system of rights serves a vital social function that further underlines the reasons that plants are subject to the same kind of social regulation as other productive resources:

> While it is well known that market activity brings with it a shifting of costs to the environment and the community, in the case study presented here, the community consensus formed by women resource owners, and community condemnation of those women who gather from the private agricultural land of others items they are forbidden to sell, help to reduce the possibility of abusing resources at the expense of the community and the environment. (pp. 111–12).

Linda Dick Bissonnette's contribution on California native peoples (Chapter 11) deals principally with issues relating to plants and women's status. She reports that gathering rights to acorns, the principal staple food, were strictly related to kinship and gender. 'In general, food resources were held in common, but individual women claimed exclusive rights to plants that required special care and management. Use rights were taken very seriously, and were made known orally as well as by sign' (p. 204). Married daughters gathered seeds from their mothers' seed localities but not from their mother-in-laws' localities. Rights were established through continuous use and by marking out gathering locations. Rights were related to the division of labour, where men were primarily responsible for hunting and fishing, and women were responsible for gathering and basket making.

Goebel (Chapter 6) explores in greater depth the gender relations and rights around plants entailed in a clearly patriarchal society. She examines gendered control, access, institutional arrangements and cosmologies in relation to woodland plant resources in rural Zimbabwe using a resettlement area as a case study. Shona women and men in rural Zimbabwe have distinct uses of woodlands and their products and differential access to and control over these resources. These gendered patterns are shaped by, and in turn reinforce, the institution of marriage and prevailing gender ideology regarding divisions of labour and intra-household rights and responsibilities. Women's access to woodland resources and land is nearly always mediated through their husbands: 'in the vast majority of cases it is married men who are assigned a homestead site, arable fields and grazing rights' (p. 119). The state has attempted to promote women's equality in resettlement areas, which has de facto if not de jure given women greater security of access to resources, at least upon widowhood. But divorce produces quite different results: divorced women in resettlement areas lose their access to communal woodland resources, whereas divorced women in communal areas maintain access if they remain in the villages where they lived with their husbands. Goebel asserts that 'Women's relationship to natural resources, particularly in patrilineal contexts, is marked by "asymmetrical entitlements" shaped by gender systems that make women's rights contingent upon their relationships with men, whereas men have primary rights' (p. 120). She argues that the most important aspect of this layer of human/environment relations for women is the persistence of certain aspects of 'traditional' beliefs about the environment that undermine women's claims to natural resources in woodlands as well as to arable land. Even in the case of the resettlement areas, when widows are granted rights to their deceased husbands' land, major conflicts arise as male relatives invoke traditional belief systems to defend their rights to take over resettlement area permits.

There are two other areas where indigenous rights systems are highly significant and are nearly always gendered, and it is in these areas that international policy debates are the most intense since legislation is being developed to create formal property systems and regulations. The first is related to rights to seed (plant genetic material), and the second is related to rights to knowledge – two areas that are, of course, interrelated. Since the 1980s, it has been argued that 'farmers' rights' to plant genetic resources should be recognized, and those who develop folk varieties or contribute substantial knowledge about local plant genetic resources should be compensated for private or public use (Fowler 1994). Currently, 'Many indigenous farmers and their supporters see a need to protect the rights of farmers to (1) grow ... and market folk variety seeds and food products, (2) be compensated when folk varieties ... are used or marketed by others, and (3) have a say in the manipulation and other use of folk varieties by outsiders, which may violate cultural and religious values' (Cleveland and Murray 1997: 482). These authors further convincingly argue that 'indigenous peoples have notions of intellectual property, and that these rights may exist at the level of individuals and/or of groups based on residence, kinship, gender, or ethnicity' (ibid.: 483).

The second area in which indigenous rights systems are significant is in relation to knowledge. There is very substantial technical environmental knowledge involved in plant management and use that might also be likened to 'intellectual property' since it is recognized, carefully protected and transmitted in accordance with social norms that are related at least in part to gender. In Part III it is clearly demonstrated that plant knowledge and rights to plant knowledge are gendered. The semi-nomadic Kel Ewey Tuareg people in Niger, West Africa present an example, where women traditionally are herders and gatherers and enjoy significant prestige. Rasmussen shows that the inheritance of herbal healing knowledge occurs along the female line and is traced back to Tagurmat, an ancestress who passed down the knowledge of trees and healing to women. The knowledge is secret, and 'it is transmitted to, belongs to, and is practised and managed by women, like property' (1998: 148). Several other researchers document the fact that women's knowledge is often held in 'secret' and passed along the female line (Herrick 1995; Browner and Perdue 1988; Descola 1994; Dick Bissonnette in this volume).

Numerous dangers attend the failure to recognize indigenous systems of rights to manage, develop and use plant genetic resources, irrespective of whether one argues that indigenous rights are best protected by 'farmers' rights' or by other rights regimes. The danger exists that outsiders will confer rights on the wrong groups, unwittingly usurping the rights of those who traditionally held them. The introduction of European land tenure systems in Africa and Asia has often resulted in the usurpation of women's customary land rights and their transfer to men. In fact, systems of rights can change without any conscious intervention. What is not clear is whether this will eventually lead to the erosion of women's control over traditional varieties, but this is a possibility given the fact that women's control is often rooted in cultural norms that are now being challenged. If women's control over traditional varieties erodes, and they are the main plant managers and repositories of knowledge, then it is likely that this knowledge will erode absolutely. Those working to implement Article 8(j) of the Convention on Biodiversity (CBD) relating to indigenous people's knowledge explicitly acknowledge the need for 'recognition of customary law as a mechanism for the protection of traditional knowledge, innovation and practices' (UNEP 2000a). However, the only explicit reference to women's indigenous rights to biological diversity in any of the CBD documents to date is a weak recommendation to 'strengthen their access to biological diversity' (UNEP 2000b, annex I). This would seem to imply that women's customary access is currently weak, which is not necessarily the case. Debates about rights to plant genetic resources, and their outcomes, cannot be considered as gender-neutral since, while women constitute the majority of those gardeners, gatherers, herbalists and plant breeders who have developed agrobiodiversity and identified useful plants, they are likely to be the last to have their rights recognized and therefore to benefit from compensation schemes or rights regimes. It may very often be incorrect to assume that the rights or compensation given to 'indigenous groups' or 'farmers' will benefit women directly.

Part III: Gendered Plant Knowledge in Science and Society

[E]thnobotanical and anthropological studies have frequently an unstated but critical male bias. (Miguel Alexiades 1999: 38)

[M]ost of the ethnobotanical writings on female health issues were by foreign men, interpreting native men in turn interpreting native women. (James Duke, foreword in Duke and Vasquez 1994: iv)

There are more ways in which the 'cult of domesticity' has affected Western scientific perspectives on women's contributions to subsistence and their relationships with plants. In the English and Latin languages, 'flora' refers to all plant life. The term comes from Roman cosmology, where Flora was the goddess of flowers, gardens and spring. Ancient Romans performed rituals and celebrations in her honour. By the Middle Ages, the Church had associated Flora's worship with paganism and sexual promiscuity and was doing what it could to eradicate her celebration. However, in eighteenth-century Western Europe, the goddess Flora was revitalized as a romantic image of nature. An explosion of interest in plants took place among the general population as well as among the scientifically and commercially inclined due to colonial plant-hunting expeditions that were introducing an extraordinary number of exotic plants to Western Europe. Due to the associations in myth and literature between women, flowers and gardens, and to the long tradition of women's medicinal herbalism and homegardening, botanical work was considered to be part of the domestic sphere, and very much in line with feminine attributes. Middle- and upper-class women were actively encouraged to pursue the study and cultivation of plants (Shteir 1996; Bennett 2000; Hyde 1998). These ideologies had an impact far beyond the domestic sphere, since the 'cult of domesticity' that prevailed in Europe in the eighteenth century also influenced the establishment of botany as an Enlightenment science.

Ann Shteir (1996) has traced the influence of the 'cult of domesticity' on the development of botany between 1760 and 1820, when the ideas of the Swedish scientist Carolus von Linnaeus (the 'Father of Botany') gained great popularity in Europe and his system of plant classification became widely accepted. He classified plants according to sex and then according to the number of pistils or stamens. This simple system, readily understood by lay persons who had a passion for plants, was based on parallels between plant and human sexuality and on concepts of masculine and feminine that were prevalent in his day. He used anthropomorphic terms to characterize the sexuality of the plant world – such as 'brides and bridegrooms', 'eunuchs' and 'clandestine marriages'. According to Shteir,

> He assigned a higher ranking to the class, a unit based on stamens (the male part), and a subsidiary ranking to the order, based on the pistil (the female part). He also represented the male part in plant reproduction as active and the female part as passive … he naturalized sex and gender ideologies of his day. (1996: 16)

The gender and anthropomorphic biases evident in Linnaeus's work went relatively unchallenged for nearly 70 years, in part since they mirrored social concepts of how nature and societies should be organized. But by the 1820s some botanists had begun to turn to plant physiology as a new area of inquiry. Scientists in Paris and Geneva were developing 'natural system' approaches to plant classification based upon a series of characteristics rather than simply plant reproduction. Linnaean botany was increasingly seen as the 'lower rung of the ladder of botanical knowledge, associated with children, beginners and women' (ibid.: 31). While Victorian England was romanticizing nature, Shteir notes, botany was becoming professionalized, a process captured in the inaugural speech of John Lindley when he became the first Professor of Botany at London University. Lindley distanced himself firmly from Linnaean botany and allied himself with the continental thinkers. He insisted that botany should be concerned with plant structure rather than identification. But this was not all: he also insisted that 'it has been very much the fashion of late years, in this country, to undervalue the importance of this science, and to consider it an amusement for ladies rather than an occupation for the serious thoughts of man' (cited in Shteir 1996: 156–7). Lindley's speech foreshadowed and rationalized the severing of the link between women and botany: Flora was once again expelled for profaning the sacrosanct, but this time the sacrosanct was declared to be the 'male' science of botany. So, according to Shteir, 'During 1830– 60, botany was increasingly shaped as a science for men, and the "botanist" became a standardized male individual … [women's] botany was in the breakfast room' (ibid.: 166).

Gender research has clearly demonstrated the presence of 'gender bias' in social and natural sciences. This means that scientists take prevailing gender norms in a society to be 'natural' and often incorporate these norms into their theories as unquestioned assumptions. It also means that scientists assume male predominance and take men's behaviour and knowledge to be 'standard', whereas the behaviour of women is downplayed or seen to be 'deviant'. Gender bias affects the theories, the questions formulated, the methods used and the research outcomes. The repercussions go far beyond the creation of biased scientific knowledge: they extend into related practices, policies and interventions that are intended to change the interactions between people, and between people and their environments. They can distort the outcomes in ways that are unanticipated and often undesirable.

Current ideas about women and plants are still linked to gender bias in the scientific pursuit of knowledge about plants. A daughter of botany is ethnobotany, 'the study of the interactions of plants and people, including the influence of plants on human culture' (Balick and Cox 1996: i). This science has become increasingly important thanks to the recent world-wide concern with biodiversity conservation and growing corporate interest in plant genetic resources. A serious shortcoming of much ethnobotanical research is that it often takes the plant knowledge of a few people, particularly of men, to be representative of the knowledge of entire cultures, in spite of the fact that the knowledge and use of plants is everywhere gender-differentiated. There are three associated errors. The first is related to the failure to research women's knowledge and use of plants, which is an error of *omission* – the species and varieties that only women know are omitted, and thus biological diversity is underestimated. I have found only one text in which the omission was acknowledged by researchers, in relation to the indigenous knowledge and vegetation use of Bedouin tribes in Egypt:

> It should be noted that these discussions and the subsequent work reported here were entirely with male respondents. The results, therefore, very much reflect a male world and there is, consequently, a need to carry out equivalent work with Allaqi women before a full understanding can be gained. (Briggs *et al.* 1999: 92)

The second error is one of *unreliability*. It is related to using sources that are not well informed, which leads to the improper identification of plants, their management, characteristics, uses and names. Numerous studies have shown that women are often more able to identify these parameters correctly in comparison with men, particularly with regard to plants that fall directly into their domains (Howard-Borjas 2002). Men and women may have some knowledge regarding the plants that are primarily used or managed by the opposite sex, but generally their knowledge is more limited or imprecise with regard to various characteristics of those plants. Such is the case in the Peruvian Andes, where Zimmerer investigated gender differences in ethnobotanical knowledge of maize and potato cultivars that he associated with the gender division of labour:

> Male cultivators tend to be less accurate and less specific in naming [different varieties].... They apply fewer names overall than women and tend to mislabel uncommon taxa.... Not only the extent of cultivar knowledge but also its focus varies

between sexes. Men know especially little about culinary properties such as mealiness or taste which are key conceptual markers of cultivars.... Variations between men and women in the identification and naming of maize cultivars exceed the gap which characterizes sex-based differences in the knowledge of potato types. This contrast parallels the division of labor, which is more pronounced in maize than in potato agriculture ... women alone provide most of the labor for maize cultivation in many households. The classification of uncommon cultivars as intermediate or diseased forms of more common taxa reflects the lack of knowledge among male cultivators concerning identification and naming. (1991: 314)

It is often difficult to determine whether the first two errors have been committed. Research results are usually presented in such a way that it is impossible to know whether women have been included, since references throughout the literature are to gender-neutral nouns such as 'farmers', 'rural dwellers', 'peasants', 'experts', 'informants' or tribal names. In the majority of cases where it is made explicit that women were included in the research (as interviewers and/or as interviewees), data are nevertheless most often not sex-disaggregated when presented, and there is no analysis made of gender differences. Unfortunately, much of the most renowned and in-depth ethnobotanical research lacks any reference to gender differences or to women – but, very fortunately, some of it does.

The third type of error is one of *interpretation*: this leads to a misunderstanding of people–plant relations since a critical component – gender relations – is not revealed. This book emphasizes throughout how gender influences people–plant relations; by inference, it also stresses the implications of *not* taking into account gender relations for scientific knowledge, for conservation policies and practices, and for women plant managers themselves.

Reasons for gender blindness

Changes in researchers' sensitivity to women and gender relations have been occurring, especially over the past decade, as is evident in the statements quoted on page 17.[9] Researchers have come to realize that knowledge is not evenly distributed throughout indigenous and peasant societies. Intra-cultural diversity in knowledge includes sex and age differences, as well as, for example, differences due to kinship, subsistence strategy, and individual competency. Alexiades (1999), an anthropologist and ethnobotanist who has done extensive research on the ethno-ecosystem and ethnomedicine of the Esa Eja (a small indigenous group living in the lowland tropical forests of Peru and Bolivia), indicated several reasons for the tendency to overlook intra-cultural knowledge diversity in much ethnobotanical research. First, it is too often assumed that knowledge is evenly distributed within communities. On the other hand, it is also frequently assumed that there are 'specialists' who are the most knowledgeable about particular subjects. 'This assumes that the pattern of distribution of knowledge in indigenous and peasant societies follows that of technical knowledge in Western science, where "experts" are consulted' (*ibid.*: 337). He makes a point similar to that made by Brij Kothari (Chapter 8) on gender bias in ethnomedicinal research: while researchers seek out indigenous specialist healers as key informants, lay persons have an extensive amount of medicinal plant knowledge that differs from that of the specialists, as well as different ways of understanding health and disease (different 'epistemologies'). Alexiades supports the contention that individual competence, motivation, experimentation and access to knowledge are important to explaining inter-cultural variation, but notes that

> these in turn are determined by age, gender, kin relations, social roles and degree of contact with other social actors and sources of knowledge. In addition, knowledge differences between women are correlated to kinship, as both plant varieties and knowledge are mainly exchanged between members of family and extended kin. (*Ibid*.: 335)

Another issue that Alexiades raises is the access that male researchers have to female informants, which is often limited due to cultural proscriptions against native women having contact with male outsiders. Kothari reported that, for a participatory ethnobotanical research project in which he was involved, having an equal number of women interviewers was crucial to obtaining access to women's knowledge, but getting women to participate as interviewers was fraught with difficulties and only really became possible when a literacy requirement was dropped. Other gender-related problems have been mentioned by researchers, such as the insistence of men that they represent the household, women's 'shyness' and inexperience in working with researchers, and restrictions on women's mobility that present difficulties when using them as interviewers (Brodt 1998; Rusten 1989; Martin 1996).

Another reason why scientists may ignore gender differences in intra-community knowledge distribution was discussed earlier: they tend to overlook women's knowledge about plants because they overlook women's contributions to subsistence. Nancy Turner's extensive research on North American aboriginal people's knowledge and knowledge transmission (Chapter 7) provides a holistic view of the range of women's technical environmental and cultural knowledge that is entailed in plant-based subsistence. Women's roles in the food production systems, including management, harvesting, processing and serving of a wide range of plant foods, were in fact essential to the health and well-being of their people. Turner (personal communication 2002) argues that, whereas women's work and knowledge were highly valued and considered as equal to men's in these societies, scientific researchers often make wrong assumptions about the importance of women's activities for subsistence. A common perception of indigenous cultures in north-western North America is that their traditional economies were based almost solely on the exploitation of salmon and other fish, and on the hunting of marine and terrestrial mammals and large birds. In many literature sources, plant foods are included as secondary products subsumed under a general category of 'berries and roots'. This marginalization of the significance of botanical food products and food processing in general has the effect of devaluing women's work and roles in these societies, since women were the main decision makers, harvesters and knowledge holders in many aspects of food use. The assumptions that Turner describes are clearly related to the gender bias that is evident in the models of human evolution that were discussed earlier.

There are yet other reasons why women's indigenous knowledge is overlooked. Many readers will be surprised at the breadth and depth of women's indigenous technical environmental knowledge that Turner describes. This surprise stems first from the fact that indigenous knowledge *per se* has been devalorized with respect to scientific knowledge and, second, from the fact that the 'cult of domesticity' has shaped notions of women's technical and environmental competencies. Weeratunge Starkloff (1998) and Kabeer (1994) relate this to the 'Western' Enlightenment framework that forged a 'mind–body' dichotomy, linking women with the body (nature, emotion and intuition) and men with the mind (culture and reason).[10] There is still little research that thoroughly and explicitly documents the full breadth of indigenous or peasant women's technical environmental knowledge, although there is more that documents this in specific domains.[11]

Of course, not all gender bias in people–plant research can be attributed to Western science. Part has to do with the relative invisibility and devalorization of women's knowledge and contributions to subsistence within non-Western patriarchal societies, as is discussed later in my introduction to Part IV (see page 27).

What is gendered plant knowledge, and why is plant knowledge gendered?

The simplest definition of gendered knowledge is that which is held either by men or by women, but not by both. Using this definition, appearances would tell us that gendered knowledge exists because men and women do different things: gendered knowledge is therefore a direct reflection of the gender division of labour. This emphasizes experience and practice as a source of knowledge, as well as the transmission of practical knowledge and skills that are required to carry out tasks. According to this line of reasoning, plant knowledge is gendered to the extent that a gender division of labour exists with respect to the use, management and conservation of plants.

But is the gender division of labour sufficient to explain gendered knowledge? In the first place, gender divisions of labour are variable over time, as well as within and between cultures and economies. Since they are variable, they must themselves be subject to explanation. In the second place, not all knowledge is experiential and practical. In all societies, the gender division of labour is related to religious and other values and belief systems, and to concepts of masculinity and femininity and norms about behaviour deemed appropriate for each sex. These value and belief systems and social norms prescribe the activities and responsibilities that are appropriate for men and women, as well as with whom men and women of different social positions can appropriately interact.

Very important for plant and other environmental knowledge, these beliefs and norms extend to men's and women's relations to different physical spaces and environments. For example, Hays reports that, among the Mauna in the Eastern

Highlands of Papua New Guinea, wild vegetable collection (mushrooms, vegetables, fruits and ferns) is carried out by women unless it involves tree climbing. However, 'the forest is primarily man's domain. Myths tell of the tragedies that occurred when women went high into the bush. Women do go in the forest to collect.... However, there is an upper limit of approximately 7,500 feet beyond which they are not supposed to go' (1974: 59). Descola (1994) reported that women's gardens are exclusively women's spaces, where men rarely venture. Goebel shows in Chapter 6 that, in east-central Zimbabwe, not only do men and women use different spaces, but they also use the same space differently. Wilson's research on women's homegardens in Bangladesh (Chapter 12) shows that the seclusion of women refers both to a limit in terms of the persons with whom women are expected to interact and to physical confinement within the homestead. Both are in turn related to the particular gender division of labour within Bangladesh homegardening. If men and women have access to different physical spaces and environments, it stands to reason that their environmental knowledge will also differ.

If men and women relate differently to different groups of people (such as mothers-in-law or male outsiders) – that is, they have different social networks – then their 'knowledge networks' also differ, which affects the type and quality of knowledge and knowledge transmission. Knowledge transmission is increasingly the subject of research because the mechanisms are poorly understood, and because plant- and environment-related knowledge transmission is eroding rapidly within many indigenous and peasant societies. Nancy Turner uses one indigenous woman's term to characterize this process: 'passing on the news'. She shows how crucial women are as educators of children of both sexes for the perpetuation of the understanding of food production systems. Her extensive research shows that knowledge transmission is not confined to instruction, but also occurs through participation, observation and conversation at times of harvesting and processing of food and related resources. Nor is this transmission confined to practical knowledge: the values and philosophies held and taught by women are an integral component of food production, and are also vital to cultural integrity and traditional ecological knowledge systems. These are transmitted through stories, songs, games and many other cultural media. In this volume, Turner, Pieroni, Dick Bissonnette, Ertuğ and Hoffmann all stress that women's knowledge is passed down along the female line. The reasons for the loss of indigenous knowledge, particularly the failure to transmit this knowledge to successive generations, are also linked to changing gender relations, and are discussed further in relation to gender and biodiversity loss and conservation in the section on Part V below.

Women and men have different access to formal and exogenous knowledge. In some societies, women have less access since they receive less formal education, have less contact with extensionists and other government agents, are less able to leave their communities, and are less able to speak languages or dialects other than their own (FAO 1993).[12] However, the opposite can also be the case: for example, in many hunting-gathering societies, women are often reported to venture further afield than men on food-gathering forays (Anderson 1983; Carlstein 1982; Fedigan 1986; Brightman 1996); the same has been reported for women herbalists who travel extensively to procure medicinal plants (Rasmussen 1998). Marketing and barter of seeds and plant materials may be women's prerogative, and women may also maintain more contact with kin in their villages of origin, all of which means they may often in fact have more contact with outsiders' knowledge and genetic resources than do men (Longley 2000; Coughenour and Nazhat 1986).

The gendered nature of knowledge, then, is not simply a function of the gender division of labour, but rather is embedded in cosmologies, beliefs and norms about appropriate behaviours. An example can be found in explanations given for what may be a cross-cultural predominance of women's labour and decision making in the management of indigenous seed. Some researchers have argued that this must be seen in terms of the relation that seed management has to post-harvest and other domestic work (Howard-Borjas 2002). But others suggest a more cosmological explanation. Zimmerer relates that, across much of the Peruvian Andes, 'Social custom forbids men to enter the storehouse or handle seed' (1991: 307). He seeks the explanation for women's control of seed in Andean cosmology, as do Tapia and de la Torre:

> The feminine and divine element represents the fruitful and prolific mother;... in the Quechua language ... all the plants useful to humans were called and adored by the name Mama (mother): Mama sara (maize), Mama acxo (potato), Mama oca (oca, a native Andean tuber), Mama coca (coca shrubs) [citing Rostworowski 1998].... The feeling about the relationship between women and seed is clearer within the tradition of Andean thinking, which is embedded in a dual conceptualization of reality ... defined by the principles of masculinity and femininity ... the man's semen is also called 'seed'... the man's 'seed' is deposited in the mother's womb, and the plant seed grown in the plot is harvested and then deposited at home. Similarly, storage at home is like the mother's womb, where the man entrusts the seed to the woman. (Tapia and de la Torre 1993: 9, 25)

In spite of the identification of women with fertility and seed that can be found across many cultures, cultural beliefs also sometimes exclude women from certain aspects of seed management. Vedavalli and Anil Kumar (1998) report that, among the Kurichiyas in Kerala, India, women's involvement in rice seed selection and storage is considered to be polluting, a phenomenon seen in other societies particularly in regard to taboos around menstruation and childbirth that also affect plant management.

Turner (Chapter 7) provides an example of the relationship between cosmology and the gender division of labour in Nlaka'pamux (Thompson) Interior Salish society. Much further south, Descola captured the intimate relationship between gender divisions of labour, knowledge, cosmology and subsistence in his work on the Achuar, a sub-group of the Jívaro who live in Amazonian Ecuador. Manioc is accorded a very special status in Achuar society, and women are the exclusive cultivators. The tutelary female spirit of women's gardens, Nunkui, resides in the topsoil, and women gardeners must have 'direct, harmonious and constant commerce with Nunkui' in order to have successful gardens (1994: 192). Nunkui is the creator and mother of all cultivated plants in Achuar gardens. Her deeds are recorded in a myth that has a similar structure among all Jívaro peoples. This myth holds that women were allowed to harvest manioc from Little Grandmother's (Nunkui-Uyush's) garden until one day a foolish woman ridiculed Nunkui-Uyush, who prohibited her from harvesting manioc. The foolish woman then took care of Little Grandmother's infant and, when the child started magically pronouncing the names of the cultivated plants, they appeared in the garden, and therefore are the offspring of Nunkui. However, the child was mistreated and all of the cultivated plants shrank until they were tiny. It was only through Nunkui's compassion that women were given seeds and cuttings to plant new gardens.

> It is therefore imperative that a woman secure Nunkui's constant presence in the garden and that she take every precaution not to offend her ... a garden's life span and productivity depend as much on the magical skills of the woman who works it as on local ecological constraints. These skills are designated by the term *anentin*, which, applied to an individual, denotes at once the scope of magical knowledge, the capacity to manipulate the symbolic fields specific to his or her sex, and the particularly fruitful relations entertained with the guardian spirits that govern the spheres of activity in which the individual engages.... To be *anentin* one needs to know a great number of *anent*, magical songs, since it is basically by means of these incantations that a woman can hope to communicate with Nunkui and with the plants in her garden. (*Ibid.*: 198)

Besides the *anent*, a woman gardener has to use gardening charms (*nantar*) in order to be successful. To be effective, the charms have to be activated by the proper *anent*: otherwise they might become uncontrollable and dangerous. There are no *nantar* for the species that men cultivate, and the use of these charms is the exclusive privilege of women. The power of *nantar* resulting in an especially fine garden is, however, proportional to their potential for harming, threatening both the offspring of the woman gardener or any other being entering her garden. 'Ownership of *nantar* is exclusive and a closely guarded secret.... Like gardening *anent*, *nantar* are inherited through the female line and are probably the most precious possession a mother can transmit to her daughter' (*ibid.*: 206–7), together with the knowledge of how to control the *nantar's* magical powers: '*nantar* are a device that permits every woman not only to maintain the individualized autonomy of her symbolic practice, but also to control concretely the very access to the exclusive domain where this symbolic practice is exercised and reproduced' (*ibid.*: 207).

This clearly illustrates that knowledge is also not equally distributed within communities because often certain types of knowledge are purposefully not shared, kept secret, or shared only with very specific groups, often of the same sex (Abbink 1993; Browner and Perdue 1988; Alexiades 1999). Just as in post-industrial societies, knowledge in indigenous and peasant societies is used to confer status, manipulate social relations, gain material advantage, and maintain control over certain aspects of one's life. Knowledge is an integral part of power relations. Gender relations are also power relations, and the distribution of ethnobotanical knowledge within societies cannot be understood without reference to belief systems that legitimize and mediate relations of power between men and women, as Shteir's analysis of the history of Western botany so clearly reveals. These power relations and the ways in which they are manifest may be relatively transparent and clearly demarcated by men's exclusive occupation of prestigious social positions. They may also be much more subtle, embedded in language and in control over the production and exchange of goods.

Brij Kothari (Chapter 8) critically examines the treatment of gender issues in medical ethnobotany, and particularly emphasizes the significance of gender power relations for understanding ethnomedical systems and the distribution of medicinal knowledge between the sexes. He describes a participatory project in which farmers from seven indigenous communities of La Esperanza, Ecuador, investigated and documented their own community's knowledge of medicinal plants. Although the project did not investigate gender relations specifically, it highlighted the importance of women's ethnobotanical knowledge in the highland communities. Prompted by the project experience, Kothari reviewed selected ethnobotanical literature, including anthropological accounts of shamanism. He argues that medical ethnobotanical research tends to ignore women's ethnomedical knowledge and therapeutic roles. He shows that 'ethnobotanists ... tend to make a beeline for the "shaman" or "magico-expert" healer, an office that in many cultures is reserved exclusively for men'. While women may hold some if not most medical ethnobotanical knowledge, by virtue of their sex they may be denied the power and status of the 'expert'. This suggests that 'gender must be explored as an integral aspect of the local power or "prestige structure" in which knowledge is held, generated and expressed' (p. 151). In contrast, ethnobotanists have paid an inordinate amount of attention to women's plant knowledge with respect to reproductive health, which they assume is exclusively the domain of women, while overlooking the breadth of their curative knowledge. Redressing this neglect of women's ethnomedicinal knowledge and the knowledge–power interface, Kothari argues, is a necessary point of departure if the relevance of gender issues in ethnobotanical knowledge is to be grasped. He discusses three theoretical models with the potential to spark a deeper conceptualization of gender power relations in ethnobotanical research.

Language has been identified as a principal vehicle of normative rules regarding gender relations within cultures. Nevertheless, it appears that little ethnobotanical research, particularly that which deals with cognition and folk-taxonomic systems, addresses the question of how the gendered nature of language may affect the ways in which people name and classify plants, and how this in turn may reflect gender power relations. Paul Sillitoe (Chapter 9), in his pioneering work on the Wola in the highlands of Papua New Guinea, was perhaps the first ethnobotanist to look at this in depth when he explored the Wola 'gender classification of crops'. In Wola society, crops are divided into male and female categories that tend to have a correspondence with the gender division of labour in plant production, which in turn is related to anthropomorphic concepts of male and female sexuality. In practice, crops are 'male only', 'predominantly male', 'both sexes', 'predominantly female', or 'female only', and sanctions are in place to ensure that 'male only' and 'female only' crops are not produced by the inappropriate sex. When discussing crops, 'the Wola distinguish between them by using two forms of the verb "to be". There is a connection between this and the sexual categorization of these plants' (p. 169). One verb is used for things that are horizontal to the ground and the other is used for things in an erect state. 'Things that stand erect are strong and masculine for them, whereas recumbent things are weaker and female' (*ibid.*). Women's crops are generally associated with the 'horizontal' 'female' plants, whereas men's crops are associated with the 'erect' 'male' plants. Crops that do not fit within this system (such as those designated with a male verb but cultivated by women) are generally those that were recently introduced to the region. The explanation for this system, according to Sillitoe, is 'the overwhelming importance of female crops in the Wola diet.... Without women and their crops the Wola could not exist, whereas they could if men's crops disappeared' (p. 178). Women produce, but men exchange wealth. 'The danger is that men, whose reputations depend on handling wealth, may be tempted to produce wealth.... Such behaviour would be antithetical to the ceremonial exchange system, which requires them to obtain valuables through transaction, not production, and then to give the items received away again' (*ibid.*). Men are therefore prohibited from producing 'women's' crops, and this prohibition is embedded in Wola language and folk taxonomy.

The above discussion makes it clear that plant knowledge, power and social status are intertwined. These relationships are also dynamic: gender power relations around plants can be contested, and social, economic and environmental change can also affect gender relations that in turn affect the knowledge, use, management and conservation of plant biodiversity, as is discussed in the following sections.

Part IV: Plants, Women's Status and Welfare

It has been suggested here and elsewhere (Howard-Borjas 2002) that plant biodiversity constitutes the greatest part of many indigenous and peasant women's wealth. It stands to reason, then, that women's welfare and social status are strongly related to their management of plant biodiversity and their plant-related contributions to subsistence and technical environmental and cultural knowledge. There is a large and growing amount of literature on the importance of plant biodiversity for the welfare of indigenous and peasant peoples, including their household income, nutrition, food security and health. Most of the chapters in this book illustrate the relation between plant biodiversity and human welfare. There is also much literature that shows how women's income and nutrition in particular are related to homegardening and wild plant collection and use.[13] A small but important body of research shows that women's income is also more closely related to indigenous crops and vegetables, whereas men's income is more often linked to exotic crop varieties.[14]

The relationship between plant biodiversity management and women's status has been far less frequently addressed. This relationship has in part to do with the question of whether the income that women earn from managing plant biodiversity contributes to enhancing their status, which is relevant to a more general debate on the relationship between women's income earning power and status (see Wilson, Chapter 12). It also has to do with women's overall contribution to subsistence. Debates about the degree to which women's contributions to subsistence are related to their status in society can be traced back to Friedrich Engels (Quinn 1977; Fedigan 1986). In particular, the relationship between plant biodiversity management and women's status is also concerned with the question of how their cultural and environmental knowledge contributions are regarded and valued. The debates about the determinants of women's status are in a sense unresolvable since no objective definition of 'status' is possible: social status is culturally, historically and contextually defined. Most of the researchers contributing to this book refer to the concepts and indicators of social status used *within* the societies in question, and also consider whether gendered social constructions of status systematically accord women an asymmetrical position in relation to men within the same societies.

Concern with the relationship between women's status and welfare and plant biodiversity management is certainly not only of academic interest. To the degree that women derive enhanced status and welfare from this role, their efforts represent a major driving force for biodiversity conservation, as the example of the Mapuche women *curadoras* attests. Externally driven policies and programmes that are intended to conserve local plant biodiversity may have positive *or* negative consequences for women's status and welfare, as is discussed further below (pp. 39ff.). One of the important determinants of the outcomes may be seen as the degree to which such policies and programmes reinforce or stimulate change in existing gender power relations and their dynamics, and whether this tends to enhance women's status or not in relation to men in their communities and to other external actors. Biodiversity conservation efforts may reinforce traditional gender relations in resource management, but these may be highly inequitable for women. On the other hand, in many cases these traditional gender relations may be more equitable for women than those that emerge as a result of the 'development' process (commoditization, acculturation, colonization, migration and so on). Ultimately, many feminists argue, only the direct participation and 'voice' of women in the decision-making processes that affect them can assure that their status is not affected in ways that are undesirable to them. In fact, this is the principle that is most strongly reflected in the working programmes of the CBD under Article 8(j).[15] The difficulty still remains, however, of how to make women's voices heard in social contexts where this is generally proscribed, or where women themselves fear that speaking out will lead to undesirable consequences.[16] What is most important here is to assert the clear relationship between women's plant biodiversity management and their welfare and social status, and to point out that their reduced access to and knowledge about plants, as well as changing gender relations, are implicated in the loss of biodiversity and of women's status (see discussion of Part V on pp. 31ff.).

Women's relations to plants are at the same time relations to people that help to define their social networks and status. Füsun Ertuğ (Chapter 10) discusses how, in a society in central Anatolia, Turkey, that is still relatively traditional and patriarchal, women's wild plant gathering contributes to the creation of social networks that effectively extend what otherwise might be a highly limited social space. Peasant women gather wild plants for food, which contributes to the diet especially during winter, as well as for other subsistence purposes, and also engage in homegardening. Processing and storing food and producing domestic handi-crafts from wild plants (cloth weaving, mat, basket and broom making) are also women's work. Ninety per cent of the informants providing information on the use of medicinal plants were women. Men and boys gather mushrooms and certain bulbous plants, but men and boys gather as individuals, whereas women gather in groups. Men do not share the fruits of their labours, whereas women give gifts of wild plants to maintain social networks that in turn sustain the labour exchange that provides necessary additional labour for gardening, harvesting, childcare, and bread and bulgur making. There are also 'women's spaces' at local markets where women sell products from their homegardens. The income that they earn from this is considered to be their own. Women expend very considerable effort collecting and processing wild plants. Their knowledge of wild food plants is 'deeply en-trenched in local cuisines, traditional tastes and women's social organization', and their skills 'as cooks, artisans, gardeners and healers give them the opportunity to exchange with others, thus simultaneously enlarging their social networks' (p. 194).

These women, then, create obligations and alliances by giving gifts of wild plants and homegarden produce, just as they do in Arbëresh communities in southern Italy, where 'Wild plant gathering and gift giving represent important elements of women's village social networks and a source of status and authority for women' (Pieroni in Chapter 3, p. 66). In both of these cases, the authors emphasize the exchange of wild plants as the factor that most contributes positively to women's status, rather than their contribution to subsistence. In his research on Wola society, Sillitoe (Chapter 9) shows that women are obliged to produce most food, but it is men's prerogative to give it away. He sees this as the fundamental underpinning for the folk taxonomic system and the gender division of labour in plant management in Wola society.

Other authors place much emphasis on women's contributions to subsistence and the value of their cultural, ethnobotanical and environmental knowledge. Linda Dick Bissonnette's research (Chapter 11) provides an example of a number of 'gender-egalitarian' indigenous societies that were essentially 'women-centred' and primarily dependent upon plant resources. Her historical research focused on the indigenous people of the central California interior who were semi-nomadic hunter-gatherers for thousands of years. She concludes that 'a shift towards male power in more recent history, combined with bias against women in anthro-pological theory, contributed to the previous categorization of these cultures as patrilineal and, by implication, patriarchal' (pp. 197–8). Her own research reveals the matrifocal residence pattern and gender egalitarianism that the acorn–basketry economy fostered. 'It was Indian women who had the most knowledge of and who managed plant resources, inherited the rights to harvest certain plant patches and trees, and obtained strong economic and social positions through the exchange and trade of baskets and basketry materials', which were increasingly central to their economy (p. 199). Positions of authority and influence weren't accessible to all women, but women elders with extensive plant knowledge held positions of high esteem and were sometimes 'chiefs'. Miwok women also occupied the position of each of the three types of healers: 'witch doctors', 'dance doctors' and 'medicine doctors', and their medicinal plant knowledge was highly valued and secret. Skilled women basket makers were also highly revered, not only for their skills but also for their artistic ability which entails the exploitation and manipulation of cultural symbols related to community well-being. Even today, in spite of the disturbance of most of their native habitat and great social change, indigenous women continue to have high social status and maintain their basket-making skills and traditions. Turner (Chapter 7) also argues in relation to aboriginal women in the Pacific North-west that 'women are ... the primary managers of plant resources, and their ability to promote and perpetuate the resources that are essential to survival brings them high status and respect' (p. 143).

However, the relationship between women's knowledge, their positions as specialists and their social status is not always straightforward. Browner (1989) performed a cross-cultural analysis of the social status of midwives, which appears to depend on a wide range of factors: no overarching theory has been able to account for all of the variation encountered. Kothari (Chapter 8) suggests that it is difficult for women to attain the status of shaman even though their medicinal knowledge may be as great as men's, since the privilege associated with this position is generally reserved for men. Pieroni (Chapter 3) echoes this when he says that 'Not all forms of knowledge are equally valued within society, and "male" forms of knowledge are often privileged over "female" forms' (p. 67). Further, as discussed earlier, women's knowledge and contributions to subsistence may be systematically devalorized. According to Margot Wilson (Chapter 12), it is patriarchy that determines whether women's welfare contributions and knowledge are valued or not – and, in Bangladesh society, it is also patriarchy that allocates to women the role of maintaining indigenous biodiversity in homegardens.

In Bangladesh, homegardens provide a viable alternative to traditional field crop production for the growing number of marginal and landless farmers. Wilson argues that patriarchal norms confine women largely to the sphere of consumption and seclude them within the home. She details the gardening patterns of men and women in rural Bangladesh as distinct yet complementary. Men's gardening patterns are reminiscent of field crop production and the Near Eastern (European) gardening tradition. Women's patterns, by contrast, more clearly resemble the South-east Asian gardening tradition and probably represent the indigenous form. Men and women tend the garden at different times of the year – men in winter, women in summer – and men's gardens are located outside of the homestead, whereas women's gardens are secluded within:

... men's and women's homegardens perpetuate and reproduce spatial and social delineations that maintain the invisibility of women's contributions to biodiversity management, to food production for family consumption, and to the transmission of culture. For women, homegardening falls within the traditional roles ascribed to them, where the invisibility of their contribution is consistent with the prevalent cultural view of women as non-productive consumers of family resources ... women's work in home-gardens does not contribute positively to their social status because this is an expected, and indeed desired, structural element of patriarchy. (p. 211–12)

Social norms about women's seclusion also prohibit them from taking their own garden produce to market. Men sometimes sell their produce for them, but this income is spent, through men, on household expenditures and does not accumulate, so it has little or no positive effect on women's status. Wilson's conclusions have quite serious implications for conservation practices and policies:

Because [women's homegardening] ... is done in seclusion, it is invisible. Because it is invisible, it is allowed. Visibility of women's homegardening would bring with it the risk of disapproval or prohibition, with all the associated negative impacts on family nutrition and culinary traditions. Moreover, if women's production was profitable, there would be a risk that it would be taken over by men. (p. 223)

The dilemmas are made quite clear: in such a patriarchal social structure, if the plant biodiversity that women manage is to be conserved, then women's status will have to remain low. If the means to preserve biodiversity are to give it significant market value, then the control over these resources may shift. This is taken up again in the following section, where shifts in women's status in relation to biodiversity conservation and loss are analysed.

Several chapters in this book (Turner, Pieroni, Hoffmann and Malaza) indicate that it is not only women's status in their own communities that is associated with their plant use and knowledge: status is also accorded to them by outsiders. In all of the cases presented, the status attributed by outsiders to indigenous and peasant women's plant use and management is low insofar as they are seen as being associated with poverty, 'backwardness' or ethnic inferiority. Acculturation and loss of cultural identity may very well lead to a loss of women's status as well as biodiversity, as is discussed below.

Part V: Gender, Biodiversity Loss and Conservation

The Food and Agriculture Organization of the United Nations (FAO), in its report entitled *The State of the World's Plant Genetic Resources for Food and Agriculture,* listed the main causes of agrobiodiversity erosion as the displacement of local varieties by improved or exotic varieties, the intensification of agricultural systems that results in habitat destruction together with the use of agrochemicals, and the over-exploitation of plant resources through overgrazing and excessive harvesting of wild plants and other forest products (1997: 36–7). The FAO also examined underlying causes of these phenomena, and listed these as: the neglect of indigenous knowledge, local institutions and management systems, the expansion of industrial agriculture and the Green Revolution, the influence of corporate interests on science and technology development, inequitable tenure and control over resources, and market pressures and the undervaluation of agricultural biodiversity (1999: 23).

Clearly, globalized markets did not create and do not sustain the world's biologically rich ethno-ecosystems. Rather, these markets tend to render them valueless (leading to neglect or destruction) because they are not recognized as useful or desirable resources outside a specific cultural and environmental context (for example, when forests are cleared for commercial timber, the wild food resources of local peoples are 'inadvertently' destroyed). When these resources do become commodities, the threat of their neglect or destruction also increases due to overexploitation. 'Modern' productivist agriculture seeks to maximize yields and minimize direct costs in the context of global market competition, where production is divorced as far as is technologically possible from natural processes, local environments and local cultures (the 'de-naturalization' and 'de-socialization' of agriculture). Globalization (representing 'de-localization'), when coupled with productivism, leads to the standardization and specialization required for mass commodity production for global trade, which undermines both cultural and biological diversity.

The loss of biodiversity is related not only to the expansion of productivist agriculture, but also to the loss of local cultures and languages and the associated changes in culinary habits and the homogenization of diets that have accompanied the expansion of the global agrofood system. The indigenous people, traditional farmers and other rural dwellers throughout the world who for millennia have dynamically maintained integrated and largely sustainable ethno-ecosystems while adapting to internal and external pressures, have recently seen their livelihoods and environments disrupted and their cultural and biological diversity dramatically reduced by economic and cultural processes accompanying the expansion of markets and, with this, the penetration of exogenous cultural and economic value systems. The future sustainability and productive capacity of these integral ethno-ecosystems depend not only on adequate management and improvement, but also on the nature of demand itself, which clearly cannot be a function of an infinitely expanding set of needs determined by an unmitigated drive toward accumulation and concomitant global homogenization. This was not the nature of consumption throughout most of human history, which was largely determined by local resource availability that shaped culture and hence consumption itself.

It is clear from the discussions throughout this book that the loss of plant biodiversity is associated not only with the expansion of productivist agriculture and global markets, but also with the invisibility of the domestic sphere and the welfare and environmental benefits that are derived from women's biodiversity management, and with unequal power relations between men and women. The 1997 FAO report acknowledged that some 1,400 million 'resource-poor' farmers, the majority of whom are women (p. 25), manage much of the world's agrobiodiversity. However, there is as yet very little recognition, among either researchers or policy makers, of the specific relationships between women, gender relations, biodiversity loss and conservation.

Two fundamental concerns need to be addressed when considering this relationship. The first is whether and how gender relations are entailed in processes that lead to biodiversity loss since, if it is to be reversed, it is essential that these relationships also be addressed. The second is how the costs of biodiversity loss and, on the other hand, the benefits of conservation, are distributed between men and women. This is clearly related to the second and third objectives of the CBD: sustainable use, and the fair and equitable sharing of the benefits.

If women are principal users and managers of plant biodiversity, then it can be expected that the costs of the erosion of plant biodiversity will fall disproportionately on them. In fact, it has been persuasively argued over the past two decades that the burden of deforestation and environmental degradation often falls on poor women's shoulders, primarily because it is women who must compensate, especially through increased labour investment, when household fuelwood, food and water supplies diminish. The disproportionate impact on women when there is a decrease in wild plant resources has been especially well documented thanks to the ample research on women and forestry.[17]

Gender relations in biodiversity loss and conservation

Some researchers have attempted to develop conceptual frameworks to assess which factors motivate indigenous or peasant farmers to conserve biodiversity, but to date these have neglected to consider gender relations as potentially significant. An example is provided by Brush *et al.* (1992) who hypothesized that, among other factors, if farmers earn income off-farm, this

> may encourage diversity by providing capital to finance the cost of maintaining diverse landraces. However, it may also create disincentives for diversity. Typically it requires the farmers' selection criteria and expertise, and hired labor is likely to be an imperfect substitute for the farmer's own labor time in this regard. (*Ibid.*: 371)

They tested this hypothesis in the Paucartambo and Tulumayo valleys of Peru and found that on-farm diversity was negatively affected by off-farm occupations. This they attributed to 'a high opportunity cost of efforts to maintain diversity where off-farm income opportunities exist' (*ibid.*: 380). But Zimmerer, in the study referred to earlier (1991), found in one of the same valleys that cultivar loss was not due to the absence of the farmer who has the principal expertise. Male off-farm labour does not decrease the expertise available for cultivar selection since it is women who mainly hold this expertise in the first place. While there are many complex transformations occurring in highland agriculture due to increasing commodity production, contract farming, and temporary male out-migration, one of the major outcomes is the 'feminization of agriculture' with the concomitant increasing pressure on women farmers' labour, which is leading to the loss of cultivar diversity (1991: 307–15).

In a later article, Brush (1995) highlighted four factors that lead to farmers' *in situ* conservation of folk varieties:

- Land-holding fragmentation means that farmers manage several fields and cultivate folk varieties in at least one or more of these fields;
- Marginal agronomic conditions mean that folk varieties are competitive with improved varieties, since they perform as well or better in these environments;
- The relative isolation of many traditional farming systems means that market imperfections are created so that improved varieties lose their commercial advantages; and
- Farmers' cultural diversity and their preferences for maintaining genetic diversity mean that they maintain folk varieties.

Whereas all of the points that Brush makes can be considered to be valid, there are important factors that would not be overlooked if gender relations were considered. With regard to the first point, Brush does not mention that men and women often manage different fields, with different responsibilities for providing plant resources and different access to technology, labour, credit, knowledge and markets. The pressures on plant biodiversity in one field may therefore be quite different from those on another field, and for different reasons (see Wilson, Malaza and Wooten, this volume). With respect to Brush's second point, it has frequently been shown that the land to which women have access for field crop production is more marginal in agronomic terms than that to which men have access. For example, in The Gambia, studies have shown that women have access to lowland swamp areas and men to upland areas, and the species and varieties that they plant correspond to these different agro-ecological conditions (Dey 1983; Schroeder 1999). Nchang Ntumngia (1997) showed that in Cameroon women traditionally produce cassava on marginal land whereas men produce cash crops on higher-quality land, but with the decrease in prices for men's export cash crops and the introduction of improved cassava varieties, men have begun to plant improved cassava cultivars on higher-quality land, leaving women to continue to produce the traditional varieties that are adapted to marginal land. With respect to Brush's third point, men and women often have access to different markets: women are mainly able to access local markets, where the demand for local varieties is often greater, while men have greater access to urban and national markets, where the demand for modern varieties is higher. Brush does not mention the fact that production for subsistence is more oriented toward varieties and species that are traditionally consumed in the local diet, and is also often in the hands of women.[18] Finally, with regard to Brush's fourth point, this book shows clearly how cultural identity, genetic diversity, women and the domestic sphere are clearly interrelated and highly important, and yet are very frequently overlooked.

There is as yet no conceptual framework dealing with *in situ* conservation or erosion of plant biodiversity that takes gender relations into account. However, the case studies presented here begin to illustrate not only the motivations that women in particular have to maintain and conserve biological diversity, but also the pressures that they in particular confront to over-exploit biodiversity or to abandon its production and use.

Wooten's research (Chapter 13) in a Bamana village in Mali, illustrates how women's subsistence production based on local plant biodiversity comes into increasing competition with men's production of exotic crops for the market, and women's production is marginalized or lost in the process. Women are traditionally responsible for producing or collecting the traditional plant varieties used to make sauces and relishes that they historically produced in homegardens. However, a market-gardening regime has developed in the community, one that is directed towards satisfying a growing urban demand for fresh produce rather than local domestic requirements. Market gardening typically involves non-traditional fruit and vegetable crops: the kinds of produce typically eaten in middle-class and elite homes in the capital, not in rural villages. Middle-aged men dominate garden leadership. Older people tend to benefit from and direct the labour of their juniors, and men tend to command the labour of women. All of the market gardeners purchase commercial vegetable seed, most of which originates in Europe. While in the past women were able to use areas alongside streams for gardening, men have displaced them, since 'there was money to be made' (p. 236). Women now must focus on the production of commodities such as charcoal and shea nut butter in order to generate income, and there is evidence that they are beginning to over-exploit these wild plant and tree resources. 'Some women clearly resent the fact that what they conceive of as traditionally a woman's sphere has now become part of a man's world.' 'As one woman put it: "Men get all the gardens. They get all the money. Yet they don't give us anything, not even money for sauce or our babies"' (p. 237).

Several other studies document such a shift as markets expand. In the Meru district in Kenya, horticulture, which was the 'traditional' domain of women, has been rapidly intensified and commercialized (Dolan 1998). Women's horticultural property, conventionally confined to very small plots or gardens, was used to produce local vegetables for household consumption and sale at local markets. As French bean production for export becomes increasingly profitable, men usurp some of women's usufruct land to cultivate the new exotic crop. 'The existence of functionally separate spheres of control such as female gardens appears to be waning. Female control ... has eroded, as men foster disputes over the gendered spheres of male and female property rights, and tension resonates over the boundaries of men's and women's economic contribution to household subsistence' (1998: 5).

Richard Schroeder (1999) presents a very different view of the relationship between women's gardening, commoditization and biodiversity conservation, that nevertheless still ignores the importance of gender inequalities and gender power relations for biodiversity conservation efforts. With the support of development aid, women's production of local crops in homegardens for home consumption in The Gambia was transformed into market gardening of exotic crops in the 1980s. This was further spurred by the decrease in prices for men's cash crops and prolonged drought, since aid for market gardening was accompanied by investment in wells for women's lowland gardens and rice plots, as well as in feeder roads and markets, all under the influence of WID (Women in Development) policies. Women's cash income for the first time represented more than men's, and women began to assume the major financial responsibilities for their households. Struggles between men and women over access to women's income soon gave way to struggles over access to land and trees. Agroforestry projects intended to enhance biodiversity and promote stabilization have had the effect of reasserting men's property rights in lowland garden areas and their control over women's labour, while threatening women's market-oriented garden production. Women therefore oppose and attempt to destabilize men's tree-planting endeavours.

Shifting resources and work responsibilities between men and women are implicated in yet other ways in biodiversity loss. There is a clear relationship between the adoption of exotic varieties and the displacement of local plant biodiversity, which is related to changing markets, resource access, and labour requirements. Export markets are a driving force behind these changes, but it is not only export demand that is important: the erosion of local cultures and culinary traditions are also highly significant here, and gender relations are clearly entailed. Several studies report that the consumption of indigenous crops and wild plant foods in many developing countries is decreasing because these foods are accorded lower status in comparison with exotic foods. For example, Astone reported that, among the Fulbe people in Fuuta Jalon, Guinea, 'Women who can afford condiments such as oil, maggi, peanuts, and meat will ignore volunteer and low-prestige crops such as the boroboro leaf and small tomato' (1996: 138). Although the mix of garden crops that these women produce has not changed greatly over the past half century, wealthier women 'no longer tend low-prestige, volunteer leaf crops, due to the availability of imported condiments such as oil and peanuts' (ibid.: 315). They purchase the ingredients to replace the traditional vegetables that are now considered to be ingredients for 'poor women's sauce'.

Daniggelis (Chapter 4) also found that issues related to social status had a negative effect on the knowledge and use of local biodiversity for food in eastern Nepal. The term 'Sanskritization' describes a process whereby a caste group undergoes cultural transformation with the hope of raising themselves higher in the Hindu caste hierarchy. In the Sanskritization process, 'wild' food resources are viewed as 'poor persons' food' and 'famine food'. However, Sanskritization has also led to poorer nutritional status among certain higher-caste children in comparison with lower-caste children who continue to eat wild foods. Ogle and Grivetti (1985) reported several reasons for people living in Swaziland to discontinue the use of wild foods, including their preferences for the taste of cultivated species, their boredom with wild species, the shortage of wild species, and perceptions that eating wild species is old-fashioned. In general there was an appreciation and high level of use of wild foods, but also an attitude that their consumption was a reflection of poverty.

But it is not only the perceived status of native crops and wild foods that is leading to changes in the culinary traditions that are so important to plant biodiversity management and women's domestic skills, knowledge and status. Millicent Malaza (Chapter 14) also carried out in-depth research on this topic in Swaziland and found additional reasons for the decline in the consumption of traditional crops such as cowpeas, jugo beans, sorghum, millet and sesame seed. Although maize is the main staple, secondary staples include sorghum, pumpkins, melons, sweet potatoes and green leafy vegetables, particularly wild species. The domestic sphere plays an important role in rural areas in the conservation of traditional crops, but women's preferences for maintaining certain traditional dishes in the diet are not based on factors like taste alone. Rather, women's time constraints play an important role, especially in processing and preparation: women emphasize that preparing most of the Swazi traditional foods is very time-consuming. Women no longer grow certain indigenous food crops such as legumes because of a shortage of land and labour. Time constraints are also very evident in urban areas. Female wage employment is negatively correlated with the consumption of legume food items and traditional vegetable items. The major reasons for higher consumption of modern food items in urban areas were convenience in terms of time preparation, change of lifestyles, lack of availability of traditional foods, processing constraints related to some traditional foods, lack of knowledge about their preparation, and lack of interest in and taste for traditional food items.

Zimmerer also reported for Peru that 'despite time-saving measures, sufficient economic and social pressures sometimes overcome agriculturalists' culinary preference for native cultivars and force the substitution of improved varieties' (1991: 504). Another study provides additional insights into the status of indigenous crops managed mainly by women. In Kenya, producing and procuring traditionally leafy vegetables are largely the tasks of women since 'women's work traditionally included vegetable and food crop production and preparation, among other reproductive roles' (Maundu et al. 1999: 69). There is an 'enormous wealth of knowledge' that 'spans all possible fields: agronomy, cultivation, seed storage and protection, food preparation and nutrition' (ibid.: 77). But there is pressure against the production and use of these vegetables due to the need to earn income, the fact that market demand is highly biased toward exotics, and that technology and extension services have strongly promoted exotic vegetable crops. Nevertheless, there is also a trend toward an increase in the production of traditional leafy vegetables due to their decrease in the wild and the existence of a market demand for a limited number of varieties.

The foregoing should make it clear that the utility of plant biodiversity for humans depends not only on the demand for these resources that is related to culture and culinary traditions, but also on the availability of labour, of knowledge of the properties of plants, and of the skills and technology for processing, preserving, preparing and storing plant materials. If for any reason these are lost, the use and knowledge of the plants concerned is also likely to be lost eventually – and this, in turn, can threaten species that depend for their existence upon human interventions. The major reasons cited for the erosion of plant biodiversity are usually not related to the kitchen or the domestic sphere, but rather to factors related to production and the environment. However, it is increasingly recognized that changing food habits that are related to migration, urbanization, globalization of food habits and expanding food commodity markets result in a decrease in the management and use of local biodiversity. The awareness that gender relations are also intimately involved must also grow.

The devalorization of traditional culinary habits and indigenous foodstuffs is part and parcel of a more general trend, where women's use of traditional crops and wild plant resources is devalorized by dominant cultures and formal educational systems that teach girls to abandon their agricultural, culinary and medicinal customs, knowledge and practices, which can also lead to a decrease in women's status. In the Venezuelan Amazon, Shirley Hoffmann (Chapter 15) shows that Arawakan women are the primary cultivators of swidden fields and homegardens. The production of bitter manioc (*Manihot esculenta*), along with small amounts of other tubers, seeds, vegetables and fruits, has provided the bulk of calories and micronutrients in the Arawakan diet. Women have the knowledge to ensure a sustainable and reliable food supply. They maintain crop and cultivar diversity, process and cook food products, and pass this knowledge on to the next generation of women. Traditional cultivation, collecting and food processing activities have provided Arawakan peoples with adequate nutrition in an extremely marginal ecosystem for thousands of years. Since their first contact with colonial explorers, Arawakans have adapted to outside influences and yet, to a great extent, have maintained their traditional subsistence activities. However, within the last 35–40 years, the government has increased its efforts to integrate Amazonas into the national economy. Although the region contributes little in terms of resources, heavy investments have been forthcoming for reasons of political and national security. Education has been encouraged, and Arawakans have had to migrate to larger population centres to ensure that children attend school. Besides disrupting traditional subsistence patterns, education has also devalorized women's traditional subsistence practices. Girls who go to school no longer learn traditional agriculture from their mothers, and are taught to think that they are destined for something better than working in the fields. In areas of in-migration, the overuse of nearby agricultural land has degraded the cultivation system. The government's use of Arawakan labour has also encouraged Arawakans to abandon traditional activities including cultivation, so the strategies that people employ to feed their families are changing significantly. Women have made decisions about cultivation based on these larger societal influences. Their roles as cultivation experts and food processers are changing as specialized skills and knowledge are left behind. This has caused a decline in the region's subsistence system, particularly in crop and cultivar diversity and in the detailed knowledge required in order to guarantee a steady and reliable food supply. The gender division of labour at household and community level has also changed. The effects on Arawakan women have been detrimental, and women's key role in the household has eroded, which has led to a restructuring of households including an increase in the number of young unwed mothers who are dependent on their parents. This has affected the quality of life for many Arawakans negatively, and created a greater dependency on an externally imposed 'welfare' economy. As the Venezuelan economy deteriorates, the welfare economy itself is disintegrating, and the Arawakans have little to fall back on.

Pieroni and Turner (Chapters 3 and 7) also cite the devalorization of women's traditional subsistence practices and cultural knowledge as a major reason for the erosion of local plant-related knowledge and practices, where formal education systems associated with the dominant cultures are implicated and women's traditional sources of status erode. In nearly every one of the above examples, women's shifting access to resources and labour, together with the devalorization of their traditional practices, knowledge and skills, have been influenced by economic, political and cultural processes accompanying the expansion of markets and, together with this, the penetration of exogenous cultural and economic value systems. Women's capacities to negotiate these changes in ways that are favourable to them are often compromised by the fact that they confront not only asymmetrical power relations with respect to dominant cultures and economic and political systems, but also asymmetrical gender power relations within their own communities and households.

What can be done? Gender and biodiversity conservation initiatives

The CBD is concerned with sustainably conserving biological diversity and ensuring the fair and equitable distribution of the benefits of its use. Much of the international debate about the achievement of this latter objective is centred on benefit sharing through different mechanisms that recognize and compensate indigenous peoples for their knowledge and contributions to plant biodiversity (as discussed above in relation to Part II) and to rights and management. It is important to emphasize that these debates do *not* address the distribution of the costs of genetic erosion, nor do they aim to compensate the affected populations for these losses. The only way currently to address these costs is indirectly, through efforts to reduce the erosion of genetic resources by means of conservation policies and initiatives.

There has in fact been much discussion relative to the distribution of the direct costs and benefits of conservation initiatives, particularly in relation to wildlife (mainly large mammals) when this has meant setting aside areas in natural parks and reserves, since this limits or prohibits local people's access to and control over natural resources. Some research has been sensitive to women in particular, and most of this has shown that women's needs are insufficiently considered in wildlife conservation programmes and policies (Hunter *et al.* 1990; Nabane and Matzke 1997; Sullivan 2000). There is much more research and discussion in the area of forest conservation and management, where the importance of women and gender issues was recognized fairly early on (Molnar & Schrieber 1989; van der Borg 1989; Wilde & Vanio-Mattila 1996; Rocheleau 1989). However, there is as yet very little research on the differential repercussions for men and women of plant biodiversity conservation efforts, and such research should be of high priority.[19]

It is also important to note that in the context of the most recent review of implementation of priority tasks under Article 8(j) and related CBD provisions on indigenous and local knowledge, use and conservation of biological diversity, 28 parties to the Convention indicated that they had fully incorporated women and women's organizations into the activities that they had undertaken, whereas 26 had not. This led the Working Group to conclude that 'much more still needs to be done in relation to increasing the participation of women in the work of the Convention' (UNEP 2000b). However, decades of experience in efforts to main-stream women's concerns and equity issues into development policies and programmes, combined with the analysis presented in this book regarding gender blindness in research and policy related to women and plants, lead one to question whether the claims of the 28 parties who have 'fully incorporated' women into conservation efforts can be fully substantiated.

Can women's needs, interests, knowledge and drives to conserve plant bio-diversity be fully and equitably dealt with in conservation initiatives? The case of the Mapuche shows that efforts to do so are occurring. Although there is as yet no certainty that creating a national market for Mapuche women's indigenous plant varieties will lead to the desired results, there may be cause for optimism. Yiching Song and Janice Jiggins (Chapter 16) present another case study exploring efforts to reverse processes leading to genetic erosion and gender discrimination. Song's earlier research in Guangxi province in South-west China showed that there has been a strong process of feminization of agriculture due to male out-migration (women now represent 80–90 per cent of farm heads), which has increased women's responsibilities for all aspects. Women in the area have always been mainly responsible for varietal selection and seed management. However, until now, owing to gender bias, this role has not been recognized by the government. Women have had less access than men to government resources and particularly to formal seed supply systems, and are experiencing severe labour constraints as well as the erosion of their maize genetic resources (Song 1998: 129–52). Song and Jiggins show that two parallel seed systems are in place: that of the formal plant breeding sector and that maintained by poor women who have developed the skills to refresh their preferred varieties through hybridization. Formal plant breeders and poor women farmers have diverse goals: the former seek higher yields and wide dissemination of genetically uniform varieties, whereas the latter seek to ensure food security by planting a range of varieties that they have carefully bred to match the diversity of agro-environmental conditions that they confront.

Chapter 16 focuses on the emerging situation and a participatory plant breeding and varietal selection project being carried out with women farmers in Guangxi province, one that Song helped to formulate in response to the situation that she encountered in her research. Up to the end of 2000, the primary stakeholder in the formal seed supply system was the Ministry of Agriculture, to which extension agents, farmers, breeders and seed companies were linked. Formerly, tensions existed among these stakeholders, but the government is moving to ease the situation by liberalizing and privatizing certain roles and functions. One approach adopted to further this is the establishment of pilot schemes under a new Seed Law that permits the division between private and public to be crossed. The project represents one such pilot scheme. It is exploring ways to create partnerships in the emerging seed system involving agricultural research, academic institutes and the provincial authority responsible for agriculture. In this project, maize breeding is carried out together with publicly employed agricultural extension workers based at grassroots extension stations and with village-based farmer technicians (FTs). Women FTs have been recruited who are known local expert maize breeders, and they have introduced other expert women farmers into the process:

> Over time, the knowledge, skills and attitudes of the breeders and extensionists, on the one hand, and of the farmers, on the other, are drawing closer together, which strengthens all participants. Routinely, 70 to 80 per cent of the participants in the collaborative activities are women, with the women professionals taking a lead role in ensuring that their male colleagues 'listen to and learn from' the women farmers. (p. 285)

Collaboration in maize varietal selection and breeding has linked women farmer maize breeders to the wider range of materials held by the research station, and has strengthened biodiversity conservation 'by widening the collection of materials accessible to farmer breeder; and by increasing the range of parental lines used by the formal breeders' (p. 287). While the project cannot change the processes that have led to the feminization of agriculture in the first place, the authors conclude that 'the lessons learned offer promise that women farmers' experience, skills and needs will be more respected as agricultural modernization proceeds' (*ibid.*).

It is certain that more resources should be invested in examining the effects of plant biodiversity conservation initiatives on women. However, such individual conservation initiatives offer only a very slim shadow of hope with respect to the global picture. In the medium and long terms, neither productivist, globalized agro-food systems, nor an economic and social order that devalorizes the domestic sphere and women, are socially, environmentally or economically sustainable. The conservation of the world's remaining plant biodiversity requires that agriculture and biological resource management be 're-localized' and that the co-evolutionary relationships between culture and nature be re-established, which in turn implies that local people will have to be enabled and empowered, partly through the recognition of their rights to access and control over resources and knowledge. This is impossible to accomplish without ensuring that these resource managers, particularly women, are able to achieve a culturally and physically acceptable level of welfare from their interactions with the environment and society. The 'sustainable use' and 'fair and equitable sharing of the benefits' from the use of biological diversity cannot be addressed at all without considering the importance of women, the domestic sphere and equity in gender relations in plant biodiversity management at local level. These can be ravaged in a single generation by commoditization and acculturation processes that place little value on them.

Women throughout the global South and in traditional communities in the North struggle to maintain their livelihoods, their cultural integrity, status and biological wealth, but are very often disadvantaged by gender inequalities and bias within households, economies and political systems. It is little wonder that many mothers want their daughters to abandon traditional occupations and knowledge, ostensibly to enjoy the advantages of the 'modern' urban world, and that their daughters are indeed massively abandoning the countryside to improve their status. The productive work, the great body of knowledge, culture and traditions that these young women leave behind are likely to be lost to them and to future generations. How, then, can it be expected that, when economic or environmental crises or democratic processes finally mandate the re-establishment of nature–culture co-evolutionary relationships across the globe, women will be able or willing to maintain and promote traditional occupations and knowledge systems?

Notes

1   See, for example http://www.soc.uu.se/mapuche/index.html and http://www.mapuche.nl/
2   There is no single internationally accepted definition of agrobiodiversity, and its boundaries are drawn differently by different agencies and in different agreements. For example, the International Treaty on Plant Genetic Resources for Food and Agriculture defines it as 'Any genetic material of plant origin of actual or potential value for food and agriculture' (CGRFA 2001). In one of the CBD Secretariat's publications, it is defined as 'the diversity at all levels of the biological hierarchy, from genes to ecosystems, that is involved in agriculture and food production ... the fundamental and distinct property of agricultural biodiversity is that it is largely created, maintained and managed by humans.... Wild species and their products used for food are not usually regarded as part of agricultural biodiversity unless there is some degree of resource management involved ... ' (CBD Secretariat 2001). However, Article 8(j) of the CBD is not restricted to 'agrobiodiversity' but refers at all times to biological diversity. Therefore, the term used throughout this book is 'plant biodiversity' rather than 'agrobiodiversity'.
3   The Convention on Biological Diversity has been ratified by 177 governments. Article 8(j) states: '(j) Subject to its national legislation, respect, preserve and maintain knowledge, innovations and practices of indigenous and local communities embodying traditional lifestyles relevant for the conservation and sustainable use of biological diversity and promote their wider application with the approval and involvement of the holders of such knowledge, innovations and practices and encourage the equitable sharing of the benefits arising from the utilization of such knowledge, innovations and practices' (CBD Secretariat 1992).
4   This literature is highly dispersed throughout a number of subject areas and disciplines. It is difficult to identify because it is often not explicitly focused on women, and is devoid of titles, keywords and descriptors that reveal its gender-specific content. Most of the chapters in this book were written by the authors specifically to present research findings that heretofore had been available only in the form of PhD dissertations or were otherwise unpublished. The literature search is based on a set of key words developed to identify a broad set of literature dealing with local management of plant biodiversity. Bibliographical reference sources are identified and fully reviewed. Descriptors and abstracts of each citation are reviewed to determine which documents are likely to contain empirical data focused on people, irrespective of whether this appears to be sex-disaggregated. Documents selected are then read to determine whether they in fact have relevant gender-related content. Some 3,000 bibliographical citations are under review. This book presents several in-depth case

studies, but still only contains a fraction of the findings.

5 See, for example, Madge 1994; Coursey 1982; Meyer-Renschausen 1991; Nicholson 1960.

6 See also Spijkers and Box 1981; Dole 1978; Chiwona-Karltun 2001.

7 See, for example, Ashby and Herpen 1991; Boster 1985; Ferguson et al. 1990; Jiggins 1986.

8 The most substantial body of research on rights to vegetation is probably represented by that focusing on 'tree tenure' (Fortmann and Bruce 1988), which also shows that there is a relationship between rights to trees and rights to land. Over much of Africa, women are not permitted to plant trees since tree planting confers ownership rights to land which is men's privilege, but women are allowed to harvest from trees.

9 It is interesting to note that gender blindness was not so obvious in people–plant research prior to the emergence of 'economic botany' around the 1940s. This is at least in part attributable to the fact that much historical ethnobotanical research was more 'anthropological' and 'ethnographic' in comparison to 'economic botany', which focuses much more on plants and their potential economic uses than on people. Much ethnobotanical research still focuses exclusively on plants.

10 See especially Weeratunge Starkloff (1998) for an in-depth discussion of contemporary global discourses on indigenous knowledge, the anthropology of knowledge and feminist debates on gendered knowledge. She examines these in relationship to the social construction of local environmental knowledge and practice among the highland Uva of Sri Lanka.

11 Notable examples include Boster (1985, 1986), Descola (1994), Norton (1985) and Denevan and Padoch (1987) on the Peruvian Bora swidden agriculturalists' management of fallows, although in this latter case this would not be evident except for a brief mention within the report of the fact that planting and much of the management of fallows is done by women.

12 FAO conducted a survey of extension services in 115 countries showing that women only received between 2 and 10 per cent of all extension contacts and a mere 5 per cent of extension resources world-wide.

13 For overviews see Rocheleau (1989); Brownrigg (1985); Scoones et al. (1992); FAO (1989).

14 See, for example, Wilson, Wooten and Malaza in this volume, as well as Nchang Ntumngia 1997; Kumar 1994; Song 1998; Chewya and Eyzaguirre 1999.

15 For example, the Preamble to the CBD calls for 'the full participation of women at all levels of policy-making and implementation for biological diversity conservation', and the review of progress focuses exclusively on this topic (see section on Part V, p. 31ff).

16 See Kabeer 1994 for a useful discussion.

17 See Molnar and Schrieber (1989); van der Borg (1989); Wilde and Vaino-Mattila (1996); Rocheleau (1989).

18 See Nchang Ntumngia (1997); Defoer et al. (1996); Chewya and Eyzaguirre (1999); Wooten, Wilson, Greenberg and Malaza, this volume.

19 The only review dealing with the gender sensitivity of biodiversity conservation policies that I have found is Kaiza-Boshe (1994) for Tanzania. Although this work must now be considered out of date, her survey of relevant implementing institutions led to conclusions that are very instructive and invite wider generalization: the government recognizes women's role in biodiversity conservation but does not provide strategies, plans and programmes specifically to involve them; conservation planners and senior biodiversity executives are not sufficiently aware of the implications of gender issues for biodiversity programmes; biodiversity conservation institutions aren't aware of the need to train their staff regarding gender issues; there are no local initiatives to involve women in formal biodiversity conservation programmes, and the only biodiversity projects established for women have been established and funded by foreigners; and institutions dealing with women's affairs don't have sufficient expertise in biodiversity conservation to manage projects in this area.

References

Abbink, J. (1993) 'Me'en medicinal, ritual and other plants: a contribution to Southwest Ethiopian ethnobotany', *Journal of Ethiopian Studies*, Vol. 26, No. 2, pp. 1–19.

Aguilar, M. (2001) 'Culinaria Mapuche: hagamos el almuerzo y no la guerra Mapuche', *El Mercurio Electronico*, Santiago, 12 October, http://www.soc.uu.se/mapuche/docs/merc011012.html

Akoroda, M. O. (1990) 'Ethnobotany of *Telfairia occidentalis* (cucurbitaceae) among Igbos of Nigeria', *Economic Botany*, Vol. 44, No. 1, pp. 29–39.

Alexiades, M. (1999) 'Ethnobotany of the Ese Eja: Plants, Health and Change in an Amazonian Society (Plant Medicinals)', PhD dissertation, City University of New York, Ann Arbor, Michigan: University Microfilms International.

Anderson, M. (1983) 'Woman as generalist, as specialist, and as diversifier in Saami subsistence activities', *Humboldt Journal of Social Relations*, Vol. 10, No. 2, pp. 175–97.

Ashby, J. and D. van Herpen (1991) 'Case study: the introduction of a new bean variety in La Merced', in D. van Herpen and J. Ashby (eds.), *Gender Analysis in Agricultural Research: Proceedings of an Internal Workshop*, Palmira, Colombia, 13–14 June 1991, Cali (Colombia): Centro Internacional de Agricultura Tropical (CIAT), pp. 5–19.

Astone, J. (1996) 'Negotiating Work Burdens: Women's Home Gardens in Fuuta Jalon, Guinea, 1930–1995', PhD dissertation, State University of New York at Binghamton, Ann Arbor, Michigan: University Microfilms International.

Balick, M., and P. Cox (1996) *Plants, People, and Culture: the Science of Ethnobotany*, Scientific American Library series No. 60, New York: Scientific American Library.

Bennett, S. (2000) *Five Centuries of Women and Gardens,* London: National Portrait Gallery Publications.

Boster, J. S. (1985) 'Selection for perceptual distinctiveness: evidence from Aguaruna cultivars of *Manihot esculenta*', *Economic Botany*, Vol. 39, No. 3, pp. 310–25.

Boster, J. S. (1986) 'Exchange of varieties and information between Aguaruna manioc cultivators', *American Anthropologist,* Vol. 88, pp. 428–36.

Briggs, J., M. Badri and A. Mekki (1999) 'Indigenous knowledges and vegetation use among Bedouin in the eastern desert of Egypt', *Applied Geography*, Vol. 19, No. 2, pp. 87–103.

Brightman, R. (1996) 'The sexual division of foraging labor: biology, taboo, and gender politics', *Comparative Studies in Society and History*, Vol. 38, No. 4, pp. 687–729.

Brodt, S. (1998) 'Learning from the Land: Local Knowledge Systems of Tree Management in Central India', PhD dissertation, University of Hawaii, Ann Arbor, Michigan: University Microfilms International.

Browner, C. H. (1989) 'The management of reproduction in an egalitarian society', in C. Shepherd McClain (ed.), *Women as Healers: Cross-cultural Perspectives*, New Brunswick and London: Rutgers University Press, pp. 58–71.

Browner, C. H. and S. T. Perdue (1988) 'Women's secrets: bases for reproductive and social autonomy in a Mexican community', *American Ethnologist*, Vol. 15, No. 1, pp. 84–97.

Brownrigg, L. (1985) *Home Gardening in International Development: What the Literature Shows*, League for International Food Education, Washington, DC.

Brush, S. (1995) '*In situ* conservation of landraces in centers of crop diversity', *Crop Science,* Vol. 35, No. 2, pp. 346–54.

Brush, S., J. Edward Taylor and M. Bellon (1992) 'Technology adoption and biological diversity in Andean potato agriculture', *Journal of Development Economics*, Vol. 39, pp. 365–87.

Carlstein, T. (1982) *Time Resources, Society and Ecology,* Vol. 1, *Preindustrial Societies*, London: George Allen and Unwin.

Cartledge, D. (1995) 'Taming the Mountain: Human Ecology, Indigenous Knowledge, and Sustainable Resource Management in the Doko Gamo Society of Ethiopia', PhD dissertation, University of Florida, Ann Arbor, Michigan: University Microfilms International.

CBD (Convention on Biological Diversity) Secretariat (1992) *Convention on Biological Diversity,*

Montreal: CBD Secretariat, http://www.biodiv.org.

CBD (Convention on Biological Diversity) Secretariat (2001) *Global Biodiversity Outlook*, Montreal: CBD Secretariat http://www.biodiv.org/doc/publications/gbo/gbo-ch-01-en.pdf

CGRFA (Commission on Genetic Resources for Food and Agriculture) (2001) *International Treaty on Plant Genetic Resources for Food and Agriculture*, Rome: CGRFA.

Chewya, J. A. and P. Eyzaguirre (eds.) (1999) *The Biodiversity of Traditional Leafy Vegetables*, Rome: International Plant Genetic Resources Institute (IPGRI).

Chiwona-Karltun, L. (2001) 'A Reason to be Bitter: Cassava Classification from the Farmers' Perspective', PhD dissertation, Department of Public Health Sciences, Karolinska Institute, Sweden.

Cleveland, D. and S. Murray (1997) 'The world's crop genetic resources and the rights of indigenous farmers', *Current Anthropology*, Vol. 38, No. 4, pp. 477–515.

Compton, B. (1993) 'Upper North Wakashan and Southern Tsimshian Ethnobotany: the Knowledge and Usage of Plants among the Oweekeno, Hanaksiala (Kitlope and Kemano), Haisla (Kitamaat) and Kitasoo Peoples of the Central and North Coasts of British Colombia', PhD dissertation, University of British Columbia, Victoria, Ann Arbor, Michigan: University Microfilms International.

Coughenour, C. M. and S. M. Nazhat (1986) 'The process of agricultural change among women farmers of North Kordofan, Sudan', *Ahfad Journal: Women and Change* (Sudan), Vol. 3, No. 1, pp. 19–28.

Counihan, C. and S. Kaplan (1998) *Food and Gender: Identity and Power*, Newark, New Jersey: Harwood Academic.

Coursey, D. G. (1982) 'Traditional tropical root crop technology: some interactions with modern science', *IDS Bulletin*, Vol. 13, No. 3, pp. 12–20.

Defoer, T., A. Kamara and H. de Groote (1996) 'Gender and variety selection: farmers' assessment of local maize varieties in Southern Mali', *African Crop Science Journal*, Vol. 5, No. 1, pp. 65–76.

Denevan, W. and C. Padoch (eds.) (1987) *Swidden-fallow Agroforestry in the Peruvian Amazon*, Advances in Economic Botany 5, New York: New York Botanical Garden Scientific Publications Department.

Descola, P. (1994) *In the Society of Nature: a Native Ecology in Amazonia*, Cambridge: Cambridge University Press.

Dey, J. (1983) 'Rice farming systems: case studies of current developments and future alternatives in upland rice and inland swamp rice', Expert Consultation on Women in Food Production, Rome, Italy, 7–14 December 1983, ESH: WIFP/83/4, Rome: FAO.

Dolan, C. (1998) 'Tesco is King: Gender and Labor Dynamics in Horticultural Exporting, Meru District, Kenya', PhD dissertation, State University of New York at Binghamton, Ann Arbor, Michigan: University Microfilms International.

Dole, G. (1978) 'The use of manioc among the Kuijuru: some interpretations', in R. Ford (ed.), *The Nature and Status of Ethnobotany*, University of Michigan, Anthropological Papers, Museum of Anthropology, Vol. 67, pp. 217–47.

Douglas, M. (1984) 'Standard social uses of food', in M. Douglas (ed.), *Food in the Social Order: Studies of Food and Festivities in Three American Communities*, New York: Russell Sage Foundation, pp. 1–39.

Duke, J. and R. Vasquez (1994) *Amazonian Ethnobotanical Dictionary*, Boca Raton: CRC Press.

FAO (Food and Agriculture Organization of the United Nations) (1989) *Household Food Security and Forestry: an Analysis of Socio-economic Issues*, Rome: FAO.

FAO (Food and Agriculture Organization of the United Nations) (1993) *Agricultural Extension and Farm Women in the 1980s*, Rome: FAO.

FAO (Food and Agriculture Organization of the United Nations) (1997) *The State of the World's Plant Genetic Resources for Food and Agriculture*, Rome: FAO.

FAO (Food and Agriculture Organization of the United Nations) (1999) 'Agricultural biodiversity', Background Paper 1, FAO/Netherlands Conference on the Multifunctional

Character of Agriculture and Land, Rome: FAO.

Fedigan, L. (1986) 'The changing role of women in models of human evolution', *Annual Review of Anthropology*, Vol. 15, pp. 25–66.

Ferguson, A., A. Millard and S. Khaila (1990) 'Crop improvement programmes and nutrition in Malawi: exploring the links', *Food and Nutrition Bulletin*, Vol. 12, No. 4, pp. 273–8.

Fortmann, L. and W. Bruce (eds.) (1988) *Whose Trees? Proprietary Dimensions of Forestry*, Boulder, Colorado: Westview Press.

Fowler, C. (1994) *Unnatural Selection: Technology, Politics, and Plant Evolution*, Langhorne, Pennsylvania: Gordon and Breach.

Hays, T. E. (1974) 'Mauna: Explorations in Ndumba Ethnobotany', PhD dissertation, University of Washington, Ann Arbor, Michigan: University Microfilms International.

Herrick, J. (edited with a foreword by D. Snow) (1995) *Iroquois Medical Botany*, New York: Syracuse University Press.

Howard-Borjas, P. with W. Cuijpers (2002) 'Gender and the management and conservation of plant biodiversity', in H. W. Doelle and E. DaSilva (eds.), *Biotechnology*, in *Encyclopedia of Life Support Systems (EOLSS)*, Oxford, UK, http://www.eolss.net.

Hunter, M., R. Hitchcock and B. Wyckoff-Baird (1990) 'Women and wildlife in Southern Africa', *Conservation Biology*, Vol. 4, No. 4, pp. 448–51.

Hyde, E. (1998) 'Cultivated Power: Flowers, Culture, and Politics in Early Modern France', PhD dissertation, Harvard University, Ann Arbor, Michigan: University Microfilms International.

Jiggins, J. (1986) 'Gender-related impacts and the work of the International Agricultural Research centers', CGIAR Study Paper No. 17, Consultative Group on International Agricultural Research, World Bank, Washington DC.

Kabeer, N. (1994) *Reversed Realities. Gender Hierarchies in Development Thought*, London/New York: Verso.

Kaiza-Boshe, T. (1994) 'Women in biodiversity conservation in Tanzania. The need for gender conscientization', paper presented at the Symposium on African Biodiversity: Foundation for the Future at the Danish Volunteer Centre, Arusha, 3 October.

Kitch, L., O. Boukar, C. Endondo and L. Murdock (1998) 'Farmer acceptability criteria in breeding cowpea', *Experimental Agriculture*, Vol. 34, No. 4, pp. 475–86.

Kumar, S. (1994) *Adoption of Hybrid Maize in Zambia: Effects on Gender Roles, Food Consumption, and Nutrition*, Research Report No. 100m, Washington, DC: International Food Policy Research Institute.

Longley, C. (2000) 'A Social Life of Seeds: Local Management of Crop Variability in North-western Sierra Leone', PhD dissertation, University College London.

Madge, C. (1994) 'Collected food and domestic knowledge in The Gambia, West Africa', *Geographical Journal*, Vol. 160, No. 3, pp. 280–94.

Martin, G. (1996) 'Comparative Ethnobotany of the Chinantec and Mixe of the Sierra Norte, Oaxaca, Mexico', PhD dissertation, University of California at Berkeley, Ann Arbor: University Microfilms International.

Maundu, P., E. Njiro, J. Chweya, J. Imungi and E. Seme (1999) 'Kenya', in J. Chewya and P. Eyzaguirre (eds.), *The Biodiversity of Traditional Leafy Vegetables*, Rome: IPGRI, pp. 48–84.

McIntosh, W. and M. Zey (1998) 'Women as gatekeepers of food consumption: a sociological critique', in C. Counihan and S. Kaplan (eds.), *Food and Gender: Identity and Power*, Amsterdam: Harwood Academic Publishers, pp. 125–44.

Meyer-Renschausen, E. (1991) 'The porridge debate: grain, nutrition, and forgotten food preparation techniques', *Food and Foodways*, Vol. 5, No. 1, pp. 95–120.

Molnar, A. and G. Schrieber (1989) *Women and Forestry: Operational Issues*, Policy, Planning, and Research Working Paper WPS 184, Washington DC: World Bank.

Nabane, N. and G. Matzke (1997) 'A gender-sensitive analysis of a community-based wildlife utilization initiative in Zimbabwe's Zambezi Valley', *Society and Natural Resources*, Vol. 10, No. 6, pp. 519–35.

Nchang Ntumngia, R. (1997) 'Gender Power Dynamics and Knowledge Systems in Household

Food Security: a Case Study of Malende and Mautu Cassava Farmers, Muyuka – Cameroon', MSc thesis, Wageningen Agricultural University, the Netherlands.

Nicholson, G. E. (1960) 'Chica maize types of chicha manufacture in Peru', *Economic Botany*, Vol. 14, pp. 290–9.

Niñez, V. (1987) 'Household gardens: theoretical and policy considerations', Part I, *Agricultural Systems*, Vol. 23, pp. 167–86.

Norton, H. H. (1985) 'Women and Resources of the Northwest Coast: Documentation from the 18th and Early 19th Centuries', PhD dissertation, University of Washington, Ann Arbor, Michigan: University Microfilms International.

Ogle, B. and L. Grivetti (1985) 'Legacy of the chameleon: edible wild plants in the Kingdom of Swaziland, Southern Africa. A cultural, ecological, nutritional study. Part III: cultural and ecological analysis', *Ecology of Food and Nutrition*, Vol. 17, pp. 31–40.

Quinn, N. (1977) 'Anthropological studies on women's status', *Annual Review of Anthropology*, Vol. 6, pp. 181–225.

Rasmussen, S. J. (1998) 'Only women know trees: medicine women and the role of herbal healing in Taureg culture', *Journal of Anthropological Research*, Vol. 54, No. 2, pp. 148–71.

Rocheleau, D. (1989) 'Gender division of work, resources and rewards in agroforestry systems', Second Kenya National Seminar on Agroforestry, Nairobi, Kenya: ICRAF.

Rusten, E. (1989) 'An Investigation of an Indigenous Knowledge System and Management of Tree Fodder Resources in the Middle Hills of Western Nepal', PhD dissertation, Michigan State University, Ann Arbor, Michigan: University Microfilms International.

Schroeder, R. (1999) *Shady Practices. Agroforestry and Gender Politics in The Gambia*, Berkeley: University of California Press.

Scoones, I., M. Melnyk and J. Pretty (eds.) (1992) *The Hidden Harvest: Wild Foods and Agricultural Systems. A Literature Review and Annotated Bibliography*, Sustainable Agriculture Programme, London: International Institute for Environment and Development.

Shellie, K. (1990) 'Food Quality and Fuelwood Conservation of Selected Common Bean (*Phaseolus vulgaris* L.) Cultivars and Landraces in Rwanda (Cooking Time)', PhD dissertation, Michigan State University, Ann Arbor: University Microfilms International.

Shteir, A. (1996) *Cultivating Women, Cultivating Science. Flora's Daughters and Botany in England, 1760 to 1860*, London: Johns Hopkins University Press.

Song, Y. (1998) '"New" Seed in "Old" China. Impact of CIMMYT Collaborative Programme on Maize Breeding in South-western China', PhD dissertation, Wageningen Agricultural University, the Netherlands.

Spijkers, P. and L. Box (1981) 'Cultivators and their crops', in Department of Rural Sociology of the Tropics and Subtropics (ed.), *Essays in Rural Sociology in Honor of R.A.J. van Lier*, Wageningen: Wageningen Agricultural University, pp. 264–304.

Sullivan, S. (2000) 'Gender, ethnographic myths and community-based conservation in a former Namibian "homeland"', in D. Hodgson (ed.), *Rethinking Pastoralism in Africa*, James Currey (Oxford), Fountain Publishers (Kampala), East African Educational Publishers (Nairobi).

Tapia, M. E., and A. de la Torre (1998) *Women Farmers and Andean Seeds*, Rome: FAO and IPGRI.

Tilzey, M. (2000) 'Natural areas, the whole countryside approach and sustainable agriculture', *Land Use Policy*, Vol. 17, No. 4, pp. 279–94.

Turner, Nancy (2002) Personal communication, April.

UNEP (United Nations Environment Programme) (2000a) 'Legal and other appropriate forms of protection for the knowledge, innovations and practices of indigenous and local communities embodying traditional lifestyles relevant for the conservation and sustainable use of biological diversity. Note by the Executive Secretary', Ad Hoc Open-ended Inter-Sessional Working Group on Article 8(j) and Related Provisions of the Convention on Biological Diversity, First meeting, Seville 27–31 March 2000, Item 3 of the Provisional Agenda, UNEP/CBD/WG8J/1/2 10 January.

UNEP (United Nations Environment Programme) (2000b) 'Report of the Working Group on the implementation of Article 8(j) and related provisions', Conference of the Parties to the

Convention on Biological Diversity, Fifth meeting, Nairobi, 15–26 May 2000, Item 11 of the provisional agenda, UNEP/CBD/COP/5/5, 12 April.

Vedavalli, L. and N. Anil Kumar (1998) 'Wayanad, Kerala', in M. S. Swaminathan (ed.), *Gender Dimensions in Biodiversity Management*, Delhi: Konark Publishers Pvt. Ltd., pp. 96–106.

van der Borg, B. 1989. *Women's Role in Forest Resource Management: A Reader*, Rome: FAO.

Weeratunge Starkloff, N. (1998) 'Trees of Desire: Gender, Environmental Knowledge and Practice in the Highland Uva of Sri Lanka', PhD dissertation, University of Toronto, Ann Arbor, Michigan: University Microfilms International.

Wilde, V. and A. Vaino-Mattila (1996) *Gender Analysis and Forestry'*, International Training Package, Forest, Trees, and People Program, Rome: FAO.

Wilson, W. (1997) 'Why Bitter Cassava (*Manihot esculenta* Crantz)? Productivity and Perception of Cassava in a Tukanoan Indian Settlement in the Northwest Amazon (Colombia)', PhD dissertation, University of Colorado at Boulder, Ann Arbor: University Microfilms International.

Zimmerer, K. (1991) 'Seeds of Peasant Subsistence: Agrarian Structure, Crop Ecology and Quechua Agriculture in Reference to the Loss of Biological Biodiversity in the Southern Peruvian Andes', PhD dissertation, University of California Berkeley, Ann Arbor, Michigan: University Microfilms International.

PART I
Culture, Kitchen and
Conservation

CHAPTER 2
Women in the Garden and Kitchen: The Role of Cuisine in the Conservation of Traditional House Lot Crops among Yucatec Mayan Immigrants

Laurie S. Z. Greenberg

Women's role in plant management and conservation may be as old as agriculture itself. Women have managed and conserved plants through the centuries because plants meet a variety of household needs for food, medicine, construction and craft materials, ornamentation, income generation, religious practice and trade, among others. Women pass on their knowledge about management and use from one generation to the next. Under women's management, some plants evolve, are conserved, and are disseminated throughout the world.

Mesoamerica is one of the major world centres of genetic diversity where numerous crops were originally domesticated and improved by indigenous peoples. Many Yucatec Mayans still cultivate traditional crop varieties in their gardens and fields. Field cultivation, historically managed by Yucatec men, in many cases no longer provides adequate food or income to meet family needs (Ewell and Merrill-Sands 1987: 97). Although many farmers still grow traditional crops, traditional Yucatec field agriculture is declining. One result is the genetic erosion of crop biodiversity, which is threatening future sources of plant genetic material long managed by the Yucatec Maya. In traditional Yucatec Mayan households, women's daily activities are centred on the house lot. Women's house lot activities include horticulture, small livestock production, child rearing, food processing and preparation, and related tasks. The house lot is known as a *solar*. Traditional Yucatec Mayan house lots contain multiple land use zones: a house and out-buildings, an outdoor kitchen, a latrine, a well, and sometimes a workshop. Small livestock, raised by women and children to ensure meat for holidays and family life cycle events, may wander free or be confined. Garden plants emerge from all corners of the lot, creating complex and diverse ecosystems. Unlike the case with field crop production, in both form and function the Yucatec house lot has changed minimally since early colonial times (Wauchope 1938: 16).

In recent decades, while field cultivation has declined in Mayan households, opportunities to migrate and earn cash wages have increased. Since 1968, inter-national tourism development in and around Cancún, Quintana Roo, on the eastern coast of the Yucatan Peninsula, has been a magnet for workers from all over Mexico.

In small communities along Quintana Roo's Caribbean coast, government land was subdivided and sold to immigrants in small urban lots. Mayan immigrants from the neighbouring state of Yucatan, who are familiar with the regional landscape, climate and natural resources, are able to transport and transplant plants and land use practices that are familiar to them. They make choices about which plant species and varieties to conserve based on many factors. Women's efforts to conserve their ethnicity through Yucatec cuisine are an important factor in the conservation of traditional crop varieties in one immigrant community.

Ethnicity and Cuisine

Eight-year-old Verónica was running down the street of her immigrant town one evening. She waved her arms and called to a friend: 'Acabo de llegar de mi pueblo. Ya tenemos huayas! Vamos a mi casa.' ('I just arrived from my hometown. We finally have *huayas*! Let's go to my house.')

Verónica reveals both her sense of ethnic affiliation and her internalization of the social practice of Yucatec cuisine. She expresses her affiliation with 'her' hometown, referring to her parents' town of origin, Chemax, in the interior of the Yucatan Peninsula. Verónica had spent all eight years of her life in La Colonia, an immigrant settlement in the town of Puerto Morelos, Quintana Roo. Verónica visited Chemax only once a year for the celebration of the town's patron saint. Yet, during those eight years, she had come to internalize a bond similar to the one that links her parents to Chemax and that contributes to their Yucatec ethnicity.

The second revealing part of the encounter with Verónica was how she called to her friend in the street, making a social event of consuming *huayas*. The *huaya* (pronounced *wy*-ah, with the emphasis on the first syllable) (*Talisia olivaeformis*) (see Table 2.1) is a small, round, green fruit the size of a cherry tomato, with a very large pit. It grows wild in the forests of the Yucatan Peninsula and has long been managed by Mayans in both rural and urban house lots. Surrounding the pit is a thin but extremely sweet orange pulp, which is what makes the *huaya* an indisputable delicacy among the Yucatec Maya. The *huaya* season is brief and in the summer. The rest of the year, Verónica and her family appreciate other fruits. But they spend the year anticipating *huayas*, pointing out progress in the branches of the tree overhead, hoping that this year it will mature enough to provide them with *huayas* of their own. Verónica's parents transplanted a *huaya* tree from their hometown when they resettled as immigrants, but the tree hasn't yet borne fruit. This year, her family took the three-hour busride back to Chemax during *huaya* season and returned with boxes full of *huayas* to eat, to share, and to sell in the immigrant community where they have resettled.

Like other garden delicacies in Yucatan and around the world, the *huaya* is appreciated by young and old. The ripening of fruits, the celebration of holidays and family events, and the practice of traditions that involve particular crops and foods mark the Mayan calendar. Young children like Verónica repeat annual rituals with their families and come to anticipate and plan for these feasts. In Yucatan,

Table 2.1: Plant Species Most Frequently Found in Immigrant House Lots and Use, La Colonia (in order of frequency)

1. sour orange (C)	*Citrus aurantium*
2. huaya (F)	*Talisia olivaeformis*
3. guava (F)	*Psidium guajava*
4. limón (C)	*Citrus aurantifolia*
5. epazote (C)	*Teloxys ambrosioides*
6. chives (C)	*Allium schoenophrasum*
7. mint (C)	*Mentha citrata*
8. zaramuyo (F)	*Annona squamosa*
9. guanabana F)	*Annona muricata*
10. banana (F)	*Musa acuminata*
11. chile habanero (C)	*Capsicum chinense*
12. coconut (F)	*Cocos nucifera*
13. avocado (F)	*Persea americana*
14. hibiscus (O)	*Hibiscus rosa-sinensis*
15. chaya (F)	*Cnidiscolus chayamansa*
16. hog plum (F)	*Spondias lutea*
17. tamarind (F)	*Tamarindus indica*

(F) – fruit or vegetable; (C) – condiment; (O) – ornamental.
Source: Greenberg 1996.

children first learn about the world's natural and social relations from inside the family house lot. The house lot ties people to the land, crops and foods that help to define who they are as Yucatec Mayans. Verónica, by inviting her friend to celebrate the joys of the *huaya* season, had internalized the Yucatec social practice of sharing *huayas* with family and friends.

The repeated practice of tasks, celebrations and everyday activities, such as those associated with Yucatec women's gardening and cuisine, result in an unconscious conditioning throughout childhood and a way of operating in the world. The practice theory of ethnicity (Bentley 1987) claims that people recognize similarities among themselves in this realm of internalized conditioning, and that these affinities are used to assert ethnicity. Some of these characteristics (which include preferences and tastes, productive activities, language and ideology) are acquired at a subconscious level and so can remain unquestioned, while guiding the ways in which people view the world, forming an 'implicit pedagogy' (Bourdieu 1977: 94) for social interaction and productivity. Bourdieu's formulation of practice theory (*ibid.*: 97–109, 143–4) emphasizes rhythmic cycles of life, routine body movements involved in work through the annual agricultural cycle, ritual foods served throughout the calendar year, and ceremonial dances as examples of con-ditioned behaviours that lead to unconscious learning and identity formation.

Verónica's mother chose to bring specific crops from Chemax and transplant them in the family's house lot, thus conserving traditional crops that meet her needs and those of her family. For Verónica's family, there were clear advantages to conserving traditional Yucatec cuisine and the associated crops. First, the house lot setting and foods were familiar, which eased some of the stress associated with migration. Plants also contribute to household income, both as subsistence food and as a source of cash from sales to neighbours. Finally, continuing traditional house lot practices allowed Verónica's family some measure of control over their lives as they faced the constant onslaught of new cultural elements in Quintana Roo.

Indigenous peoples exert cultural control in the face of a dominant culture both as a means to control the intake of new cultural elements in their lives as well as to maintain their own control over decision making (Bonfil Batalla 1996: 135). Cultural control offers some explanation of how traditional people can adopt change in some arenas of their lives and yet resist change in others. Verónica's family, like the other Chemaxeño families in this study, sought needed cash income by migrating to the tourist zone. But they also chose to resist change in their new lives by continuing some of their traditional practices. Some immigrant women retain traditional Yucatec dress, language and religious practices as well as house lot activities related to gardening and cuisine. Some of the same women adopt non-Yucatec cultural elements in their lives by trying out new crops and foods, learning to speak Spanish, and working outside the home to contribute to household income.

To analyse the relationships among women, cuisine, ethnicity and plant genetic resource conservation, in-depth research was carried out between 1993 and 1995 with 33 Yucatec Mayan immigrant women and their families originating from the town of Chemax who had resettled in La Colonia. Multiple visits were made to analyse house lot gardens, cooking and gardening practices, life histories and economic circumstances of these 33 Yucatec immigrant households. Four methods of data collection were used during multiple household visits: (1) a household survey; (2) a house lot garden inventory, including land use mapping, and a plant species inventory and specimens collection (for details on plant identification and specimens, see Greenberg 1996); (3) in-depth interviewing; and (4) participant observation. In-depth interviews and participant observation were used to collect data on household demography, family history, and current relations with Chemax, use of natural resources, household income composition, and information on practices associated with cuisine. The house lot inventory provided a list of plant species, uses of the house lot space, and a map for each of the house lots.

These 33 families had abandoned their *milpas* (agricultural fields), previously the core of household subsistence. But they still managed house lot gardens for crop cultivation and small livestock, mostly for household use. Primary informants were the women heads of households, although many men and children participated in the surveys and interviews. In most households, women were the primary managers of the garden, the kitchen and household finances. While men and children sometimes assisted in the garden and girls worked in the kitchen with their mothers, women took primary responsibility for garden food plants and livestock. Women usually kept track of household earnings and expenses and paid the bills. When interviewed alone, men were far less likely to know about women's activities than the reverse, and they could only rarely summarize household expenses.

The Mexican Caribbean and Tourism

The Yucatan Peninsula of Mexico, home to Yucatec Mayan Indians for millennia, has undergone massive change since the late 1960s. Up until this time, Quintana Roo, forming the north-eastern portion of the peninsula, was a sparsely settled, heavily forested territory of Mexico, having limited communications with the rest of the Republic.

In 1968, the Mexican government began to develop a tourist resort at Cancún to generate foreign exchange. With the development of tourism, jobs became available in construction and services. Yucatan, the Mexican state just west of Quintana Roo, supplied the majority of the labour force that built Cancún's international airport, highways, streets, hotels, restaurants and residences. In three decades, almost a million people migrated from Yucatan to Quintana Roo (INEGI 1992: 47). Labour migration had become 'a nearly universal feature of the Maya peasant economy' (Ewell 1984: 98). Some Mayans migrated seasonally, between annual agricultural harvests. Others returned to Yucatan on weekends. Still others found that the opportunity to earn cash income was reason enough to move their entire families to the coastal communities of Quintana Roo.

Today, the region boasts more than four million tourists a year. Quintana Roo's population has more than quintupled since statehood in 1974. The state now faces the challenges of massive labour immigration, pressure on natural resources, loss of native and crop biological diversity, urban sprawl and growth of slums, and the impacts of economic and social change on rural, Yucatec Mayan culture.

The immigrant settlement of La Colonia

The town of Puerto Morelos is located only 36 kilometres south of Cancún, within the tourist corridor targeted for continued development. During the 1970s and 1980s, the town grew with the extension of tourism development. Yucatec immigrant labourers spontaneously settled at the intersection of the main highway and the road that leads to the port of Puerto Morelos. The community of immigrants became a legal colony of the town of Puerto Morelos, known informally as 'La Colonia'. Federal lands along the highway were designated as a zone for future settlement and urbanization. These lands were mapped and parcelled by region and lot. Some areas are settled, while other areas remain forested and are designated for future development.

In 1993, over 90 per cent of the adult population of La Colonia were immigrants. Nearly 70 per cent of the town's residents were Yucatec Mayans, while others came from many parts of Mexico to work in the region. Among the 33 Yucatec immigrant households involved in this study, two-thirds had migrated to Quintana Roo for work. A few households migrated for other reasons, such as the chance to own land or a home, since this was rare in Yucatan where young couples often share houses or house lots with their relatives. Interviews with immigrants showed that many had lived in difficult conditions in Yucatan State. Many women recounted stories of hunger, inadequate health care and infant mortality. Men migrated weekly or seasonally to take advantage of work opportunities in Quintana Roo and eventually brought their families to settle in La Colonia. They bought lots from the government, built their homes, and then the immigrants filled house lots with structures, plants and family activities that met their economic, social and cultural needs.

For immigrants, traditional gender roles are changing. Men no longer devote themselves full-time to the intensive work of *milpa* cultivation. Many men are away during the day either working or seeking work. Some women work outside the home or have established cash-generating activities in the home. Some sell plants to neighbours, prepare food to sell along the highway, run a small store, or take in washing or sewing. Yet women immigrants experience greater continuity in their traditional responsibilities than do men. Men have lost all access to land for field cultivation, but even immigrant women who work outside the home still have access to a house lot, which continues to be a principally female domain.

Immigrant House Lots as Sites of Conservation

The house lot is the last remaining piece of land for urbanized Mayans like the Yucatec immigrants of La Colonia. Their house lots are small by Yucatec standards (only around 300 square metres in comparison to an average of around 2,500 square metres in their home town, Chemax, which were similar in size to those studied elsewhere in Yucatan) (Brown 1993: 54). On this small plot of land, Mayan immigrants must fit in a diversity of activities and land uses.

Women create spaces within the house lot for plant cultivation and food preparation. There is a well, a latrine and a *batea,* or clothes washing basin. Various pole structures are built for storage and livestock. Other areas are dedicated to childcare, entertainment, socialization and religious activities, and some areas are even rented out. Many of these elements and their designs represent continuity in house lot landscape at least from the 1930s (Wauchope 1938: 128–38) and perhaps from as long ago as pre-Hispanic times (Barrera 1980: 118).

Species diversity and use

In the 33 immigrant house lots studied in La Colonia, a total of 140 plant species were identified. The number of plant species and varieties found in any given house lot garden ranged from a high of 38 to none (for a newly arrived family that had no garden as yet). There was an average of eighteen species across the 33 house lots. Lushness, diversity and age of plants in gardens varied among households, as did the number of plants and plant species.

The most common use for the 140 plant species found in house lot gardens was for food, including fruits, vegetables and condiments. The 49 food species (35 per cent of the total species) named by the women included 36 fruits and vegetables and 13 condiments. There were 41 ornamental species (29.3 per cent) and 19 medicinal species (13.6 per cent). Eight species (5.7 per cent) were for other uses, and 23 species (16.5 per cent) were named but their uses were unknown.

The age of the house lots may have affected the number and density of plants, although it did not appear to affect crop diversity. The creation of a house lot garden appeared to be a long-term process. Immigrant house lots had a youthful appearance, tending to be sparsely planted when compared to older house lots on the Yucatan Peninsula. House lots lacked the extended canopy layer from overhead trees (as opposed to a few scattered trees) and the differentiation into zones. With time, immigrant house lot vegetation may fill in, giving them an appearance more similar to gardens in Yucatan. But the La Colonia house lots will always be much smaller, perhaps taking on the appearance of miniaturized traditional Yucatec Mayan house lots.

Location and cultivation of plants

House lot gardens in La Colonia have the same scattered appearance as home-gardens elsewhere in the tropics. Where large trees are present, they formed part of the forest that once covered the area where La Colonia stands today. Yucatec immigrants recognize useful species and preserve them when house lots are cleared. Shrubs are often located on property lines, marking boundaries and providing some privacy. Plants are rarely placed against the house where they might attract pests or provide a hiding place for snakes. Some herbaceous plants are cultivated directly in the ground, while others are planted in containers.

Limited space is always a consideration when planting, and some women never attempt to plant certain species because of space restrictions. Conflict is common between neighbours when chickens or pigs invade and destroy garden plants. Many immigrant women concluded that the small size of the house lots in La Colonia makes it difficult to accommodate both plants and animals.

Some households plant vegetation in zones. Ornamental species are placed along the street, probably for public viewing. Edible plants are grown behind the house near the kitchen for convenience. Valuable plants, such as favoured seasoning herbs and uncommon varieties of chile, are planted out of view of the street as a deterrent to theft.

Plants are cultivated in a diversity of containers: assorted aluminium cans, plastic bowls and jugs, metal or plastic buckets, wooden crates lined with plastic or cardboard, and plastic bags. Containers are recycled from purchases, gleaned from work or a neighbour, or acquired during regular pilgrimages to the dump. Containers are placed directly on the ground, propped up on a log or a pile of concrete blocks, positioned on the edge of a well, or hung from wooden poles belonging to the house or other structure. Special attention is given to each plant's need for light. For example, a bucket containing coriander (*Coriandrum sativum*) or mint (*Mentha citrata*) is placed atop a stone wall on the property line in the shade of a *zaramuyo* (*Annona squamosa*) tree, while a chile *habanero* (*Capsicum chinense*) is planted in the ground at the entrance to the house lot where the sun reaches it most of the day, and people passing by see that chiles will soon be available for sale.

Women often create seedbeds along stone walls by laying logs on three sides to retain the soil. These beds are also made from old refrigerator drawers, cartons lined with plastic, and wooden crates. Considerations in seedbed placement include light requirements and proximity to a well for ease of irrigation. Soil for the bed is carried to the house lot from the adjacent forest in buckets or sacks.

A few lots contained a traditional Yucatec elevated planter called a *ka'anché*. It is made of four vertical wooden poles, often forked at the top, that hold up a base rather like a table. The tabletop can be made of poles or a plank. Buckets and other containers are placed on top and filled with herbs and chiles. Typically at waist level, the *ka'anché* keeps animals away from the plants. It also offers a more comfortable working height.

Sources of plant material

Immigrants obtain plants, seeds and cuttings from at least three sources. Some plants are remnants of the secondary forest that was cleared to make the house lots. When clearing the forest, immigrants save plants that they know are useful. Other plants are received as gifts from neighbours or relatives both in La Colonia and in Yucatan. Still other plants are volunteers that emerge from refuse piles or from seeds dropped by humans, birds or other animals. Volunteer plants are tolerated, tended, and may grow to produce fruit. Immigrants also buy fruits from hawkers in town or Cancún, such as sour orange (*Citrus aurantium*), guava (*Psidium guajava*) or *huaya*, and then toss the seeds in the house lot, often with no conscious intention to cultivate. Modern cultivars have also been introduced, as in the case of grafted citrus varieties, certain tomato varieties, avocados, certain chile varieties and coconut.

Plant materials also come from Yucatan. Yucatec immigrants are commonly seen stepping off second-class buses and shared taxis loaded down with goods, returning from Yucatan. Among the treasures they bring back are plant cuttings and seedlings and fruits with pits or seeds that they intend to plant in their own house lots of La Colonia.

Immigrant Cuisine and Plant Genetic Diversity Conservation

While 'diet' refers to the foods and drink typically consumed by people on a daily basis, 'cuisine' encompasses much more. Cuisine refers to culturally derived patterns of behaviour associated with foods. These patterns include food selection, the particular condiments used, food preparation and the associated rules or practices (Farb and Armelagos 1980: 185). What follows is a brief discussion of different elements of Yucatec immigrant cuisine and the house lot plants women manage that contribute to traditional cuisine as observed among households of La Colonia. In their efforts to maintain traditional cuisine, immigrant women conserve special crops in their house lots, thus assuring continuity in ethnic custom and in garden and kitchen practices.

Daily meals and holiday dishes

Immigrants' diets are still based on maize, even though maize is purchased rather than cultivated as it was in Yucatan. Most families eat maize at their three daily meals. Maize is most commonly prepared in the form of *tortillas*, which are flat cakes formed out of ground maize flour and cooked on a hot griddle. In La Colonia, most families buy ready-made tortillas at the *tortillería*. Tortillas serve both as an accompaniment to the meal and as the utensil with which food is eaten.

Tamales are maize cakes: either they are filled with chicken, pork or vegetables, or the maize is combined with a variety of house lot ingredients such as *chaya* (*Cnidiscolus chayamansa*), beans (*Phaseolus* spp.), *salsa*, *epazote* (*Teloxys ambrosioides*), oregano, garlic or onion, toasted squash seed, and assorted herbs and spices. Yucatec *tamales* are then wrapped in plantain or banana leaves from the house lot and are steamed, baked or smoked. *Salbutes* and *panuchos* are two other Yucatec maize dishes. Both are thick maize pancakes formed into different shapes and piled with assorted combinations of meat, beans and vegetables, topped with fresh or citrus-pickled chile that is often harvested from the house lot.

The most common breakfast consists of eggs eaten with tortillas. Eggs are often scrambled and may be cooked with *chaya* or chopped tomato, chile or avocado produced in the house lot. Cheese, beans, ham, canned tuna, peas or leftovers may also accompany eggs. The main meal is eaten at midday if men are home, or later in the afternoon when they return from work.

For many households, a common meal is a pot of food containing little or no meat but centred on beans, which are usually black. Beans may be flavoured with any condiment paste (see *recados*, below). Stews are also common and might consist of beans, pork (in limited quantities, if cash is available), squash and potatoes, and are usually seasoned with chile, onions and spices. As many ingredients as possible either come from the house lot or are traded for ingredients from a neighbour's lot.

Special dishes are prepared for life cycle celebrations such as weddings, *quince-añeras* (fifteenth birthdays), and baptisms. *Relleno negro*, a stuffed and seasoned meat dish prepared in a traditional underground oven, is by far the favoured festival dish to serve if a family can manage to provide it. Otherwise, *tamales*, *escabeche*, *mechado*, or another distinctly Yucatec dish is prepared.

Some ingredients for speciality dishes are not available in stores in La Colonia and are available only in certain people's house lots. *Xawa*, a Yucatec chile variety and an essential ingredient in *relleno negro*, is not available for sale in Puerto Morelos. Banana leaves used to make tamales are only available in house lots. Many other holiday dish ingredients, such as sour orange, *limón* (*Citrus aurantifolia*), oregano, and chiles also come from house lot gardens. Although some are available commercially, house lot production allows immigrants to dedicate the limited cash that they earn to other needs.

House lot fruits and vegetables

Fruit trees play a special role in Yucatec life. They are planted early in a new lot to provide both food and shade. Of the 17 plant species most frequently found (see Table 2.1), nine were fruits consumed as snacks. Among the things that immigrants missed most from their hometown in Yucatan were house lot fruits that were not available in La Colonia. Children indulge in whatever fruit is mature, relishing the taste and ephemeral abundance with equal pleasure. The early Spaniards recognized the significance of fruit trees for the Mayans. When attempting to control and concentrate the Mayan population, the Spaniards not only burned Mayan homes and villages, but also cut down their fruit trees (de la Garza 1983: 86).

Among the fruit trees most commonly found in the 33 house lots studied in La Colonia were *huaya*, guava (*Psidium guajara*), *zaramuyo*, guanabana (*Annona muricata*), *zapote* (*Manilkara zapota*), banana, coconut, avocado (*Persea americana*), hog plum (*Spondias lutea*) and tamarind (*Tamarindus indica*). Both *huaya* and *zaramuyo* are frequently found in house lots throughout the Yucatan Peninsula. Both have wild forms in forests of the region (Barrera 1980: 120, 124). *Huaya, zaramuyo*, guava and banana were all eaten by Mayans in the colonial period (de Landa 1941: 199) and are prized by immigrants of La Colonia. Avocado is a common immigrant house lot tree and a favoured filling for *tortillas*, sliced or mashed and sprinkled with citrus juice. The hog plum is native to the peninsula and has wild relatives in the region (Barrera 1980: 124). Immigrants enjoy its fruit and its medicinal qualities, just as Mayans did in the colonial period (de Landa 1941: 198).

Yucatec immigrants frequently eat *chaya*, a green leafy vegetable native to the Yucatan Peninsula. It is chopped and scrambled with eggs, moulded into a special Yucatec *tamal*, steamed in stews, and added to numerous other dishes. *Chaya* grows rapidly into a tall bush, even in the shallowest and poorest of soils. There is a wild form on the Yucatan Peninsula, and it is thought that the house lot variety was domesticated in the region (Barrera 1980: 120). The Yucatec Mayans of colonial times were also fond of *chaya*: 'The Indians plant it at once wherever they are going to stay and during the whole year it has leaves to gather' (de Landa 1941: 196).

Condiments

The three most important Yucatec condiments are chile, *limón* and sour orange. Immigrants use numerous chile varieties, but the most common is the chile *habanero*, which is also found in most immigrant house lots. *Habanero* is often sliced or finely chopped and combined with citrus juice as a marinade base or to season stews or meats. Seven other chile varieties were found in immigrants' gardens. Each is used as a condiment and some are savoured as special ingredients in Yucatec holiday dishes.

Limón and sour orange are the most commonly used citrus fruits. *Limón* is the Mexican or West Indian lime (Sokolov 1983: 84), a round, deep green-coloured fruit with many seeds. Sour orange, sometimes referred to as a bitter or Seville orange, is the size of a juice orange. It is usually harvested when still green and is strictly treated as a condiment. *Limón* and sour orange are both commonly found in an accessible spot near the cooking area in most immigrant house lots. The juice from both species is used for seasoning soups or stews. Shredded cabbage or radishes, chopped purple onions, sliced *jícama* (*Pachyrhizus erosus*), and occasionally tomatoes are bathed in *limón* or sour orange and further flavoured with chile, coriander, chives and mint, and eaten as salads. *Limón* and sour orange are also squeezed onto fresh fruit, into soups and on fish. Citrus juice, combined with chile, onion, garlic and spices or herbs, is used in marinades for pork, chicken, beef or wild game.

If maize is the heart of Yucatec cuisine, *recados* are its soul. *Recados* are Yucatec condiment pastes, consisting of herbs and spices ground together in specific proportions and dissolved in *limón* or sour orange to produce distinctly Yucatec flavours. *Recados* typically require many ingredients, some of which come from the house lot. Immigrant women use a hand grinder to achieve the typical pasty texture. *Recados* can be smeared on meat before grilling, combined with citrus juice for a marinade, or simply dropped into a soup or stew to transform its flavour. *Limón*, sour orange and chile *habanero* were among the 17 plant species most commonly found in the 33 immigrant house lots. *Epazote*, coriander, mint and various varieties of chives and onions were other house lot condiment plants.

Food preparation

Yucatec cuisine is diverse in ingredients and cooking techniques, and has its origins in Spain, Mexico and the Caribbean. Yucatec women practise an eclectic combination of cooking techniques that include boiling or simmering (soups and stews), frying (eggs and *chicharrón* or pork skin), steaming (*tamales*), baking (in an underground *pib* or oven), grilling meats over charcoal, and marinating and pickling vegetables, poultry and fish. Ingredients include crop plants native to the Yucatan Peninsula and to the Caribbean, crops from elsewhere in Mexico or the Americas, and from all corners of the Old World.

Immigrant women and their daughters prepare most daily meals. For special events and holidays, meals may be prepared by a relatively small group of family members. Not everyone in the community has the knowledge and experience required to prepare certain traditional meals, and individual elders are called upon to organize meal preparation for special events. One woman in her early fifties was being trained for such meal preparations by assisting her elderly parents who were regularly called upon for such purposes. Immigrants hosting large events who had extended families in town organized cooperatively to contribute house lot ingredients, labour and cash for the festive meal.

Overall, house lots contribute numerous essential ingredients to immigrant Yucatec cuisine. About one-third of the plants that immigrants grow in their house lots are for food. All but one of the 17 species that appear with the greatest frequency are food plants (the exception is hibiscus, an ornamental). This common-ality of plant species across house lots suggests that there is a set of plants that form part of a local immigrant cuisine. Furthermore, the frequency of these 17 species in immigrant house lots reinforces the thesis that house lots are important sites for the cultivation of plants for Yucatec cuisine.

Many house lot plants are food items that are either not available for purchase in La Colonia or are available at a cost that immigrants choose not to pay. By growing these plants in the house lot, immigrant women are able to control the availability of certain ingredients. House lot fruit trees provide readily available snack foods. A steady supply of condiments and vegetable plants from house lots offers familiar tastes and essential ingredients for the preparation of traditional Yucatec dishes. Immigrant households conserve these traditional crop species in their house lots in order to assure their availability for the preparation of daily and special meals. Growing these ingredients in house lots enables women to continue to provide foods that conserve certain aspects of Yucatec cuisine and thus Yucatec ethnicity. Simultaneously, immigrant house lots become sites of *in situ* plant conservation.

Conclusions and Implications

Immigrant house lots are sites for continuity in the cultivation of traditional Mayan species and varieties in Quintana Roo. Despite the fact that immigrant families have abandoned traditional field cultivation, migrated to an urban community in Quintana Roo and now depend primarily on wage labour for their livelihoods, women choose to conserve traditional Yucatec crops in their house lots. The desire to use and easily access specific plant species clearly contributes to their conservation in house lots among Chemaxeño immigrants.

Most research on crop genetic resources has tended to emphasize field crop agriculture and the roles of male farmers in the maintenance of traditional crop varieties. House lot gardens may become even more important in the future, as is evident in the case of Yucatec immigrants in Quintana Roo. Yucatec families increasingly engage in off-farm economic activities, resulting in a reduction in the land area that is dedicated to traditional field cultivation and a loss of crop genetic diversity. Barrera, a scholar of Mayan natural resource management, confirmed this when he emphasized the role of homegardens as germplasm reserves in Yucatan (Barrera 1980: 118), and noted that this role would increase in importance over time with the general trend in agriculture towards intensive monocrop production. The present study calls attention to the role of house lots as sites for conservation and dispersal of genetic material, and as a final repository for traditional crop varieties (Wilkes 1991: 95). Homegardens represent an area of research long overlooked by many conservation biologists.

Future research could clarify certain population and evolutionary requirements if house lots are to serve a role in conserving germplasm. What is the necessary plant population size for conservation of these traditional crop varieties? Are genetic populations like those found in immigrant house lots likely to be adequate to maintain a body of healthy genetic material? For which species? Another major question concerns the adequacy of contact with native vegetation. Contact between cultivated crops and their wild or weedy relatives to ensure introgressive hybridization is important for the continued evolution of crop plants (Wilkes 1991: 94), but may not always occur in urban house lots.

Yucatec women play an important role as managers of plant genetic resources in house lots. They manage house lots and the genetic resources within them even when households migrate and adopt a household economy based primarily on cash and minimally on subsistence. Most women continue to carry out house lot activities even if family members and they themselves engage in wage labour outside the home. The persistence of women's role as resource managers, particularly through economic transitions, points to the importance of directing future research at better understanding women's work and contributions to natural resource management.

An important motivation for conserving traditional crops in house lots among immigrant women is to assure the availability of essential ingredients for the preparation of typical Yucatec dishes. Of the 17 plant species found most frequently in immigrants' house lots, all but one were used in traditional Yucatec cuisine. Of these, 11 were fruits or vegetables and six were condiments that are either native to the Yucatan Peninsula or have long histories in Yucatec cuisine. Some crop species are only available in the house lots of La Colonia; no commercial establishment sells them. The continuity of Yucatec culinary practices in La Colonia demonstrates that women have made choices to conserve these crops and dishes and thus to maintain their association with their Yucatec ethnicity and origins.

Most cultural ecological research related to food is concerned with agriculture or horticulture. These studies emphasize the role of men and focus nearly exclusively on food production, treating other aspects of cuisine as exogenous and the role of cuisine itself as negligible. The study of cuisine includes food selection prior to plant production or procurement and extends through plant cultivation and management, harvest, food preparation and consumption. Further research on the interrelationships among cuisine, female perspectives and domains of natural resource management will reveal new insights relevant to the conservation of plant genetic resources.

Yucatec immigrants maintain their ethnic identity by re-creating house lots with distinctly Yucatec characteristics, tending plants and livestock, preparing food and repeating annual rituals that were learned in their home community in Yucatan. Practice theory (Bourdieu 1977) as applied to ethnicity (Bentley 1987) suggests that continuity of these practices strengthens Yucatec identity and ethnicity after migration. The benefits associated with conserving traditional practices are that they make the transition less stressful and often contribute to the household economy. Conserving these practices also offers immigrants some measure of cultural control.[1] Cultural control emphasizes the extent to which a minority ethnic group retains autonomy in a culturally heterogeneous society by exercising decision making concerning the new cultural elements that they will adopt, reject or adapt (Bonfil Batalla 1996: 135).

House lots have multiple functions, and a better understanding of those functions can reveal much about plant genetic conservation among different ethnic groups. While this study focuses on women's practices related to crops and cuisine, there are also a variety of male practices, child-oriented activities, religious rituals, health and medical practices, and economic activities carried out in house lots that this study does not emphasize. House lots are likely to serve these multiple ethnic functions for other populations as well. Policy and programmes directed at conservation of plant genetic resources will certainly be more successful if combined with efforts to promote cultural diversity generally by encouraging ethnically significant practices, including those that sustain traditional cuisine, medicine, dance, handicrafts and religious practices.

Note

1   For some individuals, adherence to ethnic practices may not be by choice. Lack of capital for investment in alternative economic activities, limited Spanish language capability, and conventional local political systems that tend to restrict indigenous participation in certain economic activities are among the constraints faced by many indigenous people. Such constraints might result in the conservation of traditional cultural elements such as house lots and cuisine, that may not necessarily exist by preference.

References

Barrera, A. (1980) 'Sobre la unidad de habitación tradicional campesina y el manejo de recursos bióticos en el área Maya Yucatánense', *Biótica*, No. 5, pp. 115–29.

Bentley, G. C. (1987) 'Ethnicity and practice', *Comparative Studies in Society and History*, Vol. 29, No. 1, pp. 24–55.

Bonfil Batalla, G. (1996) *México Profundo: Reclaiming a Civilization*, Austin, Texas: University of Texas Press.

Bourdieu, P. (1977) *Outline of a Theory of Practice*, Cambridge: Cambridge University Press.

Brown, D. F. (1993) 'Yucatec Maya Settling, Settlement and Spatiality', PhD dissertation, University of California at Riverside, Ann Arbor, Michigan: University Microfilms International.

de la Garza, M. (1983) *Relaciónes Histórico-geográficas de la Gobernación de Yucatán*, México: Universidad Nacional Autónoma de México.

de Landa, D. (1941) [1864] *Landa's Relación de las Cosas de Yucatán*, translated, with notes, by A. M. Tozzer, Cambridge: Peabody Museum of American Archaeology and Ethnology, Harvard University.

Ewell, P. T. (1984) 'Intensification of peasant agriculture in Yucatán', Ithaca: Cornell University Department of Agricultural Economics.

Ewell, P. T. and D. Merrill-Sands (1987) 'Milpa in Yucatán: a long-fallow maize system and its alternatives in the Maya peasant economy', in B. L. Turner II and S. Brush (eds.), *Comparative Farming Systems*, New York: Guilford, pp. 95–129.

Farb, P. and G. Armelagos (1980) *Consuming Passions: the Anthropology of Eating*, Boston: Houghton Mifflin.

Greenberg, L. S. Z. (1996) 'You Are What You Eat: Ethnicity and Change in Yucatec Immigrant House Lots, Quintana Roo, Mexico', PhD dissertation, University of Wisconsin-Madison,

Ann Arbor, Michigan: University Microfilms International.

INEGI (Instituto Nacional de Estadística Geográfica e Información) (1992) *Estados Unidos Mexicanos: Perfil Sociodemográfico, XI Census General de Población y Vivienda, 1990,* Aguascalientes: INEGI.

Sokolov, R. (1983) [1979] *Fading Feast: A Compendium of Disappearing American Regional Foods,* New York: E. P. Dutton.

Wauchope, R. (1938) *Modern Maya Houses: a Study of the Archaeological Significance,* Washington, DC: Carnegie Institution of Washington.

Wilkes, G. (1991) '*In situ* conservation of agricultural systems', in M. L. Oldfield and J. B. Alcorn (eds.), *Biodiversity: Culture, Conservation and Ecodevelopment,* Boulder: Westview Press, pp. 86–101.

CHAPTER 3
Wild Food Plants
and Arbëresh Women
in Lucania, Southern Italy

Andrea Pieroni

Traditional knowledge, use and management of wild food plants in the Mediterranean are neglected areas of inquiry, as are culinary traditions and, specifically,
women's knowledge. But these are crucial to maintaining both cultural and
biological diversity in the region. Ethnic Albanian women living in three villages in
an inland area of southern Italy have, for centuries, maintained culinary traditions
based upon wild plants and have transmitted traditional knowledge (TK)[1] of these
plants across generations. Wild plant gathering and gift giving represent important
elements of women's village social networks and a source of status and authority
for women. Wild plant foods further represent a symbolic component of cultural
identity that women perpetuate through ritual foods associated mainly with
religious events. Traditional environmental knowledge (TEK) about wild plants
also reflects the dynamics of exchange between the indigenous South Italian
culture and the 'imported' Albanian culture both in terms of language and in terms
of cuisine. Italian culture has had a strong influence on the Arbëresh diet, but the
reverse is not true. Many Arbëreshë have rejected self-recognition of their cultural
and ethnic roots as Italian authorities and the media have made this recognition
very difficult. Phenomena such as emigration and wage labour employment have
also contributed to the loss of cultural traditions and wild plant TEK. For the first
time in centuries, younger women have lost their mothers' and grandmothers' wild
plant knowledge and, with it, the status and authority that these older women
enjoy. Re-instilling lost TEK will require time and will be heavily dependent upon
the positive acceptance by the younger generations of the knowledge connected
with the elderly female cosmos.

Traditional Plant Knowledge in the Mediterranean

There has been much research on traditional phytotherapy (the use of plants for
medicinal purposes) in many Mediterranean areas, especially due to the interest of
a few research centres in its potential applications in the pharmaceutical field.
These studies often tend to 'extract' the heritage of medical knowledge from its

complex socio-cultural origins and to shift it into large-scale bio-scientific evaluation circuits in a process better known as *bioprospecting*.

On the other hand, ethnobiological studies of edible plants aim to stimulate a 're-instillation' of lost knowledge and practices in the studied areas with respect to the original cosmologies (Heinrich and Gibbons 2001). They offer a wonderful opportunity to genuinely evaluate TEK as well as the distribution and nature of TEK among the sexes. Not all forms of knowledge are equally valued within society, and 'male' forms of knowledge are often privileged over 'female' forms (Parpart 1995; Kothari and Turner in this volume). Accordingly, domains involving the use of plants in traditional contexts that are mainly managed by women are often perceived as not scientifically relevant and are classified as 'folklore'. This is certainly the case for food herbs and even more so for plants used in traditional handicrafts and in religious and ritual ceremonies.

Traditional plant knowledge in Southern Europe has been the subject of several detailed surveys that have primarily focused on natural health remedies (mainly medicinal plants).[2] Very little attention has been given to Mediterranean people's traditional gathering of wild and weedy plants for food or to local culinary traditions (Forbes 1976; Paoletti *et al.* 1995; Pieroni 1999a). Also, with the exception of a few ethnobotanical surveys,[3] there has been no recent research on non-food and non-medicinal uses of plants. In the very sparse data that exists on TEK and on *gendered* TEK dynamics in the ethnobotanical literature on the Mediterranean, it becomes clear, for example, that wild vegetables and weedy greens are mainly recognized, gathered and processed by women, whereas the collection of bulbs and mushrooms is generally a male activity (Pieroni 1999a; Ertuğ this volume).

A basic role in the evolution of TEK is played by its means of transmission from one generation to another and among sexes, as well as across different ethnic groups. The survival of the complex socio-cultural mechanisms that make this transmission of knowledge possible strongly affects the types and forms of TEK that are passed along (see also Turner, this volume). There is a strong connection between TEK loss and loss of the original language that occurs with acculturation within a social environment that is influenced by a dominant culture and language (see, for example, Zent 2001 on the Piaroa of Venezuela). Precise changes in ethnobotanical competence occur between generations, and can correspond to the foundation of permanent villages and the beginning of settled, integrated and acculturated lifestyles (see also Hoffmann this volume). This could suggest that, in the presence of important turning points in local communities, TEK is dramatically affected. A similar process also took place with the disappearance of the traditional ethnic Albanian agricultural society during the 1960s and 1970s in Lucania in southern Italy.

Ethnobiological research in the Mediterranean has focused on making lists of plants used by local people, but very rarely has there been any attempt to investigate how plant TEK is distributed by age and sex, how it evolves, and which social and cultural dynamics influence these processes. The aim of this chapter is to discuss the results of a gender-sensitive study of the traditions related to wild and weedy food herbs[4] in three small ethnic Albanian (Arbëresh) communities in northern Lucania (southern Italy).[5] This survey was focused on traditional gathering, processing and cooking of non-cultivated ('wild') vegetables, as well as on local perceptions of these plants (how people classify, categorize, and perceive them by smelling and tasting), and the cultural mores associated with them, and on knowledge transmission and social dynamics affecting this process.

The Arbëreshë and Their Environment

The Arbëreshë are descendants of Albanians who emigrated in several flows from the fifteenth to the eighteenth centuries to diverse central and southern Italian inland areas (Dessart 1982). At present, it is estimated that there are no more than 80,000 Albanian-speakers, all of whom are bilingual in Italian and Arbëresh Albanian, but it is probable that the true number is much lower owing to acculturation. For example, in the predominantly Arbëreshë village of Ginestra, it is estimated that only 15–20 per cent of the current population can actively communicate using the Arbëresh Albanian language.

Arbëresh Albanian belongs to the Tosk Albanian subgroup, which represents the only surviving language from the ancient Paleo-Balkan group (Illyrian, Messapic and Thracian) of the Indo-European family (Grimes 2000). Arbëresh Albanian is classified as an 'endangered language' (Salminen 1999). Today in the (oral) dictionary of the Arbëresh language, more than 40 per cent of the words are Italian. It was only in December 1999 that the Arbëreshë – together with 11 other non-Italian-speaking groups – obtained official recognition by the Italian Parliament as an 'historical ethnic minority'. This should ensure a future for their language in local schools and should also give the people the legal right to use their language in official acts and cultural initiatives to defend their heritage (Gazzetta Ufficiale della Repubblica Italiana 1999).

The Arbëresh culture represents a wonderful example of a long intercultural exchange between an indigenous culture (South Italian) and an 'imported' culture (Albanian). This exchange has involved not only the language, but also many other aspects of social life that have probably influenced both TEK and the uses to which gathered food weeds are put.

The northern part of the Lucania region (also called Basilicata) is located in an area dominated by a former volcano: the Monte Vulture. It is characterized by a few villages sustained primarily by pastoralism and agriculture and, more recently, by a car factory that was constructed in the nearby urban centre of Melfi. The countryside is dotted with cultivated olive groves and vineyards producing a local variety that gives the name to the local wine (Aglianico). Since the 1970s the cultivation of durum wheat (*Triticum durum*) as a cash crop has become increasingly important, and the area in cultivation has significantly increased.

The Arbëreshë arrived in the Vulture area, as we have seen, during diverse immigration flows beginning in the second half of the fifteenth century. Today, three Arbëresh villages survive: Ginestra (whose inhabitants are called in Arbëresh *Zhurian*), Barile (in Arbëresh *Barilli*), and Maschito (in Arbëresh *Mashqiti*), with around 700, 3,000 and 1,800 inhabitants respectively (see Table 3.1). These villages are quite isolated from the bulk of the Arbëresh communities, which are concentrated in Calabria and Sicily, and are also isolated from the other few Albanian ethnic enclaves in southern Lucania: Apulia, Campania, Molise, and Abruzzo.

In Ginestra and Maschito, a very distinct cultural gap exists between generations, and today only the oldest members of the population are able to speak Arbëresh Albanian. The majority of the middle-aged (35–55 years) population recall some words and basic customs from their Arbëresh ancestry, but do not incorporate these facets of traditional life into their daily life. 'Modernization' – conformity to mainstream Italian culture – is marked among the population aged 35 years and younger. For the most part, this group has abandoned the traditional agro-pastoralist way of life and instead depends primarily on factory employment. In Barile, the linguistic heritage has not yet been lost and, at present, a few members of the younger generation speak Arbëresh.

An important chapter in the history of the Arbëresh communities of the Vulture area in the twentieth century is represented by emigration. During the 1950s and 1960s, nearly half of the entire male population left their villages and found jobs in the Piedmont of northern Italy, France, Germany and Switzerland, at times accompanied by their families. Those who left their families behind generally returned after a few years. This phenomenon has been central to the cultural changes occurring in the Arbëresh villages. Arbëresh men who emigrated abroad or to northern Italy did so together with many south-Italian-speaking men and a kind of standardized southern Italian became the language commonly in use in the emigrant communities.

Fieldwork was conducted in Ginestra, Maschito and Barile during April–June, August and November 2000, and March–July 2001. Ethnobotanical information was collected from 68 informants (49 women and 19 men) who retain TEK, using semi-structured and structured interviews. Most interviewees were more than 50 years old, and were mainly from families that still have a strong connection with traditional agricultural activities.

People were asked to describe precisely the methods for processing and cooking each *folk species*[6] that they had mentioned in the previous phase of research. Several fresh plant specimens or dried samples were collected during the field study, and were shown to the interviewees in order to test their ability to recognize the plants and confirm their applications.

Each wild and weedy plant species that the informants identified as used for food was collected and identified, applying nomenclature that follows the standard botanical work for Italian flora (Pignatti 1982). Voucher specimens of all the non-domesticated (wild and weedy) greens were collected and are deposited at the Herbarium of the Centre for Pharmacognosy and Phytotherapy of the School of Pharmacy, University of London.

Gathering *Liakra* among the Arbëreshë

Traditions related to gathering and cooking wild food plants are very popular in the Vulture area. More than 110 botanical taxa were identified that Arbëresh women use as food in their local culinary traditions, including about 50 non-cultivated species (Pieroni and Heinrich 2002, Pieroni *et al.* 2002a). Among wild and weedy plants, all Arbëresh women who were interviewed clearly distinguish between *liakra* (edible weedy vegetables) and *bara* (non-edible grasses and herbs). *Liakra* is used by the Arbëreshë as a synonym for 'leaves' and has an Albanian origin, even though the term no longer exists in the modern Tosk Albanian language.

Elderly Arbëreshë women remember that they used to collect *liakra* before returning home after spending the entire day working in the fields, especially while weeding fields in the spring. They removed weeds from the cultivated areas and brought home and cooked those that were edible. *Liakra* were sometimes gathered and consumed for lunch directly in the fields *all'acita* (with salt, olive oil and vinegar).

Today, the main gatherers are elderly women who normally collect wild greens on their own. Young green aerial sections of *liakra* are the most commonly gathered plant parts; they are usually dug up with a knife and stored in a plastic bag. Women collect *liakra* mainly in the ecozones located very close to the village, for example, in the *vrështë* (vineyards or olive groves) or in their proximity. A few species are also collected from hedgerows (*gardhë*). Gathering areas are today much more restricted than in the past, and all women gatherers are very concerned about the current use of pesticides in the durum wheat fields, and about the fact that their 'safe' spaces for collecting *liakra* are constantly decreasing.

Generally men collect a very few wild plants from the ecozones located further from the village surrounding wheat fields (*dheju*) and in the secondary forests (*pill*): these include tassel hyacinth (*Leopoldia comosa*) bulbs and a couple of mushroom species (*Pleurotus eryngii* and *Pholiota aegerita*). Men were attempting to semi-domesticate a very few non-domesticated species in homegardens (*kopshtë*), such as wild oregano (*Origanum heracleoticum*), Spanish salsify (*Scolymus hispanicus*), and tassel hyacinth. Gathering of these species is generally very time-consuming since they grow in areas located far from the village (this is why they are primarily gathered by men), and their natural abundance is limited. About half of these weedy greens are sold informally in local open-air markets in the nearby (Italian-speaking) villages of Rionero and Venosa.

Processing and Cooking *Liakra*

In the past, *liakra* were often eaten as snacks during fieldwork. More often they were brought home, washed at the village fountain, and then boiled in the traditional terracotta pot (*poq*). In the poorest families they were eaten raw with bread, without oil and salt. Today, very few *liakra* are eaten raw. Commonly, they are lightly boiled and then fried in olive oil together with garlic and, sometimes, a few hot chile peppers. The cooked greens are then added to boiled pasta as a kind of green vegetable sauce. In some cases, these weedy greens are boiled together with the pasta, and the entire preparation is fried in olive oil with garlic. Pasta with *liakra* is often considered to be a main dish. In some other cases, the wild species are cooked and consumed with bean soup. This is the case with the traditional preparations *luljëkuq e fazuljë* ('corn poppy leaves [*Papaver rhoeas*], and beans'), or *bathë e çikour* ('mashed fava beans [*Vicia faba*] and wild chicory [*Cichorium intybus*]'), or they are eaten in a kind of soup (*mënëstra maritatë*) prepared with mixtures of more than ten wild herbs. *Liakra* are only rarely used to prepare special meals for feast days. On Christmas Eve, anchovies or dried fish are traditionally served with boiled and fried shoots of broccoli raab that are semi-cultivated in the area (*çim de rrapë*, *Brassica rapa* ssp. *rapa* [DC] Metzg. [Group Ruvo Bailey], syn.: *Brassica rapa* L. Broccoletto Group), or of wild mustard (*sënap*, *Sinapis* sp. pl.). During Easter, a kind of pie (*verdhët*) is prepared with eggs, lamb, ricotta, sheep cheese and (previously boiled) leaf stalks of *Scolymus hispanicus*; in the village of Maschito, the young aerial parts of wild fennel (*Foeniculum vulgare* spp. *piperitum*) are used instead.

A special processing method is used only for *Leopoldia comosa* bulbs. These bulbs have a very strong bitter taste when eaten raw, and so are peeled and soaked in cold water overnight or even over several days before being fried or pickled. Women use this procedure 'to decrease the bitterness', but this is to improve taste rather than to detoxify the plant. Recently, in a few recipes, *liakra* are sometimes replaced by cultivated vegetables (in particular, beet, *Beta vulgaris*) that are bought in the market or cultivated in homegardens.

Culinary Traditions and Acculturation

There has surely been an exchange over a long period of Arbëresh and southern Italian women's knowledge of the culinary use of wild vegetables. A strong acculturation process took place in the Arbëresh centres from the 1960s onwards, when streets were improved and exchanges with other nearby southern Italian communities began to be very intense. Italian-speaking officers and civil servants arrived in the villages as local elementary schools or post offices were established, or when electricity or a sewage system was installed. This process slowly began to affect local cuisine.

Today's daily Arbëreshë diet doesn't differ substantially from that of neighbouring Italian communities. When comparing traditional Arbëresh women's cuisine in Ginestra, Barile and Maschito with that of Italian women living in Ripacandida, only a few differences are evident. Some distinct species of *liakra* (or *foglie*, as they are called in the Southern Italian dialect in Ripacandida) are gathered and, when the same plants are used, they are used in different culinary preparations. Table 3.1 lists the most salient differences between the four villages. Italian cuisine has had a strong influence on the Arbëresh diet, but very few traces of the inverse trend (Italians adopting Arbëresh dishes) can be found: the already

Table 3.1: Comparison between Arbëresh and Southern Italian Cuisine in Four Centres

	Ginestra (Zhurian)	Barile (Barilli)	Maschito (Mashqiti)	Ripacandida
Altitude	564 m	600 m	595 m	620 m
Ethnic group	Arbëreshë	Arbëreshë	Arbëreshë	Italian
Immigration flows	1470–1478	1470–1478 1533–1534 1534, 1664	1470–1478	—
Population 1998	734	3398	1928	1834
Change population 1991–8	−6.3	+4.17	−1.2	−11.5
% population 65+	25.6%	22.5%	24.1%	27.8%
Current Arbëresh speakers	10–15%	35–40%	5–10%	0%
Liakra/foglie gathering and culinary use of aerial parts of *nen* (*Amaranthus retroflexus*) and *ljabot* (*Chenopodium album*)	✓	✓	✓	—
Wild greens used in the *verdhët* (kind of timbale) on Easter Day	kardunxheljë (*Scolymus hispanicus*)	rekuljë (*Scolymus hispanicus*)	mërajnë (*Foeniculum vulgare ssp. piperitum*)	Without any vegetables
Wild greens used in *liakra e fazuljë* (weeds and bean soup)	luljëkuq (*Papaver rhoeas*)	luljëkuq (*Papaver rhoeas*)	vërajnë (*Borago officinalis*)	None
Dorzëtë (very thin home-made semolina spaghetti, cooked in milk and eaten on Catholic Ascension Day)	✓	—	—	—

mentioned *verdhët* (*verdhët* from the Albanian *verdhë*, in English 'yellow', perhaps due to the large amount of eggs used in this festival dish) is, for example, also popular in the nearby Italian villages (Rionero, Ripacandida, Venosa). A *mutual* exchange of experiences and culinary knowledge between Arbëresh and Italian women has been hindered due to the dominance of mainstream Italian culture. Historically and partly still today, the Arbëreshë have rejected self-recognition of their cultural and ethnic roots. This has surely recently been reinforced by the negative perspective portrayed by the media and the majority of the Italian population concerning the immigrant flows from Albania since 1991, and has represented a constant dynamic in collective Arbëresh psychology.

Liakra in Arbëresh Women's Social Context

Women once gathered *liakra* as they returned home from working in the fields in a sort of collective moment, as they sang together. Gathering is no longer a shared experience but, once *liakra* are gathered, they still represent an important element of women's village social networks: they are often the objects of gift giving, especially for older female neighbours. Elderly women agree that spontaneous gift-giving relations are declining, while the logic of market forces has become more pervasive and tends to replace the free exchange of goods among people as a community custom. The gift-giving dynamic is very complex and may be connected with beliefs about the 'evil eye' (envy possession).

Gallini (1973) discussed in detail the relationship between envy and possession in terms of redistribution mechanisms among social classes in Italy. The Vulture area population believes that, if one is complimented on a possession and this compliment is not followed by the response *'abbenedica'* ('that God will bless you'), the evil eye could afflict the owner of the admired possession. In order to avoid this, the possessor is then forced to share (if it is sharable) the envied object with the admirer. Gathered plants are often offered as gifts, even those plants that are considered to be rare and precious such as wild asparagus (*Asparagus acutifolius*), *Scolymus hispanicus, Leopoldia comosa* and mushrooms.

In the villages visited, people generally considered 'rare' species (see also Price this volume) to be those that are found only in special places (mainly not close to the village), whose gathering is very time-consuming, or that are fast-growing (so that the period when the plant is edible is very short). Significantly, it is mainly men who gather these particularly rare species (together with wild oregano), perhaps because they are 'rare' (although it could also be that they are 'rare' because only men gathered them). It is interesting to note that at least three of these four species are by far the most expensive in the open-air local markets and, even though women sell them, usually only men gather them. It could be hypothesized that, by this mechanism, men could gain a kind of further recognition (and power) for their economically 'fruitful' task. Moreover, it was difficult to speak with elderly men about food greens and weeds, with the exception of these four items that they considered as the only 'serious things' gathered, because they are economically very valuable.

Giving gifts of gathered *liakra* is always a female prerogative and decisions in this regard can usually only be made by the oldest woman in the household.[7] Therefore, men perhaps cannot avail themselves of the authority that accompanies gift giving in the community, but this could be compensated for by the authority they gain within the household when they make these plants available to older women for exchange.

Gendering TEK around Wild Herbs

Qualitatively, it is easy to point out that old women, as the principal wild plant gatherers, have the most extensive knowledge about weedy food greens. But, since it is also necessary to analyse TEK dynamics quantitatively among generations, 60 persons (24 men and 36 women) in Ginestra were asked to identify fresh specimens of eight locally used non-cultivated plants: four vegetables (wild chicory, *Cichorium intybus*; wall rocket, *Diplotaxis tenuifolia*; tassel hyacinth, *Leopoldia comosa*; and sow thistle, *Sonchus oleraceus*); three medicinal plants (giant reed, *Arundo donax*; mallow, *Malva sylvestris*, and white horehound *Marrubium vulgare*); and one herb that is considered among the Arbëreshë to be a prototypical food-medicinal herb (borage, *Borago officinalis*).

First, any interpretation of the cultural significance of age with respect to ethno-biological knowledge and competence is necessarily complicated by the fact that, in any cultural context, age is naturally associated with learning and accumulation of TEK. A few considerations can in any case be suggested on the basis of the recorded data.

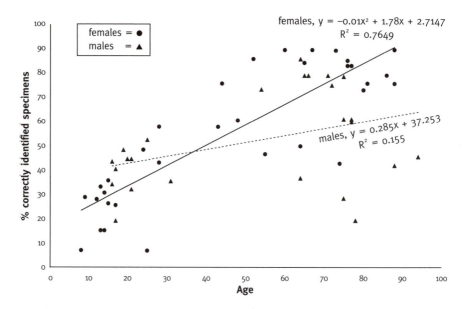

Figure 3.1: Distribution of TEK of Non-cultivated Plants by Sex and Generation in Ginestra (n=60) using a Linear or Binomial Regression Model

Figure 3.1 presents results of a linear regression of the capability to correctly identify the eight specimens relating age and sex as independent variables. The small differences among male and female trends are due to the fact that the chosen specimens are very commonly used plants. These plants were chosen because less common species could be recognized exclusively by women, while with these specimens it was easier to detect differences among generations, which could decrease the effect of age as a variable associated with the learning processes.[8]

The ability to identify a plant dramatically decreases among both men and women under age 50, even though women seem to be much more affected. Although young village men now usually work in factories, they also still work in the fields in grape, wine and olive production during weekends or holidays. The younger women, however, have completely lost their mothers' and grandmothers' knowledge: they work in the fields neither daily nor during their free time. Their younger male partners sometimes gather wild plants themselves or at least are more exposed than their wives to other people (elderly women) who gather plants.

In Ginestra, both for women and for men, the loss of TEK seems to correlate with the loss of the ability to speak the ethnic language: this has mostly affected people, particularly males, born in and after the 1940s (personal observation). As Mühlhäusler recently stated (2001: 143), there is 'an important aspect to any type of management: one can manage only what one knows; and a corollary: that one knows that for which one has a linguistic expression'. Yet it also became clear from the analysis of questionnaires that the loss of TEK and of the Arbëresh language are not necessarily associated: a few middle-aged interviewees are able to remember Arbëresh names of plants, but can't identify them or explain their traditional use.

When analysing the same recorded ethnobotanical competence by means of a curvilinear regression model, in this case among the men, the percentage of correctly identified plants reaches a maximum for those aged between 50 and 60 years; strangely, it decreases for those older than 60. This trend might be explained by the fact that most of the male population over age 65 consists of people who emigrated in search of work, often returning to the village many years later. In Ginestra, the emigration that had its major peak at the end of the 1960s and the beginning of the 1970s has certainly contributed to TEK loss, removing a generation of men from working contact with the natural environment on a regular basis. When these same men returned home, moreover, they began to work in factories rather than in agriculture. They also seem to have played a role in the positive internalization of the acculturation process and in the adoption of mainstream Italian/European cultural models. Among them are many who still tend to reject Arbëresh cultural practices. In opposition to this group of men there are elderly women who try actively to maintain the uniqueness of their culture through continued involvement in gathering weedy greens and preparing traditional meals.

Another demographic group that has certainly played a role in this process is made up of the emigrant families of the middle generation – those who left southern Italy during the 1980s to move to northern Italy, and normally come back to visit their parents or relatives in the summer. Among these people, perhaps partly because of negative media images of recent immigrant flows from Albania, the rejection of traditional culture is very strong. A man from this group tried to convince his interviewer that traditional Albanian culture is something that has to be hidden, because 'Albanians, after all, are like gypsies' (gypsies have a strongly negative connotation among ethnic Italians).

On the other hand, all of the Arbëresh villages visited had contacts with Albanians from Albania and Kosovo over the past decades, with cultural exchange and mutual visits that involved many people, and that were sustained by local municipalities. This occurred at a time when informal cultural exchanges with 'communist' Albania were very rare all over the world. Paradoxically, after the political upheaval in Albania in 1991, these contacts ended, and no interest remained in Ginestra to keep this tradition alive.

In the past, women taught their daughters how to identify the edible plants that had to be gathered while they worked in the field. This was a kind of learning by experience, where daughters observed gestures renewed daily during the spring and summer seasons. Today this mechanism of passing on cultural knowledge has broken down (see also Turner this volume). Young women no longer go into the fields but instead work at home or in factories in the surrounding areas, and do not gather wild edibles. Moreover, nutritional patterns have changed in the studied area. Young couples are now accustomed to eating meat every day and, for most of them, *liakra* represent only a kind of sporadic 'exotic' variation that is mainly prepared and provided by an elderly female (usually the mother or mother-in-law).

Dietary Traditions as Sources of Symbols and Cultural Identity

'Food is a product and mirror of the organization of society ... a prism that absorbs and reflects a host of cultural phenomena' (Counihan and Van Esterik 1997: 6). Social changes and modernization also affect food processing, storage, cooking, food habits and social relations (Counihan 1997, see also Malaza this volume). Food, then, is not only nourishment: in the study area, food botanicals represent central elements of the most important religious procession of the Catholic Holy Friday, the *processione della zingara di Barile* (Procession of the Gypsy of Barile). In this traditional procession, which is witnessed by all Arbëreshë (and southern Italians) in the Vulture area, in addition to the classical representations of the Christian tradition, a few typical Arbëreshë characters are also present. Among them, the most important is the 'gypsy lady' (*la zingara*), who is dressed in traditional costume, covered by all the (real!) gold jewels previously collected from all the families in the village. She symbolizes the temptations of Christ and, in the procession, everyone throws dried and roasted chickpeas (*Cicer arietinum*) at her. In Arbëreshë symbolism, the chickpea is considered to be 'negative' because it is believed that the sounds of its pods shaking led to the discovery of Jesus Christ during his flight to Egypt.

Another example of a ritual use of food is the dish prepared for All Souls' Night (1 November). For this occasion, elderly Arbëreshë women of Ginestra customarily boil durum wheat in grape juice (*mër kot*), adding pomegranate (*Punica granatum*) as a good omen. A bowl of this preparation is left outside the window as an offering to all the souls of Purgatory who, during the night, 'should come and eat it'. A third example is provided by the bread baked for Saint Biagio's Day (3 February): it is blessed in the Church and then eaten as a preventive for sore throats.

Culinary tradition is a popular sign of cultural identity: since 1999, for example, Ginestra's 'Pro-Loco' (the local association dedicated to promoting cultural initiatives in the village) has organized a 'festival of the typical Arbëresh kitchen'. This big feast, which takes place in the second week of August in the village *piazza*, is the result of the collective work of the whole community and especially of women. Days before, they prepare a full range of traditional dishes for the village, for visitors from nearby centres, and also for relatives who have emigrated to northern Italy and are on holiday at that time in Ginestra. This gastronomic event, of a kind quite common over the past several years in many rural areas of Italy, is a distinctive sign of the search for symbols of common identity. The result may be more 'folkloristic' than authentic folklore: many dishes presented during the festival are seen and sold as 'typical', even when they are not at all distinctive of Arbëresh traditional cuisine. As Bausinger noted: 'Folklorism is the applied version of the folklore of yesterday' (2001: 147).

While the loss of TEK has certainly contributed to the decline in the culinary use of weeds among the Arbëreshë, culinary traditions in turn play an important role in the retention of TEK. Food, food preparation and the sociability related to food directly reflect Arbëresh cultural identity. Losing these cultural traditions would certainly result in the loss of TEK and of plant gathering traditions as well.

Women and Ethnobotanical Competence: Knowledge as a Source of Authority and Power

Everyone who holds valued expertise in a specific domain receives status in a given social context (Code 1991). Elderly Arbëresh community members are respected and consulted as authorities: a distinctive sign of this is the fictive kinship terms that everyone in the village still uses when speaking with them: 'aunt' (*zia*) and 'uncle' (*zio*). The *zia*, especially, has a strong influence on the acquisition and use of traditional knowledge in household food and medicinal practices. In this latter domain, information is sometimes kept secret, only partially transmitted or trans- mitted only to special persons like particular relatives, as in the case of ritual healing by prayers (see Quave and Pieroni 2002).

The authority of these women is strong in the village whereas, by contrast, the younger female generation seems to have lost such a position, leading to a very significant change in the distribution of power within the village. From the authority of the *zie* a long series of social responsibilities is derived: managing gathering activities, organizing homegardening and cooperating with men in agricultural decisions (although these remain the final prerogative of the male community). Bearing almost total responsibility for the domestic domain and, in particular, for the kitchen, elderly women were accustomed to directing everyday life in the household. Moreover, as healers and – related to this – as religious practitioners, they played a central role in the village's ritual and religious sphere.

Today, of all these sources of authority, nothing remains in the hands of the younger generation of women. Their male partners make all decisions concerning work in the fields and their role at home is weaker than before. While all men consult the *zia* about health problems, young women are not considered able to provide such advice. Moreover, they generally do not manage homegardens (keeping only a few flowers on the balcony): they are still 'queens' of the kitchen, but the majority have lost the knowledge associated with traditional cuisine. In some ways, they no longer have the same authority as their mothers or grand-mothers had: this is perhaps the price they have had to pay for greater economic independence. If this new situation is partially accepted by their male partners, it is generally rejected by the older generation (both male and female), which at times produces deep conflicts between the generations within families. On the other hand, the majority of the young women have attended school. It seems then that their mothers' and grandmothers' TEK has been replaced by formal education without the latter having the same social implications as the former (see also Turner, this volume). At present, young Arbëresh women are very conscious of their muted role in the family and of the broader independence (both economic and psycho-logical) that they have finally attained. In the many open discussions that were held with young women in the Vulture area, the majority automatically rejected a role exclusively confined to domestic affairs, although this was 'functional' in a society conjugated in the masculine form, and in which men dominated many important decision-making processes as well as all matters related to the administration of cash income.

TEK, Arbëresh Women and Plants: Re-establishing the Links

Assuming that human nature is the result of history and society (Sahlins 1976) and that 'men make their own history, but they do not make it just as they please' (Marx 1986), it is vital to develop a vision of the future of triangular relationships among TEK, women and plants in the Vulture area.

It has to be admitted that the young women of Barile, Ginestra and Maschito will never have the same authority that their mothers and grandmothers had; at the same time, the new social contexts in which they are living will perhaps offer them new opportunities to express authority or autonomy in other ways. Regaining lost TEK will require time, and will be heavily dependent upon positive acceptance by the younger generation of the knowledge connected with the female cosmos of older women. Acculturation processes in schools and universities could generate insights and ideas for the formation of new activities that begin with the re-evaluation of the rapidly vanishing knowledge world of older relatives. Re-valorization of women's domestic knowledge has to take into account the emancipatory challenges that young women have begun to pose, especially because of their roles in sustaining family incomes.

New visions of the relations between people and nature in the area studied will depend on whether nature will become a significant political and cultural force, as has recently happened in other areas in central and northern Italy. Regional agricultural and rural development policies could support the creation of innovative income-generating activities such as the controlled gathering of weedy herbs, the re-introduction of old and archaic crops and handicrafts, the development of agro- and ecotourism, the management of natural and cultural pathways, and ethno-culinary events promoting regional and ethnic food niches.

Members of the young political class that has recently begun to administer the Lucania region, as well as many local institutions, have begun to adopt an eco-sustainable approach, especially in the valorization of typical local species and varieties ('folk varieties'), by providing financial help to new agro-tourist initiatives and to those who wish to convert traditional farms to organic agriculture. The goals of these policies include the production and marketing of biodiverse and 'speciality' food products and a kind of new 'responsible' tourism, whose circuits until recently remained far outside many inland areas of southern Italy. A few years are required to see the first concrete results.

Local women's cooperatives or enterprises, comprised of women belonging to different generations, could lead the way in taking forward the wild food plant heritage in eco-sustainable interdisciplinary projects. A few small female-run enterprises in the neighbouring region of Calabria have set an example (Alliance Project 2000). Such groups could develop strategies to enhance TEK transmission between elderly women and the younger generation in local schools, to sustain wild plant gathering and perhaps to close the gap between generations. Moreover, they could incorporate conservation of both natural and cultural/linguistic resources with economically profitable small-scale production of food plant derivatives and locally typical food products, managed by women.

Notes

1 The term 'Traditional Knowledge' or 'TK' is used in this chapter to refer to *every* traditional practice as an (original) expression of a given human culture. The term 'Traditional Environmental Knowledge' or 'TEK' is used only in relation to traditional knowledge of the natural environment. TK and TEK are the result of historically determined dynamic processes, influenced by the constant interactions between the natural environment and many aspects of language and culture. TEK in particular consists of all practices carried out by people in traditional societies to classify, categorize and organize the natural environment. The analysis of its fluctuations, changes and evolution is one of the main objects of study of modern ethnobiology.

2 See, for example, Cappelletti *et al.* 1982; Novaretti and Lemordant 1990; Bonet *et al.* 1992, 1999; Gonzáles-Tejero *et al.* 1995; Raja *et al.* 1997; Bruni *et al.* 1997; Pieroni 2000; Agelet and Vallès 2001; Corradi and Leporatti 2001.

3 Guarrera 1994; Giusti 1995; Brüschweiler 1999; Pieroni 1999b; Ertuğ 2000; and Pieroni and Giusti 2002.

4 In the perspective of ecological evolutionary biology, the plants considered are in fact 'weeds'. Weeds are plants that 'grow entirely or predominantly in situations markedly disturbed by man (without, of course, being a deliberately cultivated plant)' (Baker 1965). They represent a kind of intermediate between wild and cultivated species, and many are eco-sustainable nutritional sources (Bye 1981).

5   In other papers (Quave and Pieroni 2002; Pieroni *et al.* 2002b), women's TK related to healing practices (magic prayers and traditional phytotherapy in family primary health care) are discussed.
6   In folk classification systems, folk classifications of species don't necessarily correspond to scientific classifications (see the discussion of 'one-to-one correspondence' in Berlin *et al.* 1966; Berlin 1992): very often people name and classify a few scientific species with the same vernacular term in the same taxon ('under-differentiation'), while the contrary (diverse folk taxa corresponding to only one scientific taxon, or 'over-classification') seems to be very rare, at least in southern Europe (personal observation).
7   As in many other social and cultural contexts in southern Italy, the domestic world is dominated by women, who are exclusively involved in processing and preparing meals. That is true even among the youngest couples in the study area.
8   In ethnobiological studies of the kind attempted here, the correlation between capacity to recognize species and the age of the informants automatically contains an approximation for the youngest generation. It may be that children and teenagers do not recognize species, not because they have lost TEK, but because they have not yet learned to do so. In many studies this factor may affect assessments of the percentage of correct identifications (demonstrating 'ethnobotanical competence') among teenagers: in other words, their effective competence may sometimes be slightly underestimated. In this study, by choosing very commonly used plants, this source of possible 'misinterpretation' was minimized.

References

Agelet, A. and J. Vallès (2001) 'Studies on pharmaceutical botany in the region of Pallars (Pyrenees, Catalonia, Iberian Peninsula)', Part I, 'General results and new or very rare medicinal plants', *Journal of Ethnopharmacology*, Vol. 77, pp. 57–70.

Alliance Project (2000) Available at: http://www.artes-research.com/allianceframe.html (last visited 9 July 2002).

Baker, H. G. (1965) 'Characteristics and modes of origin of weeds', in H. G. Baker and G. L. Stebbins (eds.), *The Genetics of Colonizing Species*, New York: Academic Press, pp. 147–68.

Bausinger, H. (2001) 'Per una critica alle critiche del foklorismo', in P. Clemente and F. Mugnaini (eds.), *Oltre il Folklore. Tradizioni Popolari e Antropologia nella Società Contemporanea*, Rome: Carocci Editore, pp. 145–69.

Berlin, B. (1992) *Ethnobiological Classification*, Princeton: Princeton University Press.

Berlin, B., D. E. Breedlove and P. H. Raven (1966) 'Folk taxonomies and biological classification', *Science*, No. 154, pp. 273–5.

Bonet, M. A., C. Blanché and J. Vallès Xirau (1992) 'Ethnobotanical study in River Tenes valley (Catalonia, Iberian Peninsula)', *Journal of Ethnopharmacology*, Vol. 37, pp. 205–12.

Bonet, M. A., M. Parada, A. Selga and J. Vallès (1999) 'Studies of pharmaceutical ethnobotany in the regions of L'Alt Empordà and Les Guilleries (Catalonia, Iberian Peninsula)', *Journal of Ethnopharmacology*, Vol. 68, pp. 145–68.

Bruni, A., M. Ballero and F. Poli (1997) 'Quantitative ethnopharmacological study of the Campidano Valley and Urzulei District, Sardinia, Italy', *Journal of Ethnopharmacology*, Vol. 57, pp. 97–124.

Brüschweiler, S. (1999) *Plantes et Savoirs des Alpes. L'Example du Val d'Anniviers*, Sierre (Switzerland): Editions Monographic SA.

Bye, R. A. (1981) 'Quelites – ethnoecology of edible greens – past, present, and future', *Journal of Ethnobiology*, Vol. 1, pp. 109–23.

Cappelletti, E., R. Trevisan and R. Caniato (1982) 'External antirheumatic and antineuralgic herbal remedies in the traditional medicine of north-eastern Italy', *Journal of Ethnopharmacology*, Vol. 6, pp. 161–90.

Code, L. (1991) *What Can She Know? Feminist Theory and the Construction of Knowledge*, Ithaca:

Cornell University Press.

Counihan, C. (1997) 'Bread as world. Food habits and social relations in modernizing Sardinia', in C. Counihan and P. Van Esterik (eds.), *Food and Culture. A Reader*, New York: Routledge, pp. 283–95.

Counihan, C. and P. Van Esterik (eds.) (1997) *Food and Culture. A Reader*, New York: Routledge.

Dessart, F. (1982) 'The Albanian ethnic groups in the world: an historical and cultural essay on the Albanian colonies in Italy', *East European Quarterly*, Vol. 4, pp. 469–84.

Ertuğ, F. (2000) 'An ethnobotanical study in Central Anatolia (Turkey)', *Economic Botany*, Vol. 54, pp. 155–82.

Forbes, M. H. (1976) 'Gathering in the Argolid: a subsistence subsystem in a Greek agricultural community', *Annals of the New York Academy of Science*, No. 268, pp. 251–64.

Gallini, C. (1973) *Dono e Malocchio*, Palermo, Italy: Flaccovio Editore.

Gazzetta Ufficiale della Repubblica Italiana (1999) *Legge 15 Dicembre 1999, n. 482. Norme in Maniera di Tutela della Minoranze Linguistiche Storiche*, Rome: Ufficio Poligrafico della Zecca.

Giusti, S. (ed.) (1995) *Le Piante Magiche. Una Ricerca Storico-Antropologica*, Rome: Domograf.

González-Tejero, M. R., J. Molero-Mesa, M. Casares-Porcel and M. Martínez Lirola (1995) 'New contributions to the ethnopharmacology of Spain', *Journal of Ethnopharmacology*, Vol. 45, No. 3, pp. 157–75.

Guarrera, P. M. (1994) *Il Patrimonio Etnobotanico del Lazio*, Rome: Regione Lazio/Dipartimento di Biologia Vegetale, Università 'La Sapienza'.

Grimes, B.F. (ed.) (2000) *Ethnologue – CD ROM*, Dallas: Summer Institute of Linguistics.

Heinrich, M. and S. Gibbons (2001) 'Ethnopharmacology in drug discovery: an analysis of its role and potential contribution', *Journal of Pharmacy and Pharmacology*, Vol. 53, pp. 425–32.

Leporatti, M. L. and L. Corradi (2001) 'Ethopharmacological remarks on the Province of Chieti town (Abruzzo, Central Italy)', *Journal of Ethnopharmacology*, Vol. 74, pp. 17–40.

Marx, K. (1986) *Karl Marx. A Reader*, Cambridge (UK): Cambridge University Press.

Mühlhäusler, P. (2001) 'Ecolinguistics, linguistic diversity, ecological diversity', in L. Maffi (ed.), *On Biocultural Diversity. Linking Language, Knowledge, and the Environment*, Washington: Smithsonian Institution Press.

Novaretti, R. and D. Lemordant (1990) 'Plants in the traditional medicine of the Ubaye Valley', *Journal of Ethnopharmacology*, Vol. 30, pp. 1–34.

Paoletti, M. G., A. L. Dreon and G. G. Lorenzoni (1995) 'Pistic, traditional food from Western Friuli, N.E. Italy', *Economic Botany*, Vol. 49, pp. 26–30.

Parpart, J. L. (1995) 'Deconstructing the development "expert": gender, development and the "vulnerable" groups', in M. H. Marchand and J. Parpart (eds.), *Feminism/Postmodernism/Development*, New York: Routledge, pp. 221–43.

Pieroni, A. (1999a) 'Gathered wild food plants in the upper valley of the Serchio River (Garfagnana), Central Italy', *Economic Botany*, Vol. 53, pp. 327–41.

Pieroni, A. (1999b) 'Piante spontanee ed immaginario collettivo in Alta Garfagnana (Lucca): un centro di documentazione sulla cultura orale', *Informatore Botanico Italiano*, Vol. 31, pp. 183–9.

Pieroni, A. (2000) 'Medicinal plants and food medicines in the folk traditions of the upper Lucca Province, Italy', *Journal of Ethnopharmacology*, Vol. 70, pp. 235–73.

Pieroni, A. and M. Heinrich (2002) 'An ethnobotanical survey of the traditional food use in an ethnic Albanian community of southern Italy', in J. F. Stepp, F. Wyndham and R. Zarger (eds.), *Ethnobiology, Benefit Sharing and Biocultural Diversity*, Athens: University of Georgia Press.

Pieroni A. and M. E. Giusti (2002) 'Ritual botanicals against the evil eye in Tuscany, Italy', *Economic Botany*, Vol. 56, pp. 201–204.

Pieroni, A., S. Nebel, C. Quave and M. Heinrich (2002a) 'Ethnopharmacology of *liakra*, traditional weedy vegetables of the Arbëreshë of the Vulture area in southern Italy', *Journal of Ethnopharmacology*, Vol. 81, No. 2, pp. 165–85.

Pieroni, A., C. Quave, S. Nebel and M. Heinrich (2002b) 'Ethnopharmacy of ethnic Albanians

(Arbëreshë) in northern Basilicata (southern Italy)', *Fitoterapia*, Vol. 73, No. 3, pp. 217–41.

Pignatti, S. (1982) *Flora d'Italia*, Bologna (Italy): Edizioni Edagricole.

Quave, C. and A. Pieroni (2002) 'Magical healing. Traditional folk-medical practices of the Vulture area of southern Italy', in C. Gottschalk-Batschkus (ed.), *Ethnotherapien-Handbuch*, Munich (Germany): Institut für Ethnomedizin, pp. 109–18.

Raja, D., C. Blanché and J. Vallès Xirau (1997) 'Contribution to the knowledge of the pharmaceutical ethnobotany of La Segarra region (Catalonia, Iberian Peninsula)', *Journal of Ethnopharmacology*, Vol. 57, pp. 149–60.

Sahlins, M. (1976) *Culture and Practical Reason*, Chicago: University of Chicago Press.

Salminen, P. (1999) *UNESCO Red Book Report on Endangered Languages*: Europe, Available at: *http://www.helsinki.fi/ ~tasalmin/europe_report.html*

Zent, S. (2001) 'Acculturation and ethnobotanical knowledge loss among the Piaroa of Venezuela', in L. Maffi (ed.), *On Biocultural Diversity. Linking Language, Knowledge, and the Environment*, Washington: Smithsonian Institution Press.

CHAPTER 4
Women and 'Wild' Foods: Nutrition and Household Security among Rai and Sherpa Forager-Farmers in Eastern Nepal

Ephrosine Daniggelis

In recent decades, climatic change, other natural hazards and conflict have been increasing in severity, affecting many countries around the world and resulting in severe food shortages for their populations. For centuries, 'wild'[1] plants have been an important source of emergency food that acts as a buffer against shortage. These wild plants flourish in disturbed open areas such as fallow swidden fields (Wilken 1970). Since these wild plants have so much importance for the livelihoods of rural people, especially the poor and women, the term 'minor' labels them incorrectly: they are indeed 'major'. Wild foods are shown to be major by Lintu (1995) in India, where *mahua* flowers are a seasonal grain substitute. Fleuret (1979) argues that the label 'supplementary' is also inappropriate, because it implies that the wild leafy plant relishes used by the Shambaa people throughout the year are peripheral to the diet.

The wild environment is of great importance for impoverished rural populations – especially for women who live in remote areas of the world and have few assets in terms of land, livestock or cash, as is the case in Nepal. Outsiders often consider these wild environments as 'wasteland'. This mislabelling hides the vast biological diversity and importance of wild environments as repositories of plant genetic resources. In Nepal, those who have given attention to these environments have concentrated mainly on their importance for timber and fodder resources: they rarely allude to other plant genetic resources used for food, medicine and rituals. For example, both medicinal plants and foods are considered to have healthful properties, preventing disease by strengthening the body's defence system (Etkin and Ross 1994: 35). In addition to this, the religious and cultural aspects of the environment should be taken into account. Outsiders are unaware of the vital consequences for women forager-farmers – the gatekeepers of household food security – of the loss of wild food resources on which they depend for their survival.

The greatest impact of environmental degradation in forests and other wild environments is usually on women because they are the primary gatherers, users and managers of wild plant resources for subsistence purposes. These women have

83

a vast knowledge of wild plant resources that is apparent not only in their foraging activities, but also in processing, preservation, preparation and distribution. There is a clear adverse relationship between the consequences of natural resource degradation – decreasing availability of firewood, decreasing yields of cultivated crops and also of biodiversity in general – and the health status of vulnerable groups, especially women and children. If development agencies and conservationists turn a blind eye to these relationships, the women and children who are most dependent on these resources will be at even greater nutritional risk, and interventions intended to help will instead have negative impacts. The hidden plant genetic resources that women utilize are excellent sources of nutrients, provide local medical home remedies, and are an important source of income. The importance of these resources and of women to their management have to date been largely neglected. In the hill areas of Nepal, the significance of environmental resources needs to be viewed through the eyes of rural women forager-farmers. Those belonging to two Tibeto-Burman populations, the Kulunge Rai and Khumbu Sherpa, provide a lens through which to view these interdependencies.

The 'Hidden' Wealth of the *Jaṅgal*

Rai and Sherpa women live on the fringes of the *jaṅgal,* a 'wild wasteland' to uninformed outsiders, in the middle hills of Eastern Nepal. *Jaṅgal* is a term used by both Rais and Sherpas to refer to common property areas including all forest land, fallow swidden fields, and most grass and pasture areas surrounding their villages up to the timberline, at about 4,200 metres. Farmers view these areas as common land although they were legally declared to be government forests in 1957. Above the *jaṅgal* are high alpine meadows that are not perpetually snow-covered, referred to locally as the *lekh*. The *jaṅgal* and, to a lesser extent, the *lekh* were chosen as the focus of this research to understand how women perceive, use and manage wild plant genetic resources, and strategize to overcome household food insecurity.

Previous research in the region has focused on the forest without appreciating the inclusive complexity and extremely high biological diversity of the *jaṅgal* as defined by Rai and Sherpa women forager-farmers. *Jaṅgal* foods are especially of nutritional significance to reproductively active women and children who tend to be at greater nutritional risk than adult males. Molnar's (1981) research among the Kham Magar, a Tibeto-Burman group in north-west Nepal, found that during the winter months nettles are the main vegetable consumed, while during the monsoon, when food shortages occur, wild foods are gathered. Wild seeds and nuts are sources of energy, essential oils, minerals and protein (de Beer and McDermott 1989, Kuhnlein and Turner 1991). Tubers, roots, rhizomes and corms provide starch, and their skins provide certain minerals.

In spite of findings like this, the importance of *jaṅgal* foods has been nearly universally devalued because they are viewed as easily accessible, are associated with poverty (Wilken 1970), and are 'never sown' (Maikhuri *et al.* 2000). Another cultural perception of nettles was described by Rock (1930) who reported on the monks living in hermit quarters during the summer in eastern Tibet. These monks subsisted on *tsampa* (toasted ground barley flour rolled into balls) and boiled nettles that were 'considered the greatest sacrifice to their austere existence'.

For the Tibeto-Burman groups living in the Nepal Himalaya, the *jaṅgal* has always been an important source of edible plants. It is crucial in that it provides food during seasonal and emergency food shortage periods for hill farmers who were forced by government policies to occupy more marginal and infertile land. The Indo-Aryan rulers occupied the fertile valleys and cultivated rice on irrigated terraces, so that rice became a high-status food and a symbol of the élite (Daniggelis 2001: 9). The rights to maintain *kipaṭ* were granted by the Shah regime in the late 1700s. In the *kipaṭ* system, an individual obtained rights to land, but not owner-ship, by virtue of membership in a particular clan (Regmi 1978). Locally, *kipaṭ* means the system whereby all streams, rivers, grazing areas, steep cliffs and trees are shared by the villagers, including most *jaṅgal* resources (Daniggelis 2001: 15). Although forests officially became government property in 1957, the *kipaṭ* system is still practised and valued by Rai and Sherpa forager-farmers in the Arun Valley.

The *jaṅgal* provides food, fodder and timber resources as well as medicinal plants. An estimated 80 per cent of the Nepalese population depends upon traditional medicine as their sole or primary form of health care (Rajbhandary and Bajracharya 1994). *Jaṅgal* plant resources are also used for animal litter, compost, and building and household materials. They are valued as cash commodities and are essential for ritual and ceremonial purposes. Men occasionally play a role in collecting, managing, and trading *jaṅgal* resources but, compared to women, their participation is minor. Women are involved in the entire *jaṅgal* 'food path' that marks the flow of *jaṅgal* foods and medicinal plants from gathering to processing, distribution and consumption by household members. They are also key players in environmental management and conservation.

Jaṅgal food also has other important social dimensions. Sanskritization is a term introduced by Srinivas (1956) to describe a process whereby a caste undergoes cultural transformation with the hope of raising itself to a higher position in the Hindu caste hierarchy. This entails the prohibition of particular *jaṅgal* foods. As is shown below, Sanskritization can negatively affect the health and nutritional status of vulnerable groups. McDougal (1979: 4), pointed out that Rais have avoided Sanskritization, and in doing so, have remained essentially 'tribal', retaining a positive view of the *jaṅgal*. The Rai view themselves as '*jaṅgal* owners' because they claim to be the first human settlers in the region.

Subsistence in the Arun Valley

Research was carried out over a twenty-month period in 1993–4 on the Kulunge Rai and the Khumbu Sherpa ethnic groups living in the upper Arun Valley of eastern Nepal, within the Makalu Barun National Park and Conservation Area. Yangden, Gongtala, Dobatak and Saisima villages are seven or eight days' walk from Hile, one of the major market and trading towns in eastern Nepal. An inventory was made of how and why the *jaṅgal* is important to households in these villages; the methods used to acquire, distribute and consume *jaṅgal* foods and medicine; and the cultural categories used to identify *jaṅgal* resources. Men, women and children were interviewed at home, in the fields and in the *jaṅgal*.

The small Sherpa population living in the villages of Gongtala, Dobatak and Saisima are agro-pastoralists. They cultivate dry highland barley, wheat and potatoes. The Sherpas own high-altitude bovids (yaks and their hybrid offspring) and are heavily dependent on bovid products to meet their food needs, making them more food-secure than the Rais. The ownership of high-altitude animals is synonymous with wealth because milk and milk products (cheese, yoghurt, buttermilk and dried cheese) are important sources of protein and items for barter. Thus the Sherpas are more dependent on the *jaṅgal* for fodder than for food. Transhumance is important and high-altitude animals are taken to graze at the *lekh* during the monsoon. *Anikāl* (a term used to indicate inadequate food stores) lasts around two and a half months and is felt most acutely just before the harvest. The Sherpas belong to the Nyingmapa, the oldest Tibetan Buddhist sect. All Sherpa villages have *lamas* (Buddhist priests) who are responsible for curing illnesses and conducting ancestor rites and other ritual obligations.

The Kulunge Rai living in the lower-altitude village of Yangden practise mixed agriculture consisting of maize, millet and soybeans. Intercropping helps to ensure soil fertility and protect crops against pests. They also keep pigs and herd animals including sheep, goats, cows and oxen. Yangden's lower elevation (1,100–1,800 metres) and warmer climate allow for a greater diversity of cultivated crops that in turn provides an important means of bartering with the Sherpas. *Anikāl* for the Rai lasts nearly half a year, during which time the farmers clear the *jaṅgal* for swiddens and plant maize and millet. For several years after the crops are harvested, *chiraito* (*Swertia chirata*), a medicinal plant, flourishes in the fallow fields and provides an important source of medicine and cash income. The Rai practise an indigenous religion that is somewhat influenced by Hinduism. Village religious practitioners are *dhāmīs* (spirit mediums) and *pūjāris* (priests) who treat illnesses and perform rites to ensure the health of all household members. They are male, but women play an important role in the traditional health system by making medicinal preparations from plants.

The Gender Division of Labour in Household Food Production Systems

The gender division of labour for Rais and Sherpas is quite similar, and is not rigidly defined by sex or by social group because all family members contribute to subsistence. Domestic and subsistence activities overlap and depend on the proportion of dependent to non-dependent workers. Children from six to fourteen years old, especially girls, participate substantially in economic activities and are classified as 'partially dependent' (Daniggelis 2001: 66–7).

Men, women and children collect wild foods from the *jaṅgal* and, with the exception of children, from the *lekh*. There is no gender division of labour in digging up wild yams, which are an important staple for the Rais during the lean season. Several wild tubers require laborious processing, and Sherpas collect them from the *lekh*. Young children gather wild fruits. Both sexes and all social groups collect *chiraito*.

Women perform the majority of all agricultural tasks such as hoeing, weeding, harvesting, selecting seeds for cultivation, applying manure to the fields, husking, winnowing and grinding grain into flour. Grain processing is very time-consuming. Men, however, often assist when crops are threatened by wild animals and particularly when women are ill. It is also predominantly women who milk animals and produce other animal products, cut grass and fodder for the livestock, carry food to the fields for communal working parties, cook, clean and wash clothes. Unmarried women, youngest daughters-in-law, and children ten years of age and older usually herd dooryard animals, cows and goats.

Predominantly male tasks include: ploughing, chopping wood, collecting mālingo (*Arundinaria aristatla*), trekking, treading sheep's wool blankets, making trips to buy salt and barter for food supplies, constructing and maintaining terraces and building houses. Sherpa men also travel to neighbouring villages to collect grain or cash against outstanding loans. Men's work is considered to be of greater value than women's, evident in the fact that they receive one and a half times more food than that received by women workers.

Long-distance or seasonal labour migration increases the number of female-headed households who must rely on kin networks to carry out male-defined tasks. Because Nepali is the *lingua franca* and is spoken by only a minority of women, it can present a disadvantage for them when they trade or seek credit. Sherpa men are involved in mountain-trekking expeditions, but money is not always returned to the village and is sometimes spent on liquor and gambling. With modernity, Sherpa women are becoming involved in trekking, and a few young Rai women occasionally migrate to Kathmandu.

Household Food Security

Household food security refers to whether a household is able to access a sufficient supply of food of sufficient quality to meet its needs throughout the year. Seasonal inadequacy is a significant feature of the Rai diet and also affects the majority of Sherpa households. However, one-third of Rai households also experience chronic food insecurity, reporting *anikāl* of more than seven months' duration every year.

Households cope with chronic food scarcity by employing a combination of strategies determined by a number of factors including: the length of *anikāl*, household resources (land, livestock and gold), the availability of off-farm labour, and family members' health status. Social relationships establish ties through kin and marriage, providing for the poor and women. Sherpas and Rais establish ritual friendships very similar to kinship ties. The Buddhist religion also plays an important role because Sherpas give small amounts of foodstuffs, milking animals or chickens to destitute families to earn merit (Daniggelis 2001: 74).

Anikāl occurs during the pre-monsoon period that fortunately coincides with the abundance of *jaṅgal* foods such as *sisnu* (stinging nettle – *Girardinia diversifolia, Girardiana palmata,* and *Urtica dioica* L.), wild tubers and bamboo shoots. A period of nutritional and environmental stress occurs when male shepherds take their herds to the *lekh* during the summer months. The women and children who stay in the village are more vulnerable to protein deficiency due to the absence of animal products in their diet. They must depend upon plant protein at a time when their energy requirements are increased because this is the busiest season for planting and harvesting.

Wild Plant Use

Shrestha (1989) asserts that the knowledge involved in collecting, processing and producing wild food has not been adequately evaluated and promoted. A *jaṅgal* resource checklist was made by talking with and following men, women and children to the *jaṅgal,* and by collecting plant species that were later identified by ethnobotanists in Kathmandu. Participant observation was used to determine parameters of *jaṅgal* food acquisition and production as well as children's snacking. A household survey, a food frequency checklist and a 24-hour dietary recall were also used to collect data. Key informant interviews recorded settlement histories and perceptions of natural resource status and environmental change, and were complemented by participatory mapping of natural resources.

Data revealed that Rai women are more dependent on *jaṅgal* foods than Sherpa women and spend twice as long collecting firewood (an average of four hours daily). The types of food preserved for *anikāl* differ by ethnic group. Only Rai women ferment dried vegetables, while Sherpa women are exclusively involved in preparing yeast starters, making butter and dried cheese, and detoxifying the wild root *Arisaema flavum.* Firewood is also used for heating and for alcohol distillation that provides a source of income for some Rai and Sherpa women.

Rai and Sherpa indigenous knowledge is reflected in the more than 76 *jaṅgal* resources that were collected: 47 for human consumption, 38 for fodder, 19 for medicine, 5 for religious and ceremonial purposes, 11 to make household implements, and 11 for trade as raw and processed materials. In addition to naming plants, forager-farmers discussed the type of environment in which the plant is found and its location; the part of the plant that is used; the months that it is available; and the plant's height, flowering period and cultural value at a particular stage of maturity (Daniggelis 2001: 86–7).

Jaṅgal ethnobotanical knowledge and resource use varies according to sex, age, ethnicity and economic status. *Jaṅgal* foods consumed by the Rais and Sherpas include wild leafy greens, wild fruits, spices, condiments, bamboo shoots, seeds, nuts, roots and wild tubers. Non-floral *jaṅgal* resources include fish, honey and honey bee larvae. Wild leafy greens and berries are readily available and may be collected very close to the home. Wild greens are often gathered when Rai or Sherpa women collect firewood or water and are usually prepared for the next meal. Women and children herd cows and goats and, at the same time, gather bamboo shoots and mushrooms in the *jaṅgal*. Young children run freely near their homes and snack on wild fruits. Even though these fruits are nutritionally important, children are not often thought to be knowledge holders. These children have learned from their mothers through observation and practice.

Bamboo (*Gramineae* spp.) is abundant and has great cultural importance for Rai households. Men and women of all social groups use four species (Daniggelis 2001: 100–2). Because there are few alternative income-earning opportunities, weaving bamboo products is an important way to earn cash. Men gather, dry and weave bamboo products. One species of bamboo (*māliṅgo* – *Arundinaria aristatla*) has been overexploited and is therefore now managed communally.

Both Sherpas and Rais have a tradition of using *jaṅgal* plants for religious and ceremonial purposes. For example, *ban tarul* (*Dioscorea versicolor*) and *ghar tarul* (*Dioscorea alata* L.) are foods included in a Hindu celebration called *Maghe Sankrānti* that marks the agricultural season for the Rais. This festival coincides with *anikāl*, and the wild tubers are major staples during this period.

Male and female Rai and Sherpa herders collect medicinal plants during trans-humance at the *lekh*. *Chiraito* is traded on a large scale and is the most common source of indigenous medicine. A survey of 49 households revealed that 17 are involved in the *chiraito* trade. Sherpas use more plants for medicine than Rais (18 species, compared to ten). Both Rai and Sherpa women prepare these plants into a beverage to treat diarrhoea, headaches, fevers and coughs, or apply them directly to cuts. Medicinal plants are also used to treat livestock.

Rai and Sherpa meal patterns

The Rais' diet usually consists of a large meal in the late morning and another in the evening where the staple food most frequently consumed is *chakla*, made of boiled coarsely ground maize and sometimes millet. *Sisnu* (Himalayan or stinging nettles), wild leafy greens or soybean soup are the usual side dishes. Since *chakla* is the Rais' staple food, wild greens can supply significant quantities of the niacin that is lacking in the *chakla*. Poorer families reported one of the following as their meal: a soup made of only *sisnu* or wild greens, a maize *dhīro* (a paste-like mixture of pre-cooked flour mixed with boiling water), or a maize or millet *khole* (a thin flour porridge of water and salt). If only a few milking animals are owned, the milk is given to the youngest children.

The Sherpas eat two main meals and frequently snack throughout the day. After rising, families eat a light meal of *khole*, popped toasted maize or barley kernels, or leftovers from the previous evening meal fried in butter or oil. A pot of Tibetan tea (made of tea, butter, salt, and sometimes milk) is brewed. The large meal is eaten in late morning and usually consists of boiled potatoes served with chile, garlic, salt and occasionally wild garlic leaves, or *dhīro*, served with soybean, cheese or chicken soup. The labourers will carry a light meal to the fields or it is brought to them later by the female household head. The evening meal is similar to the late morning meal and is eaten after all the fieldwork is finished. Sherpa women continuously snack on potatoes and popped maize or barley while preparing food, visiting with friends or entertaining guests.

Jaṅgal food processing and preparation

The way that food is produced, prepared, preserved and stored, cooked and distributed can affect the nutrition of a community as much as the total quantity procured. Once jaṅgal food resources reach the household, women assume the responsibility for their flow in the food path. The methods that they use to prepare meals can positively or negatively affect the food's nutritional content. Both Rai and Sherpa women wash vegetables before they cut them, which helps to prevent nutrient loss. Pots are covered with a lid to lessen the exposure to air, which prevents the loss of ascorbic acid. Minimal nutrient loss occurs when food is boiled because the liquid is consumed in soups and stews. Boiling tubers with their skins on helps to prevent nutrients from leaching into the water because the liquid is discarded. Cast iron pans are used to fry food, which increases the amount of iron in the diet.

Seasonal wild food plants are preserved and stored for times of scarcity. As well as the labour and time needed to collect these plants, complicated, time-consuming processing techniques are used to detoxify wild tubers and make them edible. An example is *phi to* (*Arisaema flavum*), a wild root that is collected when time for processing is not a constraining factor. *Phi to* contains the same toxin (cyanogenic glycosides) that is found in bitter cassava (*Manihot esculenta* Crantz). Special techniques are used to detoxify the *phi to* and convert inulin, a complex carbohydrate, into fructose and glucose, which makes it digestible (Kuhnlein and Turner 1991). First, *phi to* roots are washed and cooked uncovered in boiling water an entire night. Open boiling hydrolyses cyanogenic glycosides into hydrogen cyanide and sugar. The hydrogen cyanide evaporates with the vapour (Standal, personal communication, 1997). The cooked *phi to* is then peeled, beaten on top of a rock, and rolled into long strips. The detoxified *phi to* is used to make bread, or is added to soup or used to make *raksī* (distilled alcohol).

Food preservation techniques

Rai and Sherpa women use food preservation techniques to store foods for *anikāl*. Drying and fermenting leaves also have a beneficial nutritional effect (Adhikari and Krantz 1989: 145). Although processing does not affect mineral content, vitamins A, C and B are somewhat reduced. Rai women make a fermented dried vegetable relish called *gundruk* out of kale, radish, rape leaves and *mangan sāg* (*Cardamine hirsuta*). The leaves are first sun-dried and then fermented for one to four weeks. The Rai also make *mulā sinki*, a fermented food made from radish roots, and store it for the winter months. Some Sherpa women collect *mangan sāg* in the *lekh* and dry it in the sun to reduce its bitter taste.

Jangal food consumption

The household survey was administered to 32 Rai and 20 Sherpa households, and encompassed both cultivated vegetables and *jangal* foods gathered during the winter months (Table 4.1) and the monsoon season (Table 4.2).

Although cultivated vegetables are available in the winter, the Rai still exploit a wide range of *jangal* foods to supplement their main staple, *chakla*. Important factors to consider in the collection of *jangal* foods are availability and proximity. *Jangal* foods are found at a lower elevation in the vicinity of the Rai village, at a time when the Sherpa villages are covered with snow. During winter months, the Rais use wild tubers (*ghar tarul*) as a substitute for *chakla*, the main source of carbohydrates (energy).

Table 4.1: Cultivated Vegetables and *Jangal* Foods Gathered by Rai and Sherpa Households during the Winter Months

Use	Local names	Description
R,S,c	*Rayo sag*	*Brassica juncea* (Leaf mustard)
R,S,c	*Mula sag*	*Raphanus sativus* (Radish)
S,c	*Pidalu sag*	*Alocasia indicum*
R,c	*Tori sag*	*Brassica napus* L. (Indian rape)
R,w	*Sisnu*	a) *Urtica dioica* L. (Stinging nettles); b) *Girardinia diversifolia* (Himalayan nettle); c) *Girardiana palmata* (Himalayan nettle)
(R,S,w)	*Bhurmang sag*	A wild leafy green
(R,w)	*Ban tarul*	*Dioscorea versicolor*
(R,w)	*Bhyakur*	*Dioscorea deltoidea* (Deltoid yam)
(R,w)	*Gitthe tarul*	*Dioscorea bulbifera* (Air tuber)
(R,w)	*Ghar tarul*	*Dioscorea alata* L. (White yam)

Key: R – Rai, S – Sherpa, c – cultivated, w – 'wild'
Source: Daniggelis 2001

Table 4.2: Cultivated Vegetables and *Jangal* Foods Gathered by Rai and Sherpa Households during the Monsoon

Use	Local names	Description
R,S,c	*Iskus sag*	*Momordica charantia* (Chayote)
R,c	*Pharsi sag*	*Cucurbita maxima* (Pumpkin)
R,S,w	*Sisnu*	a) *Girardinia diversifolia* b) *Urtica dioica* L. c) *Girardiana palmata*
R,S,w	*Gutel*	*Trewia nudiflora* L.(Bamboo)
R,S,w	*Kalo nigalo*	*Arundinaria falcata* (Bamboo)
S,w	*Niguro*	*Dryopteris cochleata* (Fiddleheads)
S,w	*Phi to*	*Arisaema flavum* (a tuber)
S,R,w	*Mangan sag*	*Cardamine hirsuta* (Bittercress)
S,R,w	*Cyau*	Various mushrooms

Key: R - Rai, S - Sherpa, c - cultivated, w –'wild'
Source: Daniggelis 2001.

During the monsoon, a greater variety of *jañgal* foods are available. Only Sherpas collect *phi to* at the *lekh* during the monsoon season. Fewer cultivated vegetables are available, and the Sherpa say that they like the variety in their diet that wild foods provide. Wild food is of utmost importance to the Rais' survival, as is apparent from the baskets of wild greens lined up along the bamboo walls of their houses.

A food frequency checklist administered to 15 Sherpa and 24 Rai women determined how often *jañgal* foods are consumed in their households throughout the year. Rai households eat more wild leafy vegetables than Sherpa households. Most Sherpa households do not rely on *jañgal* foods as much as Rai households because they own a greater number of livestock and consume the by-products. *Jañgal* foods are also associated with the poor, and the economically better-off Sherpas are becoming Sanskritized.

Both Rai and Sherpa women were interviewed about their own food consumption using a 24-hour dietary recall. Nearly half the Rai women said that they eat wild greens twice a day when they are available, as an accompaniment to *chakla*. The majority eat *sisnu* daily during the summer months and *bhurmang sāg* daily during the winter months. Not all Rai households reported consuming a staple food at their meals, and a few women lamented that their meal consisted only of soup made from wild greens. If wild greens are eaten without *chakla*, they 'do not fill the stomach', a euphemism for hunger.

Nevertheless, participant observation showed that a greater variety and frequency of *jañgal* foods are eaten than is revealed by the dietary survey methods. For example, when Rai shepherds journey to the *lekh*, they gather a number of wild leafy greens in addition to the *gundruk* and *mulā sinki* that they bring with them to eat together with the *chakla*. *Jañgal* food snacks (*gitthe* – *Dioscorea bulbifera* – and wild raspberries) are beneficial to small Rai children because they provide nutrients that are lacking in the two main meals. Although Rai women did not report any snacks in the 24-hour dietary recall, young children are frequently seen snacking on wild berries. These mothers may not consider *jañgal* fruits as food, especially when they are eaten away from the family hearth. The importance of kin networks for child nutrition should also not be underestimated because often children wander to other houses where grandmothers or other kin give them food.

Nutrient composition of *jañgal* foods

Jañgal foods boost the nutritional composition of poor forager-farmers' diets. *Sisnu* is the richest source of protein and calcium of all cultivated and wild vegetables (Adhikari and Krantz 1989, Gopalan *et al.* 1984). On several occasions, the raw weight of the wild greens was obtained before cooking. A portion of 440 grams of *sisnu* was prepared as a side dish for seven household members. Therefore, at least 60 grams of *sisnu* would be available to each person, supplying an important source of folic acid, leaf protein, vitamins A, C and K, iron, calcium and riboflavin. Wild green leafy vegetables and fruits are important sources of ascorbic acid that enhance the absorption of the non-haeme iron present in a diet consisting primarily of grains. Wild fruits are usually eaten on the spot; hence processing does not destroy the ascorbic acid present in the fruit. Wild greens have a high concentration of beta-carotene, are precursors of Vitamin A, and are high in iron.

At first appearance, fat appears to be a limiting factor in the Rai diet because the women said that vegetables are usually only boiled with salt when served as the accompaniment to *chakla*. However, it became apparent that a variety of sources of fat are available, and several are collected from the *jaṅgal*. Rai women make oil out of the seeds of *philiṅgo* (Niger seed – *Guizotia abyssinica*), the seeds of *tori* (*Brassica campestris* vartoria Duth and Full.), and occasionally eat soybeans when seasonally available. Nuts have a high fat content (Adhikari and Krantz 1989), and walnuts (*Juglans regia* L.), referred to as *okhar*, are consumed largely by Rais. Another source of fat that the Rais consume is *patle* (*Castanopsis hystryx*) (Daniggelis 2001: 161). *Patle* has a higher carbohydrate and lower fat content compared to walnuts, and is similar to chestnuts (Standal, personal communication, 1997). Thus the main problem for the Rais is the amount of fat available because, if it is not eaten in sufficient quantity, the protein available in the diet is used as energy and not for growth or to build and repair tissues. Fats are also necessary for Vitamin A absorption.

Management of *Jaṅgal* Resources

Jaṅgal resources are managed by both individual and group strategies that are influenced by Rai and Sherpa perceptions, usage, economic status and religious beliefs. Dry wood, fodder and *sisnu* are freely collected on private or community land. The use of the *jaṅgal* is controlled by closing an area to grazing at certain times of the year to permit protection and regeneration of specific resources. Depending on fodder availability, Rai and Sherpa herders decide how to allocate pastures in a yearly meeting prior to summer transhumance in the *lekh*. Traditional tenure systems prevent resource degradation, and are reinforced by social sanctions and fines. Forest watchmen are chosen by local user groups to impose fines on offenders. Individual management of the *jaṅgal* might deviate from the norm and can either positively or negatively affect *jaṅgal* resources. The effect was studied in the case of the extraction of *chiraito*, which attracted export interests and led to a local response where villagers changed land use and tenure patterns to protect it on private land.

Individual management dealing with scarcer *jaṅgal* resources includes the planting of fodder seedlings on the edges of private land, although wild species are not protected on common land. Farmers manage the yield of wild resources on common land by seasonally burning the grasses, which improves plant reproduction by increasing herbaceous production (Sauer 1969). The open areas produced by the fire provide economic benefits since bamboo flourishes as well as *chiraito*. It also prevents the invasion of insect pests. In the fallow swidden fields, *jaṅgal* foods flourish, such as *ban silam* (*Perilla frutescens*), a herb used in condiments by the Sherpas.

The images that farmers have of the landscape were used to create village- and ethnic-specific maps (Daniggelis 2001: 201–5). Rai and Sherpa men and women have different perceptions of the *jaṅgal*, and this determines whether they use methods to protect *jaṅgal* resources. Sherpa men were rather indifferent towards changes and problems related to the *jaṅgal*, but a poor Sherpa woman noted the decrease in trees and plant biodiversity. In the village with a Buddhist monastery, the farmers had a different attitude. They do not practise swidden cultivation because, in their view, many insects would die if they did so. Rai forager-farmers, who are more dependent than Sherpas on *jaṅgal* resources, have a different perspective, noting the decrease in biodiversity and in the overall extension of the *jaṅgal* area. The importance of the *jaṅgal* is apparent from their map on which they drew *sisnu*, wild greens, *lokta* and *chiraito*. Rais and poorer Sherpas are very concerned about the sustained viability of the *jaṅgal* and thus are more apt to protect it.

Religious beliefs and cultural life are intricately intertwined with the *jaṅgal*. The Kulunge Rai practise an indigenous religion minimally influenced by Hinduism and Buddhism. They believe that deities and spirits live in forests, mountains, rivers and lakes. Farmers show respect for these deities and spirits through *puja* rituals and food offerings. Rai shepherds are careful not to abuse the *lekh* pastures and anger the deities so that, once they reach the *lekh*, they hold *puja* rituals daily. Only foods considered worthy of the deities are offered (butter, ginger, rice and egg). Wild foods are considered unworthy offerings because they come from the domain of the deities.

Religious sanctions are still strong and Rai and Sherpas strictly adhere to them, particularly in the case of sacred forests, *devī than* (place of the goddess). A person can only enter a *devī than* when making a *puja* (ritual sacrifice) for the goddess. Hunting, grazing, felling trees and collecting firewood, medicinal plants and bamboo are prohibited in sacred forests. The farmers said that, if trees are cut, the goddess becomes angry and causes hail, rain, high winds and landslides. Mansberger (1991: 144) described the *ban devī*'s role as essentially that of a 'divine forest ranger(ess)'. The protector of the *devī than* is a goddess, and as such is a symbol of how women are intimately tied to the *jaṅgal*. Sacred forests in this area represent a form of environmental protection at the local level and are a rich genetic storehouse for medicinal plants.

Gender, Religion, Culture and Nutrition

Food is as much a social resource as it is a collection of nutrients, and this can have both positive and negative effects on women. Although women are responsible for their families' welfare, they themselves often neglect their own nutritional security. The burden that they bear is enormous because of their multiple responsibilities for agriculture, livestock, gathering and domestic tasks. The dire consequences for women in Nepal are shown by its position as 119th among all countries for which data are available in the Gender–Related Development Index (GDI). The GDI adjusts the life expectancy, educational attainment and income in each country in accordance with the disparity in achievement for women and men (UNDP 2000).

Overwork is recognized as a social disease that affects women in Nepal because of traditional norms. Although women's energy and nutrient needs increase during pregnancy and lactation, they do not lower their energy output during the monsoon period when male seasonal out-migration increases the demand for labour. Panter-Brick (1993) reported that working mothers attempted to protect their children from nutritional deficits at times of seasonal stress by increasing the amount of supplementary foods given, while they themselves did not increase their own food intake.

When a woman works in the fields, she takes her infant with her or leaves it in the care of an older child; she might even leave the infant alone. These infants are more prone to infections and nutritional stress because they may not be adequately fed. Diarrhoeal diseases are endemic among children throughout Nepal. Out of twenty Sherpa households, nearly half reported young child deaths. Out of 32 Rai households, ten reported 23 child deaths. Several families reported more than one death. One Rai woman had lost six children. Her breast milk ceased after three months, and three of her babies were fed only *khole* (Daniggelis 2001: 167).

Sanskritization, *jaṅgal* food resources, and nutrition

Indo-Aryan groups have a caste hierarchy based on purity and impurity with Brāhman at the top, the Tibeto-Burman groups (Rais and Sherpas) in the middle, and the untouchable castes at the bottom. High-caste Brāhmans and Chhetris refer to Rais as '*jaṅgali*' ('of the jungle') meaning 'backward' and 'uncivilized'. Food symbolically marks caste status and, in the process of Sanskritization, people begin to avoid foods associated with the *jaṅgal*.

Sanskritization is evident among rich Sherpas who show disdain for *jaṅgal* foods such as *sisnu* when foreigners and Brāhmans are present. Alcohol and prestigious foods such as meat or dairy products are usually given to high-status individuals. Sacherer (1979), in her studies in Kabre, reported on the adverse nutritional consequences of Sanskritization. While wealth may increase as one ascends the caste ladder, nutrition may suffer, since restrictions on the diet increase. On the contrary, the Rai have resisted this devaluation of *jaṅgal* food resources. An example illustrates how Sanskritization can affect a child's nutritional status. In Gorkha district, western Nepal, a primary school teacher said that some youngsters complained of night blindness, a symptom of Vitamin A deficiency. In this case it was the higher-status children who suffered, while the lower-caste children who ate *sisnu*, rich in Vitamin A, experienced no eye problems (Krantz, personal communication, 1991).

What Will Become of the *Jaṅgal*?

Women in the Arun Valley of Nepal are the key gatekeepers in the food path and have primary responsibility for farm production, and for gathering wild foods, medicinal plants, fodder, small firewood and litter for animal bedding. They are the primary holders of indigenous knowledge of *jaṅgal* resources. Rai and Sherpa women employ diverse social, economic and environmental strategies to mitigate food insecurity: relying on kin ties and ritual friendships, selling alcohol, and processing and preserving wild foods. In common property areas, Rai and poor Sherpa women gather *jaṅgal* foods that are a regular part of their diet, particularly during *anikāl* when field crops are dwindling. The use of these foods after the regular harvest helps ensure that food is available all year round. The dietary importance of *jaṅgal* foods is illustrated by the frequency with which Rai women consume them throughout the year and by the important nutrients they supply. Most of the wealthier Sherpa women gather *jaṅgal* foods seasonally for variety and taste. Even when household food security needs are met, social factors affect the allocation of *jaṅgal* foods. Sanskritization has had a negative impact on health and nutrition because *jaṅgal* foods are widely regarded as a symbol of poverty.

Outsiders often dismiss *jaṅgal* foods as weeds and, for this reason, they are omitted from programme planning. Only forests are viewed as important wild resource areas, even though the *jaṅgal* has the most biodiversity. This is a grave error. Outsiders must begin to appreciate that species having no apparent utility for economic purposes are in reality critical resources for poor women. These resources are recognized only when they are perceived as valuable outside the local environment, as in the case of *chiraito*. It is not only *jaṅgal* foods that are invisible; women forager-farmers are not recognized either. These women know the status of *jaṅgal* resources and need to become involved in natural resource management planning at all levels. They can educate outsiders about the importance of the *jaṅgal* in order to ensure that development and conservation policies and programmes reduce poverty, conserve biodiversity and are equitable for men and women.

Note

1 The distinction between 'wild' and semi-domesticated plants is blurred because all plants grow in modified environments. Throughout the chapter, 'wild' refers to those plants, fruits and other edibles found in the *jaṅgal* that are non-domesticates but may still have been intentionally or unintentionally affected by the foraging farmers' behaviour, for example in swidden cultivation.

References

Adhikari, R. and M. Krantz (eds.) (1989) *Child Nutrition and Health*, Kathmandu: Jeewan Printing Support Press.

Daniggelis, E. (ed.) (2001) *Hidden Wealth: the Survival Strategy of Foraging Farmers in the Upper Arun Valley, Eastern Nepal*, Kathmandu: Mandala Book Point and The Mountain Institute.

de Beer, J. and M. McDermott (eds.) (1989) *The Economic Value of Non-Timber Forest Products in Southeast Asia with Emphasis on Indonesia, Malaysia and Thailand*, Amsterdam: Netherlands Committee for IUCN.

Etkin, N. and P. Ross (1994) 'Pharmacological implications of "wild" plants in the Hausa diet', in Nina L. Etkin (ed.), *Eating on the Wild Side*, Tucson and London: University of Arizona Press, pp. 85–101.

Fleuret, A. (1979) 'The role of wild foliage plants in the diet. A case study from Lushoto, Tanzania', *Ecology of Food and Nutrition*, Vol. 8, pp. 87–93.

Gopalan, C., R. Sastri and S. Balasubramanian (eds.) (1984) *Nutritive Value of Indian Foods*, New Delhi: Indian Council of Medical Research.

Krantz, M. (1991) Personal communication, Kathmandu, Nepal.

Kuhnlein, H. and N. Turner (eds.) (1991) *Traditional Plant Foods of Canadian Indigenous Peoples: Nutrition, Botany and Use*, Philadelphia: Gordon and Breach Science Publishers.

Lintu, L. (1995) 'Marketing non-wood forest products in developing countries', *UNASYLVA*, Vol. 46, No. 183, pp. 37–41.

Maikhuri, R., R. Semwal, K. Rao, S. Nautiyal and K. Saxena (2000) '*Cleome viscosa, Capparidaceae*: a weed or a cash crop?', *Economic Botany*, Vol. 54, No. 2, pp. 150–4.

Mansberger, J. (1991) 'Ban Yatra: a Bio-cultural Survey of Sacred Forests in Kathmandu Valley', PhD dissertation, University of Hawaii, Ann Arbor, Michigan: University Microfilms International.

McDougal, C. (ed.) (1979) *The Kulunge Rai: a Study in Kinship and Marriage Exchange*, Kathmandu: Ratna Pustak Bhandar.

Molnar, A. (1981) 'Economic strategies and ecological constraints: case of the Kham Magar of Northwest Nepal', in C. Furer-Haimendorf (ed.), *Asian Highland Societies in Anthropological Perspective*, New Delhi: Sterling Publishers, pp. 20–51.

Panter-Brick, C. (1993) 'Mother–child food allocation and levels of subsistence activity in rural Nepal', *Ecology of Food and Nutrition*, Vol. 29, pp. 319–33.

Rajbhandary, T. and J. Bajracharya (1994) 'National status on NTFPs: medicinal and aromatic plants', National Seminar on Non-Timber Forest Products: Medicinal and Aromatic Plants, *Proceedings,* 11–12 September 1994, Kathmandu, pp. 8–15.

Regmi, M. (ed.) (1978) *Land Tenure and Taxation in Nepal*, Kathmandu: Ratna Pustak Bhandar.

Rock, J. (1930) 'Seeking the mountains of mystery. An expedition on the China–Tibet frontier to the unexplored Amnyi Machen range, one of whose peaks rivals Everest', *National Geographic Magazine,* Vol. 57, No. 2, pp. 131–85.

Sacherer, J. (1979) *Practical Problems in Development in Two Panchayats in North Central Nepal: a Baseline Study,* Kathmandu: SATA.

Sauer, C. (ed.) (1969) *Agricultural Origins and Dispersals. The Domestication of Animals and Foodstuffs,* second edition, Cambridge: MIT Press.

Shrestha, T. (ed.) (1989) *Development Ecology of the Arun River Basin in Nepal*, Kathmandu: International Centre for Integrated Mountain Development.

Srinivas, M. (1956) 'A note on sanskritization and westernization', *Far Eastern Quarterly*, Vol. 15, pp. 481–2.

Standal, B. (1997) Personal communication, Honolulu, Hawaii.

UNDP (United Nations Development Programme) (2000), *Human Development Report*, Oxford: Oxford University Press.

Wilken, G. (1970) 'The ecology of gathering in a Mexican farming region', *Economic Botany,* Vol. 24, pp. 286–95.

PART II
Gender Relations,
Women's Rights
and Plant Management

CHAPTER 5
Farm Women's Rights and Roles in Wild Plant Food Gathering and Management in North-east Thailand [1]

Lisa Leimar Price

The utilization of wild plant foods is not limited solely to hunting and gathering societies. On the contrary, the prominence of these foods is increasingly becoming recognized throughout the entire range of agricultural environments in various farming communities around the world. The evidence illustrates that the collection of wild plant foods from environments disturbed by agricultural activity occurs in heavily populated and intensively farmed areas as well as among more subsistence-oriented horticulturists, such as the indigenous populations of Amazonia. A prominent feature of wild plants that are gathered for food is that they occur in fields, fallow fields, at field boundaries, along roadsides, and in gardens and garden fallows. These 'wild' plant foods (which some would call 'weeds') are gathered by farmers in Africa, Asia and Latin America, as well as across Europe. [2]

It is mainly women who select, propagate, gather and market these wild food resources. It is unfortunate, however, that so many contemporary studies that document wild food plants lack details about the specifics of the micro-environments where these plants are collected, about the gender and age division of labour involved, about how these plants are managed, and about rights of access to wild plants (or 'gathering rights'). The historic neglect of wild plant foods in the agricultural context is in part linked to the fact that plant gathering is the work of women and children, and thus receives less attention relative to men's activities (Etkin 1994; Price 2000). It is also partly due to the fact that much of women's gathering is oriented toward daily domestic consumption, which can be easily overlooked by outsiders (Defour and Wilson 1994; see also Daniggelis, this volume). Lastly, preconceived notions that farmers are males, and the emphasis in agricultural research on increasing staple crop production for the market, have both played significant roles in keeping women's work with wild plant foods hidden (Price 2000). This, however, may be changing. There are currently a number of initiatives in the international and national agricultural research arena that are concerned with biodiversity conservation and that link women with wild plant foods found in environments disturbed by agriculture. One such initiative is a three-year research project that assesses the role of wild plant foods in Bangladesh being conducted by Policy Research for Development Alternatives (a Bangladeshi NGO) and Nayakrishi Andolon (New Agricultural Movement, which involves 50,000 women farmers). The project is funded by the International Development Research Centre (IDRC) of Canada (Eberlee 2001, Shore 2001).

This chapter examines the species-specific rights to (and limitations on) wild plant food gathering on agricultural land; the central position of women in the formation and exercise of these rights; and farm women's dynamic management of these resources in a north-eastern Thai village in Kalasin province. The research specifically addresses wild food plant gathering for domestic consumption and for market sale, and identifies the dynamics of shifting entitlements in the face of social and economic change. The case study illustrates how rights to plants and rights to land may differ, while partially reinforcing one another. Also, the dynamic rights/ prohibition system described in this study would seem to safeguard rare wild species of cultural value from over-exploitation for sale. While there are indications that gathering of selected species for consumption is often protected, there is also evidence of slow erosion of these rights with respect to rare species that have a particularly high market value. The plants identified in this study were given a status by community women based on taste desirability, species rarity, and market value. A woman's right to gather wild plant foods from agricultural land depends upon concepts of private ownership associated with land tenure and the particular plant's assigned status. Ultimately, the system of gathering rights that involves protection and partial privatization of wild plant foods as a resource can be understood in relation to the occurrence of these plants on privately owned agricultural land and the existing associated exclusive rights to domesticated plants that accompanies this ownership. Farm women's privatization rationale, however, holds only for those wild species of cultural value that women farmers perceive as rare. Perceived rarity leads to increased restrictions on gathering of selected species for market sale, and to certain prohibitions on gathering for domestic consumption. The 'value' attributed to these wild plant foods corresponds directly to the interplay between culture, economics and ecology.

Women at the Centre

The significance of wild foods for rice farming villages in north-east Thailand was illustrated in a 1988 province-wide study in Kalasin during the dry season (November–April), when little or no agricultural activity takes place. Village women were heavily engaged in gathering and marketing wild foods, including plants, insects, rats, paddy crabs, frogs and fish. Their wild food sales provided statistically significant income for their households. Food originating from paddy fields provided 43 per cent of the total wild foods sold at market (Moreno-Black and Price 1993). A 1986 time and labour allocation study done with farm women from the same province demonstrated the importance of gathering for women who do not market wild food. Thirty-one per cent of the time they spent in food production and procurement activities during March and April of the dry season was spent on wild food gathering for domestic consumption (Leimar 1987). Wild food plants originating chiefly from paddy fields make up some 50 per cent of the total food consumed by farmers in Thailand's central north-east (Somnasang et al. 1987). These foods are eaten and sold for cash all year round, and thus are a crucial source of income and nutrition in all seasons.

Somnasang's (1996) village study in the neighbouring province of Khon Kaen highlights the important difference between men and women with regard to wild food plant knowledge. Her study documents the knowledge of 32 wild food plants, five fish and two insects. Among the 64 women and men tested, women were more likely than men to identify food plants, fish and insect species. Among the 41 children aged ten to twelve, girls were more often able to identify correctly wild plant species and insects than boys were. These studies clearly point to women's predominance in wild plant food gathering, marketing and income generation. They also point to an important area of gender-based continuity in environmental knowledge. This is directly linked to gender relations in the socio-cultural organization of Thai society.

In north-eastern Thailand, daughters marry and bring their spouses to live with their family, first in the parental home and later in a separate house in the mother's compound. These daughters and their spouses and children continuously and jointly engage in farming activities with the daughter's parental household, but they begin to receive a share of the produce for their own consumption once they have a separate dwelling (usually after the birth of the first child) and their own granary. The youngest daughter and her husband and children remain in the parental household to care for the parents in their old age, and inherit the home when the parents die. Daughters inherit the land at the death of the parents. These matrilocal residential compounds thus evolve from one consisting of a mother and her daughters to one composed of middle-aged sisters and a network of their children, and ultimately to compounds including sisters, aunts, nieces and female cousins. New compounds are formed according to the same model when more space is required to permit families to expand.

Matrilocality (a married couple residing with the wife's family) gives long-term female-centred stability in the community where women live from birth to death. Women not only own property, but also earn money, hold and manage the family purse, and have freedom of mobility. Village women are forthright, speak their minds, work and celebrate as a community; and work side by side in partnership with their husbands. Women's work in agriculture is extensive and they perform all tasks, although men predominate in ploughing. Women predominate in the collection of wild plants and small protein food items like frogs, insects and rice field crabs. Both men and women fish. Women hold and transmit very local environmental knowledge that spans both their life-long residence in the village and also multiple female generations. Among these women, the enforcement of community opinion is strong regarding individual and communal gathering rights.

Gathering rights on private agricultural land are directly linked to the senior woman who holds the land in trust for generations of her daughters and granddaughters. Decision making regarding which wild plant species become 'forbidden' to gather for sale or for domestic consumption with respect to certain gathering locations, occurs through social consensus. Agreement is reached through many informal discussions that occur as women share observations and concerns about their gathering activities and about the increasing rarity and market value of selected species.

Enforcement of the consensus comes from two sources. The first is the potential threat of a loss of status within the village if the consensus is not respected. The second is the knowledge that the state recognizes private property in land, which extends to what grows upon that land. This means that there is an indigenous system of gathering rights in place that is not acknowledged or protected by the state, but that relies for its legitimacy in part on the state-sanctioned institution of private property. Women recognize and articulate both community sanction and state enforcement as incentives to restrict gathering of selected species on agricultural land. The *right* to gather on other people's private land, therefore, is dependent upon community consensus alone; whereas gathering *prohibitions* are enforced both by community consensus and by state law.

Defining the 'Wild'

Plant foods in the agricultural context exist on a continuum of human/plant interaction representing gradients of exploitation and management. One extreme of this continuum is represented by intensively cropped staple foods. Wild plant foods within the agricultural context exist along this same continuum, ranging from no noticeable human intervention to selective harvesting, transplanting and propagation. The plant-food system contains numerous species receiving various types and amounts of human attention (Harris 1989; see also Dick Bissonnette and Turner in this volume).

The edible herbaceous species common to agricultural fields exist in a commensal relationship with agricultural practices and domesticates (Vieyra-Odilon and Vibrans 2001). Other plant types, such as trees, frequently occur in pristine environments and are protected when new fields are created. Irrigation canals, footpaths, and other microenvironments are also home to the edible wild plants that women gather.

The kind of edible plants found in agricultural environments depends on the age and cultivation status of the field and on whether the plant community is located in open fields or along the field periphery near roads or canals. These plant communities are made up of species other than the field's original colonizers, as human-influenced selection procedures such as weeding and winnowing and other agricultural practices change the community composition. Barrett (1983: 256) believes that this process of 'artificial selection' through agricultural practices is most notable in areas that have been intensely cultivated for a long time, but it is also seen in areas where modern agricultural technology, such as machinery and herbicides, has been recently introduced.

Women farmers classify plants to distinguish between 'weed' and 'non-weed' as well as 'wild' and 'managed' or 'domesticated'. In the research area, the Thai/Lao phrase *geht eng*, which translates as 'birth itself', is used to indicate a wild plant. This phrase also reflects the local understanding of what a wild plant is, meaning literally that it regenerates itself. In this way, village women distinguish between domesticates and non-domesticates.

Although some domesticates do regenerate themselves spontaneously from consumption debris (tomato and eggplant are common examples), the women farmers distinguish between regeneration activity and the type of plant (plant activity versus plant type). Therefore, when there is both a domesticated and a wild counterpart to a species, villagers distinguish between the two. In the case of fruit, the wild species is frequently referred to as small (*noi*) and the domesticated cultivar as large (*yai*). In other cases, the distinction between domesticates and non-domesticates is made by adding the word for forest (*paa*) at the end of the species' name. The distinction between wild and domesticate can also be made by adding the word for village (*baan*) to indicate a non-domesticate and the word for town (*muang*) as a suffix to indicate a domesticate. In general, vegetable species names are preceded by the word *phak* and fruit names by the word *bak* or *mak*.

Research Site and Framework

The contemporary north-easterners of Thailand, like their ancestors, are primarily subsistence-oriented farmers who rely for their dietary staple on household cultivation of glutinous rice in paddy fields. The north-east is regarded as one of the most impoverished regions of the country, and contains one-third of Thailand's land area and population. The region is generally quite flat and hosts scattered swamps and wooded areas. The agricultural season depends on the annual monsoon, which occurs from May to September and provides 80 per cent of the annual rainfall. Rainy season fluctuations, droughts and floods make crops unstable. During the dry season (November to April), rainfall does not exceed 20 mm per month, and all agricultural activity effectively ceases.

Research was conducted from November 1989 to August 1990 among women farmers in a traditionally rain-fed but recently irrigated paddy rice farming village in the province of Kalasin in north-east Thailand. The farmers had access to irrigation water from a nearby dam, which was used to supplement water flow in the rainy season and facilitated a shift from single to double rice cropping in 1989. In all other respects, this village, located 10 kilometres from the provincial capital, is typical of a central north-east rural community. Inhabitants are subsistence-oriented farmers working their surrounding lands primarily with water-buffalo-drawn ploughs and a few hand tractors. Farming activity is centred on the cultivation of glutinous rice, with secondary cultivation of a cassava crop that is sold. During the study period, there were 101 houses with land (mostly under one hectare) and ten houses with no land.

Data was collected by means of an in-depth village census, focused questioning of individuals and groups, participant observation and in-depth interviews of 20 women farmers. Baseline information on plants was collected using the group informant consensus method rather than relying on individual key informants.[3] Using this format, questions were posed to a group of women who were invited to participate in a discussion. The women involved answered questions and either came to a general consensus afterwards or provided various components of the answer. This method assumes that variations in knowledge, opinion and experience exist, and that no one informant alone is an expert. At least two wild food marketers and two non-marketers were always present in the groups, and all segments of the village (including the landless poor) were also represented. The women ranged in age from 29 to 68.

Using a list of specific plant names drawn up from previous studies,[4] questions were directed to the group as a whole. The original list of plants was expanded upon during this course of questioning and through observation. A class of 'forbidden' plants (those considered to be strictly the private property of the owner of the land upon which they grow) emerged from the discussions, and these plants were ranked by the women according to criteria they identified linked to the plants, which included taste (desirability), market value (marketability and price), and rarity (easy or hard to find and gather).

Wild Food Plants: Their Environments and Propagation

Wild food plants were found in various environments: woods and swamps, paddy rice fields, upland cassava fields, planted village areas, and canal and fence borders. Communal gathering areas – those areas without specific owners – included two *koks* and eight swamps. *Koks* are wooded areas of approximately 350 *rai* (one *rai* = 0.16 hectares) and were situated seven and eight and a half kilometres from the village. Other areas that are also wooded, but are privately owned, are called *dong* (1000+ *rai*), *paa* (more than 100 but less than 1000 *rai*), and *don* (one *rai* surrounded by paddy fields or between upland and paddy fields). Swamps ranged in size from 1.5 to 18 *rai* and were 0.8 and 0.16 kilometres from the village.

Paddy fields (*naa*) and upland fields (*hai*) differ both in environment and in the wild plant species that they support. Paddy rice fields surrounding the village are flooded annually for rice cultivation. Upland fields are situated beyond the paddies and are used to grow cassava. The communal forests are beyond the upland fields. Villagers noted that the paddy fields were 100–200 years old, whereas the upland fields had been cultivated for only 30–50 years.

The village grounds also contained wild plant foods, many of which had been transplanted from outside the village to areas behind houses in residential compounds or were planted along the village paths as fencing. This phenomenon is similar to that observed by White (1989) in the same region, where villagers transplanted wild yams to their housing areas and grew them alongside yam cultivars, using identical agronomic practices for both species.

Women identified 159 plants from these areas that could be used as food. Of the 159 food plants, 77 were clearly identified as *geht eng* or 'birth itself' plant types (wild or non-domesticates). Out of this inventory of 77 plants, 15 were aquatic ferns, herbs and algae; 13 were herbaceous; 25 were trees (seven shrubby); one was a palm; one was a shrub; three were bamboo species; six were vines, and thirteen were fungi. All are referred to as 'plants' in this chapter. Thirty-eight different species and 38 different genera were represented by 44 of these 77 wild food plants; six of the 44 were identifiable only to the level of genus; and no fungi were identified by scientific name.[5]

Wild food herbs, trees and vines came predominantly from paddy fields. Some species were found in more than one environment. Thirty-five per cent of the wild food herbs were found in paddy fields (eight out of 13), 26 per cent grew in the village, and 17 per cent grew in the communal forests. Only two species were found in upland fields and none occurred in both upland and wooded areas. Only one herbaceous species occurred both in the paddy fields and in the communal woods. Of the aquatic species identified, 50 per cent were found in swamps and 36 per cent in rice paddy fields, with a third of the aquatic species occurring in both environments.

While aquatic species were predominant in swamps and ponds, trees outnumbered other plant types in all other environments. Paddy fields hosted 27 per cent (14 of 25) of wild tree food species, 23 per cent grew in communal woods, and 21 per cent in the village environs. Nine of the 25 species grew in both communal woods and paddy fields; six of these nine also grew in upland fields. Only two of the 25 tree species did not grow in multiple environments – both are *Careya arborea* but were identified in Thai by their local growth environment, the water variety *phak kadon nam* and the woods variety *phak kadon kok*.

A total of 23 per cent of all identified wild food species were transplanted, including 40 per cent of aquatic species, 28 per cent of tree species, 66 per cent of vine species and 33 per cent of bamboo species. Transplanting from paddy and upland fields to the village, and from paddy to paddy, was the norm; little was transplanted from village to paddy or to the upland fields from any source. Transplanting of edible vines and trees to housing areas was also commonplace. Transplants were watered and protected. Women were responsible for transplanting wild food plants.

Two per cent of the wild food species were seed-propagated. This percentage does not refer to the food that self-propagated from seed in consumption debris. Of the tree species, 8 per cent were propagated by seed. No fungi were propagated.

Wild Food Marketing

Only one species of wild food plant was actively propagated specifically for the purpose of sale. *Khaa paa* (*Alinia* spp.), a herb ordinarily found only in wooded areas, was mass-transplanted to residential gardens and supplied with water and fertilizer through to harvest. No other wild food was specifically cultivated for sale, although it was theoretically possible to cultivate plants that fetch high market prices.

Village women stated that wild foods have been sold at market for 50 or 60 years, and that the demand for these foods has increased over time. Whereas wild foods used to be bartered, exchanged or sold within the village, women's increased need for cash has led them to prefer selling wild foods in the market town since they fetch higher prices from buyers who are not neighbours or relatives. As one woman remarked, 'People can get money from everywhere nowadays, and people love money more than their relatives.'

Only women sell wild foods (flora and fauna) at market. When asked to report on their wild plant food marketing, women knew how much they earned from total sales, but could not recall how much they earned per plant or animal product. A comparison of the economic activities of all households in the village showed that women who sold wild foods at market (30 per cent of the households) had a higher income than those who did not. Wild food sales comprised 20.9 per cent of household income for these women, whereas non-wild food sales accounted for 6.2 per cent. In total, women sellers contributed a mean of 27.1 per cent to their households' total cash earnings, which elevated their income high above that of non-selling women villagers, who contributed a mere 5.7 per cent through miscellaneous income-generating activities. These findings are consistent with the Kalasin province-wide study that disclosed a statistically significant difference between the earnings of sellers of wild foods and non-sellers (Moreno-Black and Price 1993).

Gathering Rights and Strategies for Wild Plant Foods

A woman's right to gather wild plant foods from agricultural land depends upon:

(a) concepts of private ownership (tenure) of the land on which the plant is located; and

(b) the specific status of the species that identifies it as collectable or non-collectable, based on an evaluation of taste, market value, abundance and ease of collection.

Women's groups were asked to rank selected plants on qualities that appeared salient in their discussions. A class of 'forbidden' plants (those considered to be strictly the private property of the owner of the land upon which they are found) emerged from the discussions, and these plants were ranked by taste (desirability), market value (demand and price), and rarity (easy or hard to find and gather). Ranking was based on a scale of one to five per category with the middle position representing an average value. Level 1 ranking comprised plants that were valued as having excellent taste, excellent marketability and a high price, and that were very difficult to locate and gather. Level 5 consisted of plants that were deemed to have poor taste and marketability, and were very easy to find and gather.

The participants also ranked plants in the order of most to least prohibited. A survey of a sub-sample of 20 women selected to represent the income and land-holding variation within the village was conducted to ascertain the presence and/or propagation of selected plants on their land. These plants included the first 60 plants elicited from group consensus sessions, which contained both forbidden and non-forbidden plants. From a list of 77, consensus group informants singled out 25 wild plants that they were 'forbidden to gather from the land of others for purposes of sale'. Five of those 25 were plants they were also forbidden to gather from the land of others for domestic consumption, since all plants labelled as not to be gathered for domestic consumption are not to be gathered for marketing purposes either. In short, 'forbidden' means 'off-limits', and if one were to gather a plant labelled as 'forbidden' in the contexts outlined above, this would be perceived as stealing.

However, there were two mid-level qualifications to the restrictions on gathering 'forbidden' food items. If permission was sought and granted from the landowner where the food item was found, the food item could be gathered for consumption. A second mid-level restriction was that gathering only a small amount of the food item for consumption did not require permission from the landowner at all. Depending on the species, this permissible amount varied from a handful to be consumed on the spot to not more than a kilogram to be taken back to the household for domestic consumption. Nine plants out of the 25 within the category 'forbidden to gather from the land of others for sale purposes' also have mid-level restrictions on gathering for domestic use. In no case, however, was there a mid-level restriction on gathering for domestic consumption where there was not also a corresponding absolute prohibition on gathering for market sale.

The 25 forbidden items include 40 per cent of the aquatic species, 7 per cent of the herbaceous species, 48 per cent of the tree species, 33 per cent of the vines, 23 per cent of the fungi, and the only palm. Notably, trees and aquatic plants comprise 72 per cent (48 and 24 per cent respectively) of all forbidden plants.

Results from the ranking of forbidden plants indicated that the most forbidden were those that women identified as having better taste, greater marketability and the greatest rarity. Food items from the non-forbidden category (randomly selected as a control group) more often ranked below average or average for the same values. The combination of rarity, taste and marketability denoted the gathering status of plants for marketing purposes. The Mantel-Haenszel chi-square measure of linear association was computed for forbidden species on the ranked variable of taste, marketability and rarity, with the informants' ranking of intensity of prohibition at three levels: from most forbidden to least forbidden. There was a statistically significant linear association with the levels of the ranking (Price 1997: 218). Those species that are most rare, have greatest marketability and are most tasty, are also those ranked most strictly forbidden – having the greatest community sanctions against gathering from private agricultural land for market sale and domestic consumption. While no single factor alone was sufficient to move a plant into the 'forbidden to gather for market sale' category, without a high taste value a plant's abundance or scarcity would not be an issue and marketing would not be possible.

This quality of taste value has emerged as an important variable in food selection in studies in other cultural contexts. Wild fruit tree species in Zimbabwe have a use frequency distribution among farming households comparable to those species that people consider to be good tasting. The frequency of distribution for species considered to be easy to find and gather differs considerably from use and tastiness. In the Zimbabwean case, Campbell (1987) concluded that taste is a more important variable than ease of collection (abundance) in determining fruit species' use. Seventy-five per cent of the respondents in Campbell's study had either purchased or sold wild fruits.

The cultural significance of a plant changes over time. Stoffle et al. (1990) document from their work among the Paiute and Shoshone in Nevada that a wild plant that people perceive as being of multi-use value and 'increasingly rare in occurrence', and that 'thus should be protected', is positively associated with the development of agronomic management techniques that encourage its protection and propagation.

Plants that were classified by the women informants as 'forbidden to be gathered for market sale from the land of others' included both naturally occurring ('wild') and transplanted or seed-propagated species. Human management of a plant species and whether that plant is sold or not have no statistically significant correlation; however, statistical tests revealed that the two variables for plants that were (a) managed, and (b) forbidden for market sale are interdependent (chi-square test of independence value 12.43, significant at .00042) (Price 1997: 218). When examining the differences between wild plants that occur naturally and those that are propagated, the Pearson correlation coefficient (Phi value of 0.40, significant at .00042) indicates that gathering prohibitions for market sale are positively correlated with transplanting and seed planting. It is notable that, when these same tests were run on tree species alone, results indicated that the two variables were independent, and no significant correlation with forbidden tree species and human management practices was evident. Thus, while human management was significantly and positively correlated with gathering prohibitions, this wasn't true for all types of plant life. While the perceived rarity of a plant species provides an impetus for the management and preservation of the species, it is only partially responsible. It is the plant's multiple utility that gives it cultural significance and fuels people's desire to manage and preserve the species. In the study village, the cultural taste preference and marketability of the species together act as a multiple use factor, and thus become the impetus for the management and preservation of rarer species.

Women's Management of Wild Food Plants

Research with 20 women farmers illustrates the prodigious extent to which wild plant food management occurs and women's diverse strategies to obtain plant propagation material. Twenty-six different species out of the 60 items (43 per cent) first identified by women farmers as wild foods were transplanted by women onto their own farmland or into their privately owned swamps. Of these, half (13 species or 22 per cent) were 'forbidden' plants.

Women acquired plant material (seeds or seedlings) for propagation either through access to public lands or through social relationships. Twenty-five (35 per cent) of the wild food plants that were propagated on private agricultural land or in privately owned swamps originated from public land. Twenty-two of these 25 were 'forbidden' plants. But social relationships were equally important as a means to gain access to propagation material, since 53 per cent of the plants were propagated from material originating in privately owned agricultural land and swamps. Women villagers consciously share materials for propagation, mostly among matrilineal kin. The majority of these plants that are propagated (22 out of 38) are 'forbidden'.

Common Property Resources and Cost-Shifting Exploitation

While plants that village women perceived as rare come under a system of protection from wider community overexploitation for market sale, it is not known to what extent gathering for market sale has contributed to the rarity of these species. It is known that common resources create common interests, and common interests are shaped by common understanding and experience (Swaney 1990). Social consensus is thus pivotal to the protection of common resources and usufruct rights. It can be argued, however, that external factors can erode common concerns and shared responsibility in a community. One of the most powerful contemporary factors is the private market system that creates social costs through cost shifting:

> The commons member who degrades the commons for immediate benefit will share the eventual loss in productivity, but the primary constraint on such behaviour is the threat of lost status and reputation in the community. The private market participant, on the other hand, obtains status and reputation through the marketplace success and is constrained only by threat of punishment under the law. (Swaney 1990: 473)

Shifting the costs of the market-oriented enterprise involves manoeuvring to maintain a profit margin. The costs are often shifted to the environment. The greater the competition in the marketplace, the more the costs are shifted and the greater the cost the community must bear. A fuller understanding of the impact of the market on common resources must also include the character of the resource, regulatory procedures, and the interactions among users of the resource.

This study has shown that agricultural systems interface with wild food systems and that people's interactions with plants exists on a species-specific continuum of intensity dictated by cultural preferences and values. The protection and propagation of wild food sources are stimulated by these preferences and values. Perceived rarity stimulates restriction on rights to gather wild food plants for the market, while continuing to protect community consumption gathering rights to a certain degree.

While it is well known that market activity brings with it a shifting of costs to the environment and the community, in the case study presented here, the community consensus formed by women resource owners, and community condemnation of those women who gather from the private agricultural land of others items they are forbidden to sell, help to reduce the possibility of abusing resources at the expense of the community and the environment. In addition to losing status with their peers, gatherers of forbidden items are further constrained by an understanding that the formal legal recognition of property – that is, agricultural land and what grows upon it – exists within state law. While the village community protects gathering rights and concurrently prohibits gathering of selected species for specific purposes from privately owned agricultural land, the state prohibits but does not protect gathering rights on this same land. Women farmers recognize and articulate both community sanctions and state enforcement as incentives restricting behaviour. This system is ultimately one of convergence between traditional usufruct entitlements and a growing censure of market-oriented exploitation of natural resources through indigenous consensus and state recognition of exclusive private property rights. The privatization of selected plants corresponds to the three value qualities uncovered through group consensus sessions (taste, marketability and rarity) and the growth of a market economy. As women stated, 'Police would grab offenders as it is theft.' While community gathering rights on private property still tend to be protected overall, those plants that have gathering restrictions for domestic consumption all have corresponding absolute prohibitions on gathering for sale. Women testified that these wild foods had been bartered, exchanged or sold to neighbours for decades, but were now primarily sold in the market. This indicates that there is some shifting of the costs of market-oriented gathering within the community. The restrictions applied to plants on privately owned land, but many of the species labelled as 'prohibited' for domestic consumption were also available from communal areas. This suggests that the consumption of restricted items may not be greatly affected by limited access to resources on privately owned lands. It also suggests, however, that a decrease in the availability of wild plants in common areas will further increase gathering restrictions on private property. Those who bear the burden of increased prohibitions are those who can least afford a decline in food availability and who have the smallest voice in the community – the landless. This does not imply that the community in the case study is in the process of degrading their communal property; on the contrary, it is just as likely that they are constructively engaged in resource management.

Resource valuation and manipulation in the case under consideration have relevance to understanding how wild foods on agricultural land gain in importance and start to come under a system of protection and privatization. A direct relationship between taste and marketability in association with plant rarity triggers protection-transplanting-propagation management behaviour and leads to privatization. This study illustrates the pivotal role of women in plant resource management. Their on-farm conservation of plant food resources is important for ensuring the continued diversity in the food supply as well as the biological diversity of the planet.

Notes

1 See Price 1997 for an earlier version of this chapter that contains figures, tables and selected text omitted from this version. This version has been updated with new references, text and an enhanced focus on women.
2 Defour and Wilson 1994; Galt and Galt 1976; Moreno-Black *et al.* 1996; Ogle and Grivetti 1985; Price 2000; Price 1993; Scoones *et al.* 1992; Vainio-Mattila 2000; Vickers 1994; Wilken 1970.
3 This strategy was adapted from the process used by Biesele and Murry (1982) in their ethnobotanical elicitation from Kalahari foragers (cited in van Willigen and de Walt 1985).
4 Leimar 1987; Moreno-Black and Leimar 1988; Somnasang *et al.* 1987; Grandstaff *et al.* 1986.
5 See Price 1997 for a full species list.

References

Barrett, S. C. H. (1983) 'Crop mimicry in weeds', *Economic Botany,* Vol. 37, pp. 255–82.

Biesele, M. and R. E. Murry Jr (1982) *Morama and Other Plant Foods of Kalahari Foragers: an Applied Ethnobotanical Study*, Washington DC: National Science Foundation.

Campbell, B. M. (1987) 'The use of wild fruits in Zimbabwe', *Economic Botany*, Vol. 41, pp. 375–85.

Defour, D. L. and W. M. Wilson (1994) 'Characteristics of "wild" plant foods used by indigenous populations in Amazonia', in N. Etkin (ed.), *Eating on the Wild Side*, Tucson and London: University of Arizona Press, pp. 114–42.

Eberlee, J. (2001) 'Assessing the role of uncultivated foods in Bangladesh', *IDRC Reports on Line,* 14 December 2001: http://www.idrc.ca/reports/prn_report.cfm?article_num=536

Etkin, N. (ed.) (1994) *Eating on the Wild Side*, Tucson and London: University of Arizona Press.

Etkin, N., and P. J. Ross (1994) 'Pharmacological implications of "wild" plants in the Hausa diet', in N. Etkin (ed.), *Eating on the Wild Side*, Tucson and London: University of Arizona Press, pp. 85–101.

Galt, A. H. and J. W. Galt (1976) 'Peasant use of some wild plants on the island of Pantelleria, Sicily', *Economic Botany*, Vol. 31, pp. 20–6.

Grandstaff, S.W., Grandstaff, T. B., Athakette, P., Thomas, D.E., and J.K. Thomas (1986) 'Trees in paddy fields in northeast Thailand', in G. G. Marten (ed.), *Traditional Agriculture in Southeast Asia, A Human Ecology Perspective*, Boulder, CO: Westview Press, pp. 273–92.

Harris, D. R. (1989) 'An evolutionary continuum of people–plant interaction', in D. R. Harris and G. C. Hillman (eds.), *Foraging and Farming: the Evolution of Plant Exploitation*, London: Unwin Hyman, pp. 11–26.

Leimar, L. (1987) 'Wild Foods in an Agricultural Context: an Exploratory Study of Time and Labor Allocations of Peasant Women in Northeast Thailand', unpublished MA thesis, University of Kentucky, Lexington.

Moreno-Black, G. and L. Price (1993) 'The marketing of gathered food as an economic strategy of women in north-eastern Thailand', *Human Organization,* Vol. 52, pp. 398–404.

Moreno-Black, G., P. Somnasang and S. Thamathawan (1996) 'Cultivating continuity and creating change: women's home garden practices in North-east Thailand', *Agriculture and Human Values*, Vol. 13, No. 3, pp. 3–11.

Ogle, B. M. and L. E. Grivetti (1985) 'Legacy of the chameleon: edible wild plants in the Kingdom of Swaziland, Southern Africa, a cultural, ecological, nutritional study. Part III – cultural ecological analysis', *Ecology of Food and Nutrition*, Vol. 17, pp. 31–40.

Price, L. L. (1993) 'Women's Wild Plant Food Entitlements in Thailand's Agricultural North-east', PhD dissertation, University of Oregon, Ann Arbor, Michigan: University Microfilms International.

Price, L. L. (1997) 'Wild plant food in agricultural environments: a study of occurrence, management, and gathering rights in North-east Thailand', *Human Organization*, Vol. 56, No. 2, pp. 209–21.

Price, L. L. (2000) 'The fields are full of gold: women's marketing of wild foods from rice fields in South-east Asia and the impacts of pesticides and integrated pest management', in A. Spring (ed.), *Women Farmers and Commercial Ventures: Increasing Food Security in Developing Countries*, Boulder and London: Lynne Rienner Publishers, pp. 191–207.

Scoones I., M. Melynik and J. Pretty (1992) *The Hidden Harvest: Wild Foods and Agricultural Systems, a Literature Review and Annotated Bibliography*, Sustainable Agriculture Program, IIED: London.

Shore, K. (2001) 'Protecting uncultivated food sources in South Asia', *IDRC Reports on Line* 14 December 2001: http://www.idrc.ca/reports/prn_report.cfm?article_num=702

Somnasang, P. (1996) 'Indigenous Food Use: Gender Issues in Rural North-east Thailand', PhD dissertation, University of Oregon, Ann Arbor, Michigan: University Microfilms International.

Somnasang, P., P. Rathaketter and S. Rathanapanya (1987) 'The role of natural foods in North-east Thailand', in S. Subhadhira, G. Lovelace and S. Simarap (eds.), *Rapid Rural Appraisal in North-east Thailand: Case Studies*, New York: Routledge, pp. 20–60.

Stoffle, R. W., D. B. Halmo, M. J. Evans and J. E. Olmsted (1990) 'Calculating the cultural significance of American Indian plants: Paiute and Shoshone ethnobotany of Yucca Mountain, Nevada', *American Anthropologist*, Vol. 2, pp. 416–32.

Swaney, J. A. (1990) 'Common property, reciprocity, and community', *Journal of Economic Issues*, Vol. 24, No. 2, pp. 451–62.

Vainio-Mattila, K. (2000) 'Wild vegetables used by the Sambaa in the Usambara Mountains, NE Tanzania', *Annales Botanici Fennici*, Vol. 37, No. 1, pp. 57–67.

van Willigen, J. and B. R. de Walt (1985) *Training Manual in Policy Ethnography*, Special Publication of the American Anthropological Association, No. 19. Washington, DC: American Anthropological Association.

Vickers, W. T. (1994) 'The health significance of wild plants for the Siona and Secoya', in N. Etkin (ed.), *Eating on the Wild Side*, Tucson and London: University of Arizona Press, pp. 143–65.

Vieyra-Odilon, L. and H. Vibrans (2001) 'Weeds as crops: the value of maize field weeds in the valley of Toluca, Mexico', *Economic Botany*, Vol. 55, No. 3, pp. 264–443.

White, J. C. (1989) 'Ethnological observations on wild and cultivated rice and yams in North-east Thailand', in D. R. Harris and G. C. Hillman (eds.), *Foraging and Farming: the Evolution of Plant Exploitation*, London: Unwin Hyman, pp. 152–8.

Wilken, G. (1970) 'The ecology of gathering in a Mexican farming region', *Economic Botany*, Vol. 24, pp. 286–95.

CHAPTER 6
Gender and Entitlements in the Zimbabwean Woodlands: A Case Study of Resettlement[1]

Allison Goebel

Gender relations play key roles in the social organization of woodland use in rural Zimbabwe, Southern Africa. In this context, men and women live in somewhat different 'resource worlds'. Outlining the gendered divisions of labour serves as a useful entry point for investigating gender differences and dynamics. Crucial to understanding the overall effects of gender relations on woodland use, however, are the underlying gender power relations relating to access to and control over woodland resources. These power relations of entitlement must in turn be understood through the workings of micro institutions, especially the institution of marriage. These micro institutions must also be contextualized within broader state-driven institutional structures and practices. This examination will illustrate that concern regarding biodiversity and conservation of trees and plants must consider the complex and gendered roles of institutions and power in relation to entitlements to trees, other plants and the natural resources of the woodlands.

This discussion focuses on a resettlement area in east-central Zimbabwe.[2] In Zimbabwe's resettlement areas, local institutions are different from those in other rural areas occupied by indigenous Africans. The state has imposed gender equality policies that challenge indigenous norms and values. In some cases these state-imposed practices have expanded and strengthened women's entitlements to wood-land resources and land in general, while in other cases state actions reinforce 'traditional' practices that marginalize women's entitlements. Also, the ways in which 'tradition' is emerging in this new institutional context facilitate women's access to and control over some resources in some situations, while contributing to an overall susceptibility to loss of such access and control. The case study demonstrates the complexity of the ways in which gender is implicated in the social organization of natural resource use, and also highlights the profound challenge posed if women's entitlements are to be improved.

Land and Woodlands in Zimbabwe

Zimbabwe is divided into six basic land-use categories. One of these is the resettlement areas, which cover around eight per cent of the total land area. The category with the largest total land area is the 'communal areas'. Formerly known as Tribal Trust Lands, these are the lands designated for indigenous African use in the colonial era. Generally found in rocky or low-rainfall areas, communal areas make up about 42 per cent of Zimbabwe's total land area and serve as the rural home of the majority of the indigenous African population. After many decades of overcrowding, these areas tend to be extensively deforested. This has led to the clearance of woodlands for agricultural purposes, and hence to the current pressing problem of woodland resources scarcity. The next largest land-use category is large-scale commercial farms (mostly white-owned), which comprise about 32 per cent of the total land area. The fourth category (about three per cent) is the small-scale commercial farms of the former 'African purchase areas'. Another category (about 2.5 per cent) is the state forests, which are conserved because of their particular ecological functions such as watershed protection, or because of the commercial value of their timber resources. Finally, 'National Parks' comprise about 12.5 per cent of the total land area (Scoones and Matose 1993).

At Independence in 1980, the Government of Zimbabwe embarked on a resettlement programme that was meant to redress the racial imbalance in land distribution inherited from colonial days. Commercial farms that were abandoned during the war of liberation were designated as resettlement areas, and were mostly based on small-scale family farming. Family-farm resettlement areas are spatially organized to include nucleated village settlements where arable fields are located within each village's boundaries. Woodland and grazing areas within the boundaries of each village are treated as common property resources for the village residents. Resettlement farmers are given permits that allow usufruct rights to a homestead area, as well as to arable land and grazing land. Ultimate land owner-ship resides with the state, which can revoke permit rights if the land is not used productively or any of the resettlement rules are broken.

Woodland resources play myriad crucial roles in rural household livelihoods in Zimbabwe. Some 95 per cent of rural households use firewood for cooking (Central Statistical Office, Zimbabwe 1994: 128), and 81 per cent of all rural energy comes from fuelwood (Chimedza 1989). Domestic building depends on timber harvested from woodlands and thatching grass that grows in and around woodland areas (Matose 1994). Tree and forest products also contribute directly to household nutrition and health, especially indigenous and exotic fruits, forest mushrooms, caterpillars, honey and medicines (Fortmann and Nabane 1992; Matose 1994). Forests are also habitats for game, which provide an important source of protein for rural households (Matose 1994). Many of these products also provide income for rural men and women since they can be sold in towns or to other households in rural communities (Fortmann and Nabane 1992). In addition, woodcarving for the tourist market is a fast-growing industry (Goebel et al. 2000). Trees and forests also play crucial roles in soil and water table maintenance, which in turn affect agricultural production. Finally, woodlands provide important cultural values such as space for burial sites, places for ancestors to rest and reside, and places to enact traditional ceremonies.

In Wedza District, the woodlands characteristic of the savannah region comprise different tree-covered areas in and around human settlements.[3] The woodlands include trees in riverine areas, on and around hills or mountains, on or along the edges of arable fields, in homegardens, plantations and grazing areas, and in bush areas. The vegetation is thickest in the hills and mountains and sparsest around homesteads, arable fields and grazing areas (Goebel and Nabane 1998). Overall, the woodlands are characterized by geographical complexity related to human patterns of use and settlement. As well as woodland trees and tree products, people use other resources that grow or live in the woodlands such as herbs, grasses, wild vegetables, caterpillars and other insects, and wild animals. Woodlands also provide social-cultural spaces for recreational enjoyment, burial sites and sacred grounds.

People in Wedza District, as in other parts of Zimbabwe (Bruce *et al.* 1993), collect a wide variety of woodland products from a large number of different areas in the landscape. They collect wood for poles and firewood, thatching grass, wild fruits and vegetables, herbal medicines and fibre (for rope). They also graze their livestock and hunt wild animals. Hills, fields, river areas and tree plantations are the most important areas where many kinds of products are collected in relatively large quantities.

People collect the same product from a variety of areas. In one village, for example, people collect firewood in five different areas and medicinal herbs in eight. The use of different areas for the same product is related to seasonal patterns, the use of different plant varieties, and the types of controls and institutions operating in a certain area or for a certain product. These controls can be specific to species, area or land tenure, and can be justified by sacredness, pragmatic value, civil contracts or other recently developed institutional controls.[4] Subsistence is intimately bound up with the use of natural resources, and hence is ecologically shaped through seasonality and the physical environment, but it is also mediated through multiple layers of institutions and other social relationships.

Gender in the Woodlands

Gender emerges as a major principle of social organization in the use of different woodland resource products and geographical areas. Gender differences emerge with respect to the types of woodland products that people name, the areas where resources are collected, and the relative amounts of resources collected from different areas. For example, while both women and men name key products collected from the woodlands such as firewood, poles and thatching grass, only women mention fish and, in most cases, only women name medicinal herbs, whereas only men mention wild vegetables. Men and women mention many of the same areas for collecting resources – such as hills, fields, and grazing areas – but only men mention 'bush', whereas only women mention 'dams'. Men and women also differ in the way that they describe the relative importance of areas as sources of different products. For example, women and men have different perceptions of the places where most firewood is collected. Fields are by far the most important area for women, whereas they do not even mention bush, riverine areas or wetlands, which are the areas that men mention most frequently. Similarly, gender differences emerge in men's and women's accounts of seasonal patterns in resource use. For example, men and women have different views of when most thatching grass is used. Gender differences appear again in women's and men's lists of the uses of natural products. For example, women identify more uses for herbal medicines, while men list more uses for thatching grass.

In short, in Wedza District gender differences appear throughout women's and men's descriptions of their relationship to woodland resources (Goebel and Nabane 1998). Gendered divisions of labour serve as an entry point to explain these different 'resource worlds'. To move beyond a *description* of gender differences in people's relationships to woodlands, however, requires an analysis of gender power relations of access and control, and the institutional and ideological context that underpins these patterns.

Divisions of labour and intra-household dynamics

The study site is characterized by pronounced gendered divisions of labour and responsibilities, both in relation to woodland use and in other spheres such as agriculture, intra-household expenditure responsibilities, income-earning potential and mobility patterns (Goebel 1997; Goebel 1999a). Differences in men's and women's sense of seasonality in the use of different resources, as well as their listing of different uses for woodland products, reflect the fact that they collect things separately and sometimes use the same product for different purposes. In addition, some resources may be collected by one sex but used by both, but at different times and for different purposes. For example, it is mainly women who collect thatching material, but men actually thatch roofs. According to individual interviews, a large minority of women (36 per cent, N = 77) also sell part of the thatching material that they collect, but men do not sell thatch (Goebel 1996). Also, some products are both used and collected mainly by one sex. Poles, for example, are largely men's concern. Finally, the divisions of labour can depend on the type of technology used. Firewood collection is perceived to be women's work but, if heavy loads are transported by cart, then men and older boys assume this task.[5]

Gender differences also exist with respect to monetary exchange and control over the commercial benefits derived from certain woodland resources. In Sengezi resettlement, both women and men sell natural resource products. It is nearly exclusively women who sell thatching grass and herbs, while both women and men sell fish and wild vegetables. Children usually sell wild or exotic fruits to other children. Men sell poles and fibres, but only rarely. Men and boys sell firewood to schools, local businesses or people living in communal areas. Also, it is sometimes the case that women's relationship to a particular product is commercial, while men's relationship to the same product is domestic, as is the case with thatching grass. In local culture, women have well-recognized and protected sources of income that remain under their control. These are related to customary constructions of gender roles and responsibilities within households, wherein both women and men have (unequal) economic responsibilities and access to economic resources (Goebel 1999a).

The way in which income derived from commercial activities is distributed within the household must also be considered (see also Wilson, this volume). For example, income earned by communal area farmers from exotic fruit sales often ends up in women's hands, even though the trees and their fruits are considered to belong to men (Brigham 1994: 211, 255).[6] Similarly, in another communal area, while local conventional wisdom states that men should control income from the sale of fruit from homestead trees, women often earn this income by selling the fruit through surreptitious means, particularly in households where male migration affords women more day-to-day autonomy (Fortmann and Nabane 1992). Although no data were collected in the Sengezi resettlement about the control of men's income derived from woodland products, it is nevertheless clear that married women exercise influence over the income earned by their husbands from the sale of maize. On the other hand, 'female income', such as that earned from the sale of peanuts, is strongly protected (Goebel 1999a). These gendered dynamics of income distribution within households are largely determined by customary roles and responsibilities defined within the institution of marriage. These dynamics are well documented for Zimbabwe (ZWRCN 1994; Cheneaux-Repond 1993), and concepts of gendered incomes and responsibilities within households have long been recognized in the literature on Africa more generally (Fapohunda 1988; Folbre 1988; Guyer 1988).

Marriage and access to resources

In both resettlement and communal areas, women's access to woodlands and other resources is not only affected by the internal dynamics of marriage: it is even more fundamentally determined by marital status. The majority of Zimbabwe's indigenous Africans belong to one of a number of Shona cultural sub-groups. Shona culture is both patrilineal (inheritance through the male line) and patrilocal (women move to the husband's residence area to settle). In Shona culture, in the vast majority of cases it is married men who are assigned a homestead site, arable fields and grazing rights. This continues to be the norm in communal areas. In the early 1980s, the state made numerous legal and institutional moves to promote greater gender equality (Jacobs and Howard 1987; Maboreke 1991), which origi-nated in the socialist ideology of the revolutionary struggle and in the important roles that women played in the revolutionary war. These ideas were also expressed in resettlement policy, where state policy broke with custom and allowed a small proportion of widows and divorced women to be granted resettlement land in their own right. However, the state did not challenge the custom of granting land access to men, where women's land access depends on their husbands (Goebel 1999a). State resettlement policy decrees that, in the case of married couples, only the husband's name appears on resettlement permits. Upon divorce or widowhood, women have no legal right to remain in the resettlement area. However, in spite of the lack of a documented legal entitlement, the dominant trend in resettlement areas in the case of the husband's death has been to reassign permits to the widow. Hence, widows are able to maintain occupancy of the resettlement homestead as well as access to fields, gardens, common property woodlands and any trees planted in the homestead.

This practice of allowing widows to remain, and indeed extending permit rights to widows in resettlement areas, represents a significant difference compared with practices in communal areas. There, widows are often chased away from their homesteads and lose access to tree products and other resources, as well as most property. These practices are in accordance with customary inheritance law, which accords all rights to the property of the deceased husband to his brother or eldest male child (Maboreke 1991; Stewart 1992).

In the case of divorce in a resettlement area, however, a woman loses access to tree products in the homestead area. Trees that are commonly planted in homestead areas, especially exotic fruit trees, are used for family nutrition and income generation, and therefore represent an important household resource. This was also found to be the case in communal areas where, even if divorced women remained in the village, they lost access to homestead trees, even in those cases where it was they who had planted and tended the trees (Fortmann et al. 1997). While women are not prevented from planting trees, the social construction of tree ownership is male. In Sengezi resettlement area, it is generally men who buy tree seedlings and, in the majority of cases, the authority over fruit trees planted in the homestead is said to belong to the male head of household.

Although divorced women in communal areas lose access to homestead trees, they at least maintain access to natural resources in common property areas if they remain in the village of their former nuptial home (Fortmann et al. 1997). In resettlement areas, divorced women usually lose access to common property resources. Resettlement policy restricts residency to farmers who have permits, and to their wives and dependants, and hence divorced women must leave the area entirely, and are not allowed to set up their own households within the village as many divorced women do in communal areas. Divorced women in resettlement areas thus lose access to common property resources such as firewood, thatching grass, fish, wild fruit and herbs, as well as resources in homestead areas and arable fields. In many cases, divorced women are forced to return to their natal home areas where they become dependants of their fathers or other male relatives. These areas are unlikely to have the same abundance of natural resources as is available in resettlement villages.

These patterns support the broader theoretical point made by some feminist political ecologists regarding women's entitlements. Women's relationship to natural resources, particularly in patrilineal contexts, is marked by 'asymmetrical entitlements' shaped by gender systems that make women's rights contingent upon their relationships with men, whereas men have primary rights (Thomas-Slayter et al. 1996: 291). In the Zimbabwean context, women's access to woodland resources is vulnerable and is fundamentally mediated through marriage. Further, the ways in which marriage mediates women's access is an effect both of cultural practices and of state rules and policies.

Gender and Space

Differences in the ways that men and women talk about spaces in the landscape can also be analysed through the effects of the institution of marriage and gendered power relations. The fact that only men mention 'bush' as a place to gather resources reflects divisions of labour wherein cattle herding and hunting frequently take men and boys into bush areas. But there is also an ideological element regarding bush as a 'male space'. While no key resource-related roles would bring women into 'bush' areas, they frequently have to cross through such areas to travel to markets or other villages. Women are often fearful of venturing alone into such areas because of the danger of rape or theft. Indeed, within a three-year period, a number of women were assaulted while walking alone in the 'bush' in Sengezi resettlement area. The 'bush' therefore emerges as a predominantly male sphere, not only because of divisions of labour, but as an expression of male dominance and power over women. There is no area, however, that is clearly marked as 'female', even in reference to the domestic sphere of the homestead. There is no simple equation between place and gender as Leach found elsewhere in Africa (Leach 1994): 'domestic area' does not necessarily equal 'female'. While women wield significant power and perform many of their key activities in the domestic realm of the homestead, their control is partial and is marbled with aspects of male power, particularly the ultimate power to eject women from the homestead through divorce. The same is true for other spaces in the landscape where women are primary actors in natural resource use, and may even exercise control over the benefits derived through their use of that space (for example in wetlands, where women have their gardens). Hence, while a spatial map of the area is marked by patterns of women's use and benefits, these patterns do not present a firm demarcation of something like 'male space' and 'female space'. All 'female space' is contingent and potentially transitory, a little like their footprints everywhere in the sandy Wedza soil.

Women's Entitlements and 'Husband-Taming Herbs'

The contingent nature of women's entitlements to land and woodland resources can be read through the fascinating phenomenon of 'husband-taming' herbs. This topic also provides an example of the institutional dynamics surrounding the transformation of a natural resource into a cultural phenomenon. Women usually gather herbs for medicine and know which herbs are used for common household illnesses such as colds, influenza and stomach pains. This division of labour and knowledge is related to women's roles as caretakers of health in the family (see also Kothari, this volume). Men at times do gather herbs, but typically this is for 'men's' problems such as treatment of sexually transmitted diseases or 'to strengthen the back' – a euphemism for increasing sexual prowess. Women are also heavily involved with a category of herbs called *mupfuhwira* or 'husband-taming herbs'.

Husband-taming herbs refer to a large number of herbal preparations and regimes that women may purchase from herbalists, find and prepare themselves, or receive as gifts from family or friends. The herbs are designed to control husbands' behaviour (especially infidelity), and promote love and harmony in marriage.[7] Above all, the extensive use of *mupfuhwira*[8] indicates women's vulnerability in a context of marital instability in rural Zimbabwe. In Sengezi, women say that divorce is common, and that they are desperate to hold onto their marriages and to maintain access to their husbands' income and land where there are few other economic options. As shown earlier, if a woman living in a resettlement area is divorced, she loses her home and her entitlement to land and natural resources.

The phenomenon of husband-taming herbs also illuminates certain institutional elements in human/woodland resources relations. Not all women know how to gather and prepare husband-taming herbs. In some cases, women learn these things from their mothers, other female relatives or friends. Often, however, women must access these herbs more formally through specialist healers (both male and female healers dispense *mupfuhwira*). Hence, the knowledge is mediated through social and cultural institutions and relations in ways that help define those institutions and relations as gendered. In other words, women's relationship with a particular type of woodland resource involves engaging with and negotiating a number of social and cultural institutions and relations. In the process of looking for herbs, women may talk to friends and hence build female networks; they may try to get help from older female relatives, who may assist them or impose their power as elders to deny the needed help; or they may approach a healer who will impose his or her own analysis of proper gender relations and marital health. In the process, gender is created or reproduced. Finally, the use of *mupfuhwira* is an expression of women's agency. While it can hardly be said that the herbs have transformed gender relations in the area, women's use of them provokes fear and reflection among men and society at large. Women's extensive use of *mupfuhwira* signals deep trouble in the institution of marriage (Goebel 2001).[9]

Women's Entitlements and the [Re-]emergence of 'Tradition'

In communal areas, people settle in villages according to their lineages, and traditional ceremonies are conducted according to lineage membership. At the village level, a headman is named who is normally a relative of the chief. The headman and the chief are responsible for traditional ceremonies that are for the protection of the whole community, such as rain-making or rain-calling ceremonies that are addressed to the ancestral spirits of the ruling lineage (known as 'lion spirits' or *mhondoro*). These important spirits are thought to be able to intercede on people's behalf with the remote high God (*Mwari*) who controls rain, soil fertility and other major environmental conditions (Chavunduka 1997). These ancestors are thought of as the original inhabitants of a given territory or province, and hence the religious system has been called 'territorial cults' (Schoffeleers 1979).

Resettlement areas differ institutionally from communal areas in a number of ways. In resettlement areas, local institutions follow a democratic model designed by the post-Independence Zimbabwean state, and traditional, lineage-based institutions have no recognized role. This has produced new dynamics in local governance, including the [re-]emergence of traditional ideas and power in ways that have implications for women's entitlements to land and woodland resources. In 1984, President Mugabe created village development committees (VIDCOs) as the new basic organizational unit for rural development (Higgins and Mazula 1993; Alexander 1994). VIDCOs were easier to impose in the new resettlement areas in comparison with the already established communal areas, both because resettlement areas had no pre-existing leadership structure, and because settlers came from different home areas with different lineage affiliations. In accordance with the socialist ideology of the early post-Independence government, VIDCOs were meant to stimulate grassroots self-help development in rural areas through local-level ruling-party presence and machinery. Groups of 100 households elect a representative to the VIDCO. There are six representatives on the VIDCO, and six VIDCOs form a ward. The head of the ward is the councillor who represents villagers at District Council level. VIDCOs are meant to assist the village chairman (an elected village leader who is not a VIDCO member) in administering the villages according to resettlement rules. This includes monitoring resource use and management according to government legislation.[10] In participatory workshops, both male and female villagers consistently identified the VIDCO as the body responsible for ensuring proper woodland and agricultural management, together with the resettlement officer and agricultural extension worker (state employees). The latter live on site to work with VIDCOs and the village chairman to ensure that resettlement rules are followed and woodlands and agricultural resources are properly managed.

Nevertheless, people in Sengezi also use the term 'traditional' when they categorize or explain different rules and practices in agriculture and the woodlands. The 'traditions' that people describe are not timeless and unchanging, but rather represent people's current understandings that include reactions to institutional change. Spirit mediums, the chief and village elders are the traditional institutions. The local chief lives in a nearby communal area and has no official authority in the resettlement area. Nevertheless, some people maintain their allegiance to the chief after they resettle, and hence attribute some authority to him. People mention the chief in relation to respect for the sacred *chisi*, or the day(s) off ploughing, which are an important part of traditional culture. The chief may levy a fine (of a goat, for example) in cases where traditional rules are violated. It is said that spirit mediums and village elders prohibit cutting of *mobola* plum trees (Shona *muhacha*), which are considered to be sacred to the ancestors.[11] Traditional rules and institutions are particularly associated with herbs, small hills and river areas. Herbs are used in traditional medicine, and small hills are used as burial sites and are also sites where ancestral spirits prefer to reside. Many villagers mention that spirits[12] inhabit river areas, especially pools. Traditional rules also regulate wild fruit harvesting, where harvesting or destruction of unripe fruit is forbidden.

Local people in the resettlement area can list these traditional rules and institutions governing natural resource use with great ease and consistency (Goebel 1998). As traditional safeguards they are very similar to those found in communal areas (see Nhira and Fortmann 1993). In Sengezi, however, they seem to offer little protection for natural resources (Goebel 1999b). In some of the hill areas, for example, so many trees have been cut down that graves are exposed. The weakness of traditional institutions in resettlement areas appears to be linked to non-traditional settlement patterns (see below), to the effects of 'modern' ideas and practices that are introduced by the state institutions (VIDCOs) that dominate the resettlement structure and, to a certain extent, to the prevalence of Christianity.[13] In some places in Zimbabwe, traditional institutions and practices are strong and in others they are weak. The country is marked by profound variation in local institutional dynamics (Goebel *et al.* 2000; Sithole 1997) (also apparent in the eight villages studied in Wedza communal area) in terms of respect for local traditional leaders and adherence to traditional rules of resource use and management (Goebel and Nabane 1998). Further, certain conditions peculiar to resettlement areas contribute to and further an already profound erosion or transformation of 'tradition' in rural Zimbabwe.

In resettlement areas, people are not spatially located according to lineage, but settle among others who come from many different villages and lineage groups. In Sengezi, even though most people come from villages in the surrounding district, there is still a great diversity of origins. In each of the four study villages, most people came from villages that were not mentioned by other respondents. This is the main reason given for the view, common in Sengezi, that people in the resettlement areas follow tradition less than in the communal areas. All in all, traditional leaders appear to be virtually powerless in the resettlement area. Although most people feel that traditional leaders 'should' be involved in natural resource management (only 12 per cent of those interviewed on the topic, N = 60, said that they should *not* be involved), most feel that the VIDCOs have replaced their functions.

Despite the weakness of traditional institutions, local people maintain important elements of traditional beliefs and practices. For example, local residents link people's behaviours to the larger climatic forces that bring about drought. The endurance of certain traditional religious ideas about human–environment relations has gendered implications. Traditional Shona religion includes a division of labour among paternal and maternal ancestors. Paternal ancestors, particularly those pertaining to the ruling lineage, are associated with environmental care and management, while maternal ancestors are associated with taking care of social and physical health and issues such as fertility and nurturing (Mutambirwa 1989). Thus, when people are concerned about environmental issues such as drought, soil fertility, and deforestation, the implication is that they turn to their patrilineal ancestors. This division of labour among the ancestors mirrors (and hence provides some justification for) that among living humans. Of great significance is the association of maleness with the land, and the health of human society with the maintenance of patrilineal descent patterns. The relevance of this for women's access to natural resources is more obvious when family-based ancestral rituals are considered.

Virtually all families in the area perform the important ancestor practice of 'bringing home' the spirit (*kurova guva*) about a year after a person has died. This ceremony is usually performed only for married men, and it is normally done in conjunction with an inheritance ceremony (Bourdillon 1987: 52). These practices support the patrilocal marriage system and patrilineal inheritance practices mentioned above. Through these practices, the primary connection between men, land and other natural resources is reinforced and reproduced. The persistence of these particular practices and beliefs in resettlement areas helps to create a culturally defined ideological and moral climate regarding the 'correct' relationship to land that clearly goes against women's claims to land in their own right, either as widows or divorcees. Indeed, at the time of the field research, the resettlement officer reported that the greatest number of conflicts, and the most serious that he had to deal with, were those that arose out of granting rights to widows to remain in the resettlement area, and changing the name on permits from that of the deceased husband to that of the new widow. Male relatives of the deceased often seriously (and sometimes violently) dispute the widows' claims on the basis of 'tradition' and pressure the resettlement officer to allow a male relative of the deceased to take over resettlement permits. In general, then, despite the weakness of traditional institutions, the resettlement site presents an ontological context where the 'environment' or 'natural world' is populated by ancestors who demand attention to certain rituals and practices that underline patriarchal and patrilineal control of land and resources.

Conclusions

This discussion points to the complexity with which women's entitlements to land and woodland resources are redefined in a context of social–cultural change. State-sanctioned and -imposed policies that are designed to improve women's entitlements, such as the practice in resettlement areas of transferring resettlement permits to widows, can have important positive effects. These initiatives are played out, however, in an institutional and cultural context that dynamically resists such changes, and in which the precariousness of women's entitlements is reinforced in multiple ways, particularly in marriage and divorce practices. 'Tradition' may provide important entitlements for women, such as the protection of income gained through sale of natural resource products. However, the enduring effects of 'traditional' beliefs and practices on the reproduction of gender relations that underpin women's secondary relation to land and natural resources continue to constitute an important cultural 'bottom line'.

More generally, gender relations are central to the social organization of natural resource use in terms of the divisions of labour, commercialization, use of space and environmental knowledge (as in the case of husband-taming herbs). However, interpreting the implications of gender relations requires more than a description of the differences in men's and women's relationships to natural resources. It also requires an analysis of the cultural and institutional context and of the ways in which gender as a power relation and as a component of meaning systems is implicated in the ways in which resources are used, valued and managed. Any attempts to preserve and enhance woodland and plant biodiversity and health must therefore take account not only of the gendered patterns of people's use of the woodlands, but also of the power dynamics of entitlements within changing social contexts.

Notes

1 The data referred to in this chapter are mainly drawn from field research in Sengezi resettlement area carried out by the author between 1995 and 1998, using participatory rural appraisal (PRA), formal interviews with villagers from four villages in Sengezi, personal narrative interviews with widows and divorcees, field assistant diaries, and personal observation and informal interactions with local people. Numerous interviews were carried out with local officials and leaders. Data were also drawn from the author's work in a Social Forestry Programme implemented during 1997–8 in Wedza District by German Development Cooperation (GTZ) in cooperation with the Zimbabwean Forestry Commission. This involved documentary research at the Wedza District Council and PRA data from 10 villages in Wedza District, including four resettlement villages in Sengezi (Goebel and Nabane 1998).

2 The case study site is Sengezi resettlement area, Wedza district. Research on woodlands in Zimbabwe has focused mostly on communal areas and state forest areas, and has generally not considered gender dynamics. Important exceptions to this include Fortmann and Nabane (1992); Nhira and Fortmann (1993); Watson (1994); Elliott (1994).

3 In Wedza District, the dominant tree species in the woodlands include *Strychnos* spp., *Brachystegia* spp., *Terminalias* spp., *Syzigium* spp., *Erythrina* spp. and *Parinari* spp. (Goebel and Nabane 1998).

4 See Nhira and Fortmann (1993) for a codification of these controls in communal areas that was used as a guide in the present resettlement area study.

5 This was also found in the only other major study of wood products in resettlement areas in Zimbabwe (Elliott 1994: 26).

6 This is partly explained by the fact that most fruit is sold to middlemen who come at unpredictable times to communal areas to buy fruit, and it is the wives that are more frequently at home to sell it (Brigham 1994: 220–2).

7 In the study area, informants estimate that about 80 per cent of all married women use these herbs.

8 *Mupfuhwira* must be distinguished from the various herbal and other preparations that most married women in Zimbabwe reportedly insert into their vaginas to decrease vaginal liquids and produce a 'dry sex' experience (Civic and Wilson 1996; Ruganga, Pitts and McMaster 1992). 'Dry sex' practices appear to have many parallels with husband-taming herbs, but *mupfuhwira* encompasses more than 'dry sex' herbs.

9 A detailed discussion of the use and implications of husband-taming herbs is beyond the scope of this chapter. Interested readers are directed to Goebel 2001.

10 There are numerous relevant pieces of legislation, but the most important here are the

·Natural Resources Act (1941), the Forest Act (Amended 1981), the Parks and Wildlife Act (1975), the Water Act (1976), the Communal Forest Produce Act (1982) and the Communal Land Act (1982). See Nkala 1996.

11   Traditional healers, who may be male or female and who use roots and bark for different remedies, also use *muhacha* extensively. Fruits are also eaten (Drummond and Coates Palgrave 1973: 17–19).

12   These spirits are not ancestors *per se* but rather are translated as 'mermaids' (Shona *nzuzu*). Generally malevolent, they are thought to 'take' people, who may then re-emerge as traditional healers.

13   The Shona tend to see their traditional religion and Christianity as compatible (Bourdillon 1987: 285–307; Chavunduka 1997).

References

Alexander, J. (1994) 'State, peasantry and resettlement in Zimbabwe', *Review of African Political Economy*, Vol. 6, pp. 325–45.

Bourdillon, M. F. (1987) *The Shona Peoples*, revised edition, Gweru (Zimbabwe): Mambo Press.

Brigham, T. E. (1994) 'Trees in the Rural Cash Economy: a Case Study from Zimbabwe's Communal Areas', unpublished MA thesis, Department of Geography, Carleton University, Ottawa, Canada.

Bruce, J., L. Fortmann and C. Nhira (1993) 'Tenures in transition, tenures in conflict: examples from the Zimbabwe social forest', *Rural Sociology*, Vol. 58, No. 4, pp. 626–42.

Central Statistics Office (Zimbabwe) (1994) *Census 1992*, Zimbabwe National Report, Harare: Government Printers.

Chavunduka, G. L. (1997) *Traditional Medicine in Modern Zimbabwe*, Harare: University of Zimbabwe Publications.

Chenaux-Repond, M. (1993) *Gender Biased Land-Use Rights in Model A Resettlement Schemes of Mashonaland, Zimbabwe,* Harare: Rubecon Zimbabwe.

Chimedza, R. (1989) 'Women, natural resource management and household food security: an overview', Department of Agricultural Economics and Extension, University of Zimbabwe. Working Paper AEE 1/89.

Civic, D. and D. Wilson (1996) 'Dry sex in Zimbabwe and implications for condom use', *Social Science and Medicine*, Vol. 42, No. 1, pp. 91–8.

Drummond, R. B. and K. Coates Palgrave (1973) *Common Trees of the Highveld*, Salisbury: Longman Rhodesia.

Elliott, J. (1994) 'The sustainability of household responses to fuelwood findings', unpublished paper, Department of Geography, University of Zimbabwe/Staffordshire University.

Fapohunda, E. F. (1988) 'The non-pooling household: a challenge to theory', in D. Dwyer and J. Bruce (eds.), *A Home Divided: Women and Income in the Third World*, Stanford: Stanford University Press, pp. 143–54.

Folbre, N. (1988) 'The black four of hearts: towards a new paradigm of household economics', in D. Dwyer and J. Bruce, (eds.), *A Home Divided: Women and Income in the Third World*, Stanford: Stanford University Press.

Fortmann, L. and N. Nabane (1992) 'The fruits of their labours: gender, property and trees in Mhondoro District', Harare: Centre for Applied Social Sciences (CASS), University of Zimbabwe, Occasional Paper Series, NRM; 6/1992.

Fortmann, L., C. Antinori and N. Nabane (1997) 'Fruits of their labours: gender, property rights, and tree planting in two Zimbabwe villages', *Rural Sociology*, Vols 62, 63, pp. 295–314.

Goebel, A. (1996) 'Process, perception and power. Notes from "participatory" research in a Zimbabwean Resettlement Area', Harare: Centre for Applied Social Sciences (CASS), University of Zimbabwe, Occasional Paper-NRM Series.

Goebel, A. (1997) '"No Spirits Control the Trees": History, Culture and Gender in the Social

Forest in a Zimbabwean Resettlement Area', PhD dissertation, University of Alberta, Ann Arbor: University Microfilms International.

Goebel, A. (1998) 'Process, perception and power. Notes from "participatory" research in a Zimbabwean Resettlement Area', *Development and Change*, Vol. 29, No. 2, pp. 276–305.

Goebel, A. (1999a) '"Here it is our land, the two of us": women, men and land in a Zimbabwean Resettlement Area', *Journal of Contemporary African Studies*, Vol. 17, No. 1, pp. 75–96.

Goebel, A. (1999b) '"Then it's clear who owns the trees": common property and private control in the social forest in a Zimbabwean Resettlement Area', *Rural Sociology*, Vol. 64, No. 4, pp. 625–41.

Goebel, A. (2001) '"Men these days, they are a problem": husband-taming herbs and gender wars in rural Zimbabwe', paper presented at the International Studies Association Annual Convention, Chicago Hilton Towers, Chicago, Illinois, 21 February 2001.

Goebel, A., B. Campbell, B. Mukamuri and M. Veeman (2000) 'People, values and woodlands: a field report of emergent themes in interdisciplinary research in Zimbabwe', *Agriculture and Human Values*, Vol. 17, No. 4, pp. 385–96.

Goebel, A. and N. Nabane (1998) *Participatory Rural Appraisal Report: Wedza District*, Harare: German Development Cooperation (GTZ) and the Forestry Commission of Zimbabwe.

Guyer, J. (1988) 'Dynamic approaches to domestic budgeting: cases and methods from Africa', in D. Dwyer and J. Bruce (eds.), *A Home Divided: Women and Income in the Third World*, Stanford: Stanford University Press.

Higgins, K. M. and A. Mazula (1993) 'Community development: a national strategy in Zimbabwe', *Community Development Journal*, Vol. 28, No. 1, pp. 19–30.

Jacobs, S. and T. Howard (1987) 'Women in Zimbabwe: stated policy and state action', in H. Afshar (ed.), *Women, State, and Ideology. Studies from Africa and Asia*, New York: State University of New York Press.

Leach, M. (1994) *Rainforest Relations: Gender and Resource Use Among the Mende of Gola, Sierra Leone*, Washington, DC: Smithsonian Institution Press.

Maboreke, M. (1991) 'Women and law in post-independence Zimbabwe: experiences and lessons', in S. Bazilli (ed.), *Putting Women on the Agenda*, Johannesburg: Ravan Press, pp. 217–47.

Matose, F. (1994) 'Local People's Uses and Perceptions of Forest Resources: an Analysis of a State Property Regime in Zimbabwe', unpublished MSc thesis, University of Alberta.

Mutambirwa, J. (1989) 'Health problems in rural communities, Zimbabwe', *Social Science and Medicine*, Vol. 29, No. 8, pp. 927–32.

Nhira, C. and L. Fortmann (1993) 'Local woodland management: realities at the grassroots', in P. Bradley and K. McNamara (eds.), *Living with Trees. Policies for Forestry Management in Zimbabwe*, Washington, DC: World Bank, pp. 139–53.

Nkala, D. (1996) 'Tackling agricultural development with land dearth', in C. Lopes (ed.), *Balancing Rocks: Environment and Development in Zimbabwe*, Harare: SAPES Publishers.

Ruganga, A., M. Pitts and J. McMaster (1992) 'The use of herbal and other agents to enhance sexual experience', *Social Science and Medicine*, Vol. 35, No. 8, pp. 1037–42.

Schoffeleers, J. M. (1979) *Guardians of the Land. Essays on Central African Territorial Cults*, Gwelo, Zimbabwe: Mambo Press.

Scoones, I. and F. Matose (1993) 'Local woodland management: constraints and opportunities for sustainable resource use', in P. N. Bradley and K. McNamara (eds.), *Living With Trees: Policies for Forestry Management in Zimbabwe*, Washington, DC: World Bank, pp. 157–98.

Sithole, B. (1997) *The Institutional Framework for the Management and Use of Natural Resources in Communal Areas of Zimbabwe. Village Cases of Access to and Use of Dambos from Mutoko and Chiduku*, Harare: Centre for Applied Social Sciences (CASS), University of Zimbabwe.

Stewart, J. (1992) 'Inheritance in Zimbabwe: the quiet revolution', in J. Stewart (ed.), *Working Papers on Inheritance in Zimbabwe*, Women and the Law in Southern Africa Research Project, Working Paper No. 5, Harare.

Thomas-Slayter, B., E. Wangari and D. B. Rocheleau (1996) 'Feminist political ecology. Crosscutting themes, theoretical insights, policy implications', in D. Rocheleau, B. Thomas-Slayter and E. Wangari (eds.), *Feminist Political Ecology. Global Issues and Local Experiences*, London and New York: Routledge, pp. 287–307.

Watson, L. (1994) 'Gender and the Perceived Value of Trees on Homesites in Zimbabwe', unpublished MSc thesis, Department of Rural Economy, University of Alberta.

Zimbabwe Women's Resource Centre and Network (ZWRCN) (1994) 'The gender dimension of access and land use rights in Zimbabwe. Evidence to the Land Commission', Harare.

PART III
Gendered Plant Knowledge
in Science and Society

CHAPTER 7
'Passing on the News': Women's Work, Traditional Knowledge and Plant Resource Management in Indigenous Societies of North-western North America

Nancy Turner

Next month [October] is the month for gathering silverweed roots by the women. They will dig as many roots as they could gather.... When I was a child I would go out with the root digger. As soon as she filled the pack basket she would go home and wash the roots and dry them on a mat.... She gathers like this for many days, until she has as much as she needs for winter. Then she quits. They invited each other, I guess so they won't be lonely or sad, because they are happy, passing on the news, when they gather the roots. (Ida Jones, quoted in Turner *et al.* 1983: 18)

Ida Jones was a Ditidaht woman who lived her life along the West Coast of Vancouver Island through most of the twentieth century. Over the course of her life, she witnessed and participated in many traditional activities in relation to plant food harvesting and processing. Her words reflect a key element of these activities as described by her and by many other indigenous women, namely the social, gendered and intergenerational aspects of plant use and management. Although many traditional practices are no longer evident or dominant in aboriginal communities, there are still important plant harvesting and processing traditions featured in contemporary indigenous societies, and women still play key roles in these practices.

This chapter explores indigenous women's traditional botanical knowledge as it relates to harvesting, use, promotion and management of plant resources in north-western North America. It recognizes, at the outset, that this knowledge is part of a larger, complex, culturally mediated, applied knowledge system that inextricably links humans to the environment. The ways in which this knowledge is acquired and communicated are discussed and, finally, the contributions of women's activities to local plant resource management in the study region are examined.

Women's Activities

The traditional economic systems of indigenous societies in north-western North America, like many others around the world, are characterized by a gender division of labour where men were generally the hunters and fishers and the workers of wood and stone, whereas women were the gatherers of plant foods and shellfish, the processers of most foods for storage and consumption, and the weavers and basket makers (Turner 1996).

Many stories and narratives reflect these gendered roles. One example is in the Nlaka'pamux (Thompson) Interior Salish story, 'Old-One and the Earth, Sun and People'. After creating Earth from the body of a woman who had been abandoned by her husband, Old-One spoke to her and said,

> Henceforth you will be the earth, and people will live on you, and trample on your belly. You will be as their mother, for from you, bodies will spring, and to you they will go back. People will live as in your bosom, and sleep on your lap.... After this the earth gave birth to people.... He taught the women how to make birch baskets, mats, and lodges, and how to dig roots, gather berries and cure them. He taught the men how to make fire, catch fish, shoot, snare, trap, and spear game. (Teit 1912: 321)

Blackman (1982: 34) similarly describes the distinctive and complementary roles of men and women for Haida on the north-west coast:

> Although some economic activities, such as collecting shellfish and cooking, were performed by both males and females, in general the Haida division of labor was marked ... clam digging and the implement of procurement, the *gligú* (digging stick), were considered part of a woman's domain. The sexual division of labor was summed up for me by one elderly Massett man who offered the following comment on the essential property of the newly married couple: 'Every man's got to have his fishing line and devilfish stick and every woman her digging stick.'

Many other sources echo these gendered roles. It is important to note that women's work has been highly valued in these societies. In ensuring the well-being of families and communities, the activities of women were, in fact, considered vital and of equal importance to men's work, as confirmed by many elders today. Despite this recognition within the societies themselves, anthropologists, archaeologists and historians have sometimes been slow to focus on and acknowledge the essential contributions of women in food production. Likewise, they have tended to overlook the complexity and sophistication of the knowledge that women have held and applied as food producers, herbal medicine specialists and resource managers, as is documented in more gender-sensitive research.[1]

Women's work in harvesting and managing plants, though seldom emphasized, has been widely reported. As early as 1792, Archibald Menzies, a botanist who explored the area with Captain George Vancouver, reported root-digging activities of a number of Nuu-Chah-Nulth women at the present-day site of Tahsis, Vancouver Island:

> In the evening our curiosity was excited in observing a number of Females busily occupied in digging up a part of the Meadow close to us with Sticks, with as much care and assiduity as if it had been a Potato (*Solanum tuberosum*) field, in search of a small creeping root ... of a new species of Trifolium [*T. wormskioldii*] which they always dig up at this time of year for food ... Wherever this Trifolium abounds the ground is regularly turned over in quest of its Roots every year. (Newcombe 1923: 116 – September)

Some of the key elements inferred from this brief report include: women worked together in groups; women used digging sticks to pry up roots and till the soil; women used care and attention in harvesting clover (*Trifolium wormskjoldii*) roots (an important root vegetable along the North-West Coast) from a particular site (tidal meadow); women frequented the same digging grounds every year at the same time; and women managed a resource for sustained harvest over many years.

The various types of subsistence and cultural activities traditionally undertaken by women in indigenous societies of north-western North America are summarized in Table 7.1. They include a range of harvesting, processing, manufacturing and provisioning activities, land and resource management, household management, education and mentoring, and contributions to family and community cultural life. It is important to note that these are generalized listings: the work of an individual woman of any one language group or community will, of course, be specific to her particular role within her family, community, culture and environment.

Women's activities frequently necessitated long working hours and tremendous sustained energy, and often involved travel to distant locations. Elders of recent times recall their mothers, aunts or grandmothers journeying sometimes for many days to harvesting locations to obtain good-quality cedar (*Thuja plicata*) bark, spruce (*Picea sitchensis, Picea glauca*) roots, or edible berries or medicine. For example, Ahousaht Nuu-Chah-Nulth Elder Stanley Sam recalled that his grandmother used to go up into the mountains on the West Coast of Vancouver Island to harvest yellow cedar (*Chamaecyparis nootkatensis*) bark for weaving, sometimes remaining away for two weeks at a time. On the North Coast, Gitga'at (Coast Tsimshian) women used to travel long distances over potentially rough water to harvest edible seaweed (*Porphyra abbottae*), with some of them steering and paddling the canoe and others jumping onto the rocks at low tide to pull off the seaweed, pile it up, and put it in bags. They would then take it back to dry on the rocks near their seaweed camp at Kiel on Princess Royal Island (Helen Clifton, personal communication, 2001). On Haida Gwaii, women gathered Sitka spruce roots for basketry, requiring a long expedition from Massett to North Beach near Tow Hill. Florence Davidson recalled her mother, Isabella Edenshaw, making such a journey:

> I used to go with my mother in May for spruce roots [*hlii.ng*]. Every fine day we'd go to North Beach early in the morning before sunrise. We'd pack water and food with us and mother would cook our breakfast in the woods.... We'd collect *hlii.ng* all day long.... Sometimes other ladies would come along and we'd have a nice time together – it was just like a picnic. Then we'd gather driftwood from the beach and make a big fire to 'cook' the roots. My mother roasted them and I pulled the skin [bark] off. We'd collect piles and piles of them.... The sun would be going down when we started for home.... (Quoted in Blackman 1982: 85)

Even after returning home, Isabella Edenshaw's work was not done. Florence Davidson recalled, 'When we got home my dad would cook for us .... Soon as my mother finished eating she'd start splitting the roots in half. She bundled them up

Table 7.1: Activities Commonly Undertaken by Women in Traditional Indigenous Societies of North-western North America

General Activity	Specific Type	Examples
Harvesting	Plant foods	Root vegetables, greens, seaweed (coastal), mushrooms (interior), fruits and nuts, edible inner bark, flavourings, beverage species and famine foods
Harvesting	Edible shellfish and other marine products	Clams, mussels, chitons, limpets, sea urchins, herring eggs on kelp or hemlock (*Tsuga heterophylla*) boughs
Harvesting	Eggs and young birds for food	Mallard duck, coot, sandhill crane (interior); seagull eggs (coastal)
Harvesting	Fibrous materials for basketry, mats, clothing, blankets, bags, twine, fishnets	Cedar bark, cedar roots, cedar withes, spruce roots, basket sedge, cherry (*Prunus emarginata*) bark, basket grass (*Phalaris arundinacea*), cattail, tule, Indian hemp, silverberry (*Elaeagnus commutata*) bark; dogwood, mountain-goat wool
Harvesting	Firewood, kindling, tinder, fish spreaders, etc.	Dry branches, driftwood, cedar bark
Harvesting	Medicinal plants and health care materials	Tree bark, roots and other plant parts; moss for diapering, sanitary napkins, wound dressing
Processing	Plant foods: berries, roots, greens, inner bark, seaweed, black tree lichen (*Bryoria fremontii*)	De-stemming, mashing, drying berries; peeling, pit-cooking, drying roots; drying seaweed
Processing	Animal foods: shellfish, fish, meat, game birds, eggs, oil; meat mixtures, fish, berries, fat for travel or home use	Cleaning, smoking/curing fish; drying deer meat, ducks; making oulachen grease, fermented salmon eggs
Processing	Fibrous materials (including peeling, splitting, dyeing, drying, soaking)	Splitting cedar bark, removing outer bark, bundling, dyeing, drying, spinning plant fibres
Processing	Animal hides, wool, bird skins and feathers	Tanning buckskin, spinning goat wool, cleaning and plucking many types of game birds for meat and feathers
Processing	Plant medicines	Cleaning, splitting, making infusions, salves, powders
Storage	Overseeing storage of all types of food, materials and medicines, and household products	Preparing and filling cache-pits, raised caches, scaffolding for food baskets; wide variety of dried roots, berries, seaweed, fish, meat; basket materials, diapering, etc.
Manufacturing	Fibrous plant and animal materials into containers, blankets, clothing, mats	Weaving plant fibres into hats, mats, capes, baskets; weaving mountain-goat wool into blankets; making cradles, sanitary napkins
Manufacturing	Hides and skins into clothing, blankets, etc.	Sewing hides for clothing, blankets and footwear; making sinew thread, awls, stringing snowshoes
Manufacturing	Tools and implements for women's work	Bone scrapers, awls made from deer rib immediately after pit-cooking deer (interior); root-digging sticks and other implements used in women's work

Manufacturing	Building temporary shelters	Cattail and tule tents and bough huts for camping, girls' puberty
Provisioning	Food preparation and serving; cooking plant and animal foods for family meals, feasts and travel	Steaming clams, pit-cooking roots, making food mixtures
Provisioning	Use and care of baskets for transport, storage and other purposes	Split cedar root pack baskets; baby cradles; mats, blankets
Provisioning	Administering medicinal herbs (men also gathered and prepared medicines) and providing general health-care for family/community	Many different kinds (tree barks, roots, whole plants, etc.); preparing herbal recipes; midwifery, first aid, care of dying and dead (preparing for burial)
Land/Resource management	Habitat and population management for food production: weeding, clearing, pruning (men generally carried out large-scale landscape burning)	Clearing meadows for camas and other edible bulb production; weeding 'gardens' for clover, silverweed, riceroot, and other roots (later for potatoes, turnips, etc.); weeding and growing tobacco (Haida, Tsimshian – Turner and Taylor 1972)
Land/Resource management	Clearing, weeding, trimming, pruning for basketry materials production	Basket sedge, tule; Saskatoon and other bushes to produce withes for basketry; practising selective harvesting for roots and other plant material resources
Land/Resource management	Maintenance, monitoring and stewardship of animal resources	Tending clambeds; observing game; ensuring horses were tied or had sufficient feed (interior; recent – Teit 1900)
Household management	Building and maintaining fires (men sometimes helped)	Preparing 'slow matches'; building fires for cooking, drying and smoking food, tanning hides, heating for winter or camping
Household management	Coordinating and maintaining household activities; keeping the house or camp area clean	Maintaining and replenishing household supplies such as bedding and floor coverings, dried and preserved food, water, fuel (men sometimes helped with these); making mats, clothing
Household management	Family responsibilities: bearing, nursing and nurturing children, care-giving, storytelling	Furnishing clothing, meals and other necessities to spouse and children; care-giving for elders
Education and mentoring	Overseeing children's education and upbringing, especially for girls and young women	Teaching about safety, cultural traditions and protocols, gender roles, respect for life, conservation; enacting and teaching ritual observances, including those around puberty, menstruation, pregnancy and childbirth; teaching girls about their roles as women, appropriate behaviour, activities; sex education
Contributions to cultural life of of family and community	Participation in inter-group communications, trading, maintaining ties; organizing and participating in social events	Marrying out across language and cultural boundaries (cf. Kennedy 1993), making baskets, and processing food for trade; preparations for feasts, ceremonies, and potlatches, particularly cooking and serving food; performing major ceremonial roles, dancing, singing, etc.

Source: Information drawn from multiple sources, summarized from Boas 1921, 1930; Loewen 1998; Teit 1900, 1909; Turner 1995, 1997, 1998; Turner and Hebda 1990; Turner *et al.* 2000.

and put all the same size ones together in a bent box' (Blackman 1982: 85). Isabella used to weave baskets and hats all winter long. She would get up early each morning, prepare the roots and cook breakfast for the family, then go to work. She worked like this all day long, day after day, for the entire winter.

Although activities varied from season to season and from community to community, the intensity of women's work was always high, judging from accounts of ethnographers like Franz Boas and James Teit, and from the recollections of contemporary elders. Women's work, like men's, changed over the course of the year in a continuous seasonal round, choreographed by the times for harvesting and processing the different resources and varying with local conditions and particular needs of the family and community (Turner 1992b).

The history of settlement, European colonization, and ensuing industrial economic development resulted in changes in indigenous women's activities as many of them began applying their knowledge and skills to piecework and wage labour in fish-processing plants, fruit harvesting and cannery work, hop picking, potato growing and other agricultural endeavours (Knight 1996). Instead of making baskets for personal use or trade amongst themselves, for example, women started to manufacture baskets for sale or to trade with neighbouring settlers and tourists. Many used their basketry to obtain food or clothing from their European neighbours (Turner 1996; Turner and Loewen 1999). On Vancouver Island and in the vicinity, a new industry was developed: knitting distinctive 'Cowichan' sweaters and other clothing (Olsen 1998). The policy of Church and government, reflected in the establishment of reserves, residential schools and conversion to European-style agriculture (British Columbia Government 1875), resulted in a change in activities in order to conform to new societal norms. Nevertheless, many of the traditional activities persisted and continue in modified form into the twenty-first century.

Women's Knowledge

North-western aboriginal women's activities described here and elsewhere required an immense and complex base of knowledge and practical skills, including:

- Familiarity with ecosystems, geographic features, climate, moon cycles, tides, winds, currents and weather;
- Understanding of ecological succession, habitats and lifecycles of resource species, and of ecological indicators of these phenomena;
- In-depth knowledge of names and categories of culturally important plants and animals, and vocabulary relating to working with various resources;
- All manner of survival skills, including knowledge of wilderness survival, navigating in stormy or foggy weather, or tracking routes through rough terrain; recognition of poisonous plants and how to treat poisoning, and general first aid, midwifery, and childcare;
- Techniques required for harvesting and processing foods, materials and medicines, including dehydrating, smoking, cooking, storage, and weaving

baskets, mats, bags and clothing using a variety of techniques, materials, and designs, dyes and tanning agents;

- Knowledge of all kinds of plants, their habitat requirements, distributions, growth cycles, means of reproduction, variants, and associated plant and animal species;
- Knowledge of wildlife foods and habits, including predatory animal behaviour and where to search for root and seed caches of small mammals;
- Knowledge of various types of tinder and fuel and where to find these, and of how to kindle and maintain a fire;
- Knowledge of nutrition, foods and famine foods, including quantities required for preservation, food safety and potential toxicity of foods;
- Knowledge of the preparation, safety and effectiveness of medicinal herbs; and
- Cultural knowledge and understanding of social protocols, including rules relating to use and proprietorship of resources, privately held and confidential knowledge, family and clan crests, basket designs, songs, names and dances, and means of teaching, sharing and acquiring knowledge in culturally appropriate ways.

While some of this knowledge pertains to men as well as to women, women have held much of it primarily or exclusively, and they are the ones who have applied and perpetuated it. This knowledge not only includes practical, technical and environmental information, but also embodies 'wisdom' that accrues with training and experience, and enables women to apply the information they hold effectively and proficiently. Fundamental to traditional knowledge systems for men and women alike, is the cultural philosophy or worldview, attitudes, religious beliefs and ethics that shape and direct people's actions and activities (cf. Turner *et al.* 2000). For women, this cultural worldview is reflected in the ways in which plants are harvested; in the ceremonies and rituals enacted at the time of puberty, childbirth, marriage and death; in the ways in which women relate to one another; and in how their individual knowledge and experience is shared. As was attested to by many elders, women's knowledge is customarily passed through generations of women, from grandmother to granddaughter, aunt to niece, mother to daughter, and older sister to younger sister (Mary Thomas, Elsie Claxton, Annie York, Florence Davidson, Ruth Welsh and many others).

Teaching and Learning Women's Knowledge

In any society, knowledge is acquired and communicated in a variety of ways. Verbal communication or formal instruction is but one of many means. The accounts of many indigenous women themselves reveal that they have acquired their knowledge in large part as actual observers and participants, guided in their activities and often under the tutelage of a key individual, usually an older relative. It was through girls' and young women's journeys out on the land with their mothers and mothers-in-law, grandmothers, aunts and other family members, when they actively participated in berry picking, root digging and harvesting basket materials, and in cooking, processing and storing these resources, that they learned the details of seasonality, micro-environments, plant identification and variation, and resource processing and management techniques that they retained over their entire lives, eventually to pass along to younger generations. Norton (1985), in particular, provided major insights regarding the importance of women's work and knowledge in food storage and preparation for food security. In discussing her own learning experience, Mary Thomas recalled, for example, that 'Every time my mother would go out in the woods to gather ... her birch bark (*Betula papyrifera*) or cedar root, she was so observant. I can remember, she was always looking and she'd point out, "This is good for that."' This pattern of continuous teaching by demonstration and example, and ongoing learning by doing and practising, is a critical element in traditional knowledge systems.

There are some occasions and periods in a girl's life that offer 'teachable moments' (Katherine Fraser, personal communication, 2001): opportunities when certain knowledge is most readily and effectively taught or acquired. Puberty is a good example. Girls were traditionally kept isolated during their first menstruation, and even today this time provides the occasion for careful instruction by older women relatives about women's duties and responsibilities, including those related to plant harvesting and basketry, often reinforced in special ways (Teit 1900, 1909).

Digging roots, picking berries or chopping seaweed not only affords women the chance to 'pass on the news', but also provides teachable moments for older women to instruct girls and younger women about caring for and managing the resources that they are harvesting or processing. For example, when Mary Thomas was a child, her grandmother used to take her and her brother and sister root digging. Her grandmother would pry up the ground with her digging stick and the children would pick out the roots (among them glacier lily – *Erythronium grandiflorum* – and chocolate lily – *Fritillaria lanceolata* – bulbs and spring beauty – *Claytonia lanceolata* – corms) from the soil and place them in the basket. Then her grandmother would carefully search through the roots and replace the smaller ones or fragments, explaining to the children that these were too small to harvest and must be left to grow for the coming years. Mary and her siblings soon learned which size roots were good to harvest and which should be left behind. Mary also recalls how girls were taught about basket making and gathering food:

> I was very young when my grandmother taught me how to make a basket. Because sooner or later, we were going to become part of the food gathering. They would tie a little basket around a little girl's waist. The little girl might fill it with leaves, or dirt, or anything, but she learned that that little basket was a container and it has to be filled. And she'd go along. The bigger they got, the bigger her basket would be. And she was made at a very young age to fill one basket before she would go play.... (Mary Thomas, personal communication, February 2001)

Learning generally started from infancy, and even early childhood teachings would be remembered throughout a woman's lifetime. Learning often started with simple tasks, like twining an already-started basket, or picking reachable berries, side by side with a mother or older sister and often in the company of other learners and teachers. Children absorbed far more than practical details from such participation. They learned about attitudes and values related to conservation, discipline and sharing.

Many other women have recollections of learning from their elders, not only about practical details, but also about respecting and conserving other life forms and about being generous to others, especially to older people. For example, when Nlaka'pamux elder Mabel Joe made her first basket as a child, her mother told her to give it away. She filled it with huckleberries (*Vaccinium membranaceum*) and gave it to her uncle (personal communication, 1999). Secwepemc elder Ida Matthew recalled being taught as a child never to 'play' with animals that were being prepared for food. 'It was pitiful enough that we had to kill them. [My mother] instilled in us that we were not to waste the food, that we had to kill the poor animal. With any kinds of animal that we would hunt and eat, you have to respect them' (personal communication to Marianne Ignace, Turner *et al.* 2000).

Giving thanks to the Creator, and expressing gratitude to those life forms that give their lives or parts of themselves to sustain humans, was a part of harvesting and using plants, and women routinely demonstrated and practised these as they went about their daily activities. One of the best-known expressions of the praise and thanksgiving that women offered as harvesters is in the 'prayer' recorded by Franz Boas of a Kwakwa̱ka'wakw cedar bark gatherer:

> Look at me, friend! I come to ask for your dress, for you have come to take pity on us; for there is nothing for which you cannot be used, because it is your way that there is nothing for which we cannot use you, for you are really willing to give us your dress. I come to beg you for this, long-life maker, for I am going to make a basket for lily roots out of you. I pray, friend, not to feel angry with me on account of what I am going to do to you; and I beg you, friend, to tell our friends about what I ask of you. Take care, friend! Keep sickness away from me, so that I may not be killed by sickness or in war, O friend! (Boas 1921: 619)

Many contemporary women recall being instructed that they should give thanks to the berry bushes, the root plants, the medicine plants, the cedar tree and the birch tree, every time that they went out to harvest these resources. They were taught to leave a small gift of tobacco (*Nicotiana quadrivalvis*), or even a coin or something else of value, to signify their gratitude to the Creator for providing them with the foods, materials and medicines they needed to survive (Boas 1930; Turner *et al.* 1990).

Lessons were, and are, also taught through stories that are repeated from generation to generation, such as the Nuxalk (Bella Coola) narrative of 'The Woman Who Befriended a Wolf' (McIlwraith 1948, I: 691). In this story, a woman who was picking blueberries overheard voices calling her 'that foul-mouthed woman' and deriding her habit of munching berries as she picked instead of filling her basket. She hurried up the steep bank from which the voices came and was able to see the berries in their human forms: 'a host of goggle-eyed little boys sitting on the berry shoots'. After this she was always able to see berries in their hiding places and, having learned the lesson that they taught her about not eating berries while she picked, she became a highly successful and respected berry picker. She always respected the wishes of the fruit, never eating as she picked, but chewing dried salmon instead.

Not only stories, but also games and songs, feature in girls and young women's education. Many of these involve plants and botanical knowledge and take place in group situations where the learning of one reinforces the learning of another. Traditional education also incorporates experimentation and effective adaptation to new conditions and circumstances, and hence is responsible for maintaining a cultural group's resilience or ability to respond to change while retaining its essential characteristics. Even with the changes that have occurred since European contact and colonization, the importance of women as providers of food and other essentials for family survival, though often little recognized, has remained crucial (Norton 1985). As noted previously, women adapted their traditional harvesting and processing routines to new tasks, but were able to apply similar sets of skills. Women who worked at their family's fish camps, cutting and drying salmon or halibut, turned their training and expertise to cutting salmon in canneries. The skills of picking berries and digging roots, together with the discipline and stamina required for these tasks, were efficiently directed under the new social and economic regime to harvesting agricultural crops and growing potatoes and other vegetables.

These new ways were not always adopted willingly. When European-style agriculture was introduced to the Shuswap Lake area around Salmon Arm, Mary Thomas (personal communication, 1994) recalls that her grandmother refused to change and continued in the traditional way of gathering food from the land. However, her parents adapted, at least in part, to the new lifestyle:

> But my father and mother, I guess they were willing learners; they were really busy clearing land, which was not traditional with us, cutting down trees – you can imagine what they had to go through, because of their connection to Mother Nature. I often heard my mother talk about this, that it wasn't their way of life, but they had no choice, they had to accept the way they were taught, how to survive, was to chop down all these trees and cultivate it into European way of living. I guess that's where we began to lose a lot of the traditional food.

The knowledge described here has enabled women to serve as managers and caretakers of the land and plant resources upon which they have relied since time immemorial.

Women as Resource Managers

Evidence of women's traditional plant resource management in north-western North America is admittedly anecdotal and circumstantial. However, the combination of different types of evidence and substantiation from a variety of independent sources, provides a compelling case (Deur 2000; Turner and Peacock n.d.). In many ways, it is similar to the evidence assembled by Kat Anderson and colleagues for traditional plant management by Native Californians (Anderson 1996; Blackburn and Anderson 1993; Stevens 1999) and for resource management by other North American indigenous peoples (Minnis and Elisens 2000; Thornton 1999). In studies that reveal the sex of the resource managers (Stevens 1999, for example), women are shown to be the primary managers of plant resources, and their ability to promote and perpetuate the resources that are essential to survival brings them high status and respect (see also the chapters by Dick Bissonnette, Price and Ertuğ in this volume). The elements of complex plant resource management systems discussed below apply to women's activities in north-western North America.

First and perhaps foremost are culturally prescribed constraints against over-harvesting, taught to and practised by women. These controls can be described variously as: 'Use only what you need', 'Share with others, especially elders and those not able to get out', 'Always give thanks for the gifts of the Creator, whether food, materials or medicines', 'Honour every life and treat it with respect and dignity' (Turner 1992a; Turner and Atleo 1998). In fact, the personae of some species, such as the red alder tree (*Alnus rubra*), are themselves embodied as respected women. In the Kwakwa̱ka̱'wakw culture, for example, a red alder being approached and spoken to before its bark is harvested as a medicine is addressed as 'Supernatural Power of the River Bank', 'Healing Woman' and 'great Supernatural One' (Boas 1930: 237–8). Invoking such attitudes towards plant resources may not, on its own, prevent over-harvesting and resource depletion but, combined with other teachings and strategies, certainly would have helped to maintain species abundance.

Another important element of plant resource management pertaining to women is proprietorship or 'ownership' of resources or resource harvesting sites (see also Dick-Bissonnette and Price in this volume). In British Columbia, Nuu-Chah-Nulth, Haida and Tsimshian women, among others, were entitled through heredity to use specific berry patches, root-digging grounds and other resource sites (Deur and Turner n.d.). Although systems of ownership vary from one part of the study region to another, all peoples have defined territories where they harvest resources, and many families have specific sites to which they return year after year during the course of their seasonal rounds (Turner et al. 1990; Turner and Jones 2000; Turner 1992b). At these sites, women would harvest the plant resources, while men fished and hunted. This habituation to specific places allowed careful long-term monitoring of plant resources, including their stage of ripeness, abundance and productivity. James Teit described the former practice among the Nlaka'pamux of monitoring and overseeing the berry-picking grounds:

Among the Upper Thompsons [Nlaka'pamux] an old woman, chosen by the others or acting voluntarily, watched the larger and more important berry-patches, to see that no one picked the berries until they were ripe. When they were fit to pick, she sent word to the other women; and whoever wished picked the berries until the season was over. (Teit 1900: 294)

The women overseeing the berry patches or other gathering places were also attuned to changing weather patterns or other conditions that might cause population fluctuations or diminution of resources. For example, if the berries appeared to be small and the landscape was becoming too bushy, this would be noted by the harvesters, and would signal the need to clear or burn over the area to maintain the habitat and increase nutrient cycling (Turner 1999).

It is no accident or coincidence that the richest, most productive root-harvesting grounds, the best seaweed and eel-grass meadows, and the most diverse and productive berrying grounds, are within areas that have been visited routinely for hundreds and, in some cases, thousands of years, as indicated by the presence of archaeological features such as root-roasting pit depressions (Peacock 1998; Peacock and Turner 1999).

The plant resources that women harvested in north-western North America are, with few exceptions, perennial species that have the capacity to regenerate, not only by seed, but also through vegetative means. The timing of root harvesting is important in terms of seed dispersal. Root vegetables were usually harvested at the season when the fruiting capsules were opening and seeds maturing. The disturbance caused by harvesting thus assisted and enhanced seed dispersal. At the same time, during harvesting, women would have aerated the soil and redistributed nutrients by using their digging sticks. They also removed some of the competing weedy species while digging and, as noted previously, left intact, replanted or redistributed smaller bulbs, bulblets, corms, rhizomes or tubers of the food species. All of this would have the effect of enhancing the growth of the populations they were harvesting, thus offsetting the impact of removing some of the roots (Loewen 1998; Peacock and Turner 1999). Similar combinations of weeding, tilling the soil and replanting propagules were also applied in the management of other root vegetable populations, including springbank clover (described in the passage from Menzies's journal, quoted previously), Pacific silverweed (*Potentilla anserina* ssp. *pacifica*) and northern riceroot (*Fritillaria camschatcensis*), as well as balsamroot (*Balsamorhiza sagittata*) (Turner and Peacock n.d.; Turner *et al.* 2000), bitterroot (*Lewisia rediviva*) (Bandringa 1999), and, possibly, wapato (*Sagittaria latifolia*) (Darby 1996).

Women also practised pruning, coppicing and selective harvesting to maintain and enhance berry bushes and basketry species. Kwakwaka'wakw Chief Adam Dick (Kwaxsistala) (personal communication, 1998) described how his grandmother used to tell him to break off the tops of the red huckleberry, salmonberry (*Rubus spectabilis*) and stink currant (*Ribes bracteosum*) bushes after picking the berries for the season, so that they would be more productive the next year. Secwepemc elder Nellie Taylor and Saanich elder Elsie Claxton recalled that this practice applied to soapberry (*Shepherdia canadensis*) bushes as well (personal communication, 1994; Peacock and Turner 1999; Turner and Peacock n.d.). Mary

Thomas's mother used to look at the Saskatoon berry (*Amelanchier alnifolia*) bushes around their land and, when they became very large and bushy, she would say, 'It's time to cut them down.' She would cut them right back and, the next year, they grew long, straight shoots that were excellent for the rims of birch-bark baskets. Then, two or three years later, the remaining shoots produced quantities of large, high-quality berries (Mary Thomas, personal communication, 1998). Green shoots of cow parsnip, salmonberry and thimbleberry were also harvested selectively, and were said to grow best in places where they had been harvested in previous years.

Women who harvested the bark from cedar trees were taught to pull only one or two straps from each tree, or no more than one third of the circumference, enabling the tree to recover and sometimes continue to grow for hundreds of years. Similarly, birch-bark harvesters were instructed to take care not to cut into the tree's growing layer or cambium, but to remove only the outer bark so that the tree itself would not be damaged. Weavers digging cedar or spruce roots for basketry learned from an early age to be selective and to pull only a few roots from each tree, so as not to cause severe damage to the tree. Harvesters of cattail (*Typha latifolia*) and basket sedge (*Carex obnupta*) leaves and tule (*Schoenoplectus acutus* and *S. tabernae-montani*; syn.: *Scirpus* spp.) stems also state that those that grow best are gathered from places where they have been harvested previously and routinely. Fibre plants like stinging nettle (*Urtica dioica*) and Indian hemp (*Apocynum cannabinum*) were also maintained in designated patches, and there is some evidence that high-quality stinging nettle was cultivated and even transplanted from one site to another.

The extent of transplanting plant populations from one locality to another is well documented for other parts of the world, but is still little known in the North-west. There is evidence that indigenous people intentionally introduced other species besides stinging nettle to new areas. Blue camas (*Camassia* spp.), *wapato*, garry oak (*Quercus garryana*), springbank clover, highbush cranberry (*Viburnum edule*), cottonwood (*Populus balsamifera* ssp. *trichocarpa*), cattail and three-square tule (*Schoenoplectus olneyi*; syn.: *Scirpus olneyi*) have all been transplanted to new locations according to at least one record in each case (Turner and Peacock n.d.).

All of the management activities described above could be expected to affect the genetic and ecological diversity of plants. Although there is no firm evidence in the region of true plant domestication, there is plenty of evidence of domesticating landscapes (as defined by Blackburn and Anderson 1993 and Deur 2000) and of plant resource intensification by women harvesters from ancient to modern times.

Conclusions

Although many indigenous women in north-western North America are still very knowledgeable about traditional lifestyles and resources, the loss of traditional women's knowledge and practices as a whole has been profound (cf. Kuhnlein 1989, for an assessment of knowledge of traditional food within the Nuxalk community). The reasons for the changes are many, but certainly residential schools sanctioned by the Canadian government and run by churches of various denominations had a serious impact on traditional knowledge acquisition and on lifestyles of families and communities. In a lecture at the University of Victoria (February 2001), Mary Thomas describes her own childhood experience of being wrested away from her grandmother and from the entire way of life she had known up to the time she went to school:

> Then we begin to question, what really happened on those reservations? What effect did it have on our people? We began to forget about a lot of the natural foods, the natural medicines. When I started residential school, I was about six and a half years old when I was taken away from my grandmother. My grandmother had taken over raising the three of us, my older sister, myself and my younger brother. We practically lived with Grandma. Oh, it was so good! She was so kind to us, yet she was firm. Just out of the blue, they took us away from there and put us in the residential school. And there were nights I cried myself to sleep. I was lonely. I missed my grandmother. And in the residential school [we were not allowed to speak], in comparison with the way I grew up … we were always asking questions: 'Grandma, what is this? Grandma, what are you doing? Grandma, why do you want it?' All those questions. [With Grandma] we were allowed to talk as much as we could.

Recently, the Government and churches have apologized for the treatment of aboriginal children in residential schools: many children were abused, and virtually all were forbidden to speak their own languages. There was a general colonial policy that combined the goals of establishing reserves with that of assimilation of indigenous people within mainstream society (British Columbia Government 1875), ultimately resulting in restrictions against the practice of traditional seasonal rounds, including women's harvesting of plant foods, materials and medicines from traditional sites.

The confusion and misery for aboriginal children and adults alike caused by the combined colonial, land and residential school policies, coupled with environmental deterioration due to the industrial activities of the European newcomers, is unimaginable. One of the seldom-articulated outcomes is the disruption of entire traditional ecological knowledge systems, including many elements of the intricate knowledge and wisdom acquired, enacted and passed down by women through generations. For example, it is more difficult, given the wage economy and separate living quarters of families in contemporary aboriginal society, for groups of women of different generations to get together and 'pass on the news' as they used to do so frequently.

Loss of specialized knowledge pertaining to women and traditional societies in general is a trend that is being documented in many parts of the world (see also the chapters by Pieroni and Hoffmann in this volume). The implications for resource use and land management in the twenty-first century are momentous. Virtually every place in the world is experiencing environmental degradation and loss of biodiversity. Elders and cultural specialists maintain that this is, at least in part, because people are not caring for the land, plants and animals in the way that they did in the past. Re-instituting some of the practices and attitudes relating to the sustainable use of wild plants that are part of women's knowledge and heritage would be an obvious step towards eco-cultural restoration in north-western North America and elsewhere. Because this knowledge in all its forms is so tenuous today, the need to retain and promote what still exists is vital. Indigenous women who have retained this knowledge need recognition and support in their efforts to practise it and pass it on to future generations.

Note

1 See Anderson 1996; Deur and Turner n.d.; Hunn 1981; Lepofsky in press; Norton 1981, 1985; Peacock 1998; Peacock and Turner 1999.

References

Anderson, M. K. (1996) 'Tending the wilderness', *Restoration and Management Notes*, Vol. 14, No. 2, pp. 154–66.

Bandringa, R. W. (1999) 'The Ethnobotany and Descriptive Ecology of Bitterroot, *Lewisia rediviva* Pursh (Portulacaceae), in the Lower Thompson River Valley British Columbia', MSc thesis, Department of Resource Management and Environmental Studies, University of British Columbia, Vancouver.

Blackburn, T. C. and M. K. Anderson (eds.) (1993) *Before the Wilderness: Environmental Management by Native Californians*, Menlo Park, California: Ballena Press.

Blackman, M. B. (1982) *During My Time: Florence Edenshaw Davidson, a Haida Woman*, Seattle and London: University of Washington Press.

Boas, F. (1921) *Ethnology of the Kwakiutl*, Bureau of American Ethnology 35th Annual Report, Parts 1 and 2. Washington, DC: Smithsonian Institution.

Boas, F. (1930) *The Religion of the Kwakiutl Indians*, New York: Columbia University Press (reprinted in 1969, New York: AMS Press Inc.).

British Columbia Government (1875) *Papers Connected with the Indian Land Question, 1850–1875*, Victoria, British Columbia: Government Printer (reprinted 1987, as *Indian Land Question, 1850–1875, 1877*).

Darby, M. C. (1996) 'Wapato for the People: an Ecological Approach to Understanding the Native American Use of *Sagittaria latifolia* on the Lower Columbia River', MA thesis, Portland, Oregon: Department of Anthropology, Portland State University.

Deur, D. (2000) 'A Domesticated Landscape: Native American Plant Cultivation on the Northwest Coast of North America', PhD dissertation, Louisiana State University, Baton Rouge, Ann Arbor, Michigan: University Microfilms International.

Deur, D. and N. J. Turner (eds.) (in press 2003) *'Keeping It Living': Indigenous Plant Management on the Northwest Coast*, Seattle: University of Washington Press.

Hunn, E. S. (1981) 'On the relative contribution of men and women to subsistence among hunter-gatherers of the Columbia Plateau: a comparison with *Ethnographic Atlas* summaries', *Journal of Ethnobiology*, Vol. 1, No. 1, pp. 124–34.

Kennedy, D. (1993) 'Looking for Tribes in All the Wrong Places: an Examination of the Central Coast Salish Social Network', MA thesis, Victoria, British Columbia: Department of Anthropology, University of Victoria.

Knight, R. (1996) *Indians at Work: an Informal History of Native Labour in British Columbia, 1858–1930*, Vancouver, British Columbia: New Star Books, revised edition.

Kuhnlein, H. V. (1989) 'Change in use of traditional foods by the Nuxalk Native people of British Columbia', in G. H. Pelto and L. A. Vargas (eds.), *Perspectives in Dietary Change*, Cambridge: International Nutrition Foundation.

Lepofsky, D. (in press 2003) 'The Northwest', in P. Minnis (ed.), *Plants and People in Ancient North*

America, Washington, DC: Smithsonian Institution Press.

Loewen, D. C. (1998) 'Ecological, Ethnobotanical, and Nutritional Aspects of Yellow Glacier Lily, *Erythronium grandiflorum* Pursh (*Liliaceae*) in Western Canada', MSc thesis, Victoria, British Columbia: Department of Biology and School of Environmental Studies, University of Victoria.

McIlwraith, T. F. (1948) *The Bella Coola Indians* (2 vols.), Toronto, Ontario: University of Toronto Press.

Minnis, P. and W. Elisens (eds.) (2000) *Biodiversity and Native North America*, Norman, Oklahoma: University of Oklahoma Press.

Newcombe, C. F. (ed.) (1923) *Menzies' Journal of Vancouver's Voyage, April to October 1792*, British Columbia Archives Memoir Vol. 5, No. 8, Victoria.

Norton, H. H. (1981) 'Plant use in Kaigani Haida culture: correction of an ethnohistorical oversight', *Economic Botany* Vol. 35, pp. 434–49.

Norton, H. H. (1985) 'Women and Resources of the Northwest Coast. Documentation from the Eighteenth and Early Nineteenth Centuries', PhD dissertation, University of Washington, Ann Arbor, Michigan: University Microfilms International.

Olsen, S. V. (1998) '"We Indians Were Sure Hard Workers". A History of Coast Salish Wool Working', unpublished MA thesis, Victoria, British Columbia: Department of History, University of Victoria.

Peacock, S. L. (1998) 'Putting Down Roots: The Emergence of Wild Plant Food Production on the Canadian Plateau', PhD dissertation, Victoria, British Columbia: Department of Geography and School of Environmental Studies, University of Victoria.

Peacock, S. L. and N. J. Turner (1999) '"Just like a garden": traditional resource management and biodiversity conservation on the Interior Plateau of British Columbia', in P. Minnis and W. Elisens (eds.), *Biodiversity and Native North America*, Norman, Oklahoma: University of Oklahoma Press, pp. 133–79.

Stevens, M. (1999) 'The Ethnoecology and Autecology of White Root (Carex barbarae Dewey): Implications for Restoration', PhD dissertation, University of California at Davis, Ann Arbor, Michigan: University Microfilms International.

Teit, J. (1900) 'The Thompson Indians', Vol. 1, Part IV, in F. Boas (ed.), *The Jesup North Pacific Expedition*, Memoir of the American Museum of Natural History, New York: G.E. Stechert.

Teit, J. (1909) *The Shuswap*, Vol. II, Part VII, in F. Boas (ed.), *The Jesup North Pacific Expedition*, Memoir of the American Museum of Natural History, New York: G.E. Stechert.

Teit, J. (1912) '*Mythology of the Thompson Indians*', Vol. VII, Part II, in F. Boas (ed.) *The Jesup North Pacific Expedition*, Memoir of the American Museum of Natural History, New York, G.E. Stechert.

Thornton, T. F. (1999) '*Tleikwaani*, the "berried" landscape: the structure of Tlingit edible fruit resources at Glacier Bay, Alaska', *Journal of Ethnobiology*, Vol. 19, No. 1, pp. 27–48.

Turner, N. J. (1992a) '"The earth's blanket": traditional aboriginal attitudes towards nature', *Canadian Biodiversity*, Vol. 2, No. 4, pp. 5–7.

Turner, N. J. (1992b) 'Plant resources of the Stl'atl'imx (Fraser River Lillooet) people: a window into the past', in B. Hayden (ed.) *Complex Cultures of the British Columbia Plateau: Traditional Stl'atl'imx Resource Use*, Vancouver: University of British Columbia Press, pp. 405–69.

Turner, N. J. (1995) *Food Plants of Coastal First Peoples*, Victoria: Royal British Columbia Museum and Vancouver: University of British Columbia Press.

Turner, N. J. (1996) '"Dans une Hotte". L'importance de la vannerie das l'économie des peuples chasseurs-pêcheurs-cueilleurs du Nord-Ouest de l'Amérique du Nord', *Anthropologie et Sociétiés*, Special Issue on Contemporary Ecological Anthropology, Theories, Methods and Research Fields, Montreal, Quebec, Vol. 20, No. 3, pp. 55–84.

Turner, N. J. (1997) *Food Plants of Interior First Peoples*, Victoria: Royal British Columbia Museum and Vancouver: University of British Columbia Press.

Turner, N. J. (1998) *Plant Technology of British Columbia First Peoples*, Victoria: Royal British Columbia Museum, and Vancouver: University of British Columbia Press.

Turner, N. J. (1999) '"Time to burn": traditional use of fire to enhance resource production by aboriginal peoples in British Columbia', in R. Boyd (ed.), *Indians, Fire and the Land in the Pacific Northwest,* Corvallis: Oregon State University Press, pp. 185–218.

Turner, N. J. and E. R. Atleo (Chief Umeek) (1998) 'Pacific North American first peoples and the environment', in H. Coward (ed.), *Traditional and Modern Approaches to the Environment on the Pacific Rim, Tensions and Values,* Centre for Studies in Religion and Society, Albany: State University of New York Press, pp. 105–24.

Turner, N. J. and R. J. Hebda (1990) 'Contemporary use of bark for medicine by two Salishan native elders of Southeast Vancouver Island, Canada', *Journal of Ethnopharmacology,* Vol. 29, pp. 59–72.

Turner, N. J., M. B. Ignace and R. Ignace (2000) 'Traditional ecological knowledge and wisdom of aboriginal peoples in British Columbia', in J. Ford and D. R. Martinez (eds.), Special Issue on Traditional Ecological Knowledge, Ecosystem Science and Environmental Management, *Ecological Applications,* Vol. 10, No. 5, pp. 1275–87.

Turner, N. J. and J. T. Jones (2000) '"Occupying the land": traditional patterns of land and resource ownership among First peoples of British Columbia', CD ROM Proceedings, *IASCP 2000 (Common Property Resources)* conference, Bloomington, Indiana.

Turner, N. J. and D. C. Loewen (1998) 'The original "free trade": exchange of botanical products and associated plant knowledge in north-western North America', *Anthropologica,* Vol. 40, pp. 49–70.

Turner, N. J. and S. Peacock (in press 2003) 'Solving the perennial paradox: ethnobotanical evidence for plant resource management on the Northwest Coast', in D. Deur and N. J. Turner (eds.), *'Keeping It Living': Indigenous Plant Management on the Northwest Coast,* Seattle: University of Washington Press.

Turner, N. J. and R. L. Taylor (1972) 'A review of the Northwest Coast tobacco mystery', *Syesis,* Vol. 5, pp. 249–57.

Turner, N. J., J. Thomas, B. F. Carlson and R. T. Ogilvie (1983) *Ethnobotany of the Nitinaht Indians of Vancouver Island,* Victoria: British Columbia Provincial Museum Occasional Paper No. 24.

Turner, N. J., L. C. Thompson, M. T. Thompson and A. Z. York (1990) *Thompson Ethnobotany. Knowledge and Usage of Plants by the Thompson Indians of British Columbia,* Victoria: Royal British Columbia Museum, Memoir No. 3, and Vancouver: University of British Columbia Press.

CHAPTER 8

The Invisible Queen in the Plant Kingdom: Gender Perspectives in Medical Ethnobotany

Brij Kothari

Feminists have argued that 'gender is a pervasive principle of social organization' (Stacey and Thorne 1985: 303), and 'must remain central to the analysis of key questions in anthropology and in the social sciences as a whole' (Moore 1988: 195). Ethnobotany, being essentially a study of the relationship between humans and plants, has one foot in botany and the other in anthropology or related disciplines. It should be obvious that ethnobotanists can ill afford to ignore gender as a fundamental aspect of this relationship. Yet the ethnobotanical literature on medicinal plants, much of which is devoted to shamanism, does not generally reflect an overt consideration of gender.[1] A critical look at this issue was inspired through participatory research in the Andean communities of La Esperanza, Ecuador. This chapter begins with a brief description of the project, focusing mainly on aspects that relate to women's participation and knowledge. The project's ethnobotanical experience led to a critical look at gender as it is addressed in ethnobotanical literature on ethnomedicine (traditional medical systems based partly upon the use of medicinal plants rather than modern pharmaceuticals), in which shamanism is a major topic of research.

Women's participation as healers in ethnomedicinal systems has tended to remain invisible to ethnobotanists and other scholars. This is in spite of the fact that any child living in the sites that ethnobotanists typically visit would indicate that the first person to whom they report their illnesses and from whom they seek a cure is usually one of the women in the family who have an extensive knowledge of medicinal plants and other remedies (Finerman 1989). Women are the 'popular' or 'lay' healers who form the backbone of traditional rural health care systems, especially in areas rich in biodiversity (Kleinman 1980). A small but growing body of literature shows that, among popular healers, women are the primary actors in many societies' local health care systems (McClain 1989). Especially mothers and grandmothers are active agents in self-directed health care provision and thera-peutic knowledge generation within households and communities.[2] It also seems clear that most cases of illness are handled with fresh herbal preparations made from locally available plants. The obvious conclusion seems to be that women, in their maternal roles or as healers (herbalists and midwives, for example), must know a great deal about medicinal plants. Yet their knowledge is conspicuously under-represented in the ethnobotanical literature that focuses primarily on medicinal plants.

Gender differentiation in local knowledge is frequently conceptualized as being related to the sexual division of labour. While this has proved to be a fruitful line of inquiry, it is unable to explain islands of knowledge that belie strict demarcation based on sex roles. Women's ethnobotanical knowledge and therapeutic roles constitute one such island that is largely unexplored by ethnobotanists who tend to make a beeline for the 'shaman' or 'magico-expert' healer, an office that in many cultures is reserved exclusively for men. While women may hold some if not most medical ethnobotanical knowledge, by virtue of their sex they may be denied the power and status of the 'expert'.[3] This suggests that gender must be explored as an integral aspect of the local power or 'prestige structure' (Ortner and Whitehead 1981) in which knowledge is held, generated and expressed (Morgen 1989; Jackson 1993).

The main objective of the research project in the Andean communities of La Esperanza, Ecuador that is discussed in this chapter was for *campesinos* (farmers) to investigate and document in written form their own community's oral knowledge of medicinal plants, primarily for their own use. The intent at the outset was not to explore gender relationships explicitly. Nevertheless, the author's initial awareness of the importance of gender issues in ethnobotanical research was enhanced by the experience gained while coordinating the project. Furthermore, some of the findings confirmed that women in this area are the principal repositories of plant knowledge. The participatory methodology that was used in the project has the potential to democratize knowledge generation, at the same time that it enables the complexity of gender relations in plant knowledge to be explored. Admittedly, an exploration of this complexity was neither attempted nor accomplished in the context of the project. Even so, the gendered nature of knowledge became quickly apparent.

The La Esperanza Project

La Esperanza is located about 10 miles south-east of Ibarra, the capital of Imbabura Province in the northern sierra of Ecuador. There are several indigenous communities in the region of La Esperanza, each with a population varying from 200 to 800 people. The roughly 50 to 200 families per community are mostly subsistence farmers, or *campesinos,* with an average farm size of 1–2 hectares per family at elevations ranging from 2200 to 3200 metres. The ethnobotanical research project conducted in La Esperanza (Kothari 1996) was unconventional in two ways. First, the subject of research was *campesinos'* ethnobotanical knowledge. As Prance observed, 'Most ethnobotanical research has studied the indigenous tribal peoples of the world', and 'one of the most neglected aspects of ethnobotany today is the study of the *campesinos'* (1991: 212–13). Second, and more important, in this research the ethnobotanical knowledge of peasant farmers has been documented by the peasants to whom this knowledge belongs (see Kothari 1996; FSI and Kothari 1997).

The traditional communication channels and practices of everyday life that have successfully reproduced accumulated ethnobotanical knowledge over many generations have recently been breaking down. The loss is more than unfortunate, since this knowledge continues to be the foundation of the *campesinos'* principal health care system. Most episodes of illness continue to be handled within the traditional family and the community. The main responsibility for health care provision within the family and for the conservation of medicinal plant knowledge today rests squarely on the shoulders of women, especially in view of male emigration. Finerman (1984, 1989) confirms this for other parts of Andean Ecuador.

The investigation and documentation of medicinal plant knowledge was undertaken by the *campesinos* primarily for their own use. A grassroots organization, the Unión de Organizaciones y Comunidades Indígenas de Angochagua, La Esperanza, y Caranqui (UNOCIAE-C), provided the administrative base for the project. Seven out of the 18 communities that UNOCIAE-C represents agreed to participate. Each selected two participants, a woman and a man, to interview knowledgeable people in their own community. In retrospect, the stipulation of equal representation of men and women among the interviewers was perhaps the key decision that made it possible for women's knowledge to be fairly represented in the book that resulted. A bilingual questionnaire (in Quichua and Spanish) was designed by the coordinating members to guide the interview process. This questionnaire, to be administered for each plant remedy known by each respondent, helped to standardize the responses for comparative purposes and to ensure that information on plant remedies was complete.

The information on plant remedies distilled from more than 300 questionnaires was reviewed collectively by the participants, who also provided fresh input in the rewriting of plant remedies for which some consensus could be reached. The review sessions also triggered discussions that led to the documentation of knowledge not captured previously in any of the questionnaires. Now this knowledge is represented in a bilingual Quichua–Spanish book produced by the project and entitled *Our Medicinal Plants* (Kothari and UNOCIAE-C 1993).

Women's participation

All of the interested communities were able to nominate a male interviewer without much difficulty. Eliciting women's participation in the project was easier to plan than to accomplish, but this was not due to a lack of interest among women. Societal pressures that mainly younger women confront, combined with low levels of literacy among middle-aged and older women, made their participation difficult. In some confirmed cases, parents, families and husbands were reluctant to let their daughters or wives participate in a mixed group situation away from the community. Despite these initial obstacles, the communities were persistently urged to field a literate participant of each sex. When the communities were unable to nominate a female representative, the literacy condition was relaxed. The elimination of the literacy requirement, together with the knowledge that there was a *campesina* (female farmer) present in the coordinating group, may have created a climate that permitted seven mostly middle-aged women finally to step forward. Although literacy levels were low among the female volunteers, this did not prevent them from completing the questionnaires. Some of the women who had no or little schooling engaged the assistance of their children, husbands or other *campesinos* in order to complete the questionnaires.

The following interviewing guidelines were delineated: (1) interview *campesinos* who are knowledgeable about medicinal plants, preferably in the interviewer's own community, and (2) document an individual's knowledge exhaustively (document-ing as many remedies as possible), making sure that a new questionnaire is completed for every plant remedy. The participants mostly interviewed people from their own communities, and therefore may well have decided to interview primarily those *campesinos* whom they would normally consult, learn from, or hold in high esteem for their knowledge. The interviewers were free to select respon-dents from within their own community. From a gender perspective, it is instructive to ask who interviewed whom and what observations can be made regarding the responses obtained.

Gender variations among interviewers and respondents

Out of the 295 completed questionnaires, 63.1 per cent originated from female respondents and 36.3 per cent from male respondents. The average female inter-viewee's knowledge served to complete seven questionnaires as compared to slightly more than three questionnaires per male interviewee. These numbers may indicate: (1) the medicinal plant knowledge in conscious memory, which did not require any prodding, and/or (2) the knowledge that could be stated with some certainty given the fact that it was being recorded. The conclusion drawn is that the average *campesina* has a greater breadth of medicinal plant knowledge than the average *campesino* in the indigenous La Esperanza communities.

It is important to check whether any biases could have favoured such an outcome. First, 59 individuals, 27 of whom (46 per cent) were women and 32 of whom (54 per cent) were men, were the respondents for all of the completed questionnaires. Second, male interviewers completed 57 per cent (169) of the questionnaires as compared to the 42 per cent (125) that were completed by women interviewers. The average number of questionnaires completed by male interviewers was thus 24, and for female interviewers it was 18. Third, male inter-viewers sought responses from an equal number of male and female *campesinos* (17 each). Female participants interviewed marginally more men (15) than women (13). In summary, a comparable representation by sex in almost any category confers greater support for the assertion that, on average, *campesinas* mentioned many more plant remedies than *campesinos*.

Some of the questionnaires were self-administered – that is, completed by the participant from her/his own medicinal plant knowledge. Out of the 54 question-naires that were self-administered, 40 (74 per cent) were completed by four female participants and fourteen (26 per cent) by three male participants. This further indicates that the women in the study (both respondents and interviewers) seemed to be the principal repositories of medicinal plant knowledge.

Gender differences in plants and illnesses reported

A total of 97 medicinal plants were reported, of which female respondents reported 85 (87.6 per cent) and males 57 (58.8 per cent). In contrast, the data on illnesses for which plant remedies were reported show only a marginal difference between men and women. Cures were reported for a total of 70 illnesses – 57 (81.4 per cent) by women and 54 (77.1 per cent) by men. However, since women mentioned many more plants, this would tend to indicate that they know more plant remedies for a particular illness. The findings substantiate the earlier assertion that women's ethnobotanical knowledge in the La Esperanza indigenous communities is richer. In addition, they serve to confirm similar impressions carried away from the field. Especially during the group review sessions, the authoritative confirmation of medicinal plant knowledge was very often sought, and came from, female participants. The important thing to stress, however, is not that women know more or less than men, but to draw attention to the possibility that women and men have 'differently constituted environmental knowledge' (Jackson 1993: 1952).

In summary, the findings draw attention to the knowledge and therapeutic roles of women. The methodology employed has the potential to provide the outsider with access to both men's and women's knowledge. The participatory approach offers insights into a community's key actors and knowledge bearers without introducing the outsider's gender bias in informant selection. Although the project's achievements in gender research are extremely modest, the findings point to the need for a more involved reflection on the manner in which medical ethnobotanical literature addresses gender.

Gender and Medical Ethnobotany

The definition of ethnobotany is, and always has been, gender-neutral. A commonly accepted definition of ethnobotany is 'the study of direct interrelations between *humans* and plants, concerned with the totality of the place of plants in a culture' (Ford 1978, cited in Alcorn 1984: 3). In fact, when Harshberger (1896, cited in Alcorn 1984: 2) first used the term a century ago to refer to 'the study of plants used by primitive and aboriginal people', it was still remarkably inclusive of both women and men. Yet, in practice, it is posited that medical ethnobotany, by not adequately recognizing the gendered character of knowledge or the power–knowledge nexus, has inevitably privileged the male perspective.

Invisible healers

To a considerable extent, anthropological and ethnobotanical literature renders the female healer and her knowledge invisible. For instance, in Johannes Wilbert's long association with the Warao of Venezuela, accounts of women's herbal tradition and plant knowledge go practically unmentioned (Wilbert 1972) or, at best, merit only a cursory reference (Wilbert 1987, 1993). Werner Wilbert (1987),[4] by contrast, draws attention to the complementary role that Warao female herbalists play in non-ritual healing. According to his account, Warao women's herbal knowledge is critical to children's survival. From a gender perspective, Johannes Wilbert paints a male-oriented picture of the actors in the Warao health care system, paying exclusive attention to ritual shamanic healing (a male domain), which makes female herbal healers invisible to readers. The ethnobotanist who seeks the shaman alone may in this case easily ignore non-ritualistic herbalism, which is predominantly women's sphere of activity.

Ethnobotanical and ethnopharmacological accounts in general lack cultural and methodological detail (Croom 1983; Alcorn 1984; Etkin 1993). When the attempt is made, treatment of gender is relegated mostly to a fleeting remark, comment or paragraph (for exceptions, see Cox 1991; Kainer and Duryea 1992; South 1993). In most cases, it is difficult even to determine the sex of informants. But rather than focusing on what is lacking in the literature from a gender perspective, it may be instructive to mention examples of studies that have been sensitive to gender and that have explored the gendered nature of medical ethnobotanical knowledge (see also other chapters in this volume).

Medical ethnobotany and reproductive health

Ethnobotanists specializing in medicinal plants have given disproportionate attention to women's knowledge in the reproductive domain, which reinforces the idea that women's ethnomedical knowledge is directly related to the fact that they are physically different from men. Such a stereotype may well reflect ethnobotanists' own beliefs that women's reproductive health is an intimate and private affair that 'naturally' would only be dealt with by women, a belief that ethnobotanists unconsciously carry with them to the field. Even a limited literature search demonstrates that women's herbal knowledge has been reported for every imaginable use of plants related to reproduction. These include plants used in the course of a woman's reproductive life (Bourdy and Walter 1992; Browner 1985), antenatal remedies to induce or augment labour (Lewis and Elvin-Lewis 1990; Veale et al. 1992), abortifacients (Emmerich and de Senna Valle 1991; Nath et al. 1992), contraceptives (Emmerich and de Senna Valle 1991), enhancement of sexual experience (Ruganga et al. 1992), fertility enhancement (Valencia 1989) and emmenagogues (Browner and de Montellano 1986). Women's knowledge is of interest only due to the reproduction-centric nature of this type of ethnobotanical research. The literature in this case does not accurately reflect the totality of the place of medicinal plants in women's lives, but rather the singularity of the ethnobotanist's conceptualization of that place.

In the reproductive domain, as in all knowledge domains, the power–knowledge link is inescapable and needs to be explored. Drawing from Browner and Perdue's work (1988), Howard-Borjas (2002) discusses how reproduction-related ethnobotanical knowledge is related to gender power relations. In certain contexts, men may have more knowledge than women of medicinal plants used for reproductive health, and men may also be midwives. In specific contexts, this knowledge can afford men greater power – for example, *vis-à-vis* the ability to influence women's reproductive decision making through exclusive knowledge of abortifacients or contraceptives. The power–knowledge link is even more apparent in shamanism.

Women and Shamanism

In general, the understanding of women's knowledge and healing functions in cultures where shamanism is practised is superficial at best. Although some authors (see Harvey 1979 and Kendall 1985 for Korea) present in-depth studies on female shamans, the discussion here is confined to South American shamanism, which is of special interest to ethnobotanists. No other healing agent has aroused the curiosity of ethnobotanists and anthropologists more than the South American shaman. The list of anthropological literature on South American shamanism is long.[5] By and large, this body of literature has concentrated on shamanism as a male expression, with little or no attention to the relation of women to this institution or to the parallel expressions of women shamans. Plotkin's account of his ethnobotanical research experience in the Amazon is exceptional in that it raises popular awareness of the shaman's knowledge and the desperate need to preserve it. But, as far as women's knowledge is concerned, he admits:

> It seemed there was no way for me to walk into the forest with any woman from the tribe, and no way for me to learn about their special plants. Although I have little knowledge of the plants involved, I am convinced that there exists a wealth of ethnobotanical treatments for menstrual problems, birth control, difficult childbirth, and so on, which is simply unavailable to the male ethnobotanist. (1993: 105)

Plotkin admits the difficulty of accessing women's knowledge as a male ethnobotanist, although he is convinced that women possess tremendous knowledge in the reproductive context 'and so on'. Yet, as argued earlier, it is mostly the 'and so on' of women's knowledge that ethnobotanists tend to ignore, being largely convinced that women can only have reproduction-related medicinal plant knowledge. Admittedly, access to women's knowledge, as in Plotkin's experience, can pose difficulties for male researchers. But the relative abundance of literature on women's plant knowledge in the reproductive domain, in contrast to the paucity of studies in non-reproduction-related areas, attests to the ethnobotanists' narrow perception of the spectrum of women's knowledge rather than reflecting what women actually know or what ethnobotanists are able to access if desired. A small but growing body of literature is redressing this imbalance (see Howard-Borjas 2002, for example, and the studies in this book).

Several questions emerge, some of which arise directly from Plotkin's admission. What is the breadth of women's plant knowledge in, but also beyond the reproductive domain? What is the breadth of men's knowledge in this same area? What is the therapeutic role of women in societies where shamanism is practised, under circumstances which (1) permit women access to the shamanic office or (2) reserve the shaman's position exclusively for men? Are there any oral histories of female shamans within the culture, even if they may not be known to exist at the time of research? Is the shaman sought for all episodes of illness or are there other active agents who assume complementary healing roles, even if their status within the society is lower than the shaman's? What social, cultural and power dynamics are present when women are able or unable to become shamans? How does an ethnobotanist access women's knowledge, especially in a male-dominated shamanic ethnomedical tradition? Is a female ethnobotanist in a better position to access women's knowledge? Currently, our ability to address these questions and many other issues regarding women's therapeutic roles and knowledge in shamanic systems of healing is severely constrained. An avenue of research that holds promise for uncovering marginalized knowledge involves gaining a deeper understanding of the power–knowledge dynamics that are played out in the everyday life of a community.

Shamanism and power

According to Langdon, 'the key concept that links shamanic systems is power' (1992a: 13). In diagnosing illness, prescribing remedies and maintaining social harmony, the shaman has the power to enter into consultation with the spirits. The shaman may inhabit the spiritual and the physical worlds simultaneously. As a master mediator between the physical and the spiritual, the shaman possesses a far-reaching power and influence and may enter just about any sphere of social, political, cultural, religious/spiritual or economic life. With so much power invested in the shaman *persona*, it is not surprising that, in many patriarchal social structures, the term 'shaman' is reserved exclusively for men. The gender lines in healing are linked to power relations in social structures, as much in South American shamanism as in the health care systems of industrialized societies. Equating men's therapeutic roles with positive healing and women's with witchcraft is a phenomenon that was deeply rooted in Western medicine (Ehrenreich and English 1973). Another example is provided by the Toba in north-eastern Argentina, who have a special term for individuals who have the power to cause harm: they are thought to be mostly women, without a public *persona* (Wright 1992: 166). However, the gender lines in healing continue to shift in many cultures, albeit imperceptibly, as a consequence of constant negotiation and reproduction of power relations.

Women and the shamanic traditions

It is difficult to find an anthropological or ethnobotanical account involving a female shaman in South America, despite the fact that they are mentioned on rare occasions. Nor is there much literature on the role of women in shamanic traditions which, at least overtly, seem to be dominated by men. Yet, directly or indirectly, women do have specific roles to play in many shamanic traditions, as Pollock illustrates:

> The Culina Indians of western Brazil talk about shamanism as though it were an exclusively male institution.... Yet Culina shamanism requires the active participation of women.... While shamans are normatively men and are conceptually the critical

activators of ritual curing, the roles of women in shamanistic performance must also be underscored. (1992: 25, 34)

Not all shamanic traditions, however, allow women a key role. The Warao in Venezuela have woven women's inappropriateness to play the shaman's part into their mythology. The gods 'abhor the odor of menstrual blood', thus disqualifying all women of reproductive age (W. Wilbert 1987). In some societies that impose boundaries on women of reproductive age, post-menopausal women are able to enter the public arena, exercise influence and assume powerful roles such as that of a shaman (Brown and Kerns 1985).

The Siona, who live along the Putumayo river in the Amazon, believe that if women take large amounts of yagé regularly it will lead to sterility (Langdon 1992b). Siona shamans transport themselves into ecstasy by ingesting yagé, a hallucinogenic. It is worth noting that Siona women do consume yagé, and 'the one woman shaman remembered by the elders is said to have begun her career after she had raised a family'. Baer (1992: 53) also mentions that the occasional female shaman is reported to occur among the Matsigenka in the Peruvian Amazon. As shamans or otherwise, women's role in the shamanic séance is indispensable. According to Baer, during a séance the men drink ayahuasca. Although the women don't, 'they are vital to the séance because they sing with the shaman. In the Matsigenka's view, these ritual chants are of considerable help in inducing the appearance of the "visitor spirits"...' (pp. 86–7). The belief about the negative power of menstrual blood recurs among the Matsigenka, who claim that contact with it diminishes the shaman's power.

In Sibundoy shamanism in south-western Colombia, Ramírez de Jara and Castaño found that the 'Cultivation of magical and medicinal plants is a specialized knowledge and may be performed only by men. A garden should be fenced so that women cannot enter or touch the plants' (1992: 298). To conclude from this and similar accounts that the women have little knowledge of medicinal plants would be premature. Where circumstances place restrictions on women, they often have knowledge of other plants used medicinally, albeit (to circumvent culturally imposed taboos) outside the formal shamanic realm. If women are denied the shaman's office, what is their role when medicinal plant remedies are prepared? How are women involved in growing, gathering, selection, preparing or administering plants and remedies? What does this imply about their ethnobotanical knowledge?

While it is important to investigate the part that women play in shamanic traditions, it is even more fruitful to research possible alternatives or complementary responses to illness and cures practised in parallel. As mentioned before, literature on traditional health care systems tends to focus on 'expert' healers and 'exotic' cultural practices, with less regard for other popular healers. In many societies, the latter are mostly women, since the 'expert' role of shaman may be denied to them.

Women's healing outside the shamanistic domain

Ethnobotanists have rarely researched popular healing – that is, what people do to protect their health in their everyday lives (Kleinman 1980). In the process of gravitating towards the male 'expert', they contribute to rendering popular healers, who are very often women, invisible. Stereotypically, the existing literature on shamanism, be it popular or academic, tends to encourage the enthusiastic student, traveller or researcher to seek the male shaman in the Amazon as a storehouse of knowledge. The plant knowledge of female healers who, in many cases, are instrumental to the survival and well-being of their children and family members, may not be considered seriously. Are shamans consulted for all types of routine and extraordinary disorders, or is their expertise called upon selectively? Is there a herbal tradition to which many people relate, although in a strict sense it falls outside the shamanic tradition? Who takes care of family health needs on a regular basis, and what is their knowledge of medicinal plants?

These and other questions crop up once the focus of investigation is shifted from the shaman to other healers, but cannot be addressed satisfactorily given the shaman-centric nature of much anthropological and ethnobotanical literature. But the near absence of a discussion of women's knowledge and role in shamanistic studies is not evidence of their absence as healers. Even if women were to perform complementary functions or were equally able to mediate between the two worlds, would they be called 'shamans' or share their prestige? The Warao of Venezuela once again present a case in point.

Among Warao healers, there are three kinds of shamans, all of whom are exclusively male. Through many rituals they treat mainly spirit-related illnesses such as 'psychiatric disorders and exotic epidemic diseases' (W. Wilbert 1987). The actors in the Warao health care system also include herbalists known as *yarakota arotu*, to distinguish them from titles reserved for the three types of shamans. It is mainly women who practise non-ritualistic herbalism. Acculturation of women into herbalism starts early, continues into adulthood, and then into marriage. According to Wilbert, 'General herbalism is common knowledge among most Warao women and believed to be critical if children are to survive...' (*ibid.*: 1140).

Unlike the shamans, Warao female herbalists do not go through an initiation rite. However, they establish their status depending on whether community members outside the immediate family seek their expertise. While shamans may receive compensation and services from their clients, this was not observed for their female counterparts. The case of the Warao suggests that gender-sensitive ethnobotanical investigation entails, in part, exploring a society's macro relations of power and researching the alternate expressions of plant knowledge that exist in women's autonomous sphere of activity and influence (see references in Howard-Borjas 2002).

Towards a Power–Knowledge Framework

Reasons for the lack of attention to female healers and their herbal knowledge can be summarized as follows:

1 A preoccupation with 'expert' healers and much less emphasis on healing in the informal/popular domain (Morgan 1981; Kleinman 1980);

2 A disproportionately high interest in exotic practices and ritualistic healing;
3 Researchers and informants tend to be male;
4 Women's separate spheres of therapeutic activity may be less visible or accessible to the outsider and underplayed by the locals, including women;
5 Androcentrism, which refers to the male bias in epistemological inquiry and ethnographic accounts, that results in a tendency to neglect women's point of view.

In each case, the bias favours the exploration of men's knowledge and healing in men's sphere of activity. That women's domain of influence can be distinct from men's is not often taken into account. Even the exceptional case confirms gender bias: ethnobotanists systematically seek out women's knowledge only in that area where they expect to find it, in the realm of reproductive health. Thus, the knowledge of medicinal plants held by women in their roles as mothers, grandmothers and healers in everyday life is easily ignored or glossed over.

The fundamental problem is not one of reporting sex but of exploring gender. Recent theoretical contributions stress that 'gender' is not a discrete category (male and female), but rather a complex of shifting ideologies and identities (Rathberger 1990; Salick 1991). The description of male–female differences, perhaps a necessary component of gender research, is insufficient if the power webs that create these differences are not also explored.

Medical anthropologists have mostly employed two models to explain the intracultural distribution and acquisition of therapeutic knowledge. These are the 'status-centred' and 'interactionist' models (Browner 1991). The 'status-centred' (or role-centred)[6] model assumes that individual knowledge of medicinal plants or healing is acquired in the process of carrying out social roles. In the 'interactionist model', interpersonal interactions in everyday life are more important considerations than social roles in explaining the therapeutic knowledge of individuals. These models fall short when gender is conceptualized as a non-discrete category or as a changing complex of identities. Differential access to resources, for example, complicates the ways in which people relate to the environment. Gender roles are not merely an equal and arbitrary division of labour based upon biological differences but reflect relations of power within a multiplicity of identities, the household and the larger community. Neither the role-centred nor the interactionist models, taken by themselves or together, adequately explain the 'who knows what' and 'how' of therapeutic knowledge (Browner 1991). However, this does not mean that they have no utility as theoretical formulations. Rather, the assumption is that, unless research questions and explanations of findings are grounded in the power–knowledge framework, the understanding of intracultural differences in therapeutic knowledge will be insufficient.

Feminist scholarship consistently suggests that gender considerations in epistemological research inevitably involve framing the debate in terms of social relations of power. Therefore, to research gender issues in the differential distribution of therapeutic knowledge, a third power/knowledge-centred approach is necessary.

The question of 'who knows what' in any given society cannot be separated from micro- or macro-level power relations. In order to understand intracultural variations in knowledge, it is imperative to explore concomitantly the power–knowledge web of relations. Power is at times delegated according to the knowledge that some people hold. Conversely, one who is powerful is able to acquire more knowledge and tap into more resources. Furthermore, the power or status ascribed to an individual's knowledge is related to a society's internal value system, which is not necessarily shared by an outsider. Thus, the social definition of healers and their knowledge in any given society may at times tell us more about the power structure of the society than about the knowledge itself. This implies that it is important to explore the distribution of therapeutic knowledge at both the centre and the periphery of the local health care system. Few medical ethnobotanical studies have ventured into the power politics of therapeutic knowledge (Browner 1991 and Laderman 1981 are exceptions). This is one reason why women's thera-peutic knowledge and roles have remained relatively unexplored and hidden from the outsider.

The La Esperanza project in Ecuador demonstrated the feasibility of adopting an unconventional approach to ethnobotanical research wherein the local people participated as researchers and benefited by having investigated their own knowledge for themselves. A well-represented group of both female and male participants enabled women's knowledge and healing to become visible, despite the fact that gender issues were not explored directly. Participatory ethnobotanical research that is sensitive to power relationships between the researcher and the researched, as well as among the researched, provides a promising approach. It will remain underutilized as long as the outsider assumes, erroneously, that local people are incapable of collaborating other than as informants.

Finally, to revisit a central argument, the ethnobotanist cannot ignore the fact that women are frequently neither the 'experts' nor the ones whose knowledge is rewarded with high social status, despite the indispensability of their informal healing role. It is thus critical to investigate women's autonomous yet related spheres of healing, knowledge, influence and authority, without necessarily having to compare and contrast their roles with men's. Power often separates everyday 'lay' ethnomedicine from 'expert' ethnomedicine. Hence, a scholarly pursuit needs to understand both, independently and interactively. A full exploration of the plant kingdom needs to disclose the invisible queen.

Notes

1 Unlike in ethnobotany, in agricultural research the gendered nature of knowledge and farm activity is increasingly recognized and investigated (see, for example, Ferguson 1994; Mosse 1994).

2 See, for example, Finerman 1984, 1987, 1989; Cosminsky 1987; McKee 1987; Browner 1989.

3 Expertise is often associated with women's roles as herbalists or midwives. This does not easily translate into 'expert' status for women (but compare Dick Bissonnette, this volume).

4 Werner Wilbert should not be confused with Johannes Wilbert.
5 For a small sample, refer to Taussig 1987; Langdon and Baer 1992; J. Wilbert 1987, 1993.
6 'Role-centred' is a preferred label since 'status' implies a power dimension that is not always present in this model.

References

Alcorn, J. B. (1984) *Huastec Mayan Ethnobotany*, Austin: University of Texas Press.

Baer, G. (1992) 'The one intoxicated by tobacco: Matsigenka shamanism', in E. J. Langdon and G. Baer (eds.), *Portals of Power: Shamanism in South America*, Albuquerque: University of New Mexico Press, pp. 79–100.

Bourdy, G., and A. Walter (1992) 'Maternity and medicinal plants in Vanuatu: the cycle of reproduction', *Journal of Ethnopharmacology*, Vol. 37, No. 3, pp. 179–96.

Brown, J. K. and V. Kerns (eds.) (1985) *In Her Prime: a View of Middle-Aged Women*, Boston: Bergin and Garvey Publishers.

Browner, C. H. (1985) 'Plants used for reproductive health in Oaxaca, Mexico', *Economic Botany*, Vol. 39, No. 4, pp. 82ff.

Browner, C. H. (1989) 'Women, household and health in Latin America', *Social Science and Medicine*, Vol. 28, No. 5, pp. 461–73.

Browner, C. H. (1991) 'Gender politics in the distribution of therapeutic herbal knowledge', *Medical Anthropology Quarterly*, Vol. 5, No. 2, pp. 99–132.

Browner, C. H. and O. B. de Montellano (1986) 'Herbal emmenagogues used by women in Colombia and Mexico', in N. L. Etkin (ed.), *Plants in Indigenous Medicine and Diet: Biobehavioral Approaches*, New York: Gordon and Breach (Redgrave), pp. 32–47.

Browner, C. H. and S. T. Perdue (1988) 'Women's secrets: bases for reproductive and social autonomy in a Mexican community', *American Ethnologist*, Vol. 15, No. 1, pp. 84–97.

Cosminsky, S. (1987) 'Women and health care on a Guatemalan plantation', *Social Science and Medicine*, Vol. 25, No. 10, pp. 1163–73.

Cox, P. A. (1991) 'Polynesian herbal medicine', in P. A. Cox (ed.), *Islands, Plants, and Polynesians*, Portland: Dioscorides Press, pp. 147–68.

Croom, E. M. Jr (1983) 'Documenting and evaluating herbal remedies', *Economic Botany*, Vol. 37, No. 1, pp. 13–27.

Ehrenreich, B. and D. English (1973) *Witches, Midwives and Nurses*, Old Westbury, New York: The Feminist Press.

Emmerich, M. and de Senna Valle (1991) 'Estudios de etnobotânica no parque indígena do Xingu', *Bradea*, Vol. 6, No. 2, pp. 13–20.

Etkin, N. L. (1993) 'Anthropological methods in ethnopharmacology', *Journal of Ethno-pharmacology*, Vol. 38, pp. 93–104.

Ferguson, A. E. (1994) 'Gendered science: a critique of agricultural development', *American Anthropologist*, Vol. 96, pp. 540–52.

Finerman, R. D. (1984) 'A matter of life and death: health care change in an Andean community', *Social Science and Medicine*, Vol. 18, No. 4, pp. 329–34.

Finerman, R. D. (1987) 'Inside out: women's world view and family health in an Ecuadorian Indian community', *Social Science and Medicine*, Vol. 25, No. 10, pp. 1157–62.

Finerman, R. D. (1989) 'The forgotten healers: women as family healers in an Andean Indian community', in C. S. Shepherd McClain (ed.), *Women as Healers: Cross-Cultural Perspectives*, New Brunswick and London: Rutgers University Press, pp. 24–41.

Ford, R. I. (ed.) (1978) *The Nature and Status of Ethnobotany*, Ann Arbor: Anthropological Papers No. 67, Museum of Anthropology, University of Michigan.

FSI (Fundación Sabiduría Indígena) and B. Kothari (1997) 'Rights to the benefits of research: compensating indigenous peoples for their intellectual contribution', *Human Organization*, Vol. 56, No. 2, pp. 1–10.

Harshberger, J. W. (1896) 'Purposes of ethnobotany', *Botanical Gazette*, Vol. 21, pp. 146–54.

Harvey, Y. K. (1979) *Six Korean Women: the Socialization of Shamans*, St Paul: West Publishing Co.

Howard-Borjas, P., with W. Cuijpers (2002) 'Gender and the management and conservation of plant biodiversity', in H. W. Doelle and E. Da Silva (eds.), *Biotechnology*, in *Encyclopedia of Life Support Systems (EOLSS)*, Oxford, UK, http://www.eolss.net

Jackson, C. (1993) 'Doing what comes naturally? Women and environment in development', *World Development*, Vol. 21, No. 12, pp. 1947–63.

Kainer, K. A. and M. L. Duryea (1992) 'Tapping women's knowledge: plant resource use in extractive reserves, Acre, Brazil', *Economic Botany*, Vol. 46, No. 4, pp. 408–25.

Kendall, L. (1985) *Shamans, Housewives and Other Restless Spirits*, Honolulu: University of Hawaii Press.

Kleinman, A. (1980) *Patients and Healers in the Context of Culture*, Berkeley: University of California Press.

Kothari, B. (1996) 'Towards a Praxis of Oppressed Local Knowledges: Participatory Ethnobotanical Research in Indigenous Communities of Ecuador', PhD dissertation, Cornell University, Ann Arbor, Michigan: University Microfilms International.

Kothari, B., and UNOCIAE-C (1993) *Ñucanchic Panpa Janpicuna: Plantas Medicinales del Campo*, Quito: Ediciones Abya-Yala.

Laderman, C. (1981) 'The politics of healing in Malaysia', in *Women and Politics in Twentieth-Century Africa and Asia*, Studies in Third World Societies, No. 16, pp. 143–58.

Langdon, E. J. (1992a) 'Introduction: shamanism and anthropology', in E. J. Langdon and G. Baer (eds.), *Portals of Power: Shamanism in South America*, Albuquerque: University of New Mexico Press, pp. 1–21.

Langdon, E. J. (1992b) 'Dau: shamanic power in Siona religion', in E. J. Langdon and G. Baer (eds.), *Portals of Power: Shamanism in South America*, Albuquerque: University of New Mexico Press, pp. 41–61.

Langdon, E. J. and G. Baer (eds.) (1992) *Portals of Power: Shamanism in South America*, Albuquerque: University of New Mexico Press.

Lewis, W. H. and M. Elvin-Lewis (1990) 'Obstetrical use of the parasitic fungus *Balansia cyperi* by Amazonian Jívaro women', *Economic Botany*, Vol. 44, pp. 131–3.

McClain, C. S. S. (ed.) (1989), *Women as Healers: Cross-Cultural Perspectives*, New Brunswick and London: Rutgers University Press.

McKee, L. (1987) 'Ethnomedical treatment of children's diarrhoeal illnesses in the highlands of Ecuador', *Social Science and Medicine*, Vol. 25, No. 10, pp. 1147–55.

Moore, H. L. (1988) *Feminism and Anthropology*, Minneapolis: University of Minnesota Press.

Morgan, W. T. W. (1981) 'Ethnobotany of the Turkana: use of plants by a pastoral people and their livestock in Kenya', *Economic Botany*, Vol. 35, No. 1, pp. 96–130.

Morgen, S. (1989) 'Gender and anthropology: introductory essay', in S. Morgen (ed.), *Gender and Anthropology: Critical Reviews for Research and Teaching*, Washington, DC: American Anthropological Association, pp. 1–20.

Mosse, D. (1994) 'Authority, gender and knowledge: theoretical reflections on the practice of participatory rural appraisal', *Agriculture and Human Values*, Vol. 25, pp. 497–526.

Nath, D., N. Sethi, R. K. Singh and A. K. Jain (1992) 'Commonly used Indian abortifacient plants with special reference to their teratologic effects in rats', *Journal of Ethnopharmacology*, Vol. 36, No. 2, pp. 147–54.

Ortner, S. B. and H. Whitehead (eds.) (1981) *Sexual Meanings, the Cultural Construction of Gender*, Cambridge: Cambridge University Press.

Plotkin, M. J. (1993) *Tales of a Shaman's Apprentice*, New York: Viking.

Pollock, D. (1992) 'Culina shamanism: gender, power, and knowledge', in E. J. Langdon and G. Baer (eds.), *Portals of Power: Shamanism in South America*, Albuquerque: University of New Mexico Press, pp. 25–40.

Prance, G. T. (1991) 'What is ethnobotany today?', *Journal of Ethnopharmacology*, Vol. 32, pp. 209–16.

Ramírez de Jara, M. Clemencia and C. E. Castaño (1992) 'Sibundoy shamanism and popular culture in Colombia', in E. J. Langdon and G. Baer (eds.), *Portals of Power: Shamanism in South America,* Albuquerque: University of New Mexico Press, pp. 287–303.

Rathberger, E. M. (1990) 'WID, WAD, GAD: trends in research and practice', *Journal of Developing Areas,* Vol. 24, No. 7, pp. 489–502.

Ruganga, A., M. Pitts and J. McMaster (1992) 'The use of herbal and other agents to enhance sexual experience', *Social Science and Medicine,* Vol. 35, No. 8, pp. 1037–42.

Salick, J. (1991) 'Subsistence and the single woman among the Amuesha of the upper Amazon, Peru', *Society and Natural Resources,* Vol. 5, pp. 37–51.

South, G. R. (1993) 'Edible seaweeds of Fiji: an ethnobotanical study', *Botanica Marina,* Vol. 36, pp. 335–49.

Stacey, J. and B. Thorne (1985) 'The missing revolution in sociology', *Social Problems,* Vol. 32, No. 4, pp. 301–16.

Taussig, M. (1987) *Shamanism, Colonialism, and the Wild Man,* Chicago: University of Chicago Press.

Valencia, D. (1989) 'Fertility plants used by Kurripako Indians', *Journal of Ethnobiology,* Vol. 9, No. 2, pp. 253.

Veale, D. J., K. I. Furman and D. W. Oliver (1992) 'South African traditional herbal medicines used during pregnancy and childbirth', *Journal of Ethnopharmacology,* Vol. 36, No. 3, pp. 185–91.

Wilbert, J. (1972) 'Tobacco and shamanistic ecstasy among the Warao Indians of Venezuela', in P. T. Furst (ed.), *Flesh of the Gods: the Ritual Use of Hallucinogens,* New York: Praeger, pp. 55–83.

Wilbert, J. (1987) *Tobacco and Shamanism in South America,* New Haven: Yale University Press.

Wilbert, J. (1993) *Mystic Endowment,* Cambridge: Harvard University Press.

Wilbert, W. (1987) 'The pneumatic theory of female Warao herbalists', *Social Science and Medicine,* Vol. 25, No. 10, pp. 1139–46.

Wright, P. G. (1992) 'Dream, shamanism, and power among the Toba of Formosa province', in E. J. Langdon and G. Baer (eds.), *Portals of Power: Shamanism in South America,* Albuquerque: University of New Mexico Press, pp. 149–72.

CHAPTER 9
The Gender of Crops in the Papua New Guinea Highlands

Paul Sillitoe

An intriguing aspect of crop cultivation among the Wola highlanders of Papua New Guinea is their division of these plants into male and female categories. For them, there are some crops that only men may plant and tend, others that only women can cultivate, and a third category that members of either sex may cultivate.

This gender division of crops is found in other Highland New Guinea societies too; it occurs, for instance, among the Melpa (Powell *et al.* 1975: 14), the Maring (Rappaport 1968: 43; Clarke 1971: 124), the Kapauku (Pospisil 1963: 146) and the Enga (Waddell 1972: 51). It is noteworthy that these people tend to put the same crops into their male and female categories: sugar cane, bananas and yams are male, while sweet potato, cucurbits and certain greens are female. The pattern is not entirely consistent, however. Sometimes the same crop is classified as male by some and as female by others; for example, taro is a male crop for the Melpa but a female one for the Kapauku.

Why do the Wola, and, by extension, other people throughout the Highlands of New Guinea, categorize their crops in this way? When asked this question the Wola themselves are unable to give an answer. They simply say that this is the way their ancestors did things and so tradition dictates that they should do it. This kind of reply is all too familiar to anthropologists. Is it possible for us to go further and suggest a deeper explanation?

The Wola and Their Crops

The Wola people live in the rugged and remote Southern Highlands of Papua New Guinea. Their houses are scattered along the mountain valleys that they occupy, men living separately from women. This residential separation is another way the Wola discriminate between the sexes (Sillitoe 1979a).

In the vicinity of homesteads it is usual to see numbers of pigs, which are highly valued and reared by women. These, along with other things like pearl shells, cosmetic oil and crude salt, constitute the wealth these people hand to one another in the ceremonial exchanges that characterize all their important social events.

Table 9.1: Crops Cultivated by the Wola

Common name	Botanical ID	Wola name
Acanth greens	*Rungia klossii*	shombay
Acanth greens	*Dicliptera* sp.	omok
Amaranth greens	*Amaranthus caudatus*	mbolin komb
Amaranth greens	*Amaranthus cruentus*	paluw
Amaranth greens	*Amaranthus tricolor*	komb
Bamboo	*Nastus elatus*	taembok
Bananas	*Musa hort.* Var.	diyr
Beans: common	*Phaseolus vulgaris*	taeshaen pebway
Beans: hyacinth	*Lablab niger*	sokol
Beans: winged	*Psophocarpus tetragonolobus*	wolapat
Cabbage	*Brassica oleracea*	cobaj
Chinese cabbage	*Brassica chinensis*	kwa
Climbing cucurbit	*Trichosanthes* sp.	tat
Crucifer greens	*Rorippa* sp.	taguwt
Cucumber	*Cucumis sativus*	laek
Dye plant	*Coleus* sp.	komnol
Fig	*Ficus wassa*	poiz
Ginger	*Zingiber officinale*	shombiy
Gourd	*Lagenaria siceraria*	senem
Hibiscus greens	*Hibiscus manihot*	huwshiy
Highland breadfruit	*Ficus dammaropsis*	shuwat
Highland pitpit	*Setaria palmifolia*	kot
Irish potato	*Solanum tuberosum*	aspus
Kudzu	*Pueraria lobata*	horon
Maize	*Zea mays*	kwaliyl
Onion	*Allium cepa*	enyun
Palm lily	*Cordyline fruticosa*	aegop
Paper mulberry	*Broussonetia papyrifera*	korael
Parsley	*Oenanthe javanica*	taziy
Passion fruit	*Passiflora edulis*	ya iyl
Pea	*Pisum sativum*	mbin
Pumpkin	*Cucurbita maxima*	pompkin
Screw-pine	*Pandanus conoideus*	wabel
Screw-pine	*Pandanus brosimos*	aenk
Sedge	*Eleocharis cf. dubia*	hurinj
She-oak	*Casuarina oligodon*	naep
Spiderwort	*Commelina diffusa*	hombiyhaem
Sugar cane	*Saccharum officinarum*	wol
Sweet potato	*Ipomoea batata*	hokay
Tannia	*Xanthosoma sagittifolium*	mbolin ma
Taro	*Colocasia esculenta*	ma
Tobacco	*Nicotiana tabacum*	miyt
Tomato	*Lycopersicon esculentum*	tomasow
Watercress	*Nasturtium officinale*	kuwmba
Yam	*Dioscorea alata*	bet

These social transactions, which mark such occasions as marriages and funerals, are vital to the orderly continuance of Wola society.

An important Wola ethic is that individuals should be free to govern their own actions, but a society cannot allow free rein to this principle without ceasing to exist in the ensuing anarchy and chaos. Ceremonial exchange is vital, and the Wola accord high status to those who excel at it because, without infringing directly upon the apparent autonomy of the individual, it serves an important integrative role within their loosely organized society, binding men together in a way which promotes social cooperation (Sillitoe 1979b). There is, as this chapter argues, an intriguing connection between this and the Wola gender classification of crops.

The Wola are subsistence gardeners practising shifting cultivation. Men do the initial heavy agricultural work of clearing and fencing the areas that their families intend to cultivate. Then both sexes burn the resulting dry vegetation. The women do most of the routine garden work; preparing the soil, tending the garden and harvesting the greater part of the food grown. The staple crop is the sweet potato. It is supplemented with pumpkins, taro, bananas, several varieties of greens and a number of other vegetables (see Table 9.1).

The Gender of Crops

When classifying these plants the Wola distinguish between those which are unambiguously male or female, those which are more male than female or more female than male, and those which members of both sexes are equally entitled to plant and tend. The result is the following classificatory continuum:

MALE	MAINLY	BOTH	MAINLY	FEMALE
ONLY	MALE	SEXES	FEMALE	ONLY

Table 9.2 lists the crops grown by the Wola according to these five categories. What is the nature of this categorization for the Wola? For them, it is very wrong for a member of one sex to meddle with the crops that are the sole domain of the other. If a man, for example, found his wife cutting down his bananas or sugar cane, he would be angry and chastise her, and arguments arising over such transgressions can lead to losses of temper and beatings. So for a woman there is the threat of a physical sanction if she breaks the rules, whereas for a man there is not. Hence, for women, observance of the rules is in a different spirit to that of men; for example, a woman considers it smart if she can sneak a length of sugar cane out of the centre of a clump without her husband finding out. But she will not replant the top of such a filched cane (or indeed ever plant any all-male crop) which would advertise her behaviour; instead she will throw it away and so destroy the evidence. It is different if she is in the company of a man who authorizes her to cut down some sugar cane or bananas for them to share,[1] but the man, never the

Table 9.2 Gender Categories of Wola Crops

Male only	Mainly male	Both sexes	Mainly female	Female only
Amaranth greens (*komb*)	Amaranth greens (*paluw*)	Acanth greens (*omok*)	Cucumbers	Acanth greens (*shombay*)
Bamboo	Climbing cucurbit	Beans	Irish potatoes	Dye plant
Bananas	Tobacco	Cabbages	Onions	Highland *pitpit*
Chinese cabbage		Gourds	Parsley	Sedge
Crucifer greens		Maize	Pumpkin	Spiderwort
Fig trees		Passion fruit		Sweet potatoes
Ginger		Peas		
Hibiscus greens		Tannia		
Highland breadfruit		Taro		
Kudzu		Tomatoes		
Palm lily				
Paper mulberry trees				
Screw-pines				
She-oak trees				
Sugar cane				
Watercress				
Yams				

woman, will do any necessary replanting. Planting is thus a significant criterion in the marking of male from female crops.

Similarly, men may harvest all-female crops, and they may do so both without a female present and without her permission. For men there is no fear of a physical sanction. It is their dignity and the fear of ridicule that prompts them to observe the rules. A man may, for instance, harvest some sweet potatoes or highland *pitpit* for himself at any time, and indeed, if he is monogamously married and has no daughter old enough, nor any other female relative in his household to fill the breach, then he will do so for a few days each month during his wife's menses – a time when contact with a woman is considered polluting for a man and he cannot accept food from her (Sillitoe 1979a). But a man will usually only harvest small amounts of such crops for his own consumption; he will not bring back a load to feed his family and pigs (except in emergencies – if his wife is too ill to do so, for example, when he will receive sympathy, not ridicule, from others). However, he will never plant these crops, just as a woman will not plant those which are in the male domain. If a man did plant them, his position would be ridiculous and others would laugh at him.

The attitude of people living in some settlements on the Was river towards a man called Saemom, whose predicament they think was hilarious, illustrates clearly Wola feelings about men handling women's crops:

> In a garden which his wife Yaelten had recently planted, Saemom marked out an area from which he alone would harvest sweet potato during her periods of menstruation (a quite common practice). One day he found Yaelten digging tubers from his area and flew into a rage. He pulled up a fence stake and beat her with it, one of his blows catching

her on the neck and killing her. This murder cost Saemom and his relatives a considerable amount of wealth in compensation exchanges with Yaelten's relatives and, as a result, no one was willing to contribute to another bridewealth so that he could remarry. As a man of only average ability in manipulating wealth in ceremonial exchanges, Saemom was unable to muster a bridewealth on his own and so remained a widower until he died. The irony of the situation, and for the Wola the perversely funny side of it, was that he had killed his wife for digging tubers on his patch and as a result he had to plant his own sweet potato from then on. He had no sister to help him and his only daughter was about five years old at the time of the murder. Other female relatives (such as his elder brother's wife and daughter) helped him out, but still he had to do a considerable amount of planting himself until his daughter was old enough to take over responsibility for it. He died some twelve or so years later. This ignominious episode is remembered for Saemom having to get down on his knees and heap up sweet potato mounds. This was ridiculous.

The moral is that members of the excluded sex should never plant those crops associated exclusively with the other sex. Those crops, on the other hand, may on the odd occasion be planted by members of the excluded sex without fear of ridicule and loss of face. But such occasions are rare, the predominant sex doing nearly all the planting and harvesting. Finally, those crops which fall in the middle of the continuum are subject to no restrictions; all are free to plant them. These observations raise the following questions: what is it that qualifies any crop for inclusion in a certain category? And what is the point of this, anyway?

'To Be' a Crop

When talking about their crops, the Wola distinguish between them by using two forms of the verb 'to be'. There is a connection between this and the sexual categorization of these plants that gives significant clues to understanding the nature of these gender distinctions.

The Wola language has two verbs that can be equated approximately with the English verb 'to be'. They are *wiy* and *hae*. The word *wiy* is used for things in a recumbent state, horizontal to the ground, whereas the word *hae* is used for things in an erect state, vertical to the ground. So, for example, when talking about a raincape the Wola say *saebort wiy* (raincape is), whereas when talking about a tree they say *iysh hae* (tree is). A human being too is *ol* (or *ten*) *hae* (man [or woman] is). However, while both men and women are *hae,* this verb carries more male connotations than the *wiy* verb, which has more female ones. The Wola themselves explicitly make this equation (as do the Enga, see Brennan 1977: 13–18).[2] Things that stand erect are strong and masculine for them, whereas recumbent things are weaker and female.[3] From a male point of view, strength and erectness imply importance, such that important things are *hae*. For example, the two most important valuables of the Wola are *hae,* pigs being clearly erect but pearl shells less clearly so, although men prop them up in a vertical plane in ceremonial exchanges, and do not lay them on the ground.

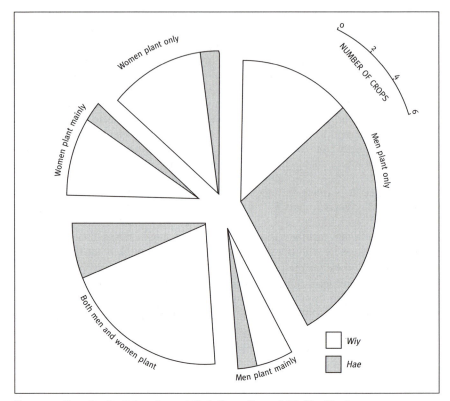

Figure 9.1: Crop Gender Categories and Their Proportions of *Wiy/Hae* Plants

Are female crops *wiy* and male crops *hae*? It is reasonable to ask whether there is such a correlation relating gender to the physical character of the plants concerned, with those standing erect as male and those lying recumbent as female. Table 9.3 lists the crops cultivated by the Wola and indicates their *wiy* or *hae* status and the sex of those who plant them. It reveals some correlation, which Figure 9.1 shows more clearly. Men do plant considerably more *hae* crops than *wiy* ones, and women the reverse. In the middle range, that is those crops that both sexes may plant, *wiy* predominates, and this fits in with the pattern that is developing because, although either sex may plant these crops in theory, it is women who do most of the planting in practice.

Although the *wiy* and *hae* status of crops correlates with their gender category, there are exceptions to this pattern that demand explanation. To discriminate simply between plants as either erect or recumbent appears somewhat gross. A refinement of the features used to divide the plants into categories may explain the anomalies in Figure 9.1. For instance, where do short erect plants fit in, which because they remain near to the earth are recumbent-like, and what about climbing ones which, without something to climb up, would become trailing and so pass

Table 9.3: Gender Categories of Crops Compared with Their *Wiy/Hae* Status

Common name	Wola name	*Wiy*	*Hae*	Men only	Men mainly	Women only	Women mainly	Both sexes
Acanth greens	omok	*						*
Acanth greens	shombay	*				*		
Amaranth greens	komb	*		*				
Amaranth greens	mbolin komb	*				*		
Amaranth greens	paluw	*			*			
Bamboo	taembok		*	*				
Banana	diyr		*	*				
Beans: common	taeshaen pebway	*					*	
Beans: hyacinth	sokol	*						*
Beans: winged	wolapat	*						*
Cabbage	cobaj	*						*
Chinese cabbage	Kwa	*		*				
Climbing cucurbit	tat		*		*			
Crucifer greens	taguwt	*		*				
Cucumber	laek	*					*	
Dye plant	komnol	*				*		
Fig	poiz		*	*				
Ginger	shombiy		*	*				
Gourd	senem	*						*
Hibiscus greens	huwshiy	*		*				
Highland breadfruit	shuwat		*	*				
Highland *pitpit*	kot	*				*		
Irish potato	aspus		*				*	
Kudzu	horon		*	*				
Maize	kwaliyl	*						*
Onion	enyun	*					*	
Palm lily	aegop		*	*				
Paper mulberry	korael		*	*				
Parsley (dropwort)	taziy	*					*	
Passion fruit	ya iyl		*					*
Pea	mbin	*						*
Pumpkin	pompkin	*					*	
Screw-pine	aenk		*	*				
Screw-pine	wabel		*	*				
Sedge	hurinj	*				*		
She-oak	naep		*	*				
Spiderwort	hombiyhaem	*				*		
Sugar cane	wol		*	*				
Sweet potato	hokay		*			*		
Tannia	mbolin ma		*					*
Taro	ma		*					*
Tobacco	miyt	*			*			
Tomato	tomasow	*						*
Watercress	kuwmba	*		*				
Yam	bet		*	*				

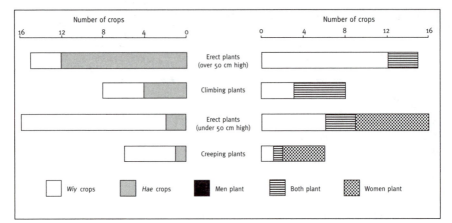

Figure 9.2: The *Wiy/Hae* Status of Crops Compared with Their Physical Appearance and the Sex of Those Who Plant Them

from erect to recumbent? Perhaps all those plants that are ambiguous in terms of their erectness or recumbency fall into the middle category, which either sex may plant. Figure 9.2 compares the *wiy/hae* status of crops with the sex of those who plant them and discriminates between plants as either erect and over 50 centimetres high, or climbing, or erect and under 50 centimetres high, or creeping.

Erect plants over 50 centimetres high may be taken as those that ought to be unequivocally *hae* and so quintessentially male, while those that are creeping ought to be unambiguously *wiy* and female. Those plants that are climbing or short and erect fall midway between these and so are not clearly *wiy* or *hae*, male or female. Figure 9.2 demonstrates a correlation along these lines, such that men plant considerably more erect plants over 50 centimetres high and climbing ones, while women only plant creeping plants and erect ones under 50 centimetres high. Similarly, significantly more climbing plants and erect ones over 50 centimetres high are *hae*, while significantly more of the creepers and erect plants under 50 centimetres high are *wiy*. Although Figure 9.2 demonstrates a more conclusive correlation than Figure 9.1 between the *wiy/hae* ascription of a crop, the sex of those who plant it, and the physical appearance of the plant in question, it nevertheless still has some aberrations from the general pattern which require explanation.

Gender Confusions

One possible source of confusion is that a number of new crops have arrived in the Wola area since European penetration of the Highlands of Papua New Guinea. Perhaps this influx of several new crops over a short period has confused the Wola into misclassifying some of them. This is feasible because they are not consciously aware of a direct correlation between the gender ascribed to a crop and its *wiy/hae* status; their classification depends upon some intuitive recognition of the apparent

Table 9.4: Gender and *Wiy/Hae* Status of Crops Compared with Their Physical Appearance and Antiquity

	Hae		Wiy		Men plant		Both plant		Women plant	
Indigenous / Introduced	IND	INT	IND	INT	IND	INT	IND	INT	IND	INT
Erect plants (over 50 cm high)	11	1	2 Hibiscus Tobacco	1 Maize	12		1 Taro	2 Tannia Maize		
Climbing plants	3	1	2 Hyacinth beans Winged beans	2 Common beans Peas	3		2 Hyacinth beans Winged beans	3 Passion fruit Common beans Peas		
Erect plants (under 50 cm high)	1 Ginger	1 Irish potato	8	6	3	3	1	2	5	2
Creeping plants	1 Sweet potato		3	2		1 Water-cress	1 Gourd		3	1

connections.[4] So, is there any evidence that the ambiguities in the previous figures have resulted from the misplacing of recently introduced crops? Table 9.4 compares the above four plant categories, their *wiy/hae* association, and the sex of those who plant them, with their status as either indigenous or introduced. This comparison indicates that, although a few of the recently introduced crops are misplaced according to the classificatory criteria suggested above, an almost equal number of the indigenous ones are also misplaced. What, then, are the reasons for these misplacements?

In an attempt to answer this question, Table 9.4, like Figure 9.2, is arranged with the plants that are most clearly of *hae* status, and therefore male, at the top, and those of unambiguous *wiy* status, and therefore female, at the bottom. The climbing plants, although more male than female, are less clearly *hae* than the self-standing and high erect ones, while the short erect plants represent the zone of transition from male to female crops (being almost equally represented on either side). The apparently misplaced plants are also identified in Table 9.4.

As shown in the table's top row, there are three of the high, erect male plants in the *wiy* class, not the expected *hae* one. Two of these are indigenous and one introduced. Both of the indigenous ones, hibiscus and tobacco, are among the shortest in this erect category and so fall near the border with the erect plants under 50 centimetres high which, with two exceptions, the Wola classify as *wiy*.

Hence the *wiy*-ness of hibiscus and tobacco. However, men plant both, which accords with the category in which they occur. Both sexes, on the other hand, plant maize, the introduced tall and erect plant of *wiy* status. A possible explanation for the designation of this crop as *wiy* is its propagation from large seeds that, in size and dibble-method of planting, are similar to those of the pulses and the gourd – crops also planted by both sexes. Furthermore, as discussed below, seeds have an intrinsically female character.

The other two plants in the erect, over 50 centimetres high category which both sexes plant, and not men only, are taro and tannia. The former is indigenous and the latter introduced, which explains why tannia occurs here. Similar to taro in many respects, it was classified with it as a *hae* crop planted by both sexes. The question remains: why was taro so classified in the first place? On currently available evidence it is reasonable to assume that, prior to the arrival of the sweet potato, taro was the staple of the Highlanders' ancestors (Bulmer and Bulmer 1964; Powell *et al.* 1975: 50; Yen and Wheeler 1968). That both sexes may plant the crop nowadays could be a throwback to bygone days, a legacy from the past which does not tally with the rationale of the current classificatory system and which has never been 'updated'.

In the climbing crop category (the second row on Table 9.4), it is the pulses that are apparently misplaced as *wiy* crops planted by both men and women. As pointed out, however, nearly all seed-propagated crops like beans are *wiy*.[5] Table 9.5 shows this by comparing the way in which crops are propagated with their *wiy/hae* status and the sex of those who plant them. This indicates why the pulses are *wiy* and planted by both sexes. The two exceptions shown in Table 9.5 of *hae* status seed-propagated crops are the passion fruit and climbing cucurbit. The former, as Table 9.4 shows, may be planted by either sex, while mainly men plant the latter. Both climb up trees and so are noticeably erect. The climbing cucurbit is further unusual in that it is propagated generally by transplanting a seedling found growing wild, not from a seed – and, as Table 9.5 shows, all seedling-planted crops are unambiguously *hae* and male; hence the sometimes seed-propagated cucurbit's *hae* status.

Table 9.5: Propagation of Plants Compared with Their Gender and *Wiy/Hae* Status

Method of propagation	Hae	Wiy	Men plant	Both plant	Women plant
Cutting	11	9	11	3	6
Seed	2	15	7	8	2
Seedling	6		6		
Lateral shoot	2	3	2	1	2
Budded rootstock	2	1	1		2

The question raised by the pulses, though, and the propagation data in general, is why are seed crops *wiy*, while neither sex predominates in their planting? This may have something to do with the intrinsic *wiy* nature of a seed as something laid

Table 9.6: Parts of Plants Eaten Compared with Their Gender and *Wiy/Hae* Status

Parts of plant eaten	Hae	Wiy	Men plant	Both plant	Women plant
Leaves	2	14	9	2	5
Fruits	6	4	5	3	2
Seeds		5		5	
Tubers	7		3	2	2
Stems	1	1	1		1
Shoots	2		2		

down in a hole and not erect in any sense, which contrasts with the intrinsic erectness of a seedling. Table 9.6 supports this suggestion. Its comparison of the parts of plants eaten with their *wiy/hae* status and the sex of the planter shows that all seed-bearing crops are *wiy* too.

This correlation and the previous one indicate that it is not only the physical appearance of a plant, its erectness or recumbency, which determines its classification. The nature of the food it yields and the parts planted also play a role. Using several such crosscutting criteria, which occasionally conflict, sometimes results in anomalous assignments when considered from the viewpoint of a single criterion. The pulse crops illustrate this. As climbers, they stand erect. But without supports they would be creepers, the epitome of recumbent plants, and this resemblance, together with the fact that they are seed-propagated and seed-producing plants, makes them, on balance, *wiy*. The crop categorization of the Wola is therefore a more complex process than initially supposed, in which a number of factors, some of them possibly conflicting between categories, are simultaneously weighed one against another.

The *wiy/hae* status of erect plants under 50 centimetres high and the planting rules covering them (recorded in the third row of Table 9.4) illustrate further how these sometimes conflicting factors are combined. The proportion of indigenous to introduced crops in each category is almost equal, as it was in the previous row of climbing plants too. Also, men and women plant these crops in almost equal proportions; they span the boundary between male and female crops (or conversely, they are the boundary, where a grey and blurred transition occurs based on the ambiguous and conflicting features of the plants). Nevertheless, all but two of these crops are *wiy*, so on balance they are more female than male. Considering the two *hae* crops, it is understandable that the introduced Irish potato was equated with the sweet potato, which is a *hae* plant, although there was more compulsion behind this equivalence than mere likeness. All tuber-producing plants are *hae*, as Table 9.6 shows, which accounts too for the otherwise anomalous *hae* status of the ginger plant, the rhizomes of which are also eaten.

Why are all the tuber-bearing crops *hae*? One of the anomalous crops on the final line of Table 9.4, which details the creeping plants, offers a clue. Creeping plants epitomize the recumbent *wiy* state and are the female crops *par excellence*. Yet the one tuber-producing crop which has creeping foliage is *hae*. This is the sweet potato, the staple of the Wola diet.

This apparent misplacement of sweet potato as a *hae* crop cannot be explained on the grounds that it is a recent introduction with confused characteristics, some of which link it with other *hae* crops. Sweet potato is, for those Wola now living, an indigenous crop which they have always grown.[6] Its categorization is not confused, either by the recent sudden influx of many new crops, or by anything else. It is part of the system and no slip.

The designation of an unambiguously female and creeping crop like sweet potato as an erect *hae* one is in direct contradiction of the classificatory system. It is blatantly wrong, and as such it serves (as do many such inversions) to emphasize and point out sweet potato. It is arguable that the great importance of this crop as the staple of the Wola diet is signalled by its anomalous *hae* status. It is so important that it must be *hae,* and this patently inverted use of the *hae* concept serves to underline its importance. Before sweet potato, the staple of the Wola ancestors was taro. This is, and presumably was, *hae,* and logically the new staple is *hae* too. This explains, perhaps, why all tuber-bearing crops are of *hae* status. The tuber has always been the mainstay of Wola subsistence.

The sweet potato is also the only female crop that is *hae* (except for the recently introduced Irish potato, which, as argued, is *hae* too because of its similarity to sweet potato). All creeping plants, as shown by the bottom row of Table 9.4, are planted largely by women. They are intrinsically female. The only exception is the very recently introduced crop of watercress, the recent arrival of which accounts in part for its misplacement. The reason for this is its appearance. Its leaves look like those of the indigenous crucifer greens that the Wola call *taguwt,* indeed they explicitly equate them (one of their names for it is 'whiteman's *taguwt'*). Men plant these greens; hence they plant watercress too as another kind of *taguwt.*

The Gender Message

The question remains: why do the Wola make these gender distinctions, anyway? Why have male and female crops, and equate this with the erectness or recumbency of plants? Clearly, the categorization of crops into those planted by men and those by women is not simply founded on something to do with the crops *per se* – their physical appearance, method of propagation or the part eaten. Rather, it is as if these latter features are amalgamated in some way to support the *wiy/hae* distinctions, which themselves in turn serve to reinforce the distinctions made between those crops planted by men and those planted by women. In other words, the *wiy/hae* status and its attendant considerations give added meaning and strength to the sexual planting distinction. Male crops are *hae,* erect and strong; female crops are *wiy,* recumbent and weak. The overall morphology of the gender distinctions made between crops does match this *wiy/hae* differentiation (the anomalies, as shown, can be accounted for in terms of conflicting criteria). So, if it has nothing to do with

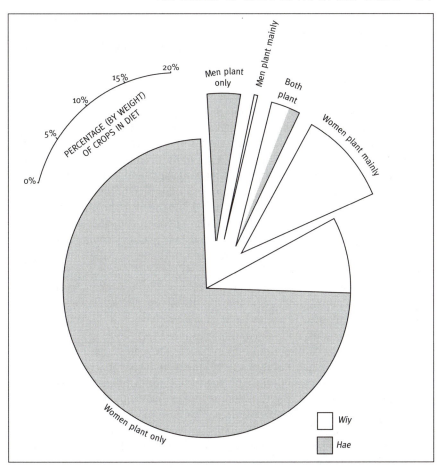

Figure 9.3: Proportional Contributions to the Wola Diet of Various Gender Categories of Crops and Their *Wiy/Hae* Status

the crops themselves, it is necessary to look elsewhere to explain why the Wola have male and female crops.

The apparently deliberate misplacement of sweet potato in the above scheme points the way to a possible explanation. This relates to the importance of this crop, and the place of the other crops, in the Wola diet. This is something not considered so far, but it is undoubtedly important because, after all, these plants are cultivated ultimately for consumption.

Figure 9.3 supports this line of approach. It compares the percentage (by weight) contributed to the Wola diet by the various classes of crop, differentiated according to the sex of those who plant them and their *wiy/hae* status.[7] All the shaded *hae* in the 'women plant only' segment of the circle (which amounts to about 78 per cent of all the plant food eaten by the Wola) is the inverted sweet potato. Otherwise women clearly plant the *wiy* crops, and the inversion of the creeping sweet potato's status to *hae* stands out markedly.[8] Men, on the other hand, are clearly responsible in this diagram for the *hae* crops. And those plants which both sexes can plant are a mix of *wiy* and *hae* plants.

This figure illustrates clearly why the sweet potato should have an inverted *hae* status to underline its unique position. In the male-dominated society of the Wola it is things masculine that are important: things erect, strong and epitomized in the concept of *hae*. Now it is obvious to anyone on the Wola diet that sweet potato is very important to their livelihood: to say that it is *wiy* (weak and unimportant) would be a mockery of the *wiy*/*hae* distinction. It has to be a *hae* status crop, but remains a creeping plant cultivated by women only; it is an aberration, a deliberate inversion to make an important point that relates to its central place in the Wola diet.

The truly startling fact revealed by Figure 9.3 is the overwhelming importance of female crops in the Wola diet. Those planted by men count for little. Without women and their crops the Wola could not exist, whereas they could if men's crops disappeared (albeit on a less varied, more boring and nutritionally poorer diet). It is here, I think, that we may be coming close to an explanation of why the Wola distinguish between male and female crops, and why they use the opposed *wiy* and *hae* statuses to reinforce and underline the distinction. In reality, as Figure 9.3 shows graphically, it is the women who plant and produce the food. What men add is no more than a luxury, an addition of some variety.

This is how the Wola understand the situation: the women produce the 'bread and butter' (or sweet potato) of the diet, and the men the appetizers and treats. All the male crops can be seen in this light: sugar cane and bananas, for instance, are relished and eaten with delight; they are the foods a man will offer a visiting friend as a treat to mark his visit. But people do not eat these male crops often, unlike the female ones which they consume daily. (In fact, for the Wola a meal is incomplete without the sweet potato: even when bloated they will say they are 'hungry' if the meal just eaten did not include some of these tubers.)[9]

Clearly, the women are the producers in Wola society, and the division into male and female crops, together with the associated *wiy*/*hae* ascriptions, relates to this. The Wola, I argue, receive a 'message' from these distinctions. They are telling them that women are the producers and men the transactors. This is a crucial point for Wola society; indeed it is one upon which its very existence depends. Its constitution stands on the exchange of wealth (Sillitoe 1979b); it is essential that men continually participate in exchange transactions and pass valuables to one another. They are the transactors; women are the producers. The danger is that men, whose reputations depend on handling wealth, may be tempted to produce wealth; for instance, to grow tubers earnestly and build up their pig herds to large sizes, or to grow surplus food and try to trade it for wealth. Such behaviour would be antithetical to the ceremonial exchange system, which requires them to obtain valuables through transaction, not production, and then to give the items received away again in other exchange transactions. The whole system depends on exchange; production is out.

In a truly acephalous society like that of the Wola, there are no enforceable laws to control behaviour, nor offices endowed with authority to see that people observed these laws if they did exist. In such societies other forces regulate and direct behaviour. One such force in Wola society is the distinction between male and female crops. This ensures that men keep exchanging wealth and do not turn their minds to its production. The distinction and its social consequences are upheld not by institutionalized and coercive sanctions but through subtle pressures involving ridicule and shame. No man wants to find himself in Saemom's ridiculous position, which is where he would be if he started planting women's crops in an attempt to boost his household's production with the intention of diverting this surplus into the exchange system in some way. This is neither possible nor tolerable in Wola society.

There are other ways in which the production of women is contrasted with the transactions of men in Wola society, so underlining the point that the two shall never meet. The relations of reproduction between men and women are hedged with taboos that also give this 'message' (Sillitoe 1979a). Interestingly, aspects of these taboos extend to the planting of crops too. A menstruating woman, for example, should not enter a garden to do any planting; neither should anyone who has indulged in sexual intercourse in the previous two or three days.[10] The implication is that too much productive effort is bad: one kind cancelling out another. The moral is that production must be controlled and not allowed to expand beyond certain limits. Women, as the producers, should not be expected to work hard to keep production at high levels. For men to compete through their womenfolk by goading them to increase production would be as harmful as for them to enter the sphere of production themselves. Unlike the rationale behind Western capitalist economies, that behind the Wola requires a certain level of production and no more.

Notes

This chapter is reprinted with permission from *Ethnography* (1981), Vol. 20, pp. 1–14.

1   These rules cover only the planting, tending and harvesting of crops, not their consumption; members of both sexes are free to eat all crops.

2   According to Brennan (1977: 14), the Enga make this equation even more explicit than do the Wola.

3   The sexual equation with the erect penis will also be clear. No Wola, however, ever made this connection verbally to me, possibly because the subject is a shameful one, to which they avoid making reference.

4   This relates to Lévi-Strauss's (1966: 16–36) elusive concept of the cultural *bricoleur.*

5   Tobacco, one of the ambiguously classified plants in the previous category, is also propagated by seed, which goes further to explain its *wiy* status.

6   There is currently some debate about the antiquity of the sweet potato in New Guinea (see Brookfield and White 1968; Yen 1974), but it certainly predated European penetration of the Wola region by several generations.

7   Data on crop consumption were collected in a survey of the food eaten by the members of 12 homesteads over a three-month period.

8   The *hae*-status Irish potato figures to such a small extent in the Wola diet that, on the scale

used, it does not show up in the 'women plant mainly' segment of the circle.

9　My wife and I found this out the first time we had some young men to eat with us. After filling them with plates of fish and rice (the most relished of introduced foods) we were surprised by their exclamations of hunger and their rush to bake some sweet potato tubers in our fire.

10　The Enga (Waddell 1972: 51) also fear that menstruating women will pollute male crops, and the Goodenough islanders (Young 1971: 149) say that sexual intercourse contaminates the hands and through them the crops.

References

Brennan, P. W. (1977) 'Let sleeping snakes lie: Central Enga traditional religious belief and ritual', mimeo, Wabag Lutheran Church.

Brookfield, H. C. and J. P. White (1968) 'Revolution or evolution in the prehistory of the New Guinea Highlands', *Ethnology*, Vol. 7, pp. 43–52.

Bulmer, S. and R. Bulmer (1964) 'The prehistory of the Australian New Guinea Highlands', *American Anthropologist,* Vol. 64, pp. 39–76.

Clarke, W. C. (1971) *Place and People: an Ecology of a New Guinean Community,* Berkeley: University of California Press.

Lévi-Strauss, C. (1966) *The Savage Mind*, London: Weidenfeld and Nicolson.

Pospisil, L. (1963) *Kapauku Papuan Economy,* New Haven: Yale University Publications in Anthropology No. 67.

Powell, J., A. Kulunga, R. Moge, C. Pono, F. Zimike and J. Golson (1975) 'Agricultural traditions of the Mount Hagen area', University of Papua New Guinea Geography Department Occasional Paper 12.

Rappaport, R. A. (1968) *Pigs for the Ancestors: Ritual in the Ecology of a New Guinea People*, New Haven: Yale University Press.

Sillitoe, P. (1979a) 'Man-eating women: fears of sexual pollution in the Papua New Guinea Highlands', *Journal of the Polynesian Society,* Vol. 88, pp. 77–97.

Sillitoe, P. (1979b) *Give and Take: Exchange in Wola Society,* New York: St Martin's.

Waddell, E. (1972) *The Mound Builders: Agricultural Practices, Environment, and Society in the Central Highlands of New Guinea,* Seattle: University of Washington Press.

Yen, D. E. (1974) 'The sweet potato and Oceania: an essay in ethnobotany', *B. P. Bishop Museum Bulletin*, No. 236.

Yen, D. E. and J. M. Wheeler (1968) 'Introduction of taro into the Pacific: the indications of the chromosome numbers', *Ethnology*, Vol. 7, pp. 259–67.

Young, M. W. (1971) *Fighting with Food*, Cambridge: Cambridge University Press.

PART IV
Plants, Women's Status
and Welfare

CHAPTER 10
Gendering the Tradition of Plant Gathering in Central Anatolia (Turkey)

Füsun Ertuğ

Archaeological remains reveal that, for at least the past nine thousand years, Central Anatolia's inhabitants have partially depended upon wild plant gathering for their survival. Although the early Neolithic inhabitants started to domesticate a certain number of cereal and legume plants, it is certain that they could not provide for their basic needs without gathering wild plants. What is perhaps surprising is that today agricultural people in Central Anatolia plant a relatively limited number of crop species and varieties and continue to use wild plants to meet many of their subsistence needs. People in Kızılkaya, a village in Aksaray Province, today use over 100 species of edible wild plants, whereas the number of cultivars planted for food is roughly half that number.[1] The wild food plants that are gathered and consumed consist of 42 greens, 28 fruits, six mushrooms, five bulbous plants and plant parts such as flowers, seeds and roots (Ertuğ 2000b: Table 2). The quantity and continuity of wild plant gathering indicates its importance in rural economies, as well as the relative importance of plant use throughout the prehistoric and historic eras.

Turkey has one of the richest floras in the Near East, with some 10,000 species of vascular plants, including 3,000 species that are endemic to Turkey and the Aegean Islands. Central Anatolia is the third most important area where these endemic species are concentrated (Ekim *et al.* 2000: 34).

Wild plant gathering in Central Anatolia constitutes not only an important cultural heritage, but also a gender heritage with clear social implications in a contemporary agricultural society. Plant gathering is often ignored in ethnographic research since gathered plants are not thought of as a basic source of food or raw materials for subsistence and are generally associated with poverty. As wild plants are, in general, women's area of interest, the level of ignorance is multiplied when research is gender biased. However, gathering contributes significantly to the economy of both poor and better-off households in Central Anatolia, and it is mainly women who manage and use wild plant resources. The identification of differences based upon 'socially constructed male and female categories' (Hastorf 1991: 132) is one of the basic prerequisites for understanding the collection of wild

183

plants in a social context. Although the role of 'woman the gatherer' is acknowledged both among hunter-gatherer societies (Dahlberg 1981; Bryce 1992) and, to a lesser extent, in agricultural societies (D'Hont 1994; Pieroni this volume), the social and economic implications of gathering are not well documented in Turkey and in the Near East in general. Men also gather certain wild plants for subsistence purposes in Central Anatolia, but women's gathering not only provides food and other materials for their households but also strengthens their social relations, providing yet another example of rural women's networks and power-building processes in specific socio-cultural settings in Turkey (Sirman 1995; Yalçın-Heckmann 1995). While men gather a limited number of species and do not draw on social networks in doing so, women gather collectively and exchange a wide range of plants for medicine, fuel, fibre and dyes.

Gender and Subsistence in Central Anatolia

In the high plains of Central Anatolia,[2] in Aksaray Province south-east of the capital city, Ankara, the main economic activities are agriculture and animal husbandry. While the western part of the country has undergone a rapid modernization process, other areas are not as developed industrially or commercially.

Most of Aksaray Province falls within the Irano-Turkanian floral region and is dominated by treeless steppe vegetation. The village of Kızılkaya, about 25 kilometres south-east of the city of Aksaray, is populated by Turkish Sunni Muslims. In the mid-1990s, around 1,500 people lived in Kızılkaya and occupied around 2,000 hectares of land. Twenty per cent of the population lived in extended families and 70 per cent in nuclear families, the remaining households consisting of single adults with or without their children.

The village agricultural economy is based on field crops and gardening, and on sheep and cattle that are grazed on common pastureland. Nine out of ten households had access to between one and nine hectares of farmland. Agriculture is primarily rain-fed, and small plots are used for wheat, barley and legumes such as lentils and chickpeas that are grown in a fallow system. A total of 70 cultivars were recorded, 55 of which were planted for food (including all vegetables and fruit trees), although some of these are only rarely planted. Some irrigated gardens and homegardens are used for vegetables and fruit trees. Most of these produce for household consumption, and no monoculture cash crops are planted. However, crops such as onions and potatoes, as well as some garden and vineyard products, provide small amounts of cash for many families.

The village's animal wealth consists mainly of sheep and cattle, supplemented by chickens, geese and turkeys. Two-thirds of the households have either a cow or some sheep for milk and cheese. Animal husbandry also provides cash: farmers sell surplus animals once a year, or sell butter and cheese in small quantities throughout the year. Milk is primarily consumed in the household in the form of yoghurt, butter and cheese. Even though villagers produce their own food, none of these activities yield enough to meet families' other needs for cash.

The main cash income of many families is derived from employment outside the village. In 1994, 15 per cent of the population, all of whom were men, lived outside the village and about 200 people lived outside the country. With the exception of young men serving in the military, these men were working in large Turkish towns or had gone abroad to work in countries such as Germany, France and Russia. The village has other ties to the national economy. Although there is no government tax on village land or animals, there are price supports for certain crops as well as education, health services, roads and electricity.

Over the past 30 years, traditional ploughs and harvesting tools in Kızılkaya have been replaced by modern agricultural machinery, but present-day agriculture still presents a combination of traditional and modern. As has been the case in many European countries, when the use of farm machinery increased, women's contribution to agricultural labour declined, especially in cereal harvesting and processing. This has given women additional time to develop gardening both for home consumption and for the market.

Turkey is moving from an agrarian and subsistence-based economy to one based on industry, services and the market, a process accompanied by a population shift from rural to urban areas. In rural areas in 1990, 82 per cent of all women were economically active, whereas the majority of urban women (71 per cent) were classified as 'housewives' (Özbay 1994: 10).[3] Although formal statistics often fail to measure informal labour, the agricultural sector continues to be the basic source of employment for most women, although their participation in non-agricultural activities is slowly increasing (Özar 1994: 33). While this transformation is expected to lead to a breakdown in traditional gender roles, in fact these roles are changing only slowly, particularly in the domestic sphere.

In rural areas, patriarchal relationships prevail despite much recent change and regional variation. Most marriages are arranged between families as a means of establishing economic and social ties, and social considerations predominate over individual choice (Kagıtçıbası 1982; Kandiyoti 1985). Women's behaviour is subject to control within the household and within the wider village community. While women in rural areas live under this yoke of double control, they nevertheless produce, reproduce, arrange marriages, bond and even lay claim to space outside the 'domestic' sphere.

Sirman's village study points out that it is not always valid to characterize Turkish society as patriarchal. Women's networks provide the means by which women are able to 'create more egalitarian relations within the household, and the community at large ... [it is] in the practice of everyday life, in the very process of negotiating these spaces, that notions of gender are redefined' (1995: 201). Wild plant gathering and use are two of the ways in which village women negotiate and extend their social space.

In spite of the fact that Turkey constitutes the richest source of plant biodiversity in the Near East, the ethnobotanical literature on Turkey is practically unknown outside the country, and there is virtually no mention of women in this research. Most research concerning plant use in Anatolia is related to medicinal plants and ethnomedicine (Sezik *et al.* 1991; Sezik *et al.* 1997; Tabata *et al.* 1988), in keeping with the emphasis on the discovery of plants that may be useful as pharmaceuticals. Although one of the more general ethnobotanical studies (Lyle-Kalças 1974) mentions that wild plants are collected and sold by women, no additional information is provided. Baytop's intensive research provides considerable information not only on medicinals but also on wild plants used for food, fodder, fuel, dyes and gums, but he only briefly mentions that edible plants are generally collected by women (1984: 5; 1994: 11). While some researchers focused on the useful plants of relatively large areas such as Eastern Anatolia (Öztürk and Özçelik 1991), with the exception of the present study, there is no other ethnobotanical research available on the variety of plants used in this geographical area of Anatolia, and no study that investigates gender relations in wild plant collection.

Ethno-archaeological and ethnobotanical fieldwork was carried out in 1994–5 to document the genetic potential of a limited area and the richness of traditional plant knowledge.[4] Information on edible and medicinal plants was collected through unstructured interviews with over 60 woman and was later confirmed in 14 surrounding villages and towns with both male and female informants. Structured interviews were conducted with a randomly chosen sample of 30 households in three income groups in the village. Male household members answered questions relating to land and animal ownership and agriculture, and female members answered those concerning plant gathering and gardening. The interviews with women also helped in the quantification of wild plant use and provided data for comparisons between different income groups. However, the most satisfactory way to collect information about plants was to accompany and question the women while they were gathering, and to participate in all agriculture-related activities such as planting, harvesting, processing and cooking. Male informants, especially herders, shepherds and hunters, were interviewed concerning various plants, and their answers were checked with other informants. One of the most important results of the fieldwork was the collection of botanical specimens[5] of the 300 locally named plants, together with data on their distribution, use and management.

Gendering the Knowledge of Wild Plant Gathering

In this region, as in many parts of the world, in addition to the care of children, the household and domestic animals, women routinely gather and process wild plants for food, medicine, fuel and handicrafts. By tradition, ploughing and seeding the land, and harvesting and threshing cereals, are men's work, which was very labour-intensive before tractors were introduced (Morvaridi 1992). Generally, men do not participate in plant gathering or processing, except when plant resources (bulbous edible plants and mushrooms, animal fodder) are found far from the village. Although men know what they eat, and what they are heated, healed and clothed by, they have neither the necessary skills and experience, nor the detailed knowledge of processes, to make all of this possible. Although many necessary jobs are shared, and everyone in a small society has general know-how, knowledge that is specific to a process is available only from those individuals actively involved.

When women gather greens, medicinals or fuel, they prefer to gather in a group. The village women agreed that they try not to go outside village borders 'in fear of the guards of other villages, or "foreigners" who might attack them'. This reflects the limits of physical space that women are supposed to respect, creating an invisible and unspoken physical and social boundary. By contrast, there are no limits on physical space for men, so that men and boys gather most of the edible bulbous plants and mushrooms that are frequently found far from the village. Their work as shepherds, hunters and village guards frequently takes them far beyond the village boundaries where they may gather wild edibles to bring home or to eat by themselves with bread.

A marked difference between men's and women's gathering practices is that women prefer to gather in social groups, and to distribute some of the plants that they have gathered as gifts to friends and neighbours. Men usually gather while they are working alone and consume what they gather, without giving wild plant materials as gifts. Men are especially careful to gather mushrooms when they are alone, as these are scarce and they don't want to reveal their sources to one another.

When women gather edible greens (locally called ot disirmek), they spend two to three hours journeying within the perimeters of their village to fallow fields, field borders, river banks and wasteland areas to collect several species of edibles that their families will consume within three to five days. Women wear aprons which they fill with gathered plants and also take a square cloth or a plastic bag and a rope to collect fuelwood. They take along with them a big knife or a short-handled adze, or sometimes both, to dig out and harvest the greens. They always leave smaller shoots in place to provide regrowth for future harvests and do not collect plants that have flowered, even though they are still edible, so that these will produce seed. Over half of the wild edibles are perennials (Ertuğ-Yaraş 1997: Table 3) that are local to specific areas. Women know where they can find them, and warn the shepherds to keep their herds from damaging these plants.

The women in the area have tried to cultivate in their gardens several of their favourite wild plants, such as chicory (Cichorium intybus) and wild spinach (Spinacia tetranda). They said that they stopped experimenting with domestication when they found that garden-grown plants did not taste 'right'. They argued that the highly prized bitter flavour of some of the wild plants is lost when they are grown in the garden. It is apparent that these women, some of whom are no longer young and all of whom have gardens, have made a conscious decision that it is worth long hours of walking, often in the wet and cold, to gather large quantities of certain wild plants.

In this particular area of Central Anatolia, women attempt to enlarge their area of influence within the household and in the society through their knowledge of plants. Women create networks among their kin and with neighbours to be able to obtain reliable help when it is needed. The necessary additional labour for garden work, bread making, childcare and the preparation of bulgur is always obtained through these networks. Labour exchange or labour payment in kind is the norm in these relationships and payment is never in money. Village women use these networks to provide labour not only for household tasks, but also to weed and harvest crops such as potatoes and onions. When the fields are large and the financial returns are high, labour has a monetary value; however, when the fields are small, women's networks provide the additional labour through reciprocal relations. These networks are not limited to the village but may also extend to friends and relatives outside the region. Freshly collected wild plants, garden products and home-made goods are given as gifts to maintain these ties. Through presents and frequent visits, women maintain relationships between various families within and outside their communities, at the same time extending the necessary information channels within their society.

Preparing food for the family is a repetitive process, but it is also creative and innovative. It requires patience, skill and experience, and this is what rural women pass on from one generation to the next. 'Traditional village food' is not constituted simply by the repetition of ancient recipes. Each woman has her own preferences and specialities as well as her collective or personal memory. Women continue to gather wild food plants as a means to provide a varied and healthy diet in accordance with their cultural traditions and environmental circumstances.

In the past, villages in the study region had little access to medical facilities and women needed to know which plants to use for healing, and how to process and apply them. Although modern pharmaceuticals have largely replaced local ways of healing, the number of women healers who remain, and the high percentage of women among the informants with knowledge of medicinal plants, indicates the importance of their roles in the folk medicine of the past.

Some of the greens and medicinals need to be chopped while others, such as red peppers and *Cannabis sativa* seeds, are pounded. All plant-processing tools (such as wooden or stone mortars and hand mills) are considered as women's property, and food preparation, cooking and storage areas are considered to be women's section of the house. Women have developed techniques to store food by drying, salting and pickling. For example, fruits such as *Celtis tournefortii* and *Prunus spinosa* spp. *dasyphylla* and wild greens such as *Polygonum cognatum* are dried for winter consumption. Women also know how to detoxify plants. Fresh acorns are stored in pits covered with earth and, when the tannin content is washed away by rains, become sweeter. The toxicity in *Arum* sp. leaves also washes away when leaves are boiled several times. Women have also evolved techniques to process various fibres into cloth, floor covers (*kilim* and carpets), sacks, mats, containers and baskets.

Some women from villages close to town sell the plants that they have locally collected and produced, creating 'women's' areas in local daily markets where they exchange goods as well as information. Although the women of Kızılkaya do not sell the wild edibles that they collect because there is no surplus, they often go to market during the summer to sell what they produce in their homegardens and orchards, as well as animal products. In addition to fresh vegetables such as green beans, tomato and cucumber, they sell grapes, apples, dried apricots, eggs, cheese and butter. This money is usually considered to belong to the women and is spent as women see fit, on themselves and on their children.

Food Gathering

Women gather edible greens primarily in winter and spring, from November until June. Small groups gather together, consisting of two to four women who are usually neighbours or relatives. During the summer and autumn, women prefer to eat greens from their own gardens or those wild greens that they gather while working in the vineyards or along the road. Each woman gathers for her own household, but also gives greens as presents to her friends and neighbours after each gathering trip. Mothers generally take one of their daughters along to show them how to identify the plants as well as where to find them. Most women consider plant gathering as a good occasion to leave the house and meet with other women, while also providing food for their families. Serving freshly collected greens and giving them as gifts are highly valued both by women and men.

Among wild edible greens, *Berula erecta, Capsella bursa-pastoris, Chondrilla juncea, Cichorium intybus, Crepis foetida, Erodium cicutarium, Lactuca serriola, Portulaca oleracea, Rorippa nasturtium-aquaticum, Sinapis arvensis,* and *Tragopogon bupthalmoides* are the most commonly consumed. While there are no more than ten leafy greens cultivated during the summer, more than 40 different leafy plants are gathered during the winter and spring. Unless there is a high snow cover, from November to March it is possible to find 13 to 16 varieties of wild plants, and this number increases to 35 in May. Three aquatic plants can be found even when the ground is snow-covered. Although the contribution of these wild plants to families' livelihoods was not quantified, it is clear that they contribute important quantities of vitamins and minerals to the diet (Ertuğ-Yaraş 1997: Table 22).

Washing and preparing the greens is also women's work. After washing, the greens are brought to each meal in a bundle. They are considered to be as essential to a meal as bread, the staple in most Anatolian village diets. A normal rural Anatolian meal seldom includes meat, except at weddings, circumcisions, memorial feasts and the religious feast of Sacrifice (*Kurban Bayramı*). The rest of the year, the village diet consists of legumes (lentils and chickpeas), cracked wheat (*bulgur*), potatoes and milk products, in addition to fresh vegetables when these are in season. Most of the wild greens are eaten raw and salted between folds of the local flat bread (*yufka*), but some greens require cooking. These are chopped on large flat wooden mortars and are cooked together with onions and cracked wheat. Such dishes (called *cacık*) are usually eaten with yoghurt.

A few greens that are gathered in the spring are dried for winter, such as *Polygonum cognatum* and *Portulaca oleracea*. *Polygonum* is found more often at higher altitudes; thus women from mountain villages give gifts of it to their friends and relatives who live in villages on the plains. These plants are more easily stored in comparison with other species. Collected in April and May when there are several other species available, they are cut into small pieces to increase their palatability, sun dried, stored, and cooked as *cacık* in the winter. Women said that, in the past, they gathered more plant species and also gathered more frequently. They have noticed that the quantity of local wild plants is decreasing and gave several reasons for this, including increasing human and animal populations, the opening of additional fields for cultivation, and drought.

There is significant variation between women's knowledge and their use of edible wild plants. The results of a questionnaire applied to a random sample of 30 women showed that the highest number of edible greens that they knew was 38, and in the whole neighbouring area, women could identify a total of 42 wild greens. Women from Kızılkaya prefer to collect only 20–25 species. About 14 of these were known by all of the women and were the most frequently collected. Ten were known by some of the women, and 18 were rarely collected. Only a few women knew or preferred other wild greens.

Women from all income groups gather wild greens. The 30 women interviewed were selected in a sample of households that was stratified to represent three income groups (Ertuğ-Yaraş 1997: Table 23). The middle and poorer groups gathered more greens than the richer households did, and the poorer women gathered a greater variety of species. It is probable that the poorer women were more dependent upon gathering and hence less selective. Both the number of known and gathered greens and the percentage of each group that gathers are high across the sample. The average of gatherers within the sample is 79 per cent for any income group. Although many people have commonly associated wild plant gathering with poverty, in this instance the gathering of wild greens is related more to preference (taste and perceived nutrition) than to poverty.

Laboratory analyses of the 12 most commonly consumed greens indicate that they are as good as if not better sources of both proteins and minerals than cultivated green vegetables (Ertuğ-Yaraş 1997: 204). Wild greens are collected in the winter and spring when fresh vegetables are scarce. They thus play an important role by diversifying the diet as well as by adding important nutritional content.

Women occasionally collect other wild edibles for teas, spices, and gums. Some of these are snacks that are eaten while women go to and from the fields or during other outdoor work. For example, seeds such as *Anchusa azurea* are usually found in arable fields and are often harvested together with wheat. When women clean the wheat before making *bulgur*, they pick out the *A. azurea* seeds and eat them because they are sweet. The plant itself is hairy and inedible. The women distinguish between two quite similar varieties of *Anchusa* and, while they gather *A. undulata* to eat, they never gather *A. azurea*. There are seven species of plants collected for herbal teas and some of them, like *Achillea teretifolia*, *Thymus argaeus* and *Thymus sipyleus* ssp. *rosulans,* are endemic to Turkey. Women in Kızılkaya also collect and use the last species as a spice. The other spices that are used most commonly in cooking are *Acinos rotundifolius* and horsemint (*Mentha longifolia* ssp. *typhoides*).

In general, children gather wild fruits such as almonds, cherries and *Crataegus* species, whereas women are not involved. Wild fruits are eaten immediately when found, and are especially eaten by boys who forage around the village. They rarely bring any fruit home. However, women and children in a village close to Kızılkaya still collect one species of Ulmaceae, the hackberry (*Celtis tournefortii*). The ripe fruit is collected in late autumn, sun dried for a few days, and then stored for winter consumption. Some elderly women in nearby mountain villages said that they still collect wild plums (*Prunus cocomilia, P. divaricata* and *P. spinosa* ssp. *dasyphylla*) for use in stews or to dry and lend a sour relish to meals. A recipe was given using *Arum* sp. leaves: after the leaves are chopped and washed with salt, they are boiled for a long time with sour wild plums (*Prunus cocomilia* or *P. divaricata* ssp. *divaricata*), whereupon *bulgur* is added, together with roasted onions and mint.

In Kızılkaya, five bulbous plants were considered to be edible. Three of them belong to the Iridaceae family, and the bulbs of *Crocus ancyrensis* are most often consumed. As these bulbs are usually found in higher altitudes and are considered to be a snack food, they are usually gathered by young boys who use a special tool that has an iron point and a long wooden handle. Often boys beg the ironsmith, or trade a few eggs with him, to have him make this iron point. They collect crocuses and sometimes bring them home. The flowers are also eaten and the bulbs are considered to be a delicacy that are eaten from mid-February to the end of March (Ertuğ 2000a).

Six different kinds of mushrooms are also known to be edible, but boys and some men collect only two species (*Agaricus subperonatus* and *Coprinus atramentarius*) on a regular basis. After every rain during the fall and spring, they search for mushrooms. Those that are collected are roasted or cooked with onions and eggs. Women usually don't know where to find the bulbous plants or mushrooms. Each of the men and boys has a secret place of his own (a hollow next to a fallen tree, for example, or a special niche in their field) which he checks as often as possible and covers with branches during the fall and spring to protect it from prying eyes.

Medicinal Plants

Although medicinal plants are seldom gathered and used today, it is clear that, in the past, women were always responsible for this domain. Across the entire study area, women provided 90 per cent of the information on medicinal plants. Only a few of these plants are still used since modern pharmaceuticals are readily available, and are generally believed to be more effective.

Forty-four medicinal plants, including 11 cultivars in 29 plant families, were documented in the area (Ertuğ 2000b: 177). Eight are endemic to Turkey. These do not include the wild edible plants that people believe to be 'good for health'. All of the folk medicinal remedies recorded came from local plants and other ingredients. Villagers did not buy drugs from herbalists in towns or barter medicinal plants. A few medicinal plants are used topically, but most are eaten or swallowed in solutions. Most are used for human skin or stomach ailments, and are only occasionally used to treat animals.

Although 44 medicinals were recorded, at the time of the study the use of these plants was apparently very limited. Within the group of 30 women, ten knew no medicinal plants, and the others knew between one and ten plants – although, when asked how many they still collect, only three reported that they collect (between one and three) plants.

Several women healers known as *ocak* (meaning 'hearth' in English) are still practising in the area. In other areas of Turkey they are called *kocakarı* (crone) or *teyze* (aunt) (Tabata *et al.* 1988: 5). Some *ocak* use plants in the healing process whereas others use stones and metal sickles or read verses from the Koran. For example, one of the women healers in the area treated a special skin disorder by reciting prayers over the roots of *Lycium anatolicum* and then gave the root to the patient, to be pounded and eaten every morning. Another woman applied burnt branches, using the juice to heal wounds. Some of these remedies may contain effective ingredients, but others are related more to magic and have only psychological effects. In addition, several women gather *Peganum harmala* seedpods when they are green and string them on thread to produce amulets to protect their homes from the evil eye.

Some elderly men were able to provide recipes to treat animal diseases (ethnoveterinary medicine), and some men were able to identify a few medicinal plants. For example, an old man identified *Eryginum campestre*, the roots of which were used for boils. However, many men said that they had not used the plants themselves, and had only learned about them from their mothers. There are also some men in the area known as *hoca* (religious teachers) who treat various illnesses by reading verses from the Koran and writing scripts on papers called *muska*. However, there were no reports that these men use medicinal plants. Tabata *et al.* (1988: 5) report that these semi-religious people, called *Sheyh* or *Shih* in eastern and south-eastern Anatolia, also use plants to treat some diseases. However, such traditions are rapidly being lost.

Animal Fodder

Male herders graze animals and many men have accompanied herders when they were young or were herders themselves. So, they have much more information about the plants consumed by animals. In addition to cultivars such as barley, rye, oats and vetch, animals graze about 170 wild species in 35 different plant families (Ertuğ 2000b: Table 1). Many of these are not collected for winter fodder, but animals graze on them most of the year. Some are cut during summer and fall and stored for winter fodder. The men who own or herd animals are also aware of the plants that are harmful, and which must be avoided because they give an unpleasant taste to milk. Although some women also know these plants, most of this knowledge is specific to males.

Fuels

Usually men cut trees and shrubs for fuel and carry them home on animals or trucks. Oak and elm were preferred for fuel before they became scarce. Now, poplar and willow trees are cultivated for fuelwood. In addition to these trees, the shrubs *Eleagnus angustifolia*, *Rosa canina* and *Crataegus* species are used for fuel. Cutting and bringing these home are men's work, but chopping and storing fuelwood are women's work. Branches of cultivars such as grape (*Vitis vinifera*) and dry stems and leaves of maize (*Zea mays*) and beans (*Phaseolus vulgaris*) are also used either as fodder or fuel and are always collected by women. Dung cakes are the basic source of fuel in Central Anatolia and are collected from grazing areas and stables and prepared by women who mix them with straw (Anderson and Ertuğ-Yaraş 1998).

About 15 plant species are gathered to start both wood and dung fires. *Astragalus elatus*, *A. elongatus* ssp. *elongatus*, and *A. kirshehiricus*, *Genista sessilifolia*, *Martubium parviflorum* ssp. *parviflorum*, *Noaea mucronata* ssp. *mucronata*, and *Salsola ruthenica* are the most commonly gathered tinder plants. Women gather them in summer and fall and store them for winter and spring.

Handicrafts

Crafts, especially domestic handicrafts such as weaving, matting, and basket and broom making, are women's work (Ertuğ 1999). When the products are meant for domestic use, women carry out all of the related work. In the study area, 30 plants were used in fibre crafts either as fibre in weaving, basketry, rope making and broom making, or to dye wool. Hemp (*Cannabis sativa*) was the main fibre plant available for domestic weaving, in which wool and goathair is also used. But as hemp cultivation was banned in the early 1970s, it is no longer used as fibre for weaving sacks, bags and floor coverings. Only a few women remember how to make fibre from hemp stems or to spin and weave hemp fibre. Women also no longer dye wool with materials extracted from plants (18 dye plants were recorded, including seven cultivars) since they prefer to buy chemically dyed, factory-spun wool for carpet weaving because it is cheap and readily available.

Reeds are used to make mats and containers, but these grow far from the village and require considerable strength to cut and carry, so men help women to harvest them although they do not help to prepare the fibres or plait the mats. Several plants, such as bulrush and cattail (*Phragmites australis* and *Typha laxmannii*) are still used to make baskets, floor coverings and ceiling mats. Mats for flat, soil-covered ceilings are still important, but floor mats and basket plaiting have lost their importance. Villagers now seldom use mat containers to carry goods on draught animals or to store dry foods such as beans, grapes and eggs. Women still use six different plants to make brooms for different purposes. Brooms from *Centaurea pulchella* are used to clean houses whereas *Chenopodium album* is used to clean threshing floors.

Men perform some village crafts such as carpentry and metalworking and sell the products. Men once cut almost all available trees for use as building material and in carpentry. Although wood is now scarce and most modern tools are made of iron, more than 70 simple wooden tools and household items were recorded in Kızılkaya village. The ownership of handicraft tools and equipment is sex-specific. Wool cleaning combs, spindles and looms are women's property, and they have the right of disposal over their tools as well as their products. Similarly, the tools and products of carpentry, metalworking and smithing are men's.

Other Wild Plant Uses

Women commonly gather a variety of plants that are used for incense, glues and gums, and as ornamentals. Women used to collect plants for glue (*Chondrilla juncea, Gundelia tournefortii*) and liked to chew the gums of *Astragalus kirshehiricus* and *Acantholimon kotschyi*, but these plants are no longer collected. Some women transplant wild tulips (*Tulipa armena*, var. *lycica* and *T. humilis*) or other attractive species to their gardens. Men were aware of plants that were used for smoking, similar to tobacco.

Some middle-aged women said that they once used *Saponaria prostrata* and *Ajuga chamaeritys* in their games as children, but these natural toys have now been replaced by more sophisticated toys bought in markets. Thus, not only the local names but also the social implications of these plants have almost been forgotten.

Conclusions

The agricultural people of Central Anatolia have retained an impressive range of knowledge of wild plants nine thousand years after basic food crops were domesticated in this area. However, in a very short period of time, due to Turkey's present rapid modernization process that presents easy access to markets for materials and food products, and also stimulates rural–urban migration, the number of plants that are used and protected by local people is rapidly decreasing. Local uses of plants and processing techniques are rapidly disappearing, and may be completely lost within the next one or two generations.

Knowledge concerning wild food plants is more likely to survive since it is deeply entrenched in local cuisines, traditional tastes and women's social organization. The new trend toward consumption of local products and 'natural foods' may encourage continuity in knowledge and use as natural food plants become popular, even in urban markets. Before the village study was initiated, it was clear that village women were responsible for processing and preparing food for their families, but it was not evident that women's traditional knowledge of plants and plant processing still makes an important contribution to village diets, and also provides a means of extending women's social space. Garden and wild plant products, milk and handicrafts are considered to be women's property, and women can give them away or sell them as they wish. These products, and the knowledge related to their production, give women the power to create new bonds, to bargain and to have some money of their own. In addition, women's skills as cooks, artisans, gardeners and healers give them the opportunity to exchange with others, thus simultaneously enlarging their social networks among neighbours and relatives, in markets, and with relatives living outside their region.

The loss of access to and knowledge of wild plant resources can erode women's social position as well as representing a loss of resources that are vital to an economy still largely based on subsistence. Ignoring the social as well as economic importance of wild plant gathering also has implications for conservation efforts since they represent major incentives to conserve traditional plant knowledge and use. Further research is needed to understand the processes whereby women begin to replace the use of local wild plant resources with non-local purchased consumption items and why they retain some of their traditions even when these are labour-intensive.

Notes

1 Among 300 locally named useful wild plants, the author's study identified about 30 per cent that had not been recorded previously in the scientific literature on Anatolia and the Near East (Ertuğ 2000b: Table 1).

2 Central Anatolia, covering 151,000 square kilometres, is the second largest region in Turkey after Eastern Anatolia, and has a population of 9 million. Among the 80 provinces of Turkey, Aksaray Province was 56th in the 'medium human development category' according to the 1997 Human Development Report (UNDP 1997).

3 Özbay noted that the rural male participation rate was also high (87.5 per cent) in 1990.

4 The aim of the original research (Ertuğ-Yaraş 1997) was to study the contemporary subsistence economy of a single village to provide comparative data for the interpretation of the archaeological remains of the Neolithic site of Aşıklı. The site was about one kilometre south of Kızılkaya village. It was excavated from 1989 to 2000 by a team from the University of Istanbul. Aşıklı is dated as early as 8900–8500 BP (8000–7550 BC calibrated). The excavations indicated that the economy of this pre-pottery Neolithic site was based on crop husbandry, hunting (with special control over sheep and goat herds) and wild plant gathering. The mud-brick architecture and related findings suggested long-term sedentarism and a large, well-organized settlement. Other early Neolithic sites were also found in close proximity (Esin 1996; Ertuğ-Yaraş 1997).

5 Some 600 plant specimens in the B5 square of the *Flora of Turkey* grid system (Davis 1965) were collected at an altitude of c.1000–2000 metres. The identifications of plants at species level were made in the Department of Biology, Gazi University, Ankara, and the samples were deposited in the Gazi University Herbarium.

References

Anderson, S. and F. Ertuğ-Yaraş (1998) 'Fuel, fodder and faeces: an ethnographic and botanical study of dung fuel use in Central Anatolia', *Environmental Archaeology*, No. 1, pp. 99–108.

Baytop, T. (1984) *Türkiyede Bitkilerle Tedavi*, Istanbul: Istanbul Üniversitesi Yayınları.

Baytop, T. (1994) *Türkçe Bitki Adları Sözlüğü*, Ankara: Türk Dil Kurumu Yayınları.

Bryce, S. (1992) *Women's Gathering and Hunting in the Pitjantjatjara Homelands*, Alice Springs NT: IAD Press.

Dahlberg, F. (1981) 'Introduction', in F. Dahlberg (ed.), *Woman the Gatherer*, New Haven and London: Yale University Press, pp. 1–33.

Davis, P. H. (ed.) (1965–1988) *Flora of Turkey and the East Aegean Islands*, Vol. 1–10, Edinburgh: Edinburgh University Press.

D'Hont, O. (1994) *Vie Quotidienne des 'Agedat: Techniques et occupation de l'espace sur le Moyen-Euphrate*, Damascus: Institut Français de Damas.

Ekim, T., M. Koyuncu, M. Vural, H. Duman, Z. Aytaç and N. Adıgüzel (2000) *Red Data Book of Turkish Plants*, Ankara: Turkish Association for the Conservation of Nature.

Ertuğ, F. (1999) 'Plants used in domestic handicrafts in Central Turkey', *The Herb Journal of Systematic Botany*, Vol. 6, No. 2, pp. 57–68.

Ertuğ, F. (2000a) 'Baharın müjdecisi: Çiğdem (*Crocus*) ya da AN.TAH.SUM.[SAR] Hititler devri Anadolu florası'na küçük bir katkı '(Harbinger of spring: *Crocus* (Çiğdem) or AN.TAH. SUM.[SAR]: A small contribution to the Anatolian flora of the Hittite period), Turkish Academy of Sciences *Journal of Archaeology* (TÜBA-AR), Vol. 3, pp. 129–36.

Ertuğ, F. (2000b) 'An ethnobotanical study in Central Anatolia (Turkey)', *Economic Botany*, Vol. 54, No. 2, pp. 155–82.

Ertuğ-Yaraş, F. (1997) 'An Ethnoarchaeological Study of Subsistence and Plant Gathering in Central Anatolia', PhD dissertation, Washington University, St. Louis, Ann Arbor: University Microfilms International.

Esin, U. (1996) 'Aşıklı, ten thousand years ago: a habitation model from Central Anatolia', in Y. Sey (ed.), *Housing and Settlement in Anatolia: a Historical Perspective*, Istanbul: Türkiye Ekonomik ve Toplumsal Tarih Vakfı, pp. 31–42.

Hastorf, C. A. (1991) 'Gender, space, and food in prehistory', in J. M. Gero and M. W. Conkey (eds.), *Engendering Archaeology*, Oxford: Blackwell, pp. 132–59.

Kağıtçıbaşı, Ç. (1982) 'Introduction', in Ç. Kağıtçıbaşı (ed.), *Sex Roles, Family and Community in Turkey*, Indiana: Indiana University Turkish Studies, pp. 1–32.

Kandiyoti, D. (1985) 'Continuity and change in the family: a comparative approach', in T. Erder (ed.), *Family in Turkish Society*, Ankara: Turkish Social Science Association, pp. 23–41.

Lyle-Kalças, E. (1974) *Food from the Fields, Edible Wild Plants of Aegean Turkey*, Izmir: Birlik Matbaası.

Morvaridi, B. (1992) 'Gender relations in agriculture: women in Turkey', *Economic Development and Cultural Change*, Vol. 40, No. 3, pp. 567–86.

Özar, Ş. (1994) 'Some observations on the position of women in the labour market in the development process of women', *Boğaziçi Journal Review of Social, Economic and Administrative Studies*, Vol. 8, Nos 1–2, pp. 21–43.

Özbay, F. (1994) 'Women's labour in rural and urban settings', *Boğaziçi Journal Review of Social, Economic and Administrative Studies*, Vol. 8, Nos. 1–2, pp. 5–19.

Öztürk, M. and H. Özçelik (1991) *Useful Plants of East Anatolia*, Ankara: SISKAV Publication, Semih Press.

Sezik, E., M. Tabata, E. Yeşilada, G. Honda, K. Goto and Y. Ikeshiro (1991) 'Traditional medicine in Turkey I: folk medicine in Northeast Anatolia', *Journal of Ethnopharmacology*, Vol. 35, pp. 191–6.

Sezik, E., E. Yeşilada, M. Tabata, G. Honda, Y. Takaishi, T. Fujita, T. Tanaka and Y. Takeda (1997) 'Traditional medicine in Turkey VIII: folk medicine in East Anatolia; Erzurum, Erzincan, Ağrı, Kars, Igdır provinces', *Economic Botany*, Vol. 51, No. 3, pp. 195–211.

Sirman, N. (1995) 'Friend and foe? Forging alliances with other women in a village of Western Turkey', in Ş. Tekeli (ed.), *Women in Modern Turkish Society: a Reader*, London and New Jersey: Zed Books, pp. 199–218.

Tabata, M., G. Honda and E. Sezik (1988) *A Report on Traditional Medicine and Medicinal Plants in Turkey (1986)*, Kyoto: Faculty of Pharmaceutical Sciences.

UNDP (United Nations Development Programme) (1997) *Human Development Report 1997*, New York: Oxford University Press.

Yalçın-Heckmann, L. (1995) 'Gender roles and female strategies among the nomadic and semi-nomadic Kurdish tribes of Turkey', in Ş. Tekeli (ed.), *Women in Modern Turkish Society: a Reader*, London and New Jersey: Zed Books, pp. 219–31.

CHAPTER 11
The Basket Makers of the Central California Interior

Linda Dick Bissonnette

For decades, many researchers thought that hunting and gathering societies were, as a rule, male-dominated. Rarely reported cases, in which senior women held positions of authority, were seen as the 'exception that proved the rule'. Even though cross-cultural studies indicated a widespread pattern of gender egalitarian or 'matrifocal' (women-centred) societies in medium-scale horticultural and fishing economies, female dominance was still thought to be a myth. In North American Indian studies in general, and in California Indian[1] studies in particular, the 'squaw drudge' stereotype has prevailed. However, recent research on the Yokuts or Yokoch, Mono, and Sierra Miwok in the central California interior reveals a regional economy based on an acorn–basketry complex and true matrifocality, both of which stem from division of labour practices that are thousands of years old.

Contemporary indigenous peoples in this area have been working with anthropologists and others to record and preserve their cultural traditions, including making baskets out of materials that come from carefully tended patches of native roots, grasses and stems, and perpetuating social traditions that pay homage to senior women and men. Some of the ethnohistorical and ethnographic research with Yokoch, Mono and Sierra Miwok descendants (here collectively referred to as central California Indians) also reveals much about the use of plant biodiversity in the indigenous valley, foothills and mountain region.

In the traditional culture,[2] plants and plant products were used as food items, medicine, for heating and cooking, and in ceremonies. For many generations, acorns, especially those of the black oak (*Quercus kelloggii*), were the dietary staple (McCarthy 1993). Basketry materials and finished baskets were important domestic and trade items, and continue to be valued today. Plant patches and groves were managed by various means, including fire (Blackburn and Anderson 1993). The most critical resources were protected through use rights, and plant knowledge was passed down through the maternal line. Control over plants played an important role in traditional social organization as a source of female status and as the focus of cooperative labour, ideology, and residence patterns. A shift towards male power in more recent history, combined with bias against women in anthropological

197

theory, contributed to the previous categorization of these cultures as patrilineal and, by implication, patriarchal (Dick-Bissonnette 1997).

If one starts from the period when the indigenous people first had contact with whites (in the late 1700s), and works both backwards and forwards in time, patterns of continuity and change emerge. The core of the research underlying the conclusions in this chapter is ethnohistorical and anthropological, including participant observation and archaeology. Genealogies and life histories were gathered from knowledgeable individuals to determine who was related to whom and how and where they lived before forced resettlement. Open-ended interviews were conducted to crosscheck data and to determine what traditions were passed on, and how they were transmitted. Twenty-two indigenous tribal groups were included in a study of the social position of Yokoch, Mono and Sierra Miwok women (Dick-Bissonnette 1997). Interviewees included 33 knowledgeable consultants who had first-hand experience with traditional cultural practices and oral history traditions, and who are life-long residents in the central California interior. Important aspects of the traditional culture, including the acorn–basketry complex, the division of labour, residence patterns, decision-making authority and ideology were analysed using ethnographic, historical, archaeological and cross-cultural data. Together, the data and analyses indicate the prevalence of complementary gender roles if not an actual cultural bias in favour of women in these traditional societies.

For example, women basket makers were obliged by custom to make or obtain special baskets to give as gifts or for use in reciprocal exchanges and ceremonial offerings. Men were obliged to hunt and fish and to share their catch with the women, who in turn provided them with cooked acorn and other wild plant foods. A case in point from the mid-twentieth century is a Yokoch man who was well thought of for hosting gatherings and serving his guests 'lots of beef'. He enhanced his standing in the Indian community by marrying a highly skilled basket maker. When she died, he married another woman who excelled in basket making from a neighbouring tribal group. While both husband and wife benefited from the marriage, Indian consultants described him as 'a lucky man'.

The Acorn–Basketry Economy

For approximately ten thousand years, the indigenous people of the central California interior were semi-nomadic hunter-gatherers. Around three to four thousand years ago, judging from the abundance of bone awls in Middle Horizon archaeological assemblages, the central California Indian economy became increasingly focused on basketry (Beardsley 1948: 172; Hull *et al.* 1999: 76). Around 3,500 years ago, wild plant foods such as seeds and acorns, supplemented by wild fish and game, were the principal food resources that supported population expansion (Hull *et al.* 1999: 93). The Yokoch, Mono and Sierra Miwok did not practise horticulture or agriculture in the traditional sense, except to grow small amounts of tobacco (*Nicotiana attenuata* and *N. bigelovi*) for ceremonial use.[3] However, they did manage wild plant resources through burning, pruning, weeding, and cultivation or tilling, as well as through conservation, storage, exchange and trade.[4] Their adaptive strategy was labour-intensive, and it both enabled and required a fairly settled village life, complex social organization, and a relatively high population density. Acorns provided the dietary staple and, together with basket making, formed the material basis of traditional central California Indian culture.

It was Indian women who had the most knowledge of and who managed plant resources, inherited the rights to harvest certain plant patches and trees, and obtained strong economic and social positions through the exchange and trade of baskets and basketry materials. Senior women played a major role in organizing plant tending and gathering activities, girls' education and the distribution of prepared foods and goods. Men were responsible for fishing and hunting; making carrying nets, stone tools, traps, and shell and soapstone beads; educating boys; pit roasting; and various other ceremonial and social duties. Prior to Euro-American contact, there was inter-tribal trade for raw materials and finished goods, but the 'domestic economy' provided the vast majority of all resources.

Basketry dates back at least 10,000 years in the western United States (Jennings 1974), and basket-making traditions are still practised by Indian people living there today (Dick *et al.* 1988). Prior to the 1700s, the central California interior environment was rich in a wide variety of wild resources, but these resources were broadly dispersed and subject to climatic fluctuations. Basketry provided a light-weight means to gather, transport, process, store, cook and trade resources both within and between tribal territories. Baby baskets also allowed women to carry infants on their backs, freeing them to travel and to do other work with their hands (Brown, personal communication, 1995).

In historic and early modern times, baskets provided an important source of income. In the 1920s, a woman could return home from selling baskets with $200, which is equivalent to $1,500 today.[5] The introduction of the cash economy in the latter half of the nineteenth century didn't create the usual gender gap. Instead, it gave women basket makers an income to support their endeavours.

Women's Status, Plants and Subsistence

For decades, many anthropologists assumed that hunting and gathering societies were patrilocal (that is, women moved to their spouses' place of residence upon marriage). The central California interior case, however, together with literature on the Canadian Montanais-Naskapi trapping–trading economy (Leacock 1955, 1958), show that these societies were horticultural and matrilocal prior to European contact. Women in many North American Indian societies inherited baskets, houses, land and other property along the female line and shared considerable influence in group decision making. In the present case, it appears that daughters and granddaughters were encouraged to stay close or return to their grandmothers' area of residence because of their resource-gathering rights, botanical and basketry expertise, cooperative labour, knowledge of traditions, birthing and childcare assistance, and their standing in the community as respected elders.

Gender roles within central California Indian society also reflect status differences between women. That is, women were not barred from high-status positions, but not all women could attain them. Economic controls, ownership and inheritance of resources, choices regarding residence location, decision making at village and tribal levels, participation in ceremonial life, and principles regarding gender as reflected in traditional ideology, all support these conclusions (Dick-Bissonnette 1997).

Women elders with extensive plant knowledge held positions of high esteem and were sometimes 'chiefs' and healers. Botanical knowledge was not exclusively women's purview, but it is fair to say that women's everyday monitoring and use of a wide variety of native plants in their home environments, and also at fairly remote locations visited on gathering and trading trips, favoured their accumulation of botanical expertise. In the early 1900s, C. Hart Merriam interviewed a Southern Sierra Miwok woman in the foothills south-west of Yosemite who was able to identify more than 500 plants, birds and animals. Her eight-year-old daughter, interviewed independently by Merriam's assistant, could name over 300 (Latta 1977 [1949]: 618).

Specialized positions held by women in traditional central California Indian society included: 'chief', 'sub-chief', healer, messenger or *winatum*, basket maker, midwife, ceremonial singer, dancer, clown and undertaker. Important women often held several specialized positions simultaneously, in addition to gathering and preparing wild plant foods, and performing other family duties. Women also specialized part-time in trade or barter to obtain basketry materials and other resources outside of their home areas. Previous researchers (Kroeber 1976 [1925]; Gifford 1926; Gayton 1948) acknowledged the occasional presence of high-ranking women but by and large saw these cases as special or temporary. However, the more than occasional occurrence of women in high office, and not just for the short term, indicates that there were no strict gender biases standing in their way. The prevalence of high-status women in matrilineal horticultural and fishing societies, including those in the central California interior, is probably due to socio-economic conditions that favoured the formation of women's work groups, supported by a gender-egalitarian ideology.[6]

Medicine women

A traditional position of influence and authority in the study area was that of healer or doctor. Indian women contributed significantly to religious life by providing special baskets for important tribal and inter-tribal ceremonies as well as by being storytellers, singers, criers, dancers, food preparers and hosts. Many Indian people knew and used herbal remedies for various illnesses and conditions, but there were certain individuals and families that knew more than others (Turner, personal communication, 1993; Jones, personal communication, 1993).

Prior to modern times, 'some of the [Yokoch] medicinal practice and all of the midwifery [were] performed by women' (Powers 1976 [1877]: 379). Traces of information about Mono women healers can be found in historical accounts, ethnographic field notes and ethnographies.[7] Miwok women were each of three types of healers: 'witch doctors', 'dance doctors', and 'medicine doctors'. The knowledge of the medicinal properties of plants was highly valued and closely guarded as a family secret (a form of 'indigenous intellectual property'), that was passed down in families.

In 1926, the Sequoia National Park superintendent wrote, 'The [Mono and Yokoch] Indians and particularly the women had a remarkable knowledge of the medicinal properties of plants' (Stewart n.d.). Sixty-seven medicinal plants were recorded for the Sierra Miwok, including various cold and flu remedies; first-aid treatments and snakebite cures; digestive, pain and rheumatism relievers; and malaria, smallpox and venereal disease abatements (Barrett and Gifford 1933: 165–76; Tadd 1988).[8]

Central California Indian women used various plants for women's health, including birth control and abortion. Then, as now, birth control gave women some ability to determine the course of their lives. Other women influenced these decisions, as is illustrated by a case in Squaw Valley (a Yokoch–Mono transition area), where there was concern about a young woman's ability to carry out her highly demanding specialist role:

> There was an attempt to make Lucy a doctor because her father was famous (Eagle lineage) and her mother's family consisted of leaders from way back. The shaman's daughter and Josephine Atwell's mother 'put a spell on her' after the birth of Frank so she would have no more children. They thought it was impossible to be a doctor if one had many children ... better not to have any. (Lynch 1953)

Basketry techniques and plants

Indian women managed numerous plants used in basketry, and employed twining, coiling and twoiling techniques. Different plant species were specifically used as background material, for rim finishes, and to provide coloured materials to weave traditional designs into the baskets. Some materials were first dyed using other plant materials such as rotting acorns or oak bark, as well as minerals found in the soil such as iron oxide, to darken bracken fern (*Pteridum aquilinum*) rhizome strands from brown to black (Heizer and Elsasser 1980: 137).

Central California Indian women basket makers used two main basketry techniques: coiling and twining. 'Sewing' is more appropriate than 'weaving' as a term to describe the coiling technique since the working strand is pushed through a hole in the previous coil and then wrapped around the working coil to form another 'stitch'. Bundles of deergrass stalks (*Muhlenbergia rigens*) provided a more flexible foundation for coils than a single- or three-rod foundation of willow (*Salix* spp.), mock orange (*Philadelphus Lewisii*), sourberry (*Rhus trilobata*), whitethorn (*Ceanothus* spp.), creek dogwood (*Cornis californica*) or maple (*Acer macrophyllum*), as used in some Sierra Miwok basketry.

The tan-coloured background material in central California Indian coiled basketry is made from sedge (*Carex barbarae*), or sawgrass (*Cladium californicum*), but *Carex nebrascensis* and *Cladium mariscus* were also reportedly used (Merriam

1903: 826; Bates 1982; Anderson 1990: 9). Split-sedge or marshgrass rhizomes, known by the basket makers as 'whiteroot' (*Carex* spp.), were used as the main sewing strand in both coiled and twined basketry. Basket makers cultivated this very pliable material in sandy soil to yield long, straight 'runners' that could be split several times into thin but durable strands. Cleaned whiteroot has different shades, from light tan or beige to golden, depending on the source area (Turner, personal communication, 1993). For that reason, it is important to have enough roots from the same source to be able to complete a basket. It has not been determined whether colour variation relates to differences in plant species, soils or growing conditions.

The dark-red basketry material used in Central Interior basket making comes from the woody stems of redbud (*Cercis occidentalis*), which can grow to the height of trees in the upper foothills of the Sierra Nevada. Redbud is gathered in autumn, 'when the sap is down' and the leaves are falling (Baty, personal communication, 1987). This is when the colour of the bark is most intense and the branches split easily. If the sticks are cut too soon, the outer bark peels away from the stronger inner layer, staying green on the edges, and making weak sewing strands (Temple, personal communication, 1987). New, one- to two-year-old shoots make the best material because they are straighter and have few or no irregularities such as lateral branches or disease discolourations (Anderson 1999).

The black element in Foothill basketry designs is called 'blackroot'. The Chukchansi Yokoch and Sierra Miwok gather and prepare blackroot from the inner rhizome of the bracken fern plant when the fronds turn yellow in late summer or autumn. A gathering party, including the basket makers' husbands or male relatives, travel together and camp near the gathering area (Spier n.d.). After gathering, the dark-brown inner strands of the fern rhizomes are dyed black by soaking them for several months in a dye mixture. When they are dark enough, the strands are rinsed, dried and stored in a dry place.

A third basketry technique in the Yokoch area, called string basketry or twoiling, was based on the use of two milkweed (also known as 'wild cotton' – *Asclepias speciosa*) fibre elements or, in modern times, commercial cotton string or raffia, with a grass bundle or rod foundation. As the name suggests, twoiling entails something like twining or weaving to produce coil-shaped baskets. Fragments of string basketry found at archaeological sites in the Chowchilla River area indicate that twoiling was an aboriginal technique (Bates, personal communication, 1986). The outsides of twoiled baskets were decorated with tufts of bird feathers in aboriginal times and coloured yarn in historic and early modern times (Dick *et al.* 1988: 19).

Basket makers

The status of a basket maker depends on her care in the preparation of materials as well as on her skills in design and weaving. Basket makers were often respected elders (Planas, personal communication, 1987). Their dedication, skill and spiritual knowledge contributed greatly to their status in the Indian community. A Chukchansi Yokoch woman reported that basket making gave some women 'more respect because of what they knew' (Charlie, personal communication, 1994).

Reports from other North American societies support the connection between knowledge and power. For instance, Pomo basket weaver and medicine woman Mabel McKay (1907–93) was considered to be a ceremonial leader 'picked from above' (Sarris 1993: 61). Woodlands and Plains Indian women who were skilled in quill work and, later, beadwork, were able to 'name their price' for items that they produced, and they were afforded 'high social standing' equivalent to that of the best male warriors (Penney 1992). Skilled California Indian basket makers, like talented specialists in other tribal societies, travelled freely to exchange materials and finished works. This gave them the opportunity to make contacts in other communities, to learn a number of dialects, and to become privy to a wider range of information. These mutually reinforcing conditions led to further enhancement of their social position.

The indigenous rationale in non-state societies for revering highly skilled specialists, in this case basket makers, is that art provided the only 'opportunity to manipulate, exploit and even create the images and ideas on which community well-being is believed to depend' (Helms 1993: 71). Central California Indian women basket makers wove age-old symbols and, in modern times, their own stylistic variations into their coiled and twined baskets, reaffirming their cultural values and heritage. In one Yokoch–Mono transition area, for example, a Morning Star design, symbolic of the creation story and of good character (because grateful, hard-working people rise before dawn and greet the morning star) and also of luck, often appears in the centre of many of their baskets.

Young women, although skilled enough before marriage to make baskets, usually did not begin serious basket making until later in life, when continued learning and seniority allowed for specialization (Planas, personal communication, 1987). The need for materials, teachers, market connections and family support continue to restrict basket making to the most capable and dedicated women.

In the late nineteenth and early twentieth centuries, native basketry became popular with white traders, and many baskets were made to order or sold to stores and hotels. In the 1890s, young women in the Yosemite region found it easier to make money by taking in washing and sewing than by making baskets for sale (Bates and Lee 1990).[9] Only the work of the most skilled, usually senior women basket makers, attracted high enough prices to make it monetarily worthwhile as a full-time specialization. But basket making continued to provide a supplementary source of income for many and a respectable livelihood for a few in the twentieth century. Today, it is a way of life more than a way to support oneself or one's family.

Basket makers preferred to gather their own materials. However, in the early twentieth century when expert weavers needed more time for basket making, their husbands and sons became increasingly involved in gathering, especially when gathering areas were located far away. Men were willing to learn to identify the desired materials and help with gathering, even though this was traditionally women's work. Contemporary basket makers discourage men who venture too far by learning basket-making skills, stressing that this is a 'female art' and domain.

Acorn gatherers

Women gathered acorns from selected oak trees in their home areas and processed them by drying, cracking, peeling and pounding, and then pouring water over the resulting flour through a twined basket or a dried pine needle or grass sieve to leach out the bitter tannic acid found in fresh acorns. In earlier times, before men went off to hunt or fish for the day, they helped harvest acorns by knocking oak branches with a pole (Spier n.d.). Different forms or consistencies of cooked acorns were prepared by small groups of women. A thin acorn soup was used as baby food and to feed the sick and very elderly. Thick acorn porridge, eaten both warm and, for up to a week, cold, was the mainstay of the diet. The gelled layer or 'skin' that forms on the top of a basket of cooked acorn when it cools was considered a treat. Acorn 'bread' was made by dipping a basket of cooked acorn in cold water, which caused round balls to form. Dried acorn bread sustained hunters and travellers on their journeys. In villages and seasonal camps, meals consisted mainly of acorns and fish,[10] while greens, berries, bulbs, freshwater mussels, seeds,[11] and pine nuts (*Pinus* spp.) added flavour and variety. Dried acorns were stored in large granaries kept by senior women near their dwellings.

In 1938, many Indian families living in the central California foothills and mountains still depended on acorns and other wild foods (Cook 1976: 468). Today, couples or family groups collect acorns for special gatherings and cultural demonstrations, but the last known individuals to regularly prepare and eat acorns have passed away.

The Matrifocal System of Gathering Rights and Wild Plant Management

The rights to gather plants from specific areas, trade relationships and baskets were all inherited matrilineally. Central California Indian women established individual harvesting rights to natural and fixed resources such as oak trees, berry bushes, whiteroot gathering areas and other basket material and grass-seed plots. In general, food resources were held in common, but individual women claimed exclusive rights to plants that required special care and management. Use rights were taken very seriously, and were made known orally as well as by sign. A digging stick or acorn-knocking pole was propped against an oak tree to indicate that its acorns were reserved (Gayton 1948: 11, 160). Fire or sweeping the ground under a *manzanita* bush (*Archtostaphylos* spp.) was a means to establish a claim to its berries. Whiteroot gathering patches as well as grass-seed plots were marked by driving stakes into the ground around the plant patch (Latta 1977: 538–9 [1949]). If another woman tried to take resources ahead of a claimant, a fight would ensue that sometimes led to a family feud (Gayton 1948: 160).

Matrilocal residence was the tradition among the central California Indian people (Aginsky 1943: 464; Gifford 1932: 32; Dick-Bissonnette 1997). The primary consideration in the choice of residence location was the quality and quantity of the food supply. If a couple lived with the husband's family, the girl returned home frequently for short visits, sometimes accompanied by her husband. This was because 'she gathered seeds from her mother's seed localities. A woman would not gather from her mother-in-law's seed-gathering areas or those that pertained to her sisters-in-law' (Gayton 1948).

Families or individuals established rights to natural and fixed resources such as oaks and bedrock mortars. The latter are sometimes deep depressions that women pounded into granite bedrock in order to process acorns into flour using stone pestles. Indian women also inherited houses along the female line (Spier n.d.). Hunting areas and fishing spots along rivers or streams could not be owned, but the use of improvements such as fish weirs, gigging platforms and pigeon booths was legitimately restricted to their makers, and passed from father to son (Gayton 1948: 221). Women controlled baskets either by making them themselves, inheriting them matrilineally, or acquiring them through exchange or trade. While individual women could own baskets, they were obliged to use food baskets to benefit the household.

Yokoch–Mono family groups gathered whiteroot in the San Joaquin River area (Wakichi Yokoch territory) in the 1920s and 1930s. Women would swim across to Cobb Island with children on their backs. They cultivated the roots with digging sticks, which loosened the sandy soil around the plants, encouraging the growth of long straight rhizomes. They also cultivated whiteroot plants by weeding around preferred specimens. Once a year, usually in the spring, enough roots were dug, broken or cut, stripped, dried and split to make several coiled baskets and to provide bundles of roots to trade for other materials. The rest of the rhizomes were left in place to keep the patch viable for future use (Sample, personal communication, 1993; Beecher, personal communication, 1993).

Habitat disturbance and private property laws have particularly contributed to the decline of whiteroot, which is rare in California today. Contemporary basket makers search for redbud and chaparral along back roads and highways, but fear that the herbicides applied by government agencies will poison them since they must handle the sticks wet, and they use their teeth to hold the ends while splitting the material. 'Blackroot' has always been in short supply due to the relative scarcity of favourable growing conditions and the added work to dye them.[12]

The Transmission of Cultural Values and Environmental–Economic Continuity

The transmission of indigenous plant knowledge in central California is gendered: it takes place through women, not necessarily but usually from grandmother to granddaughter. Those who lived on or near their former homelands were more successful in keeping their traditions alive, especially those traditions based on the knowledge and use of plants. In 1993, a North Fork Mono elder explained that the reason that she knows as much as she does is because her family has lived in the same area for many generations. 'If we went to another area, we'd know as little as strangers do here' (Bethel, personal communication, 1993). Botanical knowledge includes identification of species and good habitat management; technical aspects of food, medicine, and basketry materials preparation; the seasonality and various uses of different plants; and related spiritual beliefs and stories. Some teaching occurred on gathering trips, through storytelling and during puberty ceremonies. However, most Indian knowledge is credited to repeated observation, listening to elders and personal experience (Dick-Bissonnette n.d.; Lee 1998: 107; see also Turner, this volume). Some skills are so much a matter of dexterity, such as splitting redbud and whiteroot strands evenly or winnowing acorn, that they can be learned only through years of practice (Baty, personal communication; Ortiz 1991).

Preserving the few remaining basketry material patches, restoring others, and passing the techniques and associated beliefs and practices on to the next genera-tion are of renewed importance. 'It's a matter of respect,' contemporary leaders explain. People who learn to respect the spirits of plants and nature in general will not only preserve important resources but also learn to respect their elders and other human beings. This helps to keep families and social groups together.

Many basket makers in the area have stated that continued use and cultivation encourage these resources to flourish and to produce the best materials. By the early 1800s, much of the indigenous landscape had been overrun by European grasses and weedy annuals that were introduced by imported livestock (Huntington 1971: 316; Crampton 1974: 29–33). Further habitat disturbance occurred from mining, lumbering, ranching, agriculture, water system projects and urbanization. Private property laws and neglect have also contributed to the decline of plant biodiversity and to the decrease in sedge in particular. In recent years, however, public agencies have begun to make an effort to accommodate native basket makers by allowing them to gather plant materials in areas that were once their grandparents' homelands.

The use of traditional medicine and acorns, which were driven underground or otherwise marginalized by Euro-American hegemony, has been reduced to rituals such as smudging a reconstructed Round House with sage or tobacco as a spiritual offering, or bringing a pot of cooked acorn to an inter-tribal gathering.

Women's status in central California indigenous society continues to be high. In the mid-1990s, a Mono woman elder stated that 'there have always been more women than men on the North Fork Mono Tribal Council and on the Board of Directors of the Sierra Mono Museum' which was incorporated in 1966. Also in the mid-1990s, two-thirds of the members of the Posgisa Mono and Chukchansi Yokoch tribal councils were women. Young men are becoming more involved today as dance and spiritual leaders, to help keep young people on the right path, or the 'red road', as one elder calls it (Turner, personal communication, 1993). Indian people with business or professional degrees are valued in the 'casino economy'[13] of twenty-first-century California Indian society, while women with indigenous language, basketry and other tribal skills continue to be leaders in group decision making and intercultural matters.

Only a few basket makers in the study area can make baskets as well as their grandmothers did, but all of those who try are respected members of the contemporary Indian community. The California Indian Basketweavers' Association, with prominent leadership from the central California foothills, has become a strong voice for heritage resource protection and cultural revitalization. As long as a few individuals in each area take up the practice, the circle of central California Indian traditions will remain unbroken, and women will be recognized as expert purveyors of indigenous culture, knowledge and skills.

Notes

1   The term 'Indian' is preferred to 'Native American' by Indian people in central California, in part due to the American Indian Movement that revived pride in their ethnic and cultural heritage and in part because the term 'Native American' includes other groups, such as native Hawaiians, to whom they are not related.

2   The term 'traditional' is used here to mean indigenous culture, some of which has been handed down through the generations to modern-day descendants. The past tense is used to describe traditional Indian practices reported to ethnographers in the late 1800s to early 1900s and by various contemporary consultants.

3   Merriam noted that tobacco was 'cultivated about many of the old rancherias [small reservations] by Miwok women' (1955: 69). In the 1920s, elderly Yokoch and Mono couples were observed growing, harvesting and processing tobacco plants (Gayton 1948: 93, 155, 269). See Bean and Blackburn (1976) for theoretical comments on 'proto-agriculture' in Native California. Some plants may have been transplanted in aboriginal times, judging from their sometimes atypical distribution (Mathewson, personal communication, 2001).

4   Similar to the !Kung response to the question 'Why farm when there are so many mongongo nuts?', Central California Indians thought that planting acorns was Blue Jay's job. In other words, they understood the connection between seeds and plant reproduction, but did not adopt the practice of planting seeds. This is probably because gathering seeds with a seed-beater basket helps disburse them rather than selecting for larger seeds or a tougher rachis, as in Old World cereal grain domestication. Choice of species not suited to domestication is another important factor; oak trees have masting cycles, that is, they are irregular producers and take a generation to mature. Human selection for larger seeds, however, altered the wild plant gene pool enough to produce New World tobacco, sunflower, goosefoot and amaranth cultigens in North America, maize in Mesoamerica, and beans and potatoes in South America (Harlan 1992: 119).

5   These circumstances are in marked contrast to full-time 'attached' specialists in more hierarchically organized societies, where skilled individuals became slaves who produced goods for a ruling élite (Leacock 1972: 52; Brumfiel and Earle 1987: 5, 8, Chapter 6).

6   See Aberle 1962: 661, 703, in Schneider and Gough 1962; Murphy 1960: 181.

7   Powers 1877; Gifford 1932: 44; Dick-Bissonnette n.d., 1997: 304–11; Lee 1998: 36–7, 97, 107).

8   See also Lee (1998) on Nim (Mono) medicine, Walker and Hudson (1993) on Chumash healing, and Margolin on the Ohlone Way (1978: 19, 123–32).

9   A writer for the *Overland Monthly* in 1919 observed of the Mono: 'women are the "steady workers" and the sustainers of the social order ... taking care of the children, gathering acorns, [and] plants for basketmaking, or going here and there to wash clothes for white women' (C. H. Shinn, quoted in Bates and Lee 1990: 34).

10 King or chinook salmon (*Oncorhynchus tshawytscha*), steelhead trout (*Salmo gairdnerii*), and a dozen other kinds of fish and small game were probably more important protein sources

than deer, elk or other large game (Dick-Bissonnette 1997: 107–8).

11 Chia (*Salvia columbariae*), sunflower (*Helianthus* spp.), tarweed (*Madia* spp.) and wild rye, for example (Anderson 1993, Moratto *et al.* 1988: 312).

12 The sandy alluvial fan in Yosemite's Tenaya Creek is the outstanding exception (Bates and Lee 1990: 43). Indian women managed the plants by taking the new, straight shoots for basketry, and pruning back or coppicing the old growth to encourage more shoots for the following year (Baty, personal communication; Temple, personal communication; Anderson 1999).

13 There are at least seven Indian-owned gambling casinos in the central California interior today. The decline of wild foods has contributed to the economic need for casinos as a source of jobs in the Indian community.

References

Aberle, D.F. (1961) 'Matrilineal descent in cross-cultural perspective', in D.M. Schneider and K. Gough (eds.), *Matrilineal Kinship*, Berkeley: University of California Press, pp. 655–727.

Aginsky, B. W. (1943) 'Cultural element distributions: XXIV Central Sierra', *University of California Anthropological Records*, Vol. 8, No. 4, pp. 393–468.

Anderson, M. K. (1990) *California Indian Horticulture, Fremontia*, Sacramento: California Native Plant Society.

Anderson, M. K. (1993) *Native Californians as Ancient and Contemporary Cultivators*, Ballena Press Anthropological Papers No. 40, Menlo Park, CA: Ballena Press.

Anderson, M. K. (1999) 'The fire, pruning, and coppice management of temperate ecosystems for basketry material by California Indian tribes', *Human Ecology*, Vol. 27, No. 1, pp. 79–113.

Barrett, S. A. and E. W. Gifford (1933) *Miwok Material Culture: Indian Life of the Yosemite Region*, Yosemite National Park: Yosemite Natural History Association, Inc.

Bates, Craig (1986) Personal communication, Yosemite Museum curator.

Bates, C. (1982) 'Coiled basketry of the Sierra Miwok', San Diego Museum Papers No. 15.

Bates, C. and M. J. Lee (1990) *Tradition and Innovation: a Basket History of the Indians of the Yosemite–Mono Lake Area*, Yosemite National Park: The Yosemite Association.

Baty, Margaret (1987) Personal communication, Auberry Mono basket maker and elder.

Bean, L. J. and T. C. Blackburn (1976) *Native Californians: a Theoretical Retrospective,* Ramona: Ballena Press.

Beardsley, R. K. (1948) 'Culture sequences in central California archaeology', *American Antiquity,* Vol. 14, No. 1, pp. 1–28.

Beecher, Melba (1993) Personal communication, Auberry Mono.

Bethel, Rosalie (1993) Personal communication, North Fork Mono elder.

Blackburn, T. C., and K. Anderson (eds.) (1993) *Before the Wilderness: Environmental Management by Native Californians*, Menlo Park, California: Ballena Press.

Brown, Judith K. (1995) Personal communication, Oakland University anthropology professor.

Brumfiel, E. M. and T. K. Earle (1987) *Specialization, Exchange and Complex Societies*, Cambridge (UK): Cambridge University Press.

Charlie, Clara (1994) Personal communication, Chukchansi Yokoch cultural demonstrator.

Cook, S. G. (1976) *The Conflict between the California Indian and White Civilization,* Berkeley: University of California Press.

Crampton, B. (1974) *Grasses in California*, Berkeley: University of California Press.

Dick, L. E., L. Planas, J. Polanich, C. D. Bates and M. J. Lee (1988) *Strands of Time: Yokuts, Mono, and Miwok Basketmakers*, National Endowment for the Arts, publication sponsored by the Folk Arts Program, Fresno, California: Fresno Metropolitan Museum.

Dick-Bissonnette, L. E. (1997) 'Foothill Yokoch, Mono and Miwok Women: an Anthropological Perspective', PhD dissertation, University of California at Santa Barbara, Ann Arbor, Michigan:

University Microfilms International.

Dick-Bissonnette, L. E. (n.d.) unpublished field and research notes, 1978–96.

Gayton, A. H. (1948) 'Yokuts and Western Mono ethnography, I: Tulare Lake, Southern Valley, and Central Foothill Yokuts; II: Northern Foothill Yokuts and Western Mono', *Anthropological Records*, Vol. 10, Nos. 1 and 2.

Gifford, E. W. (1926) 'Miwok lineages and the political unit in aboriginal California', *American Anthropologist*, Vol. 28, pp. 389–401.

Gifford, E. W. (1932) 'The Northfork Mono', *University of California Publications in American Archaeology and Ethnology*, Vol. 31, pp. 15–56.

Harlan, J. R. (1992) *Crops and Man*, Madison, Wisconsin: American Society of Agronomy, Inc., Crop Science Society of America, Inc.

Heizer, R. F. and A. B. Elsasser (1980) *The Natural World of the California Indians*, Berkeley: University of California Press.

Helms, M. W. (1993) *Craft and the Kingly Ideal: Art, Trade, and Power*, Austin: University of Texas Press.

Hull, K. L. and M. J. Moratto, with contributions by H. McCarthy, C. K. Roper, W. G. Spaulding, M. R. Hale and E. Nilsson (1999) 'Archaeological synthesis and research design', Yosemite National Park, California, Yosemite Research Center Publications in Anthropology No. 21.

Huntington, G. L. (1971) *Soil Survey of Eastern Fresno County, California*, prepared for the USDA Soil Conservation Service, Washington, DC: United States Government Printing Office.

Jennings, J. D. (1974) *Prehistory of North America*, second edition, New York: McGraw-Hill Book Company.

Jones, Henry (1993) Personal communication, Chukchansi Yokoch cultural demonstrator.

Kroeber, F. (1976) *Handbook of the Indians of California*, Washington DC: Bureau of American Ethnology, Bulletin 78 (Reprint of 1925 edition), New York: Dover Publications, Inc.

Latta, F. F. (1977) *Handbook of the Yokuts Indians* (first edition 1949), Santa Cruz: Bear State Books.

Leacock, E. (1955) 'Matrilocality in a simple hunting economy (Montagnais–Naskapi)', *Southwest Journal of Anthropology*, Vol. 11, pp. 31–47.

Leacock, E. (1958) 'Status among the Montagnais–Naskapi of Labrador', *Ethnohistory*, Vol. 5, No. 3, pp. 200–209.

Leacock, E. (1972) 'Introduction', *Origins of the Family, Private Property and the State* by Frederich Engels, New York: International Publishers, pp. 7–67.

Lee, G. D. (1998) *Walking Where We Lived: Memoirs of a Mono Indian Family*, Norman: University of Oklahoma Press.

Lynch, J. M. (1953) Typed manuscript in the Anna Gayton Spier Collection, Bancroft Library, University of California at Berkeley.

Margolin, M. (1978) *The Ohlone Way: Indian Life in the San Francisco–Monterey Bay Area*, Berkeley: Heyday Books.

Mathewson, Margaret (2001) Personal communication, central California ethnobotanist.

McCarthy, H. (1993) 'A political economy of Western Mono acorn production', unpublished PhD dissertation, University of California at Davis.

Merriam, C. H. (1903) 'Basketry', *Science*, Vol. 17, No. 438, pp. 826, in C. H. Merriam papers, reel 89, BANC MSS 80/18c, Berkeley: University of California, Bancroft Library.

Merriam, C. H. (1955) *Studies of California Indians*, Staff of the Department of Anthropology of the University of California (ed.), Berkeley and Los Angeles: University of California Press.

Moratto, M. J. et al. (1988) Archaeological Excavations at Site CA-Fre-1671, Fresno County, California, Final Report prepared for California Department of Transportation, District 6, Fresno, Fresno: Infotec Research Inc.

Murphy, R. F. (1960) *Headhunter's Heritage: Social and Economic Change among the Mundurucu Indians*, Berkeley: University of California Press.

Ortiz, B. (1991) *It Will Live Forever: Traditional Yosemite Indian Acorn Preparation*, Berkeley: Heyday Books.

Penney, D. W. (1992) *Art of the American Indian Frontier: the Chandler–Pohrt Collection*, Seattle: Detroit Institute of the Arts and University of Washington Press.

Planas, Lorrie (1987) Personal communication, Choinumni Yokoch–Mono cultural liaison officer.

Powers, S. (1976) *Tribes of California. Contributions to North American Ethnology*, first edition, 1877, with an introduction and annotation by Robert F. Heizer, Berkeley: University of California Press.

Sample, Emily (1993) Personal communication, Choinumni Yokoch elder and historian.

Sarris, G. (1993) *Keeping Slug Woman Alive: a Holistic Approach to American Indian Texts*, Berkeley: University of California Press.

Schnieder, D. M. and K. Gough (eds.) (1962) *Matrilineal Kinship*, Berkeley and Los Angeles: University of California Press.

Spier, R. F. G. (n.d.) Fieldnotes, BANC MSS 79/5c. Berkeley: University of California, Bancroft Library.

Stewart, G. W. (n.d.) 'Notes and correspondence, including interviews with Jim Herington, Jim Crossmore, Joe and Mary Pohot, and Sam Garfield, 1903–1929', California Section, California State Library.

Tadd, B. (1988) *Miwok: One Miwok's View of Native Food Preparations and the Medicinal Uses of Plants,* Sonora, California: Three Forests Interpretive Association.

Temple, Ethel (1987) Personal communications, North Fork Mono basket maker and instructor.

Turner, Norma (1993) Personal communication, Auberry Mono elder.

Walker, P. L. and T. Hudson (1993) *Chumash Healing: Changing Health and Medical Practices in an American Indian Society*, Banning, California: Malki Museum Press.

CHAPTER 12

Exchange, Patriarchy and Status: Women's Homegardens in Bangladesh

Margot Wilson

In rural Bangladesh, the domestic sphere plays an especially critical role in family subsistence. Since Bangladesh is one of the poorest countries in the world, the homestead, where domestic production takes place, has become a focus for research and development programming. Since women are mainly responsible for domestic production, they are of special interest as are two of their homestead production activities that have received considerable attention: post-harvest field crop processing and care of livestock (cf. Begum 1989; Islam 1979; Wallace *et al.* 1987). Homegardening is also often mentioned as an area in which women make substantial contributions to the health and well-being of the family, not to mention its income-generation potential.[1]

Although several researchers have claimed that homegardens in Bangladesh are the exclusive purview of women (cf. Chen 1986; Huq 1979), more in-depth research indicates that this is not the case. Men invest a considerable amount of time and energy in homegardening, and substantial gender differences exist in this sphere of activity (Wilson-Moore 1990). Gender relations surrounding homegardening also have important implications in terms of human welfare, women's status and plant biodiversity management. Women manage a large diversity of mainly indigenous species of vegetables in homegardens, whereas men manage a lower diversity mainly consisting of exotic species. Men's and women's homegardens are differentiated in part by spatial definitions: cultivated areas located 'outside' the homestead are defined as fields, while cultivated areas located 'inside' are defined as homestead (*bari*) land. Men's homegardens are located 'outside', while women's homegardens are confined inside the boundaries of the homestead. Reminiscent of feminist categories of public and private spheres, these distinctions reflect prevalent attitudes towards women's proper place, which is secluded 'inside' the *bari*.

Distinct and complementary, men's and women's homegardens perpetuate and reproduce spatial and social delineations that maintain the invisibility of women's contributions to biodiversity management, to food production for family consumption, and to the transmission of culture. For women, homegardening falls within the traditional roles ascribed to them, where the invisibility of their contribution is consistent with the prevalent cultural view of women as non-productive consumers of family resources. It is argued here that women's work in homegardens does not contribute positively to their social status because this is an expected, and indeed desired, structural element of patriarchy.

Data from two rural villages in Bangladesh provide an opportunity to test feminist theories that relate women's status in society to their productive work, to societal constraints on women's production, and to women's ability to control the distribution of their produce. Structural elements that support patriarchy in Bangladesh include male control over property, income and women's labour. The kinship system and religious beliefs provide the ideological framework for patriarchy. The power of patriarchy manifests itself in land inheritance laws, in women's inability to obtain and use cash, in their reduced access to legal resources, education and political processes, and in general societal attitudes that restrict women to the domestic sphere. That the restrictive power of patriarchy does not completely dissipate women's ability to market their homegarden produce, and that women retain some degree of control over its use and distribution, is testimony to the ingenuity of the women themselves.

The following discussion details women's work in homegardens as it is rooted in concepts of patriarchy, and explores the reasons why it fails to influence their status in a positive way. It also explains why it is women, rather than men, who assume the task of maintaining indigenous biodiversity in homegardens in Bangladesh.

Homegarden Traditions

Development scholars have generated much of the information available on home-gardens, demonstrating the many benefits that accrue to gardening families. Ethno-botanists and ecologists have also studied homegardens intensively and identify them as important sites for the maintenance of plant biodiversity. In some parts of Indonesia, for example, homegardens contain a vast number of plant species and provide 40 per cent of the total calories, 30 per cent of the total protein and 65 per cent of the fuels consumed by rural households (Brownrigg 1985). Homegardens have been called by a number of different names, including kitchen garden, dooryard garden, backyard garden, dawn garden and homestead garden (see also Greenberg, this volume).

There are strong correspondences between homegardens in Bangladesh and homegardening traditions discussed in the literature. Implicit in much of the literature is the assumption that homegardens are a known and readily identifiable form of land use. To the contrary, Brownrigg (ibid.) argues that, throughout the world, a number of homegardening traditions are distinguished by distinctive garden layouts, unique constellations of plant species, and different geographical origins. Characteristic gardening traditions are found in sub-Saharan Africa, the Caribbean, Mesoamerica, and the Andes. The Near Eastern and the Asian Mixed are the two traditions most germane to this discussion.

The Near Eastern Tradition has influenced both European and Islamic garden-ing. Introduced by the Greeks and Romans to the temperate areas of Europe, this gardening tradition survived the Dark Ages within the walls of monasteries. During the Renaissance period, it developed a distinctively European style characterized by the presence of walls or fences, borders consisting of productive and protective trees, plant beds, and planting in parallel rows. It spread with European expansion throughout the colonial world, including to North America (*ibid.*). The Near Eastern tradition is also an ancestor of Islamic gardening, which spread in conjunction with religious conquest throughout the Near East, Spain, North Africa and South Asia. Here, the presence of walls became a prominent feature, guaranteeing the security of a private family domain and the seclusion of women within it. Garden vegetables in the Near Eastern tradition include lettuce, cucumber, onion and radish (*ibid.*).

The origins of the Asian Mixed tradition are closely aligned with those of wet rice agriculture. In fact, Hutterer (1982) suggests that Asian Mixed homegardens probably pre-date rice agriculture and imitate the surrounding tropical forest (see also Soemarwoto 1975; Terra 1961). Control of water is important: where Islamic and European traditions tend to be better adapted to arid and temperate climates, the Asian Mixed tradition is most commonly found in the humid tropics, where it forms 'an adaptive adjunct to the flooded rice paddy' (Brownrigg 1985: 27). Terra (1961) observed the Asian Mixed tradition in South and South-east Asia, while Hutterer (1982) has argued that the Asian Mixed tradition persists in an even broader area stretching from India to Polynesia and Oceania. Asian Mixed gardens are ecologically complex systems with multiple layers or storeys of vegetation, a high diversity of plant species, and a high ratio of perennials to annuals. Fences and hedges are rare. The plant species typical of the Asian Mixed garden include Chinese spinach (an *amaranthus* species), string bean, cassava, water spinach or *kangkong*, sweet potato, taro and yam (Soemarwoto 1981).

Islamic and European gardening traditions arrived in South Asia together with Islam in the thirteenth century and with European colonialism in the 1700s, respect-ively. Despite their long and not inconsequential influence, especially in more arid regions, the indigenous tradition, which demonstrates a distinctly Asian Mixed character, is very much in evidence today in rural areas. Since Asian Mixed gardens have a jumbled appearance, they can be completely overlooked or dismissed as disordered and inconsequential by the uninformed observer. Researchers and development planners who are influenced by European or Islamic gardening tradi-tions may have difficulty 'seeing' the Asian Mixed garden and understandably fail to appreciate the complexity of a gardening tradition so different from their own. This is particularly relevant in Bangladesh, where foreign-born or foreign-trained scientists have done much of the research and development planning. For example, one day while walking through a rural village, a colleague with many years of experience as an extension worker and planner remarked, 'So, where are the gardens? I don't see any gardens here.' When shown the small patches of vegetables and a few individual gourd plants growing over the fences and roofs of the house-hold, he expressed surprise at his inability to 'see' these 'invisible' homegardens.

Homegardens in Bangladesh

Research was conducted between 1986 and 1989 in two villages: Jalsha, a small village of about 1,500 people located in central Bangladesh some 50 miles from the capital, Dhaka; and Chuchuli, a village with a population of around 2,500 located 250 miles north-west of the capital (Wilson-Moore 1986, 1987a, 1990). Patterns of land ownership are similar to other parts of the country, where most households own a modest amount of land (three acres on average), divided into a homestead (one-tenth of an acre on average) and several small plots scattered throughout the village (Wallace *et al.* 1987; Wilson-Moore 1990). In Jalsha, it was first assumed that homegardening was exclusively women's work as the literature up to that time suggests. As a result, only women were interviewed, and research focused entirely and exclusively on women's work in homegardens. When working in Chuchuli, however, it became clear that men also produce vegetables in small gardens outside the homestead. Accordingly, both men and women were interviewed in Chuchuli, and the discussion that follows depends primarily on data from Chuchuli. Data from Jalsha are interpreted cautiously and used only comparatively.

Chuchuli is geographically more isolated than Jalsha. Electricity had not yet reached Chuchuli and transportation was primarily by foot, although some of the more affluent villagers owned bicycles. The village had a daily market, a government school and two *Madrassa* (Islamic) schools. Middle-aged villagers recalled that during their childhood there were considerably fewer people in Chuchuli. Much land was left uncultivated and there were large stands of bamboo and tangled underbrush; tigers devoured livestock; and the abundant mangoes fell to the ground and rotted. The market in Chuchuli, which is the centre of economic and social transactions in the village, is almost exclusively men's domain. Men own and operate the shops and tea stalls and, with the exception of young children and a few elderly widows, it is men who patronize them. Women, especially those from 'respectable' families, are expected to remain out of public view, and are virtually never present in the market. This restriction has important implications for women's ability to sell their homegarden produce.

In these two villages, as across much of rural Bangladesh, households consist of nuclear or extended families that are related through males, own land in common, and prepare and consume meals together. These relations are reflected in the language: *khana* (food) and *chula* (cook stove) are used interchangeably with the word *bari* (house) to refer to this configuration of people. The word *bari* also refers to the homestead, the physical place where the family resides. It includes space for housing, cooking, stabling of animals, post-harvest processing and storage of crops. Women remark upon the need to keep the courtyard in front of the house *porishkar* or 'clean': well-swept and litter-free. Women regularly plaster courtyard floors, the bases of bamboo houses and the walls of mud houses with a combination of dirt and cow dung or urine-saturated earth from under the straw in the cow barn. When dry, this mixture forms a smooth, hard, durable surface particularly suitable for threshing, winnowing, and sun-drying rice, wheat, pulses and mustard seed.

Women's homegardens are typically located in any clear space inside or immediately adjacent to the *bari*. The need for a clean, flat courtyard means that women's vegetables must be tucked into the corners and alleys between and behind the buildings. Planted singularly or in clusters and climbing over the walls, along the fences and across the roofs of the buildings, they must be unobtrusive and out of the way.

Plant species are highly diverse, there are no beds or rows, and the delineation of boundaries between species is vertical rather than horizontal. Tall and medium-height trees, smaller bushy shrubs, upright plants, and creepers and root crops form vertical layers. Weeding is minimal, and it is often difficult to differentiate the homegarden from the surrounding undergrowth of voluntary plants. The overall impression is one of an edible jungle. In fact, even the husbands of the women in Chuchuli failed to recognize the gardening efforts of their wives. When asked what their wives were cultivating, they invariably answered 'nothing at all', even when the proof was crawling across the roofs and walls of the homestead.

Clearly, men identify vegetable cultivation on the basis of total number of plants and the amount of earth required for their upkeep. Although a single gourd plant can generate a sizeable harvest, men maintained that their wives were generally 'lazy' and uninterested in vegetable cultivation. Men's failure to acknowledge a woman's productive labour in homegardens is attributable in large part to more general societal attitudes toward women who are seen not as producers, but as consumers. This view of women as non-productive is pervasive, and undoubtedly has a significant bearing on the failure of women's homegarden production to enhance their status. Men are not 'untrained' observers, like the extension agent mentioned above. They are aware of women's production, but the small scale and jumbled appearance that helps to keep it 'invisible' to outsiders makes it appear to be 'domestic' rather than 'productive' work. Thus neither men nor women consider women's homegardening to be 'productive' work, which is, by their definition, almost exclusively men's work.

Women cultivate mainly indigenous vine or gourd species that spring up readily. They are produced from seed that women select and store from the previous year. Being well adapted to seasonal climatic fluctuations, they flourish inside and around the homestead with a minimum of labour or other inputs. The majority of species grown by women are cultivated in the summer months (Table 12.1).

In comparison with men's gardens, women's gardens contain a higher diversity of plant species and a smaller number of plants of any particular type. The quantities produced are smaller and more varied, and are intended mainly for family consumption. This high-diversity, low-volume output is the predominant characteristic of women's homegardening patterns in Bangladesh, and reflects a strategy that is oriented towards meeting local nutritional and culinary require-ments. It is no coincidence that the vegetables most commonly grown in women's homegardens are those that the villagers prefer to eat and that form part of local culinary tradition (see also Greenberg, this volume). The diversity of vegetables grown helps to offset the boredom of eating the same food every day. Women

Table 12.1: Women's Vegetable Species in Homegardens in the Bangladesh Study Villages

Bangla name	English name	Scientific name	Season
Chal kumra	Wax gourd	*Benincasa hispida*	Summer
Dhunduli	Marrow	*Cucurbita pepo*	Summer
Jhangi Alu	Sweet potato	*Dioscorea* spp.	Summer
Kankrol	Bitter cucumber	*Momordica cochinensis*	Winter
Kira	Cucumber	*Cucurbita anguina*	Summer
Koita	Snake gourd	*Trichosanthes anguina*	Summer
Korla	Bitter gourd	*Momordica charantia*	Summer
Lau	Bottle gourd	*Lagenaria vulgaris*	Winter
Man kochu	Giant taro	*Alocasia macrorrhiza*	Summer
Mas koliy	String bean	*Vigna sinensis*	Summer
Maz alu	Yam	*Dioscorea* spp.	Summer
Misti Kumra	Sweet pumpkin	*Cucurbita maxima*	Summer
Ole kochu	Elephant foot	*Amorphophallus campanulatus*	Summer
Potal	Pointed gourd	*Trichosanthes dioeca*	Summer
Pui shak	Indian spinach	*Basella alba*	Summer
Seem	Country bean	*Dolichos lablab*	Summer
Torui	Ribbed gourd	*Luffa acutangula*	Summer

Note: Local names for vegetables were translated into English by the author. Scientific names are taken from Ahmad (1982) and Burns (1988).

Table 12.2: Men's Vegetable Species in Homegardens in the Bangladesh Study Villages

Bangla name	English name	Scientific name	Season
Adda	Ginger	*Zingiber officinale*	Winter
Begun	Eggplant	*Solanum melongena*	Both
Bhada kopi	Cabbage	*Brassica oleracea*	Winter
Data	Amaranthus	*Amaranthus lividus*	Summer
Derosh	Okra	*Hibiscus esculentus*	Summer
Gajor	Carrot	*Daucuc carota*	Winter
Gol alu	Potato	*Solanum tuberosum*	Winter
Holud	Turmeric	*Curcuma domestica*	Both
Kacha morich	Chili pepper	*Capsicum* spp.	Both
Kochu	Taro/arum	*Colocasia* spp.	Both
Kolmi shak	Water spinach	*Ipomoea aquatica*	Summer
Lal shak	Amaranthus	*Amaranthus lividus*	Winter
Lapa shak	(none)	*Malva verticillata*	Winter
Mula	Radish	*Raphanus sativus*	Winter
Palong shak	Chinese cabbage	*Spinacia oleracea*	Winter
Pat shak	Jute leaf	*Corchorus capsularis*	Summer
Peyaj	Onion	*Allium cepa*	Winter
Roshun	Garlic	*Allium sativum*	Winter
Shalgom	Turnip	*Brassica campestris*	Winter
Tomato	Tomato	*Lycopersicon esculentum*	Winter

Note: Local names for vegetables were translated into English by the author. Scientific names are taken from Ahmad (1982) and Burns (1988).

carefully stagger planting times so that plants mature at different times and are available throughout the summer. Some gourds can be stored for a short time, but most vegetables are eaten as they mature. If more vegetables ripen than can be consumed, they are given away, traded with neighbours or sent to the market for sale. Women living in separate households who are related by kinship coordinate their planting times and species in order to maximize access through sharing. In this way, the garden acts as a living larder, providing fresh produce on a daily basis.

Homesteads throughout rural Bangladesh are clustered together and surrounded by plots for field crops. All of the men's homegardens in Chuchuli were located within the homestead clusters in small plots near to but outside the boundary of the homestead itself, usually within 10 metres of the house. Men's garden plots are clearly delineated and easily identifiable. Square or rectangular beds are raised or fenced and are normally monocropped with exotic species (Table 12.2). In this way, the pattern of men's vegetable cultivation is strongly reminiscent of field crop production patterns.

Many of the winter vegetables that men produce are exotic species and varieties that require extra inputs such as fertilizer, pesticides and irrigation. Some are temperate species that pose an additional risk in terms of crop failure if growing conditions are not optimal. Men's vegetable crops are grown in winter, with a few exceptions. Villagers like to eat most of the species that men grow but, more important, they also command a high price in the market. Furthermore, many can be transported easily without damage over rough roads.

Men's vegetable production requires more land than does women's vegetable production, in the sense that men's gardens occupy small plots (the largest was 22 by 10 metres, the smallest two metres square), while women's gardens are tucked into the corners of the homestead. Men who own more land devote more to vegetable production and cultivate a larger number of vegetable species. In general, men strategize to produce a surplus, and plant a single crop in each garden plot or multi-crop several species in separate subsections of a single plot. This results in synchronized maturation and harvesting times. The produce is packed up and carried off to the market in bulk. By contrast, women's vegetable production yields many individual plants with staggered maturation times. Harvesting on a piece-meal basis is entirely determined by the day-to-day needs of the household.

Overall, the men surveyed cultivate a total of 20 different species of vegetables, three more than the total produced by the women interviewed. Nevertheless, within individual households, men rarely cultivate as many species as their wives do. Whereas most women have a minimum of five or six species growing inside the family compound over the course of a year, their husbands might only cultivate two or three species during the same period. In fact, where 59 per cent of women grow five or more species, 52 per cent of men grow fewer than three.

The distinction between vegetable species grown in winter and summer is not, in itself, very surprising, especially given wide seasonal variations in weather conditions in Bangladesh. However, summer species are predominantly Asian Mixed types that tend to be heat- and moisture-tolerant, and are grown almost exclusively by women. This suggests that women's gardening patterns may be older, traditional and indigenous. Conversely, winter vegetables are Near Eastern species adapted to cooler, drier conditions, and are grown almost exclusively by men. Recently, men have adopted some temperate winter species associated with European gardening traditions. These species probably reflect the preferences of the people who introduced them (Western development workers), and represent an expansion of the traditional vegetable repertoire.

Men's and women's garden patterns in Jalsha and Chuchuli reflect traditional delineations in production (men for sale and women for consumption), and do not replicate other cases in which men take on more lucrative cash crop production while women manage subsistence (homegarden) production. In Chuchuli and Jalsha, men are not investing extensive resources (such as large amounts of land, external labour or other inputs) in their homegardens; rather, these resources are reserved exclusively for field crop production. Nevertheless, the greater opportunity for income generation, and the relatively rare and valuable nature of temperate vegetables, may explain why men have accepted vegetable gardening so readily when it appears traditionally to have been women's work (see also Wooten, this volume).

Tradition, Change and Food

Generally, women in both villages cultivate the same vegetable species in the same seasons. Some differences exist in the names used to designate particular vegetable species, and several species grown in Jalsha were not grown in Chuchuli. Despite these differences, however, similar cultivation patterns are found in both villages. In Chuchuli, a few women experimentally grow some species out of season, but this is not the usual pattern. A few cultivate species that are normally considered to be men's crops, but these are grown inside the *bari* and are for family consumption only. Occasionally, both husband and wife cultivate the same crop, the wife inside and the husband outside in a small plot. More often, however, the species cultivated inside and outside the homestead are complementary, providing both summer and winter vegetables, food and income.

Like their counterparts in Chuchuli, some women in Jalsha cultivate 'men's' vegetable species inside the *bari* at some time during the year. What is remarkable is that over 80 per cent of the women in Jalsha report that they are doing this. For example, one woman displayed a homegarden plot that was planted in beds with straight rows, each of which was marked with the name of the vegetable. When questioned, she admitted that she 'worked together' with her husband in this homegarden, and that her 'own' garden was inside the homestead. When asked about vegetable production, she had proudly shown the 'joint' garden rather than her own.

These behaviours appear to contradict the patterns described above and to challenge distinctions between homegardening and field crop production. However, women's cultivation of exotic species is far more prevalent in those households where other evidence of collaboration between men and women cultivators is apparent, including women's market purchase of seed rather than use of own seed, women's use of fertilizer and pesticides, and women selling the produce rather than consuming it at home. Although no development agency was officially working in either village at the time of the research, some farmers have received inputs and training from one of the many development programmes operating in nearby villages. Some programmes (cf. CARE's LIFT Programme, see Wilson-Moore 1987b, 1988) encourage farmers with small landholdings to grow vegetables as an alternative to traditional field crops. No farmers in Jalsha or Chuchuli had consciously adopted this strategy and, since the scale remains small, men's vegetable production can still be considered as homegardening.

Thus, data from Chuchuli reflect more traditional patterns of homegardening in more isolated areas, while homegardens in Jalsha demonstrate the continuing presence of indigenous patterns that are nevertheless changing under the influence of development programming and market demand. Jalsha is clearly more closely integrated into the capitalist economy by its relatively close proximity to the capital and access to the transportation system. A demand for large volumes of both indigenous and exotic species in city markets has undoubtedly had an influence on vegetable cultivation patterns in Jalsha. Villages throughout Bangladesh can be expected to range somewhere between the two ends of a continuum represented by these two villages.

These distinctive village patterns also parallel differences in women's and men's homegardens, where women maintain indigenous varieties even under conditions of increasing commoditization, whereas men are readily adopting exotic species. Women in Jalsha are experimenting with exotic species but only in the context of 'working with' their husbands. This is an important issue considering women's roles in biodiversity conservation. Certainly, women's seclusion inside the homestead presupposes more traditional homegardening practices: they simply aren't exposed to new ideas and species. Women also have virtually no access to the market, so commodity production may be less appealing to them. By contrast, men are the primary agents in the marketplace and are more readily exposed to information about new species and varieties, new production techniques, market demand and opportunities for training.

Beyond opportunity, however, women choose to cultivate those species that are required by local culinary preferences and which people 'like to eat'. Food preparation influences women's decisions not only because they prepare family meals, but also owing to the influence of traditional food preparation technology. A *chula* is an earthen stove excavated in the kitchen floor and fuelled by straw, jute and bamboo sticks, dried cow dung or, occasionally, firewood. Three triangular points around the edges of the central opening support the traditional round-bottomed aluminium or terracotta cooking pots. Lighting the *chula* is a costly affair, especially for poorer families. In fact, a reasonably good indicator of the socio-economic status of rural households is the number of times that the *chula* is lit during a single day. Women cultivate those vegetable species and varieties that cook quickly, and lend themselves to meals produced in a single pot or in pots that can be juggled or stacked on top of one another. Most indigenous vegetables meet these requirements, whereas many exotic species do not. Women's garden production is intended to produce nutritious, preferred and economical meals for their families, and traditional species more readily fill this need.

Patriarchy and Marketing

Feminist theorists argue that women are social actors who have goals and strategies to achieve these goals (cf. Rosaldo and Lamphere 1974; Brettell and Sargent 1993). However, women in rural Bangladesh demonstrate very little ability to influence the decisions made in their households, even those that impact directly on themselves (Alamgir 1977). Unable to mitigate the pervasive influence of patriarchy, women continue to be treated as chattels. They have virtually no decision-making power in terms of choosing marriage partners, either their own or their children's. Decisions about childbearing are primarily in the hands of husbands and mothers-in-law and, although this may be interpreted as a form of power for older women, young women have no control over their own bodies. They gain power only as mothers-in-law and then only in the case that they have sons. Women have no legal recourse against a husband who takes a second wife or who fails to provide for the family. They cannot divorce except with their husbands' permission or under special circumstances determined by the court. Women do not inherit or own property. Education is generally considered unnecessary, and women's literacy rates are half those of men. At election time, if women vote (and most do not), their choices are dictated by their husbands.

Purdah is but one institutionalized form of patriarchy applicable specifically to Muslim women. Fundamentally, *purdah* calls for the physical seclusion of women within the boundaries of the household and is ostensibly intended to protect their virtue and the prestige of the family, which is predicated upon that virtue. Beyond this, however, *purdah* represents a series of behaviours and attitudes toward women that effectively prevent them from entering into the mainstream of community life. They are barred from participation in social, religious or political processes and are confined to the private sphere of the household. Although economic need presents an obstacle to women's ability to observe *purdah*, it remains an ideal toward which most rural Muslim women strive (McCarthy 1977). Men and women alike generally agree that the world 'outside' is not a safe place for women, and that they are protected and happier when they remain 'inside', as Chuchuli villagers attested:

> Women are always inside and men are always outside. Something bad might happen to them if they go outside. Why would a woman want to go outside? (A Muslim housewife.)

> Women don't go outside unless they have to work to eat. (A Muslim farmer.)

Syncretism of Islamic and Hindu beliefs in Bangladesh has resulted in restrict-ions that apply only slightly less rigorously to Hindu women. These restrictions contrast with the relative freedom enjoyed by Hindu women in India. And, despite the serious implications that these restrictions have for women's ability to generate income for the family, respectable Hindu women are also expected to remain inside the physical boundary of the homestead or at least in its immediate vicinity. One villager expressed the ramifications for women's agricultural production in this way:

> Women can't plough the fields so they do not go outside. If they were to plough, Loki [a goddess] would be angry and no plants would grow. (A Hindu housewife.)

As a result of these attitudes, women in rural Bangladesh don't engage in agri-cultural (field crop) production, and it is generally considered unseemly for women to engage in any productive activities outside the confines of the homestead. Ostensibly, only the most destitute woman would undertake such work. Neverthe-less, time allocation research indicates that women in rural Bangladesh do contribute a substantial proportion (23–39 per cent) of the total time spent in subsistence activities, including post-harvest field crop processing, livestock care and home-gardening, all of which take place inside the homestead. The relegation of women's work to the homestead devalues their productive contributions by rendering them invisible. Furthermore, women are not able to go to the market. In Chuchuli, only small girls go to the local market with their fathers; some elderly widows also may go there to sell rice or wheat flour. However, respectable women of reproductive age do not go to the market. In Jalsha, the market is located in the next village, and women do not go at all. Accordingly, women in both villages must negotiate with a male family member or neighbour to take their homegarden produce to market for them.

Control and exchange of valued goods and services outside of the household have been correlated to show improved status for women (cf. Sanday 1974; Friedl 1975). Therefore, who produces food may be less important than who creates obligations and alliances through food distribution (see Sillitoe, Pieroni, and Ertuğ, this volume). Accordingly, one might suspect that, in rural Bangladesh, women's lack of self-determination is related to loss of control over the distribution of their homegarden produce. However, this is not the case. Extensive redistribution and exchange systems operate in both Chuchuli and Jalsha. Wealthier women give extra produce to less well-off neighbours and relatives, or to beggars who come to the door. Gifts of homegarden produce given to equally wealthy neighbours or relatives incur obligations for reciprocal returns at some point in the future. Through donation and reciprocal obligation, women control the distribution of homegarden foods outside the family and create networks of alliance throughout the community.

Surplus homegarden produce (over and above what can be eaten, given away or exchanged) is routinely sold in the market. One might postulate that, because women depend upon men to market their produce, they lose control at the marketing level; however, this also does not appear to be the case. More than 75 per cent of the women interviewed reported that, when they turn over the produce to a man for sale, they also provide a shopping list. Although women do not go to the market, they know the value of both the produce they send and the items on their lists. Some women confided that, if they are 'very clever', they arrange for the shopping list to be worth more than the produce that they supply. In this way, they try to ensure that their husbands obtain a good price for the produce or pay the difference from their own pocket. Generally, shopping lists include household items that are not produced at home, such as soap, tea, sugar, salt and other spices, cooking oil, hair oil and kerosene. Occasionally, if the produce that she provides for sale is valuable, the woman may ask her husband to buy *sindor*, the red powder that Hindu women wear in their hair, or *churis*, the glass bangles that Muslim women favour.

Men are compliant with this arrangement. When asked what becomes of the money generated by the sale of women's homegarden produce, only six out of 22 men replied that the money belonged to the women; only four stated that the cash was actually given to women. The rest reported that the money belonged to the man who sold the produce. This issue generated considerable discussion between the village imam (the local Islamic religious leader) and one of the village men. The imam maintained that, if the woman grows the produce, then the money is rightfully hers. The village man, on the other hand, claimed that men never give money to their wives: they either keep the money or use it to purchase items for the household. Finally, the two men reached a compromise, agreeing that, although it is technically the women's money, since women have little use for cash, it would not normally be given to them. Women agreed with this conclusion, commenting that there is no point in having cash since they cannot go to the market to spend it. However, when women do control cash, they use it to participate in savings societies, save it to purchase larger household items, or give it to their children to purchase sweets.

All women cultivate homegardens. They control the distribution of their garden produce through consumption, exchange and sale. The constancy of this contribution and its structural importance to subsistence should affect their status positively. Why then does this appear not to be the case? Possible explanations are offered and discussed in the following section.

Homegardens and Women's Status

Women's homegarden production is consumed primarily within the homestead. Thus, women's produce finds its way invisibly into the cooking pot. If a surplus is produced, women may trade it, give it away or send it to the market for sale. This surplus is relatively small and is available only sporadically. Thus, women's market production appears to be minimal compared to men's. Beyond this, redistribution and exchange of homegarden produce is informal and takes place only among women. The social alliances formed in this way do not involve men, and men are unlikely to be aware of them. Thus, like the produce itself, these networks of alliance and obligation remain invisible.

Produce from women's homegardens is recycled back into the household on a daily basis as food, gifts, and cash. It is not stored and does not accumulate over time, and its value is not recognized. Indeed, when questioned on this point, women were unable to assign a value to their cumulative homegarden production on a yearly, monthly or even weekly basis, although they know very well the value of individual products and can recall the quantities eaten, exchanged or sent to market. Similarly, men are unable to assign a value to women's homegarden production despite their active participation in its marketing and consumption. Cash is generated almost as an accidental by-product of production for consumption and is immediately recycled back into small purchases for the household. Because cash is not the primary objective of women's production and, since it never accumulates, it is never assigned a 'value'. So, as the vegetables themselves grow invisibly over the rooftops and walls, disappear into the cooking pot, and are traded away to neighbours and relatives, so too the cash that women generate vanishes into the family food budget. Women's homegarden produce is not recognized as an asset, and thus has no impact on women's status.

Yet, women predominate in homegardening because it is an acceptable productive activity for them. Indeed, it may be one thing that patriarchal restrictions on behaviour allow them to do. Because it is done in seclusion, it is invisible. Because it is invisible, it is allowed. Visibility of women's homegardening would bring with it the risk of disapproval or prohibition, with all the associated negative impacts on family nutrition and culinary traditions. Moreover, if women's production was profitable, there would be a risk that it would be taken over by men (see also Wooten, this volume). Thus, the small-scale 'invisibility' of women's homegarden production shouldn't be surprising: rather, it represents a desired structural quality within a patriarchal society.

Women's homegardens complement men's work in agriculture. Through homegardening, women enhance family nutrition, conserve culinary traditions, economize on the use of domestic resources, contribute to subsistence and create alliances among themselves. Yet, being invisible, these activities conform to the traditional values and roles ascribed to women by patriarchy. Thus, women's homegardens are defined as just another aspect of domestic work, construed as simply a part of the homestead like the kitchen or the cow barn. Since women are not supposed to engage in productive work (which is considered to be men's responsibility), women's homegardens are merged into the domestic sphere and women's work in them is defined as domestic work. The reason that women's homegarden production doesn't increase their status is because it is integral to the construction of patriarchy.

So, why do women engage in homegardening if it doesn't improve their status? Possibly it is because manifestations of status are of greater concern among academics than among rural Bangladeshi women. Alternatively, these women live within (and subtly manipulate) the strictures of patriarchy: the same characteristics that keep women's work in homegardening invisible allow women to continue to exercise these productive roles. Because they go unnoticed, they persist. To draw attention to the importance or profitability of women's homegardens would be to jeopardize them. Women cultivate homegardens because of patriarchy, not in spite of it.

In a material sense, homegardens allow women to meet total household food needs. In a social sense, women create alliances and exchange networks among themselves through distribution of homegarden produce. Equally significant for Bangladesh society, women's homegardens contribute to the maintenance of plant genetic diversity and perpetuate cultural identity by providing necessary indigenous ingredients for traditional foods. Since men's vegetable production is focused largely on exotic species and is directed almost entirely toward the market, it doesn't contribute to maintaining any of these important aspects of rural Bangladeshi culture. If women had other options, such as coming out of seclusion and engaging in agriculture or wage labour, perhaps they would emulate men's home-gardening patterns or abandon homegardening altogether. But, for now, the maintenance of horticultural biodiversity, good family nutrition, exchange networks between women and the perpetuation of culinary tradition all depend on women's interest in maintaining this apparently unrewarding (in terms of status) activity. Thus, women's continuing engagement in homegardening finds its explanation in aesthetic, nutritional and cultural processes, and in the sanctions of patriarchy.

Note

1 Abdullah and Zeidenstein 1982; Martius-von Harder 1981; Schoustra-van Beukering 1975; Wallace *et al.* 1987.

References

Abdullah, T. and S. Zeidenstein (1982) *Village Women of Bangladesh: Prospects for Change,* New York: Pergamon Press.

Ahmad, K. U. (1982) *Gardener's Book of Production and Nutrition,* Dhaka: Dacca Press Sangstha.

Alamgir, S. F. (1977) *Profile of Bangladeshi Women: Selected Aspects of Women's Roles and Status in Bangladesh,* Dhaka: USAID.

Begum, K. (1989) 'Participation of rural women in income-earning activities: a case study of a Bangladesh village', *Women's Studies International Forum,* Vol. 12, No. 5, pp. 519–28.

Brettell C. and C. Sargent (eds.) (1993) *Gender in Cross-cultural Perspective,* Englewood Cliffs: Prentice Hall.

Brownrigg, L. (1985) *Home Gardening in International Development: What the Literature Shows,* Washington: League for International Food Education.

Burns, B. (1988) *Wild Edible Plants in the Greater Noakhali District of Bangladesh: an Introductory Report,* Dhaka: Mennonite Central Committee Report.

Chen, M. A. (1986) *A Quiet Revolution: Women in Transition in Rural Bangladesh,* Cambridge: Schenkman Publishing Co.

Friedl, E. (1975) *Women and Men: an Anthropologist's View,* New York: Holt, Rinehart and Winston.

Huq, J. (1979) 'Economic activities of women in Bangladesh: the rural situation', in Women for Women (eds.), *The Situation of Women in Bangladesh,* Dhaka: BRAC Printers, pp. 139–82.

Hutterer, K. (1982) *Interaction between Tropical Ecosystems and Human Foragers: Some General Considerations,* Hawaii: The East–West Center, Environment and Policy Institute.

Islam, R. (1979) *Some Aspects of Female Employment in Rural Bangladesh,* Dhaka: National Foundation for Research on Human Resource Development.

Martius-von Harder, G. (1981) *Women in Rural Bangladesh,* Fort Lauderdale: Verlag Breitenback Publishers.

McCarthy, F. (1977) 'Bengali women as mediators of social change', *Human Organization,* Vol. 36, No. 4, pp. 363–70.

Rosaldo, M. Z. and L. Lamphere (eds.) (1974) *Woman, Culture and Society,* Stanford: Stanford University Press.

Sanday, P. (1974) 'Female status in the public domain', in M. Z. Rosaldo and L. Lamphere (eds.), *Woman, Culture and Society,* Stanford: Stanford University Press, pp 189–206.

Schoustra-van Beukering, E. J. (1975) 'Sketch of the daily life of a Bengali village woman', *Plural Societies,* Vol. 6, No. 4, pp. 51–66.

Soemarwoto, O. (1975) 'Unifying concepts in ecology', in W. H. van Dobben and R. R. Lowe-McConnel (eds.), *Rural Ecology and Development in Java,* The Hague: Dr W. Junk BV Publishers, pp. 275–81.

Soemarwoto, O. (1981) 'Homegardens in Indonesia', paper presented at the Fourth Pacific Science Inter-Congress, Singapore.

Terra, G. J. (1961) 'Characteristics of tropical horticulture in relation to food patterns', *Chronica Horticulturae,* Vol. 1, No. 3, pp. 37–40.

Wallace, B. J., R. M. Ahsan, S. H. Hussain and E. Ahsan (1987) *The Invisible Resource: Women and Work in Rural Bangladesh,* Boulder: Westview Press.

Wilson-Moore, M. (1986) 'Women's work in homestead gardening in rural Bangladesh: a preliminary analysis', consultancy report, Dhaka: Winrock International.

Wilson-Moore, M. (1987a) 'Homestead gardening in rural Bangladesh: method and definition', consultancy report, Dhaka: Winrock International.

Wilson-Moore, M. (1987b) 'LIFT baseline survey: a report of LIFT participant farmers in three sub-offices', LIFT Monitoring Series Report No. 1, Dhaka: CARE International.

Wilson-Moore, M. (1988) 'LIFT monitoring and evaluation: measuring progress and implementing change', LIFT Monitoring Series Report No. 3, Dhaka: CARE International.

Wilson-Moore, M. (1990) 'Subsistence, Patriarchy, and Status: Women's Work in Homestead Gardens in Northwest Bangladesh', PhD dissertation, Southern Methodist University, Ann Arbor, Michigan: University Microfilms International.

PART V
Gender, Biodiversity Loss and Conservation

CHAPTER 13
Losing Ground: Gender Relations, Commercial Horticulture, and Threats to Local Plant Diversity in Rural Mali

Stephen Wooten

In a Bamana farming community in central Mali, two male elders, Nene and Shimbon Jara, reported that their fathers were among the first people in the region to produce exotic fruits and vegetables for sale. They said that, in the early 1960s, these enterprising men began to cultivate crops such as banana and tomato in the low-lying stream areas around the community. Their activities were a response to a growing demand for fresh produce on the part of élite urban dwellers in the nearby capital city, Bamako. Over the years, other young men entered into the domain by clearing and incorporating what Nene referred to as 'unused areas'. Market gardening (the cultivation of fruits and vegetables for sale) has now become a key means to generate personal income in the community.

While the comments that Nene and other older men offered provide an important perspective on the development of commercial gardening activities in the community, they contrast with the historical insights provided by local women — especially when it comes to the idea that the garden lands were 'unused'. Indeed, older women reported that, prior to men's development of the low-lying areas for commercial gardening activities, women had in fact cultivated traditional crops and collected wild plants in at least some of those areas. For example, Wilene Diallo, the community's oldest woman, said that she and the other village wives used these areas to cultivate traditional vegetable crops for their sauces. A middle-aged male contemporary market gardener, Mamari Jara, noted that big changes have occurred in the gardening domain during his lifetime. What was once a woman's activity is now largely a man's affair, and commercially valuable, largely exotic crops have eclipsed traditional garden crops and plants in gardening niches.

This chapter examines the changing nature of gardening activities in a Bamana community in rural Mali. Using ethnographic field data collected between 1992 and 1998, it describes the transformation of gardening from a production-for-use activity associated with women to a commercial enterprise in which men predominate. It documents the contours of the contemporary commercial gardening sector, showing that men are the principal actors and revealing their prevailing focus on non-local fruit and vegetable crops. This chapter also addresses the implications that this shift in horticultural production has for women's ability to meet household obligations in terms of sauce production, and identifies a series of potential threats to local plant diversity and overall environmental stability that are likely to arise as a result of the process.

The Setting

Niamakoroni is a farming community located on the Mande Plateau in south-central Mali, approximately 35 kilometres from Bamako. The nucleated settlement consists of a series of closely clustered adobe brick structures and associated shade trees. According to community elders, the settlement was founded at the close of the nineteenth century when a lineage segment from a nearby community settled there in order to gain access to new farmland. Contemporary residents of Niama-koroni, like their ancestors before them, assert a Bamana (Bambara) ethnic identity.

As is the case in most Bamana communities, the people of Niamakoroni live in a small, tightly knit rural community (Becker 1990; Lewis 1979; Toulmin 1992). During 1993–4, the community had a total resident population of 184. Descent in Niamakoroni is traced patrilineally and control over productive resources is generally corporate in nature. Age and sex are important characteristics in social, political and economic contexts, with elders dominating juniors and men typically holding more power than women. Becker (1990: 315) refers to this as 'a patrilineal geronto-cracy'. The dominant residence pattern is patrilocal (women move to the husband's residence upon marriage), and marriages are frequently polygynous. In the community, the primary domestic group (residential and food production and con-sumption unit) is called a *du* (*duw*, plural) in the Bamana language (*Bamanankan*).

Niamakoroni's *duw* are multi-generational, joint families in which junior males and their spouses and families typically live and work under the authority of the group's eldest male, the *dutigi*. As senior members of their lineage groups, *dutigiw* have access to arable uplands and the authority to direct the labour of those who live with them in the subsistence realm. The members of each *du* live close to one another and share meals throughout the year.

Women in the community are responsible for food processing and cooking, as well as for all household maintenance tasks. Men typically have few domestic obligations aside from building and maintaining houses (see also Creevey 1986; Thiam 1986). This clear gender division of labour characterizes the wider agrarian economy as well.

Gendered Domains in the Food Economy

Most of the relatively sparse rains (900–1,200 mm per year) in Niamakoroni fall in a short span of three to four months from June to September. People depend upon rain-fed agriculture for subsistence, and therefore work diligently during these few short months in order to meet most of their food needs. Each rainy season, the vast majority of able-bodied, working-age villagers focus their productive energies on the cultivation or collection of food crops and plants, which they refer to as *ka balo* (for life) activities.

Very clear gender relations of production and domains of experience and knowledge mark this food production process. The men in each household work collectively in their group's main upland field (*foroba*), which is located in bush areas at least a few kilometres from the settlement. Here, they produce a suite of staple crops including sorghum (*nyo – Sorghum bicolor*), millet (*sanyo – Pennisetum glaucum*), corn (*kaba – Zea mays*), cowpeas (*sho – Vigna unguiculata*), peanuts (*tiga – Arachis hypogaea*), and Bambara groundnuts (*tiganinkuru – Voandzeia subterranea*). As is the case over most of the region, sorghum and millet account for the most acreage (PIRL 1988).

Women, on the other hand, are responsible for the cultivation and collection of plants that make up the sauces that accent men's grain crops in the daily meals. During the rainy season, married women in each domestic group work individually in upland fields assigned to them by the *dutigiw* to produce *nafenw*, or 'sauce things'. In most cases, women inter-crop peanuts (*tiga – Arachis hypogaea*), cowpeas, kenaf (*dajan – Hibiscus cannabinus*), roselle (*dakumun* or *dabilenni – Hibiscus sabdariffa*), okra (*gwan – Abelmoschus [Hibiscus] esculentus*), and sorghum. There is a clear focus in their cropping patterns on traditional leaf and vegetable items that complement the staples produced on the *forobaw*. The vast majority of women's crops are destined for direct consumption although, from time to time, some items are sold to generate income that is typically used to purchase commercial sauce ingredients such as bouillon cubes, vegetable oil or salt (Wooten 1997).

In addition to cultivating relish crops in upland fields during the rainy season, throughout the year women also gather various wild or semi-wild plant resources from their fields or from bush areas for use in their sauces. For example, they gather and process the leaves of the baobab tree (*Adansonia digitata*) to make a key sauce ingredient and use the fruit of the shea nut tree (*Butryospermum parkii*) to make cooking oil and a lotion for skin care. As reported elsewhere in the region (Becker 2000, 2001; Gakou *et al.* 1994; Grisby 1996), women maintain these productive trees in their fields, and make use of species in the bush areas around the community. A wide variety of wild and semi-wild greens is regularly used for their sauces.

This general pattern of distinct gender contributions to the food economy, with men providing grains and women providing sauces, is widespread among the Bamana (Becker 1996; Thiam 1986; Toulmin 1992). However, there is another typical production activity and niche associated with Bamana women: gardening. Accounts from across the Bamana region suggest that women regularly use low-lying areas near streams to establish and maintain homegardens, and to collect wild plants for sauce ingredients (Grisby 1996; Konate 1994). Indeed, *nako*, the Bamana word for garden, is often translated literally as 'sauce stream', which relates both to the type of produce and to the production site. Considering that, for generations, women in most Bamana communities have had the responsibility to produce *nafenw*, a historical association between the women of Niamakoroni and *nakow* (sauce streams) seems entirely logical. Yet today, they do not typically garden in such areas around their village. Instead, they grow their sauce crops in upland fields and gather wild food plants in nearby bush areas. Over the past few decades, gardening, a domain that was once closely associated with women and the food economy, has become a man's affair and a commercial venture.

Gardening for Cash: Meeting the Demands of Urban Consumers

In addition to labouring within the context of their respective *duw* for domestic consumption, individuals of all ages in Niamakoroni have the option to engage in independent commodity production activities that will earn them personal incomes. These are typically referred to as *ka wari nyini* (for cash/money) activities.

While a variety of income-generating activities occurs in the community, people are uniform in viewing market gardening as the premier avenue available for income generation and potential accumulation. Men and women alike commonly identified market gardening as the preferred strategy for earning income, and note that urban consumers in Bamako, the capital city, provide the main market for the garden produce (see also Konate 1994: 122).

Bamako has grown dramatically since the French set up their administrative headquarters in the city at the end of the nineteenth century. In 1994, it was estimated to be home to more than 800,000 people (Diarra *et al.* 1994: 230), and more recent estimates place the number at just over one million. Furthermore, according to Diarra and colleagues (*ibid.*: 239), only seven per cent of the population of Bamako is now engaged in agriculture or livestock production. Clearly, urbanization in Bamako, as in other contexts around the world, has been associated with a major shift in production and consumption patterns. There is now a well-established regional market for cereals, and most urban consumers depend on rural producers to supply their basic staples such as sorghum and millet. Moreover, there is an increasing demand for specialized horticultural produce.

Over the decades since the French colonial forces began to consume fresh fruits and vegetables produced in the colonies, Bamako's residents have become increasingly interested in acquiring and consuming exotic fruits and vegetables (République du Mali 1992; Villien-Rossi 1966). A number of factors have contributed to this consumption shift: the expansion of governmental nutritional campaigns that highlight the nutritional value of fresh fruits and vegetables; the emergence of a middle class that considers Western dietary patterns to be a sign of culture and wealth; and the growth in the number of foreign aid workers who wish to consume fruits and vegetables native to their home countries. Together, these create strong demand for specialized non-traditional horticultural items in the capital. Communities such as Niamakoroni that are within market distance of the capital are well placed in this overall context (see also Becker 1996; Konate 1994).

Market gardening is now a central component of the local livelihood system in Niamakoroni. In the mid-1990s, there were 22 distinct market gardening operations in the community, each with its garden leader (*nakotigi*). Married men managed the vast majority of garden operations (19 out of 22, or 86 per cent). Each of the three women *nakotigiw* had the position of first wife within a polygynous unit. As such, they had all retired from direct engagement in the food production realm, and their activities were no longer managed by their respective *dutigiw*. Compared to other *nakotigiw*, these women operated relatively minor enterprises, working on small plots in peripheral locations. Most *nakotigiw* are helped by younger brothers or sons and daughters and, in some cases, wives. The *nakotigiw* establish cropping patterns, organize labour, make decisions regarding harvest and marketing, and sell the produce and distribute the proceeds as they see fit.

In the mid-1990s, Niamakoroni's 22 *nakotigiw* operated a total of 34 different garden plots ranging in size from 378 to 9,720 square metres, with an average of 3,212 square metres. The vast majority of these plots were located in low-lying areas immediately surrounding the community. Most were well delineated and fenced to protect them from livestock damage. The plots controlled by the three women gardeners were unfenced and were the smallest (378–650 square metres). Moreover, their plots were located deep in the bush along relatively minor streams.

Market gardens produce a wide variety of vegetables and fruits, most of which are non-traditional exotics. The most common types of vegetables grown in Niama-koroni were tomatoes, bitter eggplant (*Solanum incanum*), common beans, hot pepper and cabbage. Of these, tomatoes and bitter eggplant were the most popular. At one point or another, all 22 *nakotigiw* cultivated these crops. Other vegetable crops included onion, European eggplant (*Solanum melongena*), green pepper, squash and okra. Fruit crops also play a major role in these gardens. Often these fruit plantings occupy a large percentage of an enclosed garden area, mainly as pure orchards or, less frequently, integrated into a diversely planted garden. Except for the plots belonging to the three women *nakotigiw*, all garden plots contained at least some mature (productive) fruit plantings including banana, papaya, mango and various citrus species. In all cases, banana was the most abundant fruit crop. Papaya was the next most common and was cultivated by all nineteen male *nakotigiw*. All male *nakotigiw* also had mango (*mangoro*) trees. Most gardeners had citrus stock including lemons, oranges, mandarins, tangelos and grapefruit, with lemons the most common. With the exception of bitter eggplant, hot pepper and mango, these crops are non-traditional garden plantings. All of the garden crops, traditional and non-traditional alike, are in high demand in the capital city.

Gardeners frequently use a range of commercial inputs. All 22 *nakotigiw* purchase commercial vegetable seed for their market gardens. In interviews, they specifically mentioned purchasing tomato, cabbage, and bitter eggplant seed. Except for traditional crops such as bitter eggplant, the seed typically originates in France or Holland. Respondents uniformly reported that they buy seed at distribution sites in the capital where vendors (street-side table merchants and storefront operators) tend to specialize in hardware and agricultural supplies. In fact, there are several shops in the area catering specifically to market gardeners. These shops supply both the fully commercial market gardening operations that exist within the city itself and rural market gardeners such as those in Niamakoroni. Several of

Niamakoroni's gardeners stated that they purchase seed from *tubabu* boutiques (European-style stores) in the Dibida area. Expatriates, including some French businessmen, run many of the specialized garden supplies operations.

In addition to purchasing vegetable seed and seedlings, Niamakoroni's *nakotigiw* also regularly purchase orchard stock. All 19 male *nakotigiw* reported that they purchase orchard stock, banana plantings, citrus seedlings or citrus grafting stock. The Badala market along the Niger River was their main source. They also mentioned obtaining items such as banana sprouts, orange tree seedlings and tangelo grafts from the Badala vendors. Some of the male *nakotigiw* noted that they also obtained such items from *nakotigiw* in neighbouring communities where longer-established orchards exist. The three women *nakotigiw* had not planted any citrus trees in their plots and the bananas that they were cultivating had been obtained locally.

All 19 male *nakotigiw* said that they purchase chemical fertilizer for their plots. Fourteen also stated that they purchase animal manure (mainly chicken – *she nogo*). A few male *nakotigiw* purchase chemical pesticides from time to time. The gardeners are usually unaware of the health risks of these materials and thus fail to protect themselves.

Gardeners were unanimous when asked about their production goals. All 22 *nakotigiw* indicated that they viewed their horticultural activities as a way to earn income. They noted that all of the produce from their gardens is destined for sale. Indeed, garden produce only very rarely appeared in the local diet and, when it did, it was either damaged or deteriorating. The bulk of the produce from Niamakoroni's gardens was directed to Bamako's markets. The produce was typically brought to a suburban site where urban market traders – mostly young women — purchased it from gardeners or their helpers. There was always a stable cohort of buyers at these markets and, on some occasions, these buyers even travelled directly to the gardens to secure produce, which indicates the strong demand in the capital city.

In order to get a sense of the potential income levels from market gardening, a series of crop value estimates were made based on a systematic count of the number and assessment of the reproductive status of fruit plantings in each garden. The gross value of certain crops could be estimated by knowing how many productive trees there were, how much fruit a tree could yield in a year, and average sale prices. This analysis showed that the total value of the banana crop alone across all gardens during 1993–4 was approximately US$35,000. The individual with the largest number of banana plantings (736) could have taken in approximately US$4,400 from this crop alone. The individual with the fewest banana plantings (36) could have earned US$216. The projected value of the total papaya crop for the year was approximately US$9,500. The individual with the most mature plantings (76) could have taken in about US$1,600 from this crop, whereas the individual with the fewest mature plantings (4) could have earned US$85.

These examples indicate that potential incomes from market gardening are relatively high for Mali, which has a very low per capita income (US$260 in the early 1990s, Imperato 1996). Based on proceeds from banana and papaya alone, if shared equally among all 184 Niamakoroni residents, the gross per capita income would be approximately US$244, or nearly the national average. However, figures are based on gross value and not net income. Furthermore, income generated through gardening is most definitely not distributed uniformly in the community. Rather, because the vast majority of garden leaders are married men, they are the primary benefactors of this relatively lucrative livelihood diversification strategy (Wooten 1997; n.d.).

Contrasting Views on the Development of Commercial Horticulture

Clearly, market gardening is a very significant endeavour in contemporary Niama-koroni. It is also very clearly a male-dominated commercial activity and one that focuses on an array of largely exotic, non-traditional crops. However, as we have seen, gardening has not always been male-dominated, market-oriented, and based on exotic plants. Moreover, not all people have quietly accepted market gardening, nor is it likely to affect everyone in the same way. Indeed, men and women in the community tended to narrate the story of the development of market gardening and current garden tenure patterns in quite different ways. The juxtaposition of their accounts highlights a significant change in the nature of gardening over time.

From a male elder's perspective, garden tenure in Niamakoroni shares a character-istic with the settlement of the community: first farmers made first claims. When the initial Jara settlers began farming in Niamakoroni, male lineage heads estab-lished themselves as guardians of the land (Wooten 1997). Male descendants of these founding Jara patrilineages retained the right to distribute upland tracts to the community's household heads. However, it appears that the original Jara claim did not necessarily include lowlands, which men at that time did not see as being central to the food production regime. From the commentaries provided by Nene Jara and Shimbon Jara, the two male elders, it seems that control over these areas fell to those who opened them for cultivation, in most cases to the first generation of market gardeners: their fathers.

Others subsequently joined the first wave of gardeners in the community as they began to see the advantages of garden cultivation. Young men entered the domain by clearing what Nene referred to as 'unused areas'. In addition, over time, some young men who had worked for the original garden heads established their own operations, either by claiming 'unused' land or by obtaining a section of their fathers' or elder brothers' holding after death or retirement. Later still, some indi-viduals obtained plots from non-related individuals. Rent was not mentioned, although short-term, non-monetized loans of plots have been made. Nene and Shimbon noted that, most recently, a few women had begun gardening activities far into the bush on lands that they said men deemed to be too distant for serious horticulture activities. The women cleared these areas themselves in order to garden.

Women offered a quite different perspective on the development of market gardening. Various older women reported that, prior to men's development of the low-lying areas for commercial gardening activities, women had in fact cultivated crops and collected plants in some of those areas. Wilene Diallo, the community's oldest woman, said that she and the other village wives used plots in these areas during the rainy season to cultivate traditional vegetable crops for their sauces (*naw*). She also indicated that village women sometimes planted rice in low-lying areas during the rainy season. The rice produced was a traditional variety that was used in special meals or marketed. Wilene's assertion was echoed by a number of other senior women, and the pattern is also noted in published accounts about rural production patterns in other areas of Mali (see, for example, various papers in Creevey 1986; Becker 1996).

Thus, before the first generation of market gardeners became established, it appears that women used at least some stream areas freely and without direct competition from men, and did so with the primary goal of producing local sauce crops. Such uncontested use of these areas may relate to the fact that a ready market for specialized horticultural produce had not yet developed, and that men perceived low-lying areas to be less desirable. A comment offered by one of Niamakoroni's contemporary male garden leaders supports this general position. With regard to the development of his own garden plots, Mamari Jara said that, perhaps a generation ago, he thought, some of the land was originally used by some of the village women to produce leaves and vegetables for sauces.

Mamari went on to say that, as market demand for horticultural produce grew, men in the community became more aware of the potential value of the low-lying stream areas and eventually displaced women in the cultivation of these areas. He said that they began to clear the areas and then proceeded to fence and claim them as their holdings. After all, he said, 'There was money to be made!' As he finished saying this, he and his younger brother Konimba laughed and added that, after all, 'Men are thieves!'

Lost Ground, Threatened Resources

Whatever the exact historical particulars, it is clear that today women are largely excluded from the community's garden spaces. To establish their commercial enterprises, men have appropriated the physical space of the lowlands as well as the garden production niche itself. In the process, the women of Niamakoroni have lost important ground. Men's movement into the gardening domain has been facilitated by broader inequalities in local gender relations of production. According to Davison (1988: 3), gender relations of production are the 'socioeconomic relations between females and males that are characterized often by differential assignment of labour tasks, control over decision making, and differential access to and control over the allocation of resources – including land and income'.

In Niamakoroni, as in most rural African settings, gender relations of production generally favour men. As noted above, it is a community in which descent is traced patrilineally and control over productive resources is generally corporate in nature, with elders dominating juniors, and men typically holding more power than women. Married men have exploited their privileged position in this structure to establish themselves as market gardeners. They have laid claim to land where their mothers and wives once cultivated and collected plants for the household saucepot. This has important implications for women's contributions to the food economy and for their relative standing in the community.

Women's marginalization from the gardening niche in Niamakoroni limits their ability to produce traditional foodstuffs. The women endeavour to grow sufficient sauce crops on the upland fields allocated to them by their *dutigiw*, but their productivity there is limited. They have a wide range of domestic obligations that limit the time that they have available to cultivate these fields and, moreover, some of their traditional crops may not grow well in upland environments. The upland fields can only be cultivated during the rainy season, while sauces typically require fresh plant material throughout the year. Thus, even if the women are fortunate enough to secure a solid harvest of some sauce crops from their fields, they still need to locate additional local plant resources for their sauces. With access to the low-lying areas constrained, their ability to procure these items is hindered. Their marginalization from the gardening realm also limits their access to financial resources that could be used to purchase some of the sauce ingredients they are unable to secure locally.

Women's near exclusion from this important income stream may have broader implications as well. Numerous studies in Africa (Clark 1994; Fapohunda 1988; Gordon 1996) have shown that income autonomy can enhance an individual's status in various social settings. In particular, an independent income that parallels their husband's earnings seems to provide a foundation for women's empowered negotiation within African families and communities. This certainly appears to be relevant in the Bamana context. As Turrittin (1988: 586) notes, 'control over their own economic resources is an important resource for women when bargaining with men'. She goes on to show how Bamana gender relations of production constrain women's opportunities to gain access to such resources through trading activities. Like the women of Niamakoroni, the female traders in Turrittin's study were unable to establish themselves in a prized income-generating niche. In both cases, men used existing gender relations of production to lay claim to a relatively lucrative enterprise. Their actions were supported by an established institutional framework in which men, as patrilineage members, have priority access to productive resources and economic opportunities.

It should be noted that this shift has not gone unnoticed or unchallenged by the women of Niamakoroni. In the course of interviews, several women voiced clear dissatisfaction with the situation. As one woman said, 'Men get all the gardens. They get all the money. Yet they don't give us anything, not even money for sauce or our babies.' Some women clearly resent the fact that what they conceive of as traditionally a woman's sphere has now become part of a man's world. Moreover, it is important to keep in mind the fact that there were three female *nakotigiw*. Their gardens were very small and located at considerable distance from the village on relatively minor streambeds, but they had gardens nonetheless – commercially oriented gardens at that. However, unlike most married women in the community, these women gardeners were senior wives who were retired from most of the regular duties associated with the household food economy. Their accomplishments, meagre as they might be, are not likely to be widely replicated.

In addition to the emergence of a series of social and economic challenges, women's exclusion from the garden realm may lead to detrimental shifts in a number of other important domains. The shift documented here points to changes in culinary patterns and to the possibility of declines in nutritional status (see also Daniggelis, this volume), local plant diversity and overall environmental stability. While these issues were not specifically evaluated in the study, the data presented do reveal a number of significant threats.

The expansion of men's market gardening may lead to a decrease in the availability of local plants for the diet. Men have pushed women and women's crops out of the gardening niche. In the process, many garden plants maintained by men and associated with urban consumers have replaced local plants linked with women and the saucepot in Niamakoroni gardens. Today's male market gardeners are not interested in maintaining women's sauce crops unless there is a suitable urban market for them, as is the case with bitter eggplant. Indeed, most men see most women's plants (especially traditional leaf crops and wild sauce plants) as weeds to be removed in favour of income earners such as tomatoes or bananas. The well-manicured market gardens now only very rarely contain traditional vegetables and wild or semi-domesticated plants. In short, lacking access to traditional gardening and collecting areas, women have fewer options when it comes to making their sauces. While it is not documented as yet, a change in local culinary patterns may be under way as a result – ironically, by growing and selling garden crops, male gardeners may be contributing to a decline in the nutritional value of their own meals.

Studies from a range of contexts reveal that shifts toward commercial agriculture can result in declining nutritional standards at the local level as nutritious traditional crops are replaced by non-food items, food items of lesser nutritional value, or by items that, while quite nutritious, are sold rather than consumed (von Braun and Kennedy 1994; de Walt 1993). Specifically, in the light of research that shows the nutritional significance of traditional leafy vegetables in the diet (Chweya and Eyzaguirre 1999; Nesamvuni et al. 2001; Thaman 1995; see also Daniggelis, this volume), the transformation in Niamakoroni may well lead to nutrient deficiencies and related health problems. (Indeed, recent work in southern Mali has documented the nutritional importance of local plant resources typically associated with women. Nordeide et al. (1996) have shown that traditionally gathered and locally produced crops contribute valuable nutrients, particularly in rural settings like Niamakoroni.) This kind of decline is especially likely because so little of the 'new' replacement garden produce ever finds its way into the local diet. The market gardeners view their operations as money-earning endeavours and their produce strictly as a means to that end. They neither use their incomes to purchase food nor provide their wives with cash that could be used to purchase traditional sauce ingredients or local medicinal herbs (Wooten 1997).

If studies of commercialization processes in other contexts are any indication, additional problems having both local and global repercussions are likely to arise in the longer term. In order to ensure the long-term viability of locally adapted plant resources, experts in plant genetic resource management are calling for in situ conservation (Altieri and Merrick 1987; Qualset et al. 1997). This is seen as the most effective way to conserve genetic resources, ensuring their continued adaptation to local environments over time and continued access to locally adapted resources. Research has shown that, while they may be small in size, women's homegardens around the globe typically hold a tremendous range of useful, locally adapted plants (Howard-Borjas 2002). Women use such spaces as experimental plots and as sites for rare plant conservation. In fact, it has been noted that African women's gardens may be one of the most significant reservoirs of local plant genetic material (Chweya and Eyzaguirre 1999). However, the potential for in situ conservation of plants traditionally linked to women in Niamakoroni is threatened by the expansion of commercial gardening. Without access to appropriate gardening niches, women lack the opportunity to maintain traditional plant resources in situ. While some of their traditional plants may be suitable for upland cultivation during the rainy season, there are many more wild or semi-domesticated plants that are adapted to the low-lying stream areas. This situation presents a challenge for the maintenance of viable locally adapted plants and, over time, to the continuity of local knowledge of these tried and true species. Without continuous management, it is possible that these species may erode locally. Loss of plant genetic resources and associated knowledge at the local level would represent a significant loss to the wider realm of global plant biodiversity as well. In general, very little is known about the genetic characteristics of traditional African crops. In fact, until recently, they have been ignored by ex situ gene banks and commercial prospectors (for a discussion see Chweya and Eyzaguirre 1999). Thus, plants that slip into obscurity or become extinct at the local level run the risk of being lost completely.

The threat to local plant biodiversity is not limited to garden areas, however. There are a number of important secondary environmental effects related to the development of men's market gardening in Niamakoroni. Without access to lowlands for sauce production or other alternatives for income generation, women are increasingly focusing their attention on the exploitation of other local, bush-based plant resources for food as well as for income generation in support of their domestic cooking obligations (Wooten 1997). Specifically, they are expanding their commercial production of charcoal, shea nut butter and toothbrushes made from plants. In interviews, several women noted that they use the proceeds from these activities to secure sauce items for their household meals. All these activities are dependent upon the use of wild native plant resources. Women's expanding use of such resources reveals what may represent a vicious cycle: without access to garden spaces, women may be overexploiting bush resources to acquire income that they can use to obtain sauce ingredients they can no longer produce locally.

Women uniformly identified charcoal as their primary commodity: like market garden produce, charcoal is a highly desirable product in urban Bamako. An arduous production process generates a relatively low return (Wooten n.d.). However, because it is one of the very few income-generating activities open to women, charcoal pits are becoming very common. At the same time, there has been a noticeable decrease in mature woody growth around the village. Women's actions are likely to be increasing the rate of deforestation of key charcoal-linked species. Indeed, women were already lamenting the fact that it was increasingly difficult to find appropriate species and volumes for charcoal production. They indicated that they were beginning to use younger and less desirable tree species, and to cut whole trees. A study in the region suggests that, because rural women have few durable land rights, they are not likely to invest in the long-term stability of such land-based enterprises (Grisby and Force 1993). This is ironic considering that studies in the area indicate that women are the primary users and benefactors of land-based activities (Driel 1990; Gakou et al. 1994). With increasing urban demand and few other options, it is likely that women will continue to exploit the woody resources necessary for charcoal production and that this process will contribute to deforestation in the area. In this case, it may not be long before women lose the meagre benefits of this marginal income-generating activity and become fuelwood-deprived themselves. Furthermore, with the continued loss of woody cover comes the possibility of increased soil compaction and erosion and associated environmental degradation (see official Malian reports cited in Becker 2001).

Gender, Commercialization and Threats to Local Plant Genetic Resources

In the face of mounting evidence of the rapid and escalating loss of plant bio-diversity across the globe, a wide range of individuals and organizations are now devoting attention to the twin tasks of documenting and conserving local plant genetic resources. As a result, understanding of the diversity and significance of locally adapted plants has increased considerably over the last decade. This expansion has often come through a growing appreciation of the extensive body of local or indigenous knowledge in this realm of biocomplexity. However, as research in this area has progressed, it has become clear that there is often a substantial degree of differentiation within local populations with regard to knowledge about local plant biodiversity, for example depending upon ethnicity or mode of livelihood. In short, researchers have shown that there are frequently local plant 'knowledges' rather than a monolithic local plant knowledge.

Thus, in order to gain insights into these different realms of people–plant relations it is critical to identify relevant local specialists and to learn from them about the plant resources that they know best. Unfortunately, it has become increasingly apparent that a significant group of key knowledge holders has been largely ignored in this process. Despite their critical roles in various plant management arenas, women's knowledge of local plants has been sorely under-represented in research (for a review see Howard-Borjas 2002). The result is a skewed and incomplete picture of local knowledge of the plant world.

To address this lacuna, it is imperative to identify and document situations in which women have discrete responsibilities and knowledge of plant resources and to document the cases in detail. Moreover, it is critically important that close attention is paid to those cases in which women's plant resources and knowledge base are under threat. This case study offers a clear example of the type of process that can lead to the deterioration of women's access to plant resources and, subsequently, knowledge.

As women's productive spaces, such as the homegardens of Niamakoroni, are shifted over to commercially viable exotic crops and market garden production, traditional plant resources may decline and knowledge of these crops may be lost. This threat has been identified as a key concern by the International Board for Plant Genetic Resources and other organizations concerned with the long-term viability of locally adapted plant biodiversity. It is clear from the case of Niamakoroni that gender-linked commercialization dynamics can pose a threat to local plant biodiversity and that the loss of these resources can provoke further detrimental effects on the environment and on human welfare.

References

Altieri, M. and A. Merrick (1987) 'In situ conservation of crop genetic resources through maintenance of traditional farming systems', Economic Botany, Vol. 41, No. 1, pp. 86–96.

Becker, L. (1990) 'The collapse of the family farm in West Africa? Evidence from Mali', Geographical Journal, Vol. 156, No. 3, pp. 313–22.

Becker, L. (1996) 'Access to labor in rural Mali', Human Organization, Vol. 55, No. 3, pp. 279–88.

Becker, L. (2000) 'Garden money buys grain: food procurement patterns in a Malian village', Human Ecology, Vol. 28, No. 2, pp. 219–50.

Becker, L. (2001) 'Seeing green in Mali's woods: colonial legacy, forest use, and local control', Annals of the Association of American Geographers, Vol. 91, No. 3, pp. 504–26.

Braun, J. von and E. Kennedy (1994) 'Introduction and overview', in J. von Braun and E. Kennedy (eds.), Agricultural Commercialization, Economic Development, and Nutrition, Baltimore, Maryland: Johns Hopkins University Press.

Chweya, J. A. and P. Eyzaguirre (1999) The Biodiversity of Traditional Leafy Vegetables, Rome: IPRGI.

Clark, G. (1994) Onions Are My Husband: Survival and Accumulation by West African Market Women, Chicago, Illinois: University of Chicago Press.

Creevey, L. (1986) 'The role of women in agriculture in Mali', in L. Creevey (ed.), Women Farmers in Africa: a Study of Rural Development in Mali and the Sahel, Syracuse, New York: Syracuse University Press.

Davison, J. (1988) 'Land and women's agricultural production: the context', in J. Davison (ed.), Agriculture, Women, and Land: the African Experience, Boulder: Westview Press.

de Walt, K. (1993) 'Nutrition and the commercialization of agriculture: ten years later', Social Science and Medicine, Vol. 36, pp. 1407–16.

Diarra, S., A. Sékouba Kouame, R. Marcoux and A. Camara (1994) 'Mali', in J. Tarver (ed.), Urbanization in Africa: a Handbook, Westport, Connecticut: Greenwood Press.

Driel, A. van (1990) 'A tree is more than only fuelwood with leaves', Bos Nieuwsletter (Netherlands), Vol. 9, No. 20, pp. 19–26.

Fapohunda, E. (1988) 'The non-pooling household: a challenge to theory', in D. Dwyer and J. Bruce (eds.), A Home Divided: Women and Income in the Third World, Stanford, CA: Stanford University Press.

Gakou, M., J. Force and W. McLaughlin (1994) 'Non-timber forest products in rural Mali: a study of villager use', *Agroforestry Systems*, Vol. 28, pp. 213–26.

Gordon, A. (1996) *Transforming Capitalism and Patriarchy: Gender and Development in Africa*, Boulder, Colorado: Lynne Reiner.

Grisby, W. (1996) 'Women, descent, and tenure succession among the Bambara of West Africa: a changing landscape', *Human Organization*, Vol. 55, No. 1, pp. 93–8.

Grisby, W. and J. Force (1993) 'Where credit is due: forests, women, and rural development', *Journal of Forestry*, Vol. 91, No. 6, pp. 29–34.

Howard-Borjas, P. with W. Cuijpers (2002) 'Gender and the management and conservation of plant biodiversity', in H. W. Doelle and E. Da Silva (eds.), *Biotechnology*, in *Encyclopedia of Life Support Systems (EOLSS)*, Oxford, UK, http://www.eolss.net.

Imperato, P. (1996) *Historical Dictionary of Mali*, Lanham, Maryland: Scarecrow Press.

Konate, Y. (1994) 'Household Income and Agricultural Strategies in the Peri-Urban Zone of Bamako, Mali', PhD dissertation, State University of New York, Binghamton, Ann Arbor, Michigan: University Microfilms International.

Lewis, J. (1979) 'Descendants and Crops: Two Poles of Production in a Malian Peasant Village', PhD dissertation, Yale University, Ann Arbor, Michigan: University Microfilms International.

Nesamvuni, C., N. P. Steyn and M. J. Potgieter (2001) 'Nutritional value of wild, leafy plants consumed by the Vhavenda', *South African Journal of Science*, Vol. 97, pp. 51–4.

Nordeide, M., A. Harloy, M. Folling, E. Leid and A. Oshaug (1996) 'Nutrient composition and nutritional importance of green leaves and wild food resources in an agricultural district, Koutiala, in Southern Mali', *International Journal of Food Sciences and Nutrition*, Vol. 47, pp. 455–68.

PIRL (Projet Inventaire des Ressources Ligneuses et Occupation Agricole des Terres au Mali) (1988) 'Notice de cercle, cercle de Kati, région de Koulikoro, Bamako', Ministère de l'Environnement et de l'Élevage, Direction Nationale des Eaux et Forêts.

Qualset, C., A. Damania, A. Zanatta and S. Brush (1997) 'Locally based crop plant conservation', in N. Maxted, B. V. Ford-Lloyd and J. G. Hawkes (eds.), *Plant Genetic Conservation: the* in situ *approach*, New York: Chapman and Hall.

République du Mali (1992) *Rapport National sur la Nutrition, Conférence Internationale sur la Nutrition,* Rome – December 1992.

Thaman, R. (1995) 'Urban food gardening in the Pacific Islands: a basis for food security in rapidly urbanising small-island states', *Habitat International*, Vol. 19, No. 2, pp. 209–24.

Thiam, M. (1986) 'The role of women in rural development in Segou region of Mali', in L. Creevey (ed.), *Women Farmers in Africa*, Syracuse, New York: Syracuse University Press.

Toulmin, C. (1992) *Cattle, Women and Wells: Managing Household Survival in the Sahel,* Oxford: Oxford University Press.

Turrittin, J. (1988) 'Men, women, and market trade in rural Mali, West Africa', *Canadian Journal of African Studies*, Vol. 22, pp. 583–604.

Villien-Rossi, M. L. (1966) 'Bamako, capitale du Mali', *Bulletin d'IFAN*, series B, Vol. 28, Nos 1–2, pp. 249–380.

Wooten, S. (1997) '"Gardens Are for Cash, Grain Is for Life": the Social Organization of Parallel Production Processes in a Rural Bamana Community (Mali)', PhD dissertation, University of Illinois, Ann Arbor, Michigan: University Microfilms International.

Wooten, S. (in press 2003) 'Women, men and market gardens: gender relations and income generation in rural Mali', *Human Organizations*.

CHAPTER 14
Modernization and Gender Dynamics in the Loss of Agrobiodiversity in Swaziland's Food System

Millicent Malaza

Over much of the world, diets have undergone dramatic changes, especially in the last three decades. Highly industrialized countries are converging towards a dietary pattern that is high in saturated fat and sugar and in low-fibre refined foods (Regmi 2001). In developing countries, exotic food crops and many industrially processed foods have become dominant features in the diet of both the poor and the rich (Popkin 1993; Regmi 2001). For most of Africa, this process of change involves the displacement of traditional staple crops and wild and cultivated indigenous fruits and vegetables. The implications include increasing dependence upon imports of food and agricultural inputs, declining nutritional status, weakened food systems, and the devalorization of traditional diets and crops, together with those who produce and procure such native foods, the majority of whom are women (Howard-Borjas 2002).

In many countries in sub-Saharan Africa a diet based on traditional coarse grains has shifted to one based on non-traditional grains in response to structural changes related to the twin processes of agricultural modernization and urbanization. For example, in Dar es Salaam, Tanzania, urban dwellers have switched from sorghum, millet and cassava to maize, rice and wheat. Other studies point out that wheat bread has become the principal breakfast food, particularly among younger people (Goody 1982; Kennedy and Reardon 1994).

Various African countries also report a loss of agrobiodiversity and a decline in the consumption of both wild and cultivated indigenous vegetables due to deforestation, overgrazing, land degradation and the expansion of agriculture (Chweya and Eyzaguirre 1999). However, the most important reasons cited for the loss of agrobiodiversity, especially of food crops, are the commercialization of agriculture and the neglect of indigenous plant species on the part of policy makers and researchers, followed by changes in lifestyles and cultural values associated with modernization (Chweya and Eyzaguirre 1999; Howard-Borjas 2002). These developments result in structural transformations that drastically transform the lives of Africa's populations, and particularly the lives of the women who are still the major food producers and providers of traditional foodstuffs in most of Africa.

In Africa, so-called 'modernization' is linked to urbanization, formal education and the adoption of Western values and practices, all of which lead to changes in the economic sphere, including new occupational roles and increasing market opportunities for both men and women, an increase in the value of time, the acquisition of new tastes and attitudes towards food and the adoption of new status symbols (Goody 1982). Furthermore, the influence of Western cultures that has been exerted by colonization and Western education has led various social groups to assign a lower status to indigenous crops and food patterns and a higher status to those that are exotic, where the former represent 'backwardness', 'primitive practices' and poverty (Guarino 1997; Ogle and Grivetti 1985; Chweya and Eyzaguirre 1999; Guinand and Lemessa 2001).

The impact of modernization and its connection to the loss of agrobiodiversity and knowledge about the production, procurement and use of indigenous food crops in Africa's food systems is more intense among younger and formally educated age groups. Studies from Botswana, Zambia, South Africa, Mozambique and Kenya all emphasize that young people, particularly in urban areas, are no longer familiar with many indigenous fruits and vegetables, nor with the preparation of traditional food items (Chweya and Eyzaguirre 1999; IUCN ROSA 2001). This has come about through changes in lifestyles, occupations and attitudes towards indigenous practices that young people acquire in part through the formal education system. For example, the fact that many of them spend more time in school and urban centres has affected the intergenerational transmission of knowledge about indigenous food crops and plant resources (IUCN ROSA 2001).

The commercialization of agriculture has added yet another set of challenges for both men and women farmers. These include a growing dependency on the cash economy to meet basic needs and, particularly for women, increased workloads and loss of access to land and seed. In spite of these problems, however, rural women continue to produce a large number of traditional crops and to collect and use wild plant resources. These food crops and wild plant foods are frequently used to prepare relishes and sauces that are essential complements to the starchy grains that form the major component of meals across much of Africa. They also provide food sources to fall back upon in times of drought and crop failure, which is an ongoing challenge for Africa's agricultural systems. Furthermore, traditional crops and plant species are usually more affordable and nutritious than exotic food crops, and many also have medicinal properties as well as significant cultural meanings.[1]

However, the very significant role that women and agrobiodiversity play in achieving food security, and the barriers that women face in conserving agrobiodiversity in Africa's food systems, are virtually invisible to policy makers and researchers. Hence, problems of food shortage and depletion of genetic resources continue to plague many African countries (FAO 1999; Howard-Borjas 2002). Yet while the various dynamics related to the loss of agrobiodiversity have had the same impact on many African societies, there is considerable variation in the extent of this loss and in the difficulties posed if agrobiodiversity is to be conserved. This chapter discusses the loss of agrobiodiversity in the food system in Swaziland as a result of modernization and of gender dynamics, and particularly as a result of the changes in women's lives in both rural and urban communities.

The Research Setting

Swaziland is a small, landlocked country in Southern Africa that shares borders with the Republic of South Africa and Mozambique. In 1996, the population was estimated to be around one million. In distinction to other African countries, Swaziland consists of basically one tribal group, the Swazi.

Urbanization and 'modern' influences came with British colonial rule, which set the stage for many changes in the Swazi way of life, including living standards, status symbols and dietary patterns. One of the major changes introduced was in the Swazi subsistence pattern, which was centred around traditional food crop production and the use of wild plant resources (Ogle and Grivetti 1985). The colonial era diversified the economy through commercial agriculture, wage employment and imported goods. Swazi farming practices and crops continued to change over time with the development of a commercial sector. Cash crop production was increasingly based on the use of imported high-yielding varieties and other inputs, and 'improved' farming practices, all of which reduced the number of crops that farmers planted in their fields. As in other African countries, the pace of urbanization accelerated over the years, drawing both men and women into wage employment and greater reliance on imported food items. Compared to other African countries, Swaziland has a highly developed road network, which facilitates the transportation of goods into and out of the country. A network of centres for distributing farm inputs in remote rural areas also introduces a variety of modern food crops. Industrialization and wage labour opportunities have led to even greater changes in women's lives in terms of occupational roles and education levels, particularly for the younger age groups. In the process, the link between education, Westernization, and Christianity has led to a rejection of traditional cultural practices among young and educated people. Those who are able to access better jobs through education tend to emulate the former British settlers' dietary practices and adopt their status symbols. Economic opportunities have allowed households in both urban and rural areas to purchase exotic foods, which have become the staples in many households, particularly in urban areas. Furthermore, work away from home allows women little time for food preparation.

Swaziland's current staple food, consisting of a stiff maize porridge (*liphalishi*) and a relish side dish (*sishibo*) composed mainly of vegetables (*umbhidvo*) or meat and other relish items, emerged from this colonial experience. Before the colonial encounter, the traditional Swazi diet consisted of one-dish meals prepared by mixing traditional grains with legumes or vegetables, fruits and sometimes meat. At that time, it was also very common to consume one type of food in a meal without serving it with a relish.

With the emergence of urban centres and strong class divisions, dietary patterns reflecting rural versus urban and rich versus poor have emerged. To meet these multiple dietary patterns, the country relies heavily on foreign imports. The new cereals (rice and wheat) come from South Africa. Maize is primarily produced by subsistence farmers (particularly women), as are traditional vegetables and other crops such as legumes and tubers that are consumed mainly by rural households. Women's farming activities are carried out on small plots of land that are communally distributed, where their usufruct rights depend upon their husbands or male heads of households. Since there is a high rate of male migration to urban centres for wage employment, agricultural activities in rural households have increasingly fallen to women who are left to manage subsistence crops and even the cash crops that belong to their husbands. Some women also produce their own cash crops, including exotic vegetables (Malaza 1993).

Swaziland consists of four agroecological zones (Highveld, Middleveld, Lowveld, and the Lubombo Plateau) that represent different topographies, climatic conditions, natural habitats for wild plants, and agricultural production systems. Maize, which is the main staple food crop, only performs well in the Highveld, parts of the Middleveld, and the Lubombo Plateau. The remaining areas therefore tend to produce mainly cash crops.

In spite of Swaziland's heavy reliance on food imports, basic food requirements are still not met and nutritional problems are prevalent among rural and lower-income urban households (Swaziland Government 1996). These problems have increased over the years, especially following recurring incidences of drought and crop failure. One source of these problems is the gradual loss of agrobiodiversity that has been taking place, driven by structural transformations related to urbanization and the commercialization of agriculture. The next section discusses these transitions and in particular how they relate to women.

The discussion draws mainly on a field study conducted in Swaziland in 1993, following one of the country's worst drought periods. The study focused on the extent of change in the Swazi diet and on the reasons underlying this change, as well as on existing food practices and preferences. In-depth interviews were conducted with farmers, government officials and focus groups, and a survey was completed. Twelve focus group discussions were conducted in the country's four ecological zones. Nine of the focus groups were from rural areas; of these, five groups consisted of middle-aged women, two of young adult women, and two of adult men. All of the members of the rural focus groups were engaged in farming and other income-generating activities, including wage employment. In the case of the urban groups, one consisted of young educated adult men and women who were teachers at a school in the capital, while the other consisted of men and women who were teachers at a college, also in the capital. The third urban group consisted of young adult women who were students at a vocational training centre. The survey covered 424 households (200 from rural areas, 176 from the urban low-income and middle-income categories, and 48 from the urban upper-income category) (Malaza 1994). The questionnaire was administered at household level, and in that setting women provided the answers because they are responsible for food preparation.

Table 14.1 Major Food Crops and Wild Food Plant Resources in Swaziland Indigenous Diets

Swazi name	English name	Scientific name
Legumes		
Tinhlumaya	Cowpea	*Vigna sinensis*
Tindumba	Cowpea	*Vigna unguiculata*
Tindlubu	Jugo beans	*Voandzeia subteranea*
Mgomeni	Mung beans	*Phaseolus mango*
Emabhontshisi	Beans	*Phaseolus vulgaris*
Ludvonqa	Sesame seed	*Sesame indicum*
Emantongomane	Groundnuts	*Arachis hypogaea*
Grains		
Emabele	Sorghum	*Sorghum vulgare*
Lunyawodzi	Bush millet;	*Pennisetum typhoides*
	Finger millet	*Eleusine coracana*
Umbila wesintfu	Black people's mealies	*Zea mays (open pollinated, dark colour)*
Tubers		
Bhatata	Sweet potato	*Ipomoea batata*
Ematabhane	n.a.	*Unknown*
Emadumbe	Taro	*Colocasia antiquorum*
Umjumbula	Cassava	*Manihot* spp.
Umhlata	n.a.	*Coleus esculentus*
Cultivated vegetables		
Ematsanga	Pumpkin	*Cucurbita pepo*
Emajoti	Melon	*Citrullus* spp.
Emaselwa	Gourd	*Cucurbita* spp.
Wild vegetables		
Umdzayi	n.a.	*Asclepias affinis/Xysmalobium acerateoides*
Emahala	n.a.	*Aloe saponaria*
Inshubaba	n.a.	*Momordica foetida*
Imbuya	n.a.	*Amaranthus* spp.
Chuchuza	Spanish needle	*Bidens pilosa*
Ligusha	n.a.	*Corchorus* spp.
Umshuku	n.a.	*Riocreuxia picta/R. burchelli*
Sibhadze	n.a.	*Annesorhiza flagellifolia*
Sikhwa	n.a.	*Tulbaghia* spp.
Ingabe	Sowthistle	*Sonchus oleracea*
Inkakha	n.a.	*Momordica involucrata*
Umsobo	Black nightshade	*Solanum nigrum*
Silele	Common purslane	*Portulaca oleracea*
Wild fruits		
Tincozi	Water berry	*Syzyguim cordatum*
Emakhiwa	Cape fig	*Ficus capensis*
Emaganu	Marula tree	*Sclerocarya birrea* ssp. *caffra*
Emantulwa	n.a.	*Vangueria cyanescens*
Emagwava	Guava	*Psidium guajava*

Note: The names of indigenous food plants are based on the local language (Siswati). Many of these plant species, particularly the wild species, do not have an English name (noted as 'n.a.'). Also, there are some indigenous wild food plants that the Swazi claim to use that have not yet been identified by scientists. These are noted here as 'unknown'.

Source: Malaza (1994), pp. 64–6.

The Swazi Food System and Agrobiodiversity Loss

Elderly men and women's historical accounts indicated that, before the colonial encounter with the British, the Swazi diet consisted of a variety of foods based upon multiple species of legumes, tubers, cereals, succulent vegetables, green leafy vegetables (mainly wild species), wild fruits and a small number of animal products (Table 14.1).

Ogle and Grivetti (1985) confirmed the existence of many of these food plant resources, but highlighted the fact that many of the indigenous leafy vegetables had become less popular, and that numerous species had been rendered extinct or reduced in availability by overgrazing and land clearing for agricultural production and construction. They also observed that none of the existing species were used today to their maximum benefit. Research in 1993 showed that the Swazi diet continued to lose diversity after 1985. Traditional food plant resources are now found mainly in the diets of rural households, lower-income households, older people, less-educated people, and households with a lower proportion of female members engaged in wage employment. Also, traditional food crops have been replaced by non-traditional food crops in urban households and among the better-educated, higher-income and younger-generation households (Malaza 1994).

Rural Diets

In all of the rural adult focus groups it was emphasized that there was a decrease in the consumption and production of indigenous food crops. With respect to traditional leafy vegetables, both men and women reported that they no longer ate many of the wild species they used to collect and prepare before intensive agricultural and cash crop production came to prevail. The major reason given was that women, who are the primary collectors, no longer have time to go to the mountains, bush lands and river basins to collect wild foods. Very few wild vegetables were still a major part of rural diets. The plants that were reported to be included today include *Corchorus* spp., *Amaranthus* spp. *Bidens pilosa*, *Momordica foetida* and *Momordica involucrata*. Consumption of even these few plant species appeared to be lower than the levels reported by Ogle and Grivetti in 1985.

All of the rural adult focus groups also emphasized that a decline had occurred in the production and consumption of succulent vegetables. The major reason that was cited for this decline was the shortage of seed. All of the succulent vegetables are preferred both for their leaves and fruit. Seed collection and preservation, and planting of all of the succulent vegetables, are strictly a woman's domain. Men are not even allowed to harvest these crops because they represent the power of a woman in the household, as maize represents the power of a man. Also, the Swazi yearly harvest ritual is conducted around the succulent vegetables. Men's participation in vegetable production only emerged with the introduction of exotic species such as cabbage and carrots, which are grown for the market (see also Wooten and Wilson, this volume). Of the three species of cultivated vegetables listed in Table

14.1, *Cucurbita pepo* was reported to be most popular, perhaps because this species produces leaves for a longer period of time than the other species. All of these succulent vegetables are usually intercropped.

The focus group members also attributed curative properties to many of the traditional vegetables (both wild and cultivated). For example, *Momordica foetida* and *Momordica involucrata* are used to treat high blood pressure and diabetes. *Portulaca oleracea* and *Aloe cooperii* are said to be good for pregnant women (Malaza 1994). In spite of these properties, however, use of wild vegetables has declined, in part reflecting the low status rural people accord these plants as a result of their colonial experience. As Ogle and Grivetti reported (1985), wild vegetables are associated with poverty, and people are embarrassed to admit that they eat them or to serve them to visitors. Rural women further stated that the seasonal availability of traditional vegetables also affects their consumption levels, since they do not have the time to preserve enough vegetables to last them through the year. Preservation is basically done by sun drying. Women also admitted that they now substitute exotic vegetables, especially spinach and cabbage, for traditional ones. A study conducted by Huss-Ashmore and Curry (1988) showed that the nutritional status of rural women and children was at its lowest level during the seasonal periods when traditional green leafy vegetables are not available. The superiority of traditional vegetables (wild and cultivated species) over most of the exotic vegetables in terms of nutritional elements such as proteins, calcium and vitamins has been documented for Swaziland and other African countries (Ogle and Grivetti 1985; Mnzava 1997).

All of the rural adult groups also reported a decline in the production and consumption of traditional cereal crops, tubers and legumes. In the case of cereals, hybrid maize was said to have replaced millet and sorghum. Millet was now a 'forgotten crop'. Some adult members were not even familiar with the crop. Sorghum production and consumption was also said to have declined a great deal since very few people still produce it. Its production was confined mainly to the Lowveld, where maize production was poor because of the climate. The men stated that sorghum and millet were very low-yielding and are labour-intensive, whereas maize had higher yields and demands less labour. The labour constraints of sorghum production were also echoed by women, who pointed out that sorghum production came to a halt when the children who used to help in production and by chasing birds away started to attend school (Malaza 1994). The women also emphasized that harvesting and processing sorghum demands a lot of labour and is not an easy task. Women still use a grinding stone to achieve the texture of sorghum powder that is required for certain dishes. The men also highlighted the fact that the maize commanded the best price in the market, and that traditional grains, particularly the dark ones, were not in demand. Certain local maize varieties were said to have fallen out of favour because of low yields and the dark colour of the grains. According to both men and women, white maize has become a symbol of 'civilization' (Malaza 1994). Sorghum, on the other hand, was associated with backwardness. Both men and women said that sorghum symbolized the past, and that they are no longer eager to produce it because they now live in the modern era (Malaza 1994). Women further stated that stiff porridge prepared from sorghum no longer appealed to them. The use of sorghum is now restricted to breakfast and to brewing an alcoholic beverage that is used in many Swazi ceremonies. Men stated that, if the price of sorghum were competitive with that of maize, they would consider producing it. They also emphasized the fact that they now grow crops that provide them with the cash needed to buy farm inputs. For example, an increase in the price of sweet potatoes has increased men's participation in the production of tuber crops, which were traditionally 'women's' crops. The shortage of seed for traditional tuber crops and cereals was cited as a problem. Women also cited a lack of access to land. The women stated that they try to grow the traditional tuber crops whenever they can because they are very 'handy in the kitchen'. For example, tuber crops can be served without a relish, in mixed dishes or with relish food items, which reduces the dependency on stiff maize porridge.

All of the rural focus groups stated that they had reduced the production of legumes, particularly jugo beans and mung beans. As the major legume producers, women gave the shortage of land and seed as the main reason they no longer produced them. The women also emphasized labour constraints: they first have to start by planting the men's cash crops (including maize) before they can plant their own legumes and, by the time they finish, it is too late to plant the legumes because the rains are gone. One woman illustrated this vividly when she stated that the men would often ask them if they had ever seen a cowpea granary (Malaza 1994). In other words, filling the granary with maize not only means cash income, but is also a symbol of status and power. However, women mentioned that, in the past (before commercial farming), men and women used to share land resources more equitably because the men also attached great importance to women's relish crops.

Women also emphasized the labour demands involved in processing legumes, including concerns about the availability of fuel for cooking legumes and other traditional food dishes. In all of the rural focus groups, women stated that preparing traditional dishes takes up a lot of time. One woman stated that they now enjoy the convenience offered by commercial soup and tinned food items, such as fish. However, women strongly emphasized the crucial role played by legumes in rural diets. The various species of legumes are used extensively to make a nutritious relish item that blends well with the stiff maize porridge. They are used in various types of mixed dishes and also as seasoning to improve the taste and texture of various dishes. Therefore, in spite of the fact that modern food items have been introduced, all adult members of the rural focus groups stated that they consumed more traditional food crops than modern food items. Some of the focus group members stated that rice and bread were luxury foods to them because these foods did not satisfy their hunger. The groups admitted that their food supply was heavily affected by the drought in 1992 because they had abandoned many of their traditional food crops as well as the use of wild plant resources. When suggesting crops that they would like to produce to improve their food security in times of drought, the women mentioned all of the traditional legume crops, tuber crops, succulent vegetables and sorghum, as well as cash crops. The women argued that today's lifestyles force them to depend on some of the modern food items. For example, they stated that bread has become a major part of their breakfast diet because their children have become accustomed to it.

Discussions with younger women in the rural focus groups indicated that they depend heavily both on traditional and modern food crops. However, unlike the adult members in their families, their choice of modern food crops was based on more than the convenience offered by modern foods with respect to preparation. The younger women admitted that they had become accustomed to eating modern food crops. They also stated that they do not know how to prepare some of the traditional dishes because wage employment and school attendance mean that they no longer spend a lot of time with their mothers. Unlike the adult members, they had never seen some of the indigenous crops, including many of the wild plant species. The knowledge of indigenous plant species had apparently declined drastically since Ogle and Grivetti wrote in 1985. When naming foods that they considered to be healthy, all of the young women named only modern items, which appeared to reflect both the issue of status and their ignorance about the nutritional value of traditional food plant species.

Urban Diets

Focus group discussions in urban areas confirmed that urban diets consist mainly of imported food items and exotic food crops. Rice and wheat products have become the most common staple foods in many households, except for the low-income households where maize is still the dominant cereal. Exotic vegetables such as cabbage, spinach and Irish potatoes, as well as meat, have replaced traditional vegetables as the staple relishes. The main reasons given for high consumption of modern food items were the convenience offered by modern processed foods in terms of ease of preparation, and the lack of traditional foods in the formal market sector. Both men and women (even though women still do most of the cooking) expressed the concern that traditional dishes take a lot of time to prepare, and that women, now in wage employment, no longer have much time to spend in the kitchen. Women also stated that they preferred to spend their time on other activities in the household. Like their rural counterparts, urban women expressed concern over fuel costs for food preparation, in this case since electricity is expensive. Some of the women further admitted that they do not know how to prepare many of the traditional dishes since they attended boarding schools where they ate and prepared only modern foods. Depending on where they were raised, some were unfamiliar with a number of traditional food crops and dishes. The issue of status also came out strongly among the urban focus groups. Men and women shared the sentiment that they would feel embarrassed or ashamed if they partook of traditional foods in public. When describing her eating habits, one woman stated that she tastes *sjabane* (a traditional Swazi mixed dish) only when she visits rural areas, but eats rice and salads regularly at home (Malaza 1993). However, all of the focus group members emphasized that income dictates what they eat. For example, they indicated that, when money is a problem, one eats soft porridge for breakfast, stiff maize porridge and sour milk for lunch, and stiff maize porridge and beans for dinner (Malaza 1994). There were a few people, however, who admitted that they enjoy eating traditional foods whenever they can find them. For example, many urban residents are often seen purchasing traditional leafy vegetables and boiled groundnuts and cowpeas from rural women in roadside markets. The urban groups further stated that they were not affected a great deal by the 1992 drought because they are accustomed to substituting rice, wheat products and Irish potatoes for maize.

The diets of younger urban people also consisted almost entirely of modern food items. Some mentioned that they tasted traditional food items (such as boiled groundnuts and beans) only once in a while because they liked them. The young people claimed that they have not been exposed to traditional foods. Some, however, stated that they do not like the taste of some of the traditional foods. Many did not know many of the traditional food crops and dishes. In their list of foods they considered to be good for one's health, they all mentioned modern foods, which reflected their domestic science curriculum in school and also the issue of status. They stated that their cooking ideas come mainly from magazines, cookbooks, domestic science classes and observation of their parents and friends.

All of the food practices and attitudes towards the use of indigenous food crops and plant resources highlighted by the urban and rural focus groups were confirmed by the survey, which revealed the following about the Swazi food system:

1. Modern cereals were the most frequently consumed food crops. In the diet of the people who reported eating these foods twice or more per week, maize was the most prevalent (86 per cent), followed by wheat bread (66 per cent), and rice (51 per cent). At least 73 per cent of the population reported that they never ate sorghum and 99 per cent never ate millet.
2. With respect to succulent vegetables, pumpkins and melons were the most frequently consumed (36 per cent reported that they ate succulents on a more frequent basis). At least 72 per cent of the people reported that they never ate the gourd species. Pumpkin consumption has been boosted by the sale of exotic species (butternut) in supermarkets.
3. Of the modern types of vegetables, 53 per cent of the people surveyed reported that they consumed cabbage on a more frequent basis. Spinach, lettuce, carrots and beetroot, respectively, were eaten by 38, 37, 35 and 27 per cent of households on a frequent basis.
4. Of tuber crops, the Irish potato was consumed frequently by the highest percentage of people (53 per cent). Sweet potatoes were second at 34 per cent. Cassava was the least popular tuber, with 93 per cent of households reporting that they never ate it. Taro root was the choice of (at most) 31 per cent of people on an occasional basis (three times or more per month). The preference for sweet potatoes has been boosted by supermarket sales.

5. As for legumes, a maximum of 47 per cent of households reported putting them on the menu, while beans were eaten more frequently. Eighteen per cent reported that they chose cowpeas on a more frequent basis. Jugo bean food dishes were occasionally eaten by 23 per cent (highest estimate) of households. At least 89 per cent of households reported that they never cooked dishes with mung beans. Groundnuts were eaten on an occasional basis by at most 50 per cent of the households. At least 82 per cent reported that they never ate sesame seed. Bean consumption has also been boosted by supermarket sales.

6. The number of wild vegetable species in the diet had been reduced to around five common species. *Corchorus* spp. was cooked on a frequent basis by at most 53 per cent of the households, *Amaranthus* spp. more frequently by 42 per cent, and *Bidens pilosa* by 30 per cent. Both *Momordica foetida* and *Momordica involucrata* were eaten by approximately fifteen per cent of the households on an occasional basis.

From the above results, it is clear that the Swazi food system has moved toward great reliance on fewer food crops to meet food needs, and that many of the indigenous wild plant species have been eliminated in most people's diets. Modern food crops are replacing traditional food staples and plant resources in many Swazi households. As highlighted in the focus group discussions, the loss of agrobiodiversity in the Swazi food system is related to gender differences regarding the needs for, use of, and value attributed to plant genetic resources. Men valorize these resources mainly on the basis of market values and status, while women's valuation of them is based on household dietary needs, culinary qualities of the crops and plants, convenience, labour, land shortages, cash needs, and status. Women's needs are undermined by their lack of control over production resources and time constraints (see also Howard-Borjas 2002).

Devalorization of Indigenous Diets and Gender Blindness in Swaziland's Agricultural Policies

Swazi government policies have also contributed greatly to the loss of agrobiodiversity. Swaziland's agricultural development policies are still strongly influenced by the British colonial system which chose to elevate the status of men as farmers, and relegate women to the status of helpers (Easton and Ronald 2000). Where the government has acknowledged women's status as fully fledged farmers in their own right and as food producers, this has remained largely a political recognition, without commitment in terms of application (Oppong 1995). Research stations and seed companies have maintained a bias against indigenous food crops and focused on producing hybrids only. As noted above, women reported problems with the supply of seed for the production of indigenous food crops. It is only in the 1990s that women's crops have become a major topic of discussion in prominent agricultural conferences after the country's experience with recurring drought episodes and crop failure (Swaziland Government 1996; Mkhatshwa and Dlamini 1997).

Besides making women farmers 'invisible' for many years, the government has intensified women's land problems. Its development policies have intentionally or unintentionally institutionalized barriers and constraints that were previously dictated by custom alone into formal laws and policies that regulate farmers' access to credit (Gladwin et al. 2000). Credit assistance for agriculture is tied to economic assets that women don't have and to cash crops. In this context, women's crops are denied access to agricultural support programmes since they are labelled 'supplementary crops' (Swaziland Government 1996). This has allowed the government to avoid making a commitment to meeting women's agricultural needs.

Women's traditional crops have also been systematically discriminated against because their market prices are lower than those of non-traditional crops, which consequently reduces the incentive to produce these crops (Easton and Ronald 2000). In addition, Swaziland's food security policy is anchored to the Southern African regional strategy of achieving self-sufficiency in maize production and in cereals in general (Gladwin et al. 2000; Regmi 2001). The focus on cereals has worked against promoting the production of root crops and legumes in dry areas where people depend on these foods to meet most of their energy requirements (Swaziland Government 1996).

The concept of 'supplementary crops' has also helped to promote the view that women's crops provide only a secondary income. In this context, the increasing financial needs of Swazi women as they assume more responsibility for paying school fees, purchasing food items and fulfilling other family needs through the market, continue to go unnoticed. Furthermore, over the last few years, the number of female-headed households has increased in Swaziland. Government programmes also continue to be blind to the increasing labour constraints that rural women face. These relate no longer only to identified issues such as male migration and school attendance, but now also to changes in the aspirations of young women and men who no longer find farming rewarding given the existence of other economic options (Oppong 1995). In the focus groups, rural women highlighted the fact that the young people and family members who are engaged in wage employment are no longer keen to provide labour for agriculture. Instead, they prefer to help by sending money home to hire labour and purchase other farm inputs. One woman commented that their young daughters-in-law would run away from home if they subjected them to hard agricultural work (Malaza 1994). This means that abundant free labour is no longer available to rural households, and particularly to enable women to produce all of the food crops that they need. In spite of all of these developments, research stations and the private sector have done very little to identify technologies that can resolve some of the production and food processing constraints that women face. Nutrition programmes in Swaziland also devalorize indigenous food crops. As is the case with agricultural programmes, they also neglect needs to promote, preserve and store indigenous vegetables and fruits. In the process of modernizing Swazi diets, more attention has been paid to exotic vegetables that lend themselves to Western-style recipes. Also, unlike other African countries such as Kenya, Swaziland did not promote the use of homegardens to enhance the production of traditional vegetables in either rural or peri-urban areas. Instead, homegardens were encouraged in order to produce exotic vegetables such as spinach, cabbage and tomatoes. All of these gender-blind developmental policies have greatly affected the production and use of a variety of traditional food crops in Swaziland.

Conclusions

The findings that have been presented in this chapter pose serious challenges to Swaziland's contemporary food system. Swaziland is confronted by the loss of agrobiodiversity and indigenous plant materials and by the need to meet the nutritional needs of different population groups, especially in rural areas and among the urban poor. Its dependency on food imports and on exotic varieties has serious repercussions for food security and nutrition.

The case of Swaziland has demonstrated that the specific needs and agricultural activities of men and women in an economy that is rapidly becoming urbanized and market-led, together with specific government policies that favour this process, drive the processes of loss of agrobiodiversity. To deal effectively with these challenges, Swaziland will have to invest heavily in agricultural infrastructure and in the promotion of local farming practices, diets and agrobiodiversity; it must also commit itself to addressing gender dynamics more seriously, particularly the needs of rural women who are the principal food producers and gatherers. The first issue is to acknowledge the fact that Swaziland now has multiple diets, mainly reflecting different rural and urban lifestyles. The second is the need to accept the fact that people rely upon a range of cereal and non-cereal crops to meet their physiological, mental and cultural dietary requirements. By ignoring this fact, the emphasis on cereal crops and the neglect of non-cereal crops and wild food plants in food security policies represents a serious weakness. Rural women must constitute the central figures in any intervention that is aimed at addressing both these issues and the loss of agrobiodiversity, because it is women who manage all household fields and provide diet-enhancing relish foods (Ogle and Grivetti 1985; Oppong 1995). Their production and processing constraints demand attention, particularly those related to labour, which will become more critical in the years to come because of the HIV/AIDS pandemic that has hit Swaziland and other countries (Haslwimmer 1996).

Given the changes in food culture and the new tastes that people have acquired over years of exposure to processed food items, as well as the changes in living conditions and women's occupational roles, there should be an emphasis on providing processed traditional foods to suit the new living conditions (Malaza 1994). In this case, small-scale village technology improvements might no longer be adequate to expand the production and consumption of some of the traditional foods (Swaziland Government 1996). This ought to be accompanied by strong and elaborate marketing programmes that will promote the nutritional and social value of the various traditional crops, and also create and promote a new image of traditional staple foods (Chweya and Eyzaguirre 1999). The nutritional value of traditional food crops has to be emphasized in all health-related programmes that deal with diet and nutrition. Programmes can also determine the importance of traditional food crops and wild plant resources for the management and treatment of diseases such as hypertension, diabetes, gout and HIV/AIDS, which currently affect large numbers of people in Swaziland (Mender 1998; Naur 2001).

Important key factors in this new venture are drastic measures to dignify women's food production and procurement activities and knowledge. First, agricultural policies and projects have to reflect the fact that women produce crops that are not 'supplementary' but rather constitute a major part of the nutritional spectrum for numerous families in Swaziland (Malaza 1994; Fleuret 1979; Easton and Ronald 2000). Second, rural women are the major custodians of knowledge about the stock of food plant resources available in various parts of the country, including knowledge about herbal plants and food crops that help to maintain everyday health (Ogle and Grivetti 1985; Howard-Borjas 2002; Chweya and Eyzaguirre 1999). The dignity to be accorded to women's agricultural activities and knowledge has to begin in the agricultural sectors and go as far as the classrooms of schools, colleges and universities. Otherwise, much of the knowledge about traditional foods and plant biodiversity will not be maintained, much less recovered (Chweya and Eyzaguirre 1999; IUCN ROSA 2000).

Sustaining healthy nutritional standards across different population groups consisting of different economic classes also presents formidable challenges to the Swazi food system, given its heavy reliance on food imports and reduced resilience to phenomena such as drought that are related to the predominance of exotic, high-yielding crop varieties. Rural populations and low-income groups, particularly women, suffer most from market fluctuations and food shortages. One way of minimizing the negative impact of the market and of drought on nutritional standards is to promote local agrobiodiversity in the food system so that people do not rely on uniform diets. Swaziland can achieve this by capitalizing on the already existing diversity of cultivated and wild staple and relish foods that characterize various regions and the diets of different social groups (Swaziland Government 1996).

The last challenge would be to enhance the supply of these foods, an achievement which will depend upon women's time investment in gathering, cultivating, processing, storage and preparation. Improved technologies for production and processing that make these tasks easier to perform will become critical. Also important is the need to compensate women for their time spent performing these functions (Guarino 1997; Howard-Borjas 2002). Increasing cash demands on women, along with the aspirations of the younger generation, mean that the compensation for agricultural work must be comparable to that afforded in other economic sectors. In the final analysis, strategies to strengthen Swaziland's food system and to address the loss of agrobiodiversity effectively must focus squarely on gender dynamics.

Note

1 Chweya and Eyzaguirre 1999; Guinand and Lemessa 2001; Howard-Borjas 2002; Gladwin *et al.* 2001; Easton and Ronald 2000; Mender 1999; Guarino 1997.

References

Chweya, J. A. and P. Eyzaguirre (eds.) (1999) *The Biodiversity of Traditional Leafy Vegetables*, Rome: IPGRI.

Easton, P. and M. Ronald (2000) 'Seeds of life: women and agricultural biodiversity in Africa', *IK Notes*, No. 23, Washington DC: World Bank.

FAO (Food and Agricultural Organization of the United Nations) (1999) 'Women – users, pre-servers and managers of agrobiodiversity', on-line at www.fao.org/sd/2001/pe1201a_en.htm

Fleuret, A. K. (1979) 'The role of foliage plants in the diet: a case study from Lushoto, Tanzania', *Ecology of Food and Nutrition*, Vol. 8, pp. 87–93.

Gladwin, H., M. Thomson, J. Peterson and A. Anderson (2000) 'Addressing food security in Africa via multiple livelihood strategies of women farmers', *Food Policy*, Vol. 26, pp. 177–207.

Goody, J. (1982) *Cooking, Cuisine and Class: A Study in Comparative Sociology*, Cambridge, UK: Cambridge University Press.

Guarino, L. (ed.) (1997) *Traditional African Vegetables: Promoting the Conservation and Use of Under-utilised and Neglected Crops*, Proceedings of the IPGRI International Workshop on Genetic Resources of Traditional Vegetables in Africa: Conservation and Use, 29–31 August 1995, ICRAF-HQ, Nairobi, Kenya.

Guinand, Y. and D. Lemessa (2001) 'Wild food plants in Ethiopia', United Nations Development Programme, Addis Ababa.

Haslwimmer, M. (1996) 'AIDS and agriculture in Sub-Saharan Africa', FAO Farm Management and Production Economics Service (ACSP), Rome: FAO.

Howard-Borjas, P. with W. Cuijpers (2002) 'Gender and the management and conservation of plant biodiversity', in H. W. Doelle and E. Da Silva (eds.), *Biotechnology*, in *Encyclopedia of Life Support Systems (EOLSS)*, Oxford, UK, http://www.eolss.net.

Huss-Ashmore, R. and J.J. Curry (1988) 'Report of the Food Consumption Survey Part Two: Nutritional Content of Women's Diets', Paper prepared for the Swaziland Cropping Systems Project, Swaziland Ministry of Agriculture and Malkerns Research Station, Swaziland.

IUCN ROSA (2001) 'Indigenous knowledge systems (IKS)', online at www.iucnrosa.org/zw/networks/sarniks.html

Kennedy, E. and T. Reardon (1994) 'Shifts to non-traditional grains in the diets of East and West Africa: role of women's opportunity cost of time', *Food Policy*, Vol. 1, pp. 193–208.

Malaza, M. (1993) 'Changing dietary patterns in Swaziland', transcripts from focus group discussions, Malkerns, Swaziland.

Malaza M. (1994) 'Food Security in Swaziland: Factors Influencing Dietary Patterns', PhD dissertation, Pennsylvania University, Ann Arbor, Michigan: University Microfilms International.

Mender, M. (1998) 'Marketing of Indigenous Medicinal Plants in South Africa: A Case Study Prepared in Kwazulu-Natal', FAO Forest Products Division, Rome: FAO, on-line at www.fao.org/forestry/fop/foph/marketing/doc/w9195e00.htm

Mkhatshwa, P. and G. M. Dlamini (1997) 'Indigenous under-utilised crops in Swaziland', paper prepared for the Agricultural Research Division, Malkerns, Swaziland.

Mnzava, N.A. (1997) 'Vegetable crop diversification and the place of traditional species in the tropics', in L. Guarino (ed.) *Traditional African Vegetables: Promoting the Conservation and Use of Under-Utilized and Neglected Crops*, Proceedings of the IPGRI International Workshop on Genetic Resources of Traditional Vegetables in Africa: Conservation and Use, 1–15 August 1995, ICRAF-HQ, Nairobi, Kenya.

Naur, M. (2001) 'Indigenous knowledge and HIV-AIDS: Ghana and Zambia', *IK Notes*, No. 30, Washington DC: World Bank.

Ogle, B. M. and L. E. Grivetti (1985) 'Legacy of the chameleon: edible wild plants in the Kingdom of Swaziland, Southern Africa. A cultural, ecological, nutrition study', Parts II–III, *Ecology of Food and Nutrition*, Vol. 17, pp. 1–64.

Oppong, C. (1995) *Gender and Population Issues in Swaziland's Development*, ILO/UNFPA/TSS/June/95/C.O.

Popkin, B. M. (1993) 'Nutritional patterns and transitions', *Population and Development Review*, Vol. 9, No.1, pp. 285–95.

Regmi, A. (2001) *Changing Structure of Global Food Consumption and Trade*/WRS-01-1, Economic Research Service. Washington DC: USDA.

Swaziland Government (1996) *The National Development Strategy: Agriculture, Land and Rural Development*, Ministry of Economic Planning, Mbabane.

CHAPTER 15
Arawakan Women and the Erosion of Traditional Food Production in Amazonas Venezuela

Shirley Hoffmann

Both the evolving role of women in the Guainia-Negro region of the Venezuelan Amazon and the erosion of plant genetic diversity in the late twentieth century can be understood only by examining the range of responses of indigenous societies to a changing economic, political and cultural context. In the north-west Amazon,[1] throughout history, women have been the principal guardians of plant diversity both in homegardens and in *conucos* (manioc swidden fields). Their relationships with plants and with household reproduction have changed with the incursion of 'modern' *criollo*[2] life into the furthest reaches of the Venezuelan Amazon region. The Arawakans are the indigenous peoples who have lived in the region since several centuries before Christ. Although they have had various degrees of contact with outsiders and *criollos* for over 400 years, traditional subsistence practices continued as the foundation of economic and cultural life. However, over the past 20–30 years, the extent and intensity of change occurring due to increased outside interest in the region has eroded this subsistence foundation.

Gender relations and the gender division of labour are developed within the context of household survival strategies. In the Guainia-Negro region, these survival strategies have been increasingly influenced by *criollo* practices and priorities, which are changing Arawakan gender relations. Arawakan women now go to school, work in *criollo* jobs, and move to larger population centres, all of which have eroded the importance of their traditional activities. Their knowledge of agriculture and plant biodiversity, which for centuries has been essential to household food security, has become less important. The 1970s were boom years in Venezuela's Amazonas region, accompanied by a strong increase in non-traditional employment and the introduction of government entitlement and food subsidy (welfare) programmes. During this period, the knowledge of traditional agricultural crops and their cultivation was no longer perceived to be relevant, especially for the younger generation that more quickly took advantage of new opportunities. This perception, which appeared to be reasonable and profitable during the boom years, has now jeopardized food security since, by the end of the 1980s, government subsidies had decreased and alternatives to traditional activities also began to disappear. How will the younger Arawakan women, who did not learn the knowledge and skills necessary to engage in traditional agriculture, cope when they find that they must attempt to return to the agricultural practices of their foremothers? How will the loss of knowledge about crop varieties affect the success of agriculture in the future? How does the loss of women's traditional knowledge affect their status and roles within Arawakan society?

History and Ecology of the Guainia-Negro Region

The geographical focus of this study is on an agricultural system characterized by very low productivity in the south-western corner of Amazonas in Venezuela. The area is drained by the Guainia and Negro rivers, a major tributary system of the Amazon River. The Guainia-Negro region forms a distinctive part of the Venezuelan Amazon because most of Amazonas is in the Orinoco drainage basin.

The low nutrient level of the Guainia-Negro watershed creates very low soil fertility and determines the types of crops and crop varieties that can be cultivated successfully. As a result of heavy precipitation and high temperatures, the soils are heavily leached, sandy and nutrient-deficient, with low pH. Many ecologists consider the region as the poorest in the Amazon Basin in terms of nutrients (Herrera *et al.* 1978: 223). The vegetation is less varied and smaller in size. The majority of the land is flooded for part of the year. Once the land is cleared for planting, heavy rainfall quickly leaches nutrients from the soil. Only crops that require fewer nutrients (most importantly calcium, magnesium, potassium and phosphorus) can be grown immediately after clearing and burning, before these nutrients are leached out. Only manioc (*Manihot esculenta*) and limited amounts of pineapple (*Ananas* spp.) can be produced after the initial harvest.

Almost all people living in the Guainia-Negro region are from the Arawakan language group, which has five related languages. Only a handful of *criollos*, or people originally from outside the region, have settled in the Guainia-Negro region (Catholic mission personnel, Navy personnel), and it is mainly these people who hold important official positions in the communities.

Subsistence activities are similar among the ethnolinguistic groups throughout the entire north-west Amazon[2] and include fishing, hunting, agriculture and other traditional activities. However, there are differences in the seasonal timing of activities, varieties of cultivars and some working techniques that distinguish the different groups' activities.

Historically, the life of the Arawakans in the region was based on fishing, hunting and gathering; agriculture only developed as population density increased. There were trade networks with other peoples, with some specialization in the production of goods such as *curare* (arrow poison), quartz stones used for grating manioc, and pottery and basketry. People sometimes travelled long distances to trade in these specialized goods. Settlements were formed with family groups living in communal longhouses. Manioc was the cornerstone of the agricultural system, but details about its cultivation and the cultivation of other crops are unknown both before and after colonial domination (Vidal 1987: 36; Wright 1981: 102–3). The history of the indigenous groups in the Guainia-Negro region was one of exploitation and population consolidation along the larger, most travelled rivers, and a slowly increasing dependence on imported goods from the time of first contact with the Portuguese and the Spanish.

Subsistence practices were undoubtedly affected by *criollo* influences. However, indigenous people remained fully self-sufficient in food production until very recently, when a relatively wealthy Venezuelan government began to provide support to the region in the form of jobs, welfare and social services for reasons of national security, and without expecting economic returns (Hill 1983: 391–2; Pérez 1988: 423–4; Sweet 1974; Clark and Uhl 1984: 358–65).

Today, the Arawakans still rely mainly on fishing and agriculture although, as is discussed below, they increasingly depend upon wage labour. Plant and insect gathering are of tertiary importance, and hunting is of minor importance. The gender division of labour is not extremely rigid, but tasks are quite clearly defined. If a man or woman takes on a task normally performed by the opposite sex, it usually indicates that there is a social or economic problem in the household. Men clear the fields for agriculture and sometimes assist with other agricultural tasks. They fish and infrequently hunt, and at the same time collect wild foods and other products in the forest. Women supervise the *conucos* and homegardens and have the detailed knowledge of cultivation and crops. They alone process manioc and prepare meals. They also collect wild foods. Women who have specialized knowledge make manioc graters and clay cooking pans. Men weave manioc sifters and manioc dough squeezers, although both men and women weave carrying baskets. The gender division of labour is apparently becoming increasingly flexible under the influences of school, religion and government. For example, men have begun to make wooden craft products to generate income, and women look for odd jobs to help pay for their children's school expenses.

Currently, men's primary job is to fish, thereby providing the main protein source in the diet. Because of the low nutrients in blackwaters and the low fish population density, fish are neither plentiful nor easy to catch, so the men spend most of their time fishing or performing related activities (Clark 1982: 347–9). As mentioned earlier, both men and women collect wild food. Men generally do more ranging through the forest when hunting and are responsible for selecting new agriculture sites. Because there are social and cultural taboos about women travelling through forested areas on their own, they mainly collect close to the trails that lead to their agricultural fields. Collecting provides additional nutrients and dietary variety, but the quantity of food collected in comparison to fishing and agriculture is low. Both men and women have a broad knowledge of forested area vegetation and usually snack on a wide variety of wild foods while working.[3]

Other activities that people engage in besides food acquisition and preparation include house building, handicraft production, housework and socializing. The first two activities depend primarily on plant materials collected from the area. Through the combined efforts of men and women, the people of the Guainia-Negro can supply themselves with sufficient food and many other basic goods. However, there are several key products that they must purchase: sugar and salt, clothing and boots, fishing gear and metal implements such as machetes, axes and knives, kitchen utensils, and shotguns and shells. Even the most self-sufficient families are to some extent tied into the national economy. This connection, which has steadily increased over the last 25 years, has changed the traditional subsistence system, particularly agriculture.

The Agricultural System

Conucos are small plots in the forest that are cleared for agriculture. Cultivation is a relatively straightforward process involving site selection, clearing, burning, planting, weeding, harvesting, replanting and, finally, fallowing. Swidden systems are found throughout the world's tropical regions. However, since they are adapted to locally specific ecological and cultural conditions, each swidden system is both complex and unique. The system in Amazonian Venezuela is distinguished by the flexibility that cultivators have in scheduling *conuco* tasks, and the limited number of crops that can be cultivated as a result of low soil-nutrient levels. Women have developed many distinctive techniques and practices related to both ecological and social factors to ensure the sustainability of *conuco* productivity over time (see Hoffmann 1993).

The major crop in the Guainia-Negro region is bitter manioc (*Manihot esculenta* Crantz), the major staple of the Arawakan diet, which constitutes over 80 per cent of all *conuco* production. Bitter manioc is a calorie-rich carbohydrate that requires extensive processing to remove the poisonous alkaloids from the roots. Other crops that provide some variety and additional nutrients for the diet that are not available from manioc include, in order of frequency, pineapple, *mapuey* (*Discorea* spp., a tuber), cashew (*Anacardium* sp.), sweet manioc (a non-toxic or 'sweet' *Manihot esculenta* variety that is boiled and eaten), sugar cane (*Saccharum* spp.), banana and plantain (*Musa* spp.), chile pepper (*Capsicum* spp.), *tupiro* (*Solanum* spp.), other tubers (*laigreng* – sweet potato, yam; *ocumo* – *Calathea, Ipomoea, Dioscorea, Xanthosoma* spp.), tree fruits such as guava (*Psidium* spp.), palm fruits (*Astrocaryum, Eurterpe* spp.), and *guama* (*Inga* spp.). With the exception of pineapple, these secondary crops are grown only in newly cleared old-growth forest *conucos*. Soil nutrients are sufficient to sustain only one planting cycle for crops other than manioc.

In comparison with *conucos*, homegardens have traditionally provided greater variety for the diet. Since they are located close to the house, plants can be tended more closely, new varieties can be tried out, and more valuable plants (which can be stolen from the *conuco*) are better protected. Homegardens contain not only food plants, but also medicinal, magic, ornamental and other non-food plants (see also Greenberg and Wilson, this volume).

Women are the primary cultivators. While men spend much of their time providing protein through fishing, women provide the bulk of the households' calories and micronutrients. They also process and store food and prepare meals.

As supervisors of cultivation both in *conucos* and homegardens, they are the decision makers in almost all facets of cultivation. Men provide some knowledge and skill in *conuco* site selection and the brute force needed to cut large trees (women also help in land preparation), but women decide when to burn, what and how to plant, and when to harvest and process manioc; they also identify and preserve cultivar varieties.

As food processers, women are responsible for the major task of rendering the poisonous manioc safe to eat. This requires a tremendous amount of effort on a regular basis: processing takes approximately the same amount of time overall as cultivation (Uhl and Murphy 1981: 13). Men's only support for this task is to collect weaving material and weave some processing tools. Manioc processing is usually done every couple of months and takes a week to complete. First, fresh roots are harvested and soaked anywhere from three days to a week to soften and ferment them. When they are ready, an equal amount of fresh roots are harvested. Both types of roots are peeled and the fresh roots are grated to a fine mush. The fermented and fresh pulp are mixed, and then the poisonous juice is squeezed out. The damp dough is then sifted and cooked until dry into manioc cakes (*casabe*) or grains (*manioco*). The ratio between raw product and finished manioc is about 4.6: 1 (Hoffmann 1993: 204). Women normally process a fairly large quantity of manioc at one time, to obtain about 10–20 kilograms of finished product.

Agricultural Biodiversity

A high diversity of crop cultivars is a hallmark of the entire north-west Amazon.[4] Arawakan women cultivate over 70 varieties of bitter manioc. At least two varieties of most other crops are commonly used, even though they may be of minor importance (*ibid.*: 104–6 and Appendix 2). Arawakan women classify the huge range of bitter manioc varieties into just two basic categories, based on characteristics pertaining to yield and growth (*ibid.*: 103). One manioc category has a root that is quicker to mature and enlarge (in as little as six months) and that decays quickly in the soil (12–18 months after planting). The other category has roots that take longer to mature (12–24 months) and that can be left in the soil as the roots continue to enlarge for long periods without decaying (36–42 months after planting). These root growth times are also somewhat dependent on the type of *conuco* in which they are planted: longer for newly cleared and burned old-growth forest, shorter for subsequent plantings in an old *conuco*. Women take these factors into account when determining which varieties of manioc to plant in order to have a steady supply of manioc over both the short and long terms.

Other manioc characteristics that have some importance in other regions of the Amazon – such as cultivar hardiness, ease of processing, productivity or pest resistance[5] – are not distinguished by Arawakan cultivators. Differences in colour, root shape, taste, texture, level of toxicity, ease of processing and nutritional content are also not characteristics that Arawakan women appear to consider when selecting planting material (*ibid.*: 107). Nonetheless, they maintain multiple manioc varieties. The differences that women use to distinguish bitter from sweet manioc varieties are visual only, consisting of root peel and flesh colour, stem colour, petiole and new foliage colour, and branching of the stems. Other minor characteristics that are sometimes used to distinguish cultivars are root peel texture and root shape, colour of the inner layer of the root peel, and overall plant height. All of these differences can be quite subtle; it is the combination of characteristics, or the 'gestalt' of the plant, that is used to identify the variety (see Boster 1985: 31). There is a relatively strong congruence between Arawakan women's varietal characteristics and the classification system developed by Rogers and Fleming to identify varieties of manioc from both South and Central America (Rogers and Fleming 1973).

Although differences between ethnic groups have decreased, there is still a reasonably strong correlation between the manioc types that a woman manages and her village and ethnic group affiliation. An Arawakan woman also collects manioc varieties through her kin and family connections and sometimes acquires varieties from sources outside the immediate region such as Brazil, Colombia or the Orinoco Basin. There is a lively exchange of varieties between members of extended families, and mothers pass down their varieties to their daughters. Serious full-time cultivators maintain on average eight to twelve manioc varieties. Thus, Arawakan women cultivators use manioc varieties as a medium of social exchange and as a source of group and family identity. Cultivators who supply the subsistence needs of their families have a keen interest in learning about new varieties and find a *conuco* with multiple varieties to be aesthetically pleasing.

Only a small to moderate number of crops other than bitter manioc are planted in a newly cleared and burned old-growth forest *conuco*. Usually only pineapple is sown in older *conucos* or *conucos* that are cleared from younger successional forest. Another class of plant found in *conucos* are those that are not planted but kept because they have edible fruit or leaves, such as *tupiro* or *caruru*, and palms such as *moriche* (*Mauritia flexuosa*) or *comare* (*Astrocaryum* spp.).

The greatest variety of crops is found in the homegarden. The most commonly grown tree crops include *manaca* palm (*Euterpe precatoria*), avocado (*Persea americana*), banana, *copuasú* (*Theobroma grandiflorum*), *pejiguao* palm (*Bactris gasipaës*), *temare* (*Pouteria caimito*), orange (*Citrus* spp.), and *guama*. Condiments, such as herbs and chile peppers (*Capsicum* sp.), and medicinal plants are also cultivated. The mild tropical climate means that people spend most of their time out of doors, so homegardens are actually an extension of the house. Arawakan women take pride and pleasure in their homes and put in extra effort to keep a variety of ornamentals and magic plants around the house.

Although experienced cultivators can identify the crop varieties, there are no apparent agronomic advantages to growing one variety over another. Experienced cultivators enjoy having multiple crops and multiple varieties, and go out of their way to achieve a broad mix of plants and varieties in their gardens and fields. People sometimes explain that specific varieties are perceived as a family and cultural heritage, so cultural and aesthetic decisions play an important role in traditional agriculture in the Guainia-Negro (see also Greenberg this volume). Women will put in a considerable amount of extra work for little or no return in terms of product simply for the pleasure of trying something new or having an attractive plant. This interest is not only a manifestation of their detailed knowledge of agricultural cultivation, but also demonstrates their pride in the key economic and cultural role that they play in the Arawakan family and society.

Traditional Agriculture and Socio-Economic Change

Traditional subsistence agriculture is changing together with women's roles in maintaining crop biodiversity, as can be seen in the village of San Carlos de Río Negro, with a population of about 600. San Carlos is the national government's district hub for the southern portion of Amazonas State, functioning as a medical, military, religious and educational centre. In addition to traditional subsistence activities, people in San Carlos have other opportunities and responsibilities. Women attend school, find jobs or marry someone who has a paid job. They sometimes become connected with the Catholic Mission, with its attendant benefits and requirements. The process of *creolization* is exemplified in San Carlos. The strategies that different women develop and the choices that they make affect their interest and involvement in maintaining agricultural biodiversity. These changes are a result of decreased time investment in traditional agriculture, the participation of younger women in formal education, a general devaluation of the traditional skills and way of life, and the increasing concentration of population with a consequent deterioration in the surrounding environment. Knowledge of plant biodiversity and maintenance of crop cultivars are decreasing as households become incorporated into the national economy. The latter process is expressed in social factors such as length of residence in San Carlos, the schooling level of daughters, and the increase in out-of-wedlock births among the younger generation of Arawakan women, all of which affect women's cultivation strategies. Three women with differing family circumstances illustrate this point.

Lucymar, a part-time cultivator, has a full-time job cooking at the local Navy installation. Her *conucos* are a ten- to fifteen-minute walk from town and are planted in young successional forest clearings that can only support manioc cultivation. Although her job pays well, she supports a household of 15 people, so that she must supplement food purchases with cultivated manioc. She has two unmarried daughters with children who do not help her to cultivate and have not learned cultivation techniques because they spent their younger years in school. Now they have no interest in supporting their mother's agricultural work and stay at home to take care of their children. Because the *conucos* are located on overused soil near town, Lucymar's *conucos* produce low yields, and she must apply an insecticide to control the leaf-cutter ants that infest frequently used fields with very short fallows. She cultivates six types of manioc but still needs to buy additional manioc to feed the household. There are times when she feels overworked and readily admits that her *conucos* are poor, but she says that even a little manioc helps.

She may well abandon her *conuco* as she gets older and, if so, there will be no one in the household who will take over.

Rosa cultivates full-time, although her husband has a prestigious job as a nurse in a village near San Carlos. Because she can count on a variety of purchased foods from her husband's income, she focuses on producing manioc supplemented by a few other crops. She has a greater interest in and spends more time on her *conucos* than does Lucymar, and cultivates thirteen types of manioc. Her *conucos* are quite distant from the town – at least a half-hour by canoe. Her manioc production meets the entire demand of her five-person household. Her children are not learning how to cultivate and, with a daughter already living in the city of Puerto Ayacucho and a husband who could transfer to the city, it is probable that she will give up cultivation completely and move to the city when their son is ready to attend high school.

Dolores, a new immigrant who came from a small village on the Guainia, practises her traditional tasks and works full-time in *conuco* cultivation. She keeps her household of six fully supplied with basic foodstuffs so they only need to purchase salt, sugar and other 'luxury' foods. She cultivates nine types of manioc as well as a number of other crops, and has a very diverse and complex home-garden. She plans to increase the number of manioc varieties as she lost several when the family moved to San Carlos. She also plans to continue to cultivate in the future. Two adult children live at home and her daughter has a small child, although she isn't married. Dolores does not expect her children to cultivate with her and, although they know some rudiments of *conuco* cultivation, their focus and that of their parents has been on their formal education. Although Dolores and Carlos will probably remain in San Carlos, their children are looking for opportunities in the city of Puerto Ayacucho and will move on when the opportunity arises.

These three women demonstrate that, with increasing dependence on resources from outside the traditional subsistence system, the importance of agriculture and the specialized cultivation skills required to maintain a dependable food source are lost as other priorities take their place. Also notable is the loss of knowledge about agricultural biodiversity and the capacity to cultivate that happens within a generation if the transfer of critical skills and knowledge is interrupted as a child matures. It is doubtful whether these skills can be fully recovered once the older generation is gone.

Cultures world-wide (including so-called modern societies) have lost many of the skills that were once vital to survival but that became obsolete (Lee *et al.* 2001). The question is whether the Arawakans are making the right choice by providing formal schooling instead of traditional training for their girls (it applies to boys also, but to a lesser extent), particularly given the instability of the local economy. For the last 25 years, national government programmes that were provided in this very isolated area in the interests of security and territorial control have created a welfare economy. Resources have come into the area in the form of municipal jobs, social services and economic development programmes with no expectation of an economic return to the rest of the country. With Venezuela's economic crisis in 1980, the devaluation of the bolívar and rising inflation, the government had to scale back welfare and subsidy programmes. There were subsequently cutbacks in the local economy in Amazonas. What previously had made economic sense for residents is not necessarily sustainable now as jobs are disappearing, social services are cut, and funding for economic schemes has dried up.

Agrobiodiversity Loss and Women's Work and Status

It is clear that an important subsistence agricultural system is deteriorating and that there is a concomitant loss of knowledge about and use of agricultural biodiversity. What might be the long-term effects? Women's key gender role as agriculturists is changing and their skills and knowledge now have less value in Arawakan society. How does this affect women's status in the society in general?

Although Arawakan women don't necessarily think that cultivating and conserving many different varieties of manioc or other crops has a specific utility, the overall maintenance of a variety of plant genetic resources, irrespective of whether specific characteristics are consciously preserved or not, promotes greater overall hardiness, adaptability and sustainability in agricultural systems (National Research Council 1982: 89). Cultivators' apparently stronger focus on aesthetic differences demonstrates that they consider biodiversity to be important and part of their wealth and cultural heritage, even though they may not provide specific utilitarian reasons for maintaining many varieties. Since some deterioration in the traditional agriculture system has been occurring for much longer than the past 25 years, at one time there may have been specific utilitarian reasons for maintaining certain cultivars, but those reasons have been forgotten. Even so, a cultural definition of beauty that includes objects that are important, useful and familiar helps to preserve biodiversity even though it doesn't appear to have a practical purpose (Zimmerer 1991: 342; Wilson 1997: 152). For Arawakan traditional cultivators, beauty is found in the technical skills that set cultivators apart from others, demonstrating their abilities and key role in society (Hapke 2001: 325).

In contrast, part-time cultivators have little interest in investing the extra effort to grow crops other than manioc or to maintain multiple varieties of manioc in their *conucos*. Young women who have only cultivated on a part-time basis may not even be able to distinguish manioc types. One result is the eventual loss of crop varieties. This is, of course, gradual, and the current number of 70 manioc varieties is probably lower than what would have been evident 20 years ago. Thus, *conucos* become a less rich source of manioc biodiversity and a less reliable source of food overall, since they only supply calories through manioc without providing micronutrients through other crops. The decrease in cultivar biodiversity is also reflected in homegardens. A comparison of homegardens in San Carlos between *conuco* cultivators and non-*conuco* cultivators showed that homegarden biodiversity was less for those who did not cultivate *conucos*. Of the three women discussed above, Dolores, who was a full-time cultivator, had the greatest variety in her homegarden and Lucymar, a part-time cultivator, the least (Hoffmann 1993: 157).

Homegardens continue to provide a variety of foods for cultivators (full-time or part-time) and non-cultivators alike in San Carlos, but the level of knowledge, interest and investment in them decreases with increased non-subsistence responsibilities. Some traditional subsistence knowledge is retained but not to the same breadth or depth as in previous generations (see also Turner, Pieroni and Greenberg, this volume).

Another outcome of socio-economic change is the loss of women's status as cultivators. Their gender role is changing as both macro-economic conditions and micro-level factors affect them (Hapke 2001: 325). When those changes are perceived as critical to household welfare, they can occur in a single generation. For Arawakan women, a formal education (at the expense of learning traditional cultivation), non-traditional means of earning a living and the encroaching ideologies of outside *criollo* culture have meant that traditional cultivators no longer have the high status that they once enjoyed. As other means of acquiring food become available, the role of the traditional cultivator loses much of its perceived importance. The increasing number of unmarried mothers who live with their parents partially reflects the fact that creating a separate nuclear household is not necessarily considered an optimal choice for young men or women. Without agricultural skills, they cannot afford to set up a separate household, especially when neither has a job. The resulting larger households create extra burdens on the food providers, ironically increasing the importance of cultivated food. In most cases, even with more people in the household, there isn't an increase in income sources, which creates even greater difficulties in procuring enough food for everyone. Because the household food level is less stable, the household has less rather than more capacity to withstand economic shocks such as job loss or medical emergency. The decreasing stability of food supply then encourages migration to Puerto Ayacucho, the state capital, where opportunities are perceived to be better. However, if the cultivator role is not considered to be important, even though production is both needed and expected, chances are that the finer points of cultivation practice will not be passed on to succeeding generations. The result is a partial system of swidden cultivation (see, for example, Conklin 1962) which may not be sustainable in the long term, either for the environment or to support the family.

There is a tendency to attribute the deterioration of traditional knowledge systems to the influences of modern society. However, even if such an attribution is correct to a certain extent, it assumes that traditional knowledge would otherwise be unchanging and always beneficial and sufficient for the people who hold that knowledge. This view, or various versions of it, is at best naïve and at worst simplistic and paternalistic. The importance of traditional knowledge, in this case women's knowledge of swidden cultivation, lies in its utility for supporting indigenous peoples as they move into the twenty-first century. This requires an acknowledgement by those who promote modernization that traditional systems can continue to be an important part of the social and economic system. In the case of San Carlos, people have been encouraged to give up subsistence production without considering whether the alternatives are viable in the long run.

In the Guainia-Negro region, a key factor influencing gender relations and agrobiodiversity conservation is the formal Venezuelan education system. Girls need a formal education: one of the few propositions that has been demonstrated empirically many times is that women who have at least a rudimentary formal education have healthier, smaller and more prosperous families (World Bank 2002; USAID 1999; Summers 1994; Schultz 1998). However, this does not appear to be the case in the Guainia-Negro. The current educational system encourages (both directly and indirectly) the abandonment of traditional activities in favour of a basically unproven modification of activities based on *criollo* values and perceptions (see also Turner, this volume). The message received by schoolchildren is that traditional activities and values are not important or correct, and should be abandoned. Another example from San Carlos illustrates the last point. The school in San Carlos keeps a couple of *conucos* and the children go out, as part of their classes, to care for them. However, these *conucos* are cultivated on the basis of the *criollo* principal's ideals of a 'proper' field. The teacher is from northern Venezuela, which has a completely different agroecosystem. She considers the abandonment of fields after only three years to be wasteful and indicative of laziness on the part of the indigenous people (they aren't willing to spend the time weeding older *conucos*). However, she doesn't take into account the fact that she has a free labour supply in the students and that, by the end of the third year, the productivity per unit of labour drops considerably. She doesn't need to consider the labour costs of food production (any cultivated food shortages are replaced by purchased goods) and the incursion of leaf-cutter ants when a *conuco* is cultivated for too long a period. She has pesticides available and the money with which to purchase them.

The message to the children is that their parents are lazy and inefficient and practise an antiquated and obsolete form of cultivation. After years in school, with a constant message that *conuco* cultivation is unskilled, menial and physically hard, most teenage girls actually refuse to help their mothers and live in expectation of 'greater' things. At the same time, viable and reasonable replacements for traditional activities are not widely available since, in reality, salaried permanent jobs are relatively few, and those that are lucky enough to have these are very careful to keep them. In addition, key traditional knowledge that is not learned in girlhood is not being recovered later in life. Either girls have lost their mothers by the time they are ready to learn agricultural skills or they have migrated to Puerto Ayacucho, to be met not only by a completely different ecosystem but also by land tenure regulations that prevent newcomers from acquiring *conuco* space near the large city. There is a resulting trend toward greater dependence on parents or on extended older families during young women's adulthood, a decline in nuclear families with fewer marriages between young people, and generally less prosperity in the extended family. Finally, schooling has helped spur migration to larger towns and cities in the hope (not borne out in towns like San Carlos, Maroa and the state capital, Puerto Ayacucho) that Arawakan youth may find greater opportunities for employment and a better life. These larger towns, which have provided more easily accessible welfare (subsidies, social services) to offset the fact that economic opportunities are limited throughout Amazonas State, are now having to decrease support to people who have become dependent on that welfare.

In part what is needed is a serious re-examination of the formal education system in the region, the subjects taught and the values imbedded within those subjects. Besides the basic skills of reading, writing and arithmetic, an education most useful to Arawakan women would also include key traditional knowledge – basic cultivation skills and techniques, manioc processing, and use of crop varieties. These skills must be based on what works within their agroecosystem and social structures, and therefore must be provided by senior Arawakan women. This type of integrated education, respectful of the usefulness of both old and new knowledge, would provide hope for the preservation of agricultural biodiversity while providing skills needed for today's modern world. It would reinforce the status of women cultivators as critical contributors to economic, subsistence and family life.

Conclusions

There is a continuing loss of knowledge of agrobiodiversity in Arawakan swidden agriculture, which jeopardizes the livelihoods of the Arawakans living in the Guainia-Negro region of Venezuela. The effects on Arawakan women, the traditional keepers of this knowledge, have also been detrimental. There is no modern replacement for this knowledge, which has been abandoned among many families along with sustainable agriculture, with a resulting instability in food supply. Women's key role in the household has also eroded. This has resulted in a restructuring of households, with fewer new nuclear households being formed and a dependence on the traditional skills of the older generation without the younger generation learning these skills or taking on these responsibilities. This trend will not be sustainable in the long term. Effects of this erosion can be seen in increased migration to larger towns and cities, where migrants have no real prospects of earning a living; household food supply variability, which at times results in hunger and malnutrition; and the *creolization* of Arawakan indigenous culture, which puts Arawakans at the margins of Venezuelan society and of their own traditional society.

Notes

1 This region is defined as the drainage system of the Río Negro, which includes portions of Colombia, Venezuela and Brazil. This study is focused on a small part of the north-west Amazon – the lower Guainia River in Colombia and Venezuela and the upper Negro River

that forms the border between Venezuela and Colombia.

2 González-Ñañez 1977; Jackson 1983; Goldman 1963; Meggers 1971; Marquez and Perez 1983.

3 Although I refer to collecting in the 'forest', it is often difficult to know the degree to which indigenous peoples have managed forested areas, especially around villages like San Carlos de Río Negro, which has been a permanent settlement since the sixteenth century. People are collecting food in the sense that they have not deliberately planted or tended the products they are gathering. They collect from former *conucos* in the process of succession to mature forest, or from areas that have been manipulated by people for many years such as along old, well-used trails or former house sites.

4 Carneiro 1983; Johnson 1983; Boster 1980; Jackson 1983; Goldman 1963.

5 Johnson 1983; Dufour 1981; Carneiro 1983; Boster 1980; Goldman 1963.

References

Boster, J. S. (1980) 'How the Exceptions Prove the Rule: an Analysis of Informant Disagreement in Aguaruna Manioc Identification', PhD dissertation, University of California at Berkeley, Ann Arbor, Michigan: University Microfilms International.

Boster, J. S. (1985) 'Selection for perceptual distinctiveness: evidence from Aguaruna cultivars of *Manihot esculenta*', *Economic Botany*, Vol. 39, No. 3, pp. 310–25.

Carneiro, R. (1983) 'The cultivation of manioc among the Kuikuro of the upper Xingú', in R. Hames and W. Vickers (eds.), *Adaptive Responses of Native Amazonians*, New York: Academic Press.

Clark, K. E. (1982) 'Subsistence fishing at San Carlos de Río Negro, Venezuela', in *An Annual Report and Renewal Proposal for the National Science Foundation Supported Project: Nutrient Dynamics of a Tropical Rain Forest Ecosystem and Changes in the Nutrient Cycle Due to Cutting and Burning*, Athens, Georgia: Institute of Ecology, University of Georgia, April.

Clark, K. E. and Uhl, C. (1984) 'Decline of subsistence life style in San Carlos de Río Negro (Venezuela)', *Interciencia*, Vol. 9, No. 6, pp. 358–65.

Conklin, H. C. (1962) 'An ethnoecological approach to shifting agriculture', in P. Wagner and M. Mikesell (eds.), *Readings in Cultural Geography*, Chicago: University of Chicago Press.

Dufour, D. L. (1981) 'Household Variation in Energy Flow in a Population of Tropical Forest Horticulturalists', PhD dissertation, State University of New York, Binghamton, Ann Arbor, Michigan: University Microfilms International.

Goldman, I. (1963) *The Cubeo*, Urbana: University of Illinois Press.

González-Ñañez, O. (1977) 'Los indígenas de las riberas del Guainía-Río Negro: etapas de un proceso de aculturación en la Amazonia Venezolana', Departamento de Antropología, Universidad Central de Venezuela, April.

Hapke, H. M. (2001) 'Gender, work, and household survival in south Indian fishing communities: a preliminary analysis', *The Professional Geographer*, Vol. 53, No. 3, pp. 313–31.

Herrera, R., C. F. Jordan, H. Klinge and E. Medine (1978) 'Amazon ecosystems. Their structure and functioning with particular emphasis on nutrients', *Interciencia*, Vol. 3, No. 4, pp. 223–32.

Herrera, R., E. Medina, H. Klinge, C. F. Jordan and C. Uhl (1981) 'Nutrient retention mechanisms in tropical forests: the Amazon Caatinga, San Carlos Pilot Project, Venezuela', in F. DiCastri, F. W. Baker and M. Hadley (eds.), *Ecology in Practice Part I: Ecosystem Management*, Dublin: Tycooly International Publishing, Ltd., pp. 90–4.

Hill, J. (1983) 'Wakuenai Society: a Processual-Structural Analysis of Indigenous Cultural Life in the Upper Río Negro Region of Venezuela', PhD dissertation, Indiana University, Ann Arbor,

Michigan: University Microfilms International.

Hoffmann, S. (1993) 'Subsistence in Transition: Indigenous Agriculture in Amazonas, Venezuela', PhD dissertation, University of California at Berkeley, Ann Arbor, Michigan: University Microfilms International.

Jackson, J. E. (1983) *The Fish People: The Linguistic Exogamy and Tukanoan Identity in Northwest Amazon*, Cambridge: Cambridge University Press.

Johnson, A. W. (1983) 'Machiguenga gardens', in R. Hames and W. Vickers (eds.), *Adaptive Responses of Native Amazonians*, New York: Academic Press.

Lee, R. A., M. Balick, D. L. Ling, F. Sohl, B. Brosi and W. Raynor (2001) 'Cultural dynamism and change – an example from the Federated States of Micronesia', *Economic Botany*, Vol. 55, No. 1, pp. 9–13.

Marquez, C. and A. Perez (1983) 'Los curanderos y santeros del Alto Río Negro como exponentes de un sincretismo cultural Amazonico', *Revista Española de Antropología Americana*, Vol. 13, pp. 173–95.

Meggers, B. (1971) *Amazonia: Man and Culture in a Counterfeit Paradise*, Chicago: Aldine Atherton, Inc.

National Research Council (1982) *Ecological Aspects of Development in the Humid Tropics*, National Academy Press, Washington, DC.

Pérez, A. (1988) 'Los Balé (Baré)', in W. Coppens (ed.), *Los Aborígenes de Venezuela*, Vol. III, *Etnología Contemporánea*, Caracas: Fundación La Salle de Ciencias Naturales, Instituto de Antropología y Sociología, Monte Avila Editores, CA.

Rogers, D. J. and H. S. Fleming (1973) 'A monograph of *Manihot esculenta* with an explanation of the taximetric methods used', *Economic Botany*, Vol. 27, pp. 1–113.

Schultz, T. P. (1998) *Returns to Women's Education in Developing Countries*, Baltimore: Johns Hopkins Press.

Summers, L. H. (1994) 'Investing in all the people: educating women in developing countries', World Bank Paper No. 45, Washington DC: World Bank.

Sweet, D. G. (1974) 'A Rich Realm of Nature Destroyed: the Middle Amazon Valley', PhD dissertation, University of Wisconsin, Madison, Ann Arbor, Michigan: University Microfilms International.

USAID (United States Agency for International Development) (1999) 'Girls' education: good for boys, good for development', Office of Women in Development, Gender Matters Information Bulletin No. 5, October, Washington DC: USAID.

Uhl, C. and P. Murphy (1981) 'A comparison of productivities and energy values between slash and burn agriculture and secondary succession in the upper Río Negro region of the Amazon Basin', in *Nutrient Dynamics of a Tropical Rainforest Ecosystem and Changes in the Nutrient Cycling Due to Cutting and Burning*, an Annual Report for the National Science Foundation Supported Project, Institute of Ecology, University of Georgia, Athens, Georgia, April.

Vidal, S. (1987) *El Modelo del Proceso Migratorio Prehispánico de los Piapoco: Hipótesis y Evidencias*, Tesis para Magister Scientiarum, Biología mención Antropología, Instituto Venezolano de Investigaciones Científicas (IVIC), Julio.

Wilson, W. M. (1997) 'Why Bitter Cassava (*Manihot esculenta* Crantz)? Productivity and Perception of Cassava in a Tukanoan Indian Settlement in the Northwest Amazon (Colombia)', PhD dissertation, University of Colorado at Boulder, Ann Arbor, Michigan: University Microfilms International.

World Bank (2002) *Engendering Development through Gender Equality in Rights, Resources, and Voice*, New York: Oxford University Press.

Wright, R. (1981) 'History and Religion of the Baniwa Peoples of the Upper Río Negro Valley', PhD dissertation, Stanford University, Ann Arbor, Michigan: University Microfilms International.

Zimmerer, K. S. (1991) 'Seeds of Peasant Subsistence: Agrarian Structure, Crop Ecology and Quechua Agriculture in Reference to the Loss of Biological Biodiversity in the Southern Peruvian Andes', PhD dissertation, University of California at Berkeley, Ann Arbor, Michigan: University Microfilms International.

CHAPTER 16
Women and Maize Breeding: The Development of New Seed Systems in a Marginal Area of South-west China

Yiching Song & Janice Jiggins

Maize (*Zea mays*) has been grown for many thousands of years in south-west China; some even claim that the region is one of the world's 'centres of origin' for maize. In the remote upland areas of the region, which is the centre of maize genetic diversity in China, maize today is the main staple food crop of the poor. This genetic diversity is of great interest to maize breeders, who are seeking to develop higher-yielding varieties for human consumption as China's population grows, and for use as a nutrient supplement in animal feed.

The first research report on farmers' own maize breeding activities was published by Song (1998). Four years of field study documented profound structural changes in agriculture in the poor rural areas of the south-west, revealing the hidden knowledge and skills of poor women farmers. Over generations they had acquired, refreshed and bred new varieties of maize, using many of the simpler techniques and skills familiar to professional plant breeders. This work opened the door to a second phase of research and action to involve men and women farmers directly in the emerging, market-oriented seed system as China cautiously opens up its agricultural markets to private sector and local government participation.

Before the introduction of a new Seed Law at the end of 2000, women farmers were marginalized by a formal seed system that neither recognized nor acknowledged their skills and experience in crop breeding and varietal selection. Poor women living in remote areas unfavourable for growing the modern high-yielding hybrids introduced by the formal system were simply not in the picture. The system also failed to perceive how fundamentally the political and socio-economic changes brought about by the gradual opening to the market system had affected women's position in marginal areas in rural society. As more and more of their menfolk have left the farms to seek work elsewhere, women have taken on the major responsibility for household food security and production. Today, the roles, responsibilities and leadership of women farmers have become central to the success of the initiatives currently on trial in south-west China.

The efforts of the professional plant breeders to work together with poor women farmers in varietal selection and breeding nevertheless poses a dilemma. The national interest is conceived in productivist terms, which pushes the professional breeders to select for higher yields and wide dissemination of genetically uniform varieties. The poor women farmers in the rocky, mountainous areas of the south-west ensure their food security by planting the small pockets of fertile soil with a range of varieties that are carefully bred to match the diversity of conditions. The reconciliation of productivist and biodiversity conservation goals is one of the surprising outcomes of the collaboration.

The Feminization of Agriculture and the Implications for Maize Development

The research carried out in the mid-1990s made visible to international and national maize breeders, as well as to local authorities in south-west China, the rapid socio-economic changes that were taking place in farming, and the implications of these changes for the conservation, development and use of maize genetic materials. The most profound changes were found in the structure of rural households and farming systems, and in related changes in the role of women in farm production (Song and Jiggins 2000). These changes could be characterized as the 'feminization of agriculture', which in China has multiple causes and effects. As pressure increases on poor rural households to participate in the cash economy, men are migrating in ever-larger numbers to seek wage employment in cities, local industries or irrigated agriculture in the lowlands. The bias towards male migration is formed in part by the patriarchal expectations of the family. The husband is supposed to provide for his family economically, guide the household's decisions, and mediate its relations with the outside world. Male migration is also favoured by gender discrimination in the wage labour market, which favours men over women in terms of job opportunities, and pays men higher wages even for the same work. Women thus are assuming a larger and larger responsibility for meeting the household and food needs of the rural family, while men seek to make their way in the modern economy, creating a system known as 'two households, one family'. Rural women are also assuming the costs of bringing up children, at a time when China's 'one child' policy has reduced the amount of household and farm labour available to support women's efforts. In the absence of their male relatives, women are also taking on unfamiliar roles in community leadership at a time when the certainties of government provision are giving way to the uncertainties and challenges of the market. The traditional division of labour between farm men and women, captured in the folk slogan 'the men till and the women weave', is surrendering to the new reality of 'women till and the men work in industry'. A survey of farmers has shown that, in selected areas of the three south-west provinces of Guangxi, Yuman and Guizhou, women comprise more than 85 per cent of the agricultural labour force (Song 1998). At the same time, the traditional expectation that 'men control the outside world, and women the inner world of the home' is giving way to the reality that women must stretch their 'inner world' to include farming and community responsibilities.

Two of the most difficult challenges that women farmers face in their new roles as farm heads were shown to be: (1) accessing viable improved seed from the public sector agencies responsible for seed management; and (2) maintaining a range of varieties that have the particular characteristics suited to women's preferences and farming conditions. Song also noted that two parallel seed systems were in place: one that is supported by the formal plant breeding sector, and one that is maintained by poor farm women themselves. The formal sector is focused on the breeding and dissemination of hybrid, high-yielding varieties, and is driven by the government's push to raise yields per hectare. In favourable conditions, these hybrids provide stable and high yields. However, many of the formal sector's hybrid products were the result of single crosses and lacked the buffering capacity to withstand environmental shocks or to sustain yields in the face of production constraints (Li 1990). In most smallholder farming areas in south-west China, the conditions are not at all favourable, and farmers also experience great difficulties in getting access to hybrid seed. Therefore, they rely upon exchanging the seed from their own harvests amongst themselves and on their indigenous maize-breeding practices.

Women Farmers as Expert Maize Breeders

In the case study village of Wenteng, women farmers definitely preferred open pollinated varieties (OPVs) for a number of reasons:

- The seeds can be saved and used again the following year, whereas hybrids lose their vigour after one cropping cycle;
- Farmers can manipulate the genetic material themselves to produce varieties that have desired characteristics related, for example, to yield, stress resistance, taste, storage, cooking qualities and the intensity of crop management;
- OPVs offer the continuing potential for evolution at the local level. The 1998 study was one of the first to document in detail the practices by which women acquired, maintained and refreshed their preferred varieties through OPV hybridization;
- OPVs can be crossed with materials brought into the farming system from elsewhere, including those obtained through the formal seed system. The word 'creolization' is used in this context to refer to the processes by which farmers maintain and improve introduced cultivars.

Women who were known in the village to be expert maize breeders skilfully control the breeding process from field design and seed selection through to pollination. The women claim that they have maintained their landraces (traditional varieties) through generations by separating the planting of landraces in space and time. The seed that is destined for the following year's planting is harvested, cultivar by cultivar, in a three-step process known as 'mass selection'. The first step is to select the best plants from the middle of the field, that is, healthy, vigorous plants with big maize ears. Step two is to select the best ears based on cob size, length and the number of seed rows. Step three is to select the best grains from the middle portion of each ear, based on kernel size, shape, quality and colour.

The women maize breeders also make new seed crosses using manual and mechanical methods to remove tassels from the seed plants before they shed pollen, and to collect the pollen from male plants for artificial pollination. In this way, women managed to maintain the vigour of one OPV variety, called Tuxpeño 1, which the government had released through the formal seed system in the early 1980s but subsequently neglected since new hybrids were coming on stream. One woman farmer breeder not only maintained the variety's vigour, but also adapted it better to local conditions. By 1998, more than 80 per cent of Wenteng's maize-growing area was planted to the women's improved Tuxpeño 1 which had spread through women's social and family networks, through women-to-women exchange, and through sales at local markets.

The curious point is that, with respect to the custodianship of seed and the management of local agrobiodiversity, for generations women have played a central role. It is only as labour and commodity markets have penetrated into the remotest areas of the south-west that this role has come to light. While plant-breeding expertise certainly existed and continues to exist among male farmers, and individual male enthusiasts take pride in their knowledge and management of plant diversity, it is the men's skills and knowledge that are eroding as they move off the farm. Yet, so long as the formal seed system is staffed mainly by men and remains focused on productivist goals, its products more nearly match male farmers' seed preferences than those of women. Thus, the choice of seed characteristics in the two seed systems reflects differences in responsibility and focus between women and men.

Maize Breeding and Seed Supply before the New Seed Law

From women farmers' point of view, the almost exclusively male networks of influence and communication in the formal system that persisted up to the end of 2000 were impossible to penetrate. Women's needs, skills and knowledge were ignored. The primary stakeholder in the formal plant-breeding process was the Ministry of Agriculture. The Ministry in turn was linked to public service extension agents, so-called 'leading' farmers, government plant breeders and government-controlled seed companies. At the same time, the government's policy of increasing yields through the development and release of hybrids failed to deliver products that were adapted to the real farming conditions in the smallholder sector (Lin 1998).

There were also institutional problems. The breeders tended to blame the extension workers for not communicating the advantages of the modern varieties (MVs) strongly enough and hence not getting them into the hands of sufficient numbers of farmers. The extension workers blamed the farmers for the poor adoption of MVs in more marginal farming areas. Further, since extensionists working in these areas communicated almost exclusively with the minority population of male farmers, they provided distorted feedback to higher authorities regarding the changes taking place in the structure of farming and regarding farmers' needs. In addition, local governments, Ministry officials and seed companies were rewarded on the basis of the number of new hybrid seed varieties released and planted, which biased the formal system towards agricultural areas that were more favourable for the production of released varieties. At the same time, some official voices began to express concern about the loss of biodiversity in the more favoured areas where the more genetically uniform MVs were displacing farmers' own varieties. The tensions created by divergent interests, communication blocks and deteriorating institutional relations between the central and local authorities began to threaten the continuing functioning of the formal seed system. At the same time, the political authorities were concerned that millions of poor farmers remained beyond the reach of the formal system and at risk of hunger, while the scientific capacities of the formal system did not seem to be able to reconcile production and conservation goals.

The New Seed Law: Opening to Innovation

Towards the end of the 1990s, the government began moving to ease the situation by liberalizing and privatizing certain roles and functions. The People's Congress approved a new Seed Law that became effective on 1 December 2000. It allowed the establishment of pilot schemes in order to test local options for a more effective seed system that might reconcile production and conservation goals, and to test ways to bring the formal seed system and poor farmers' seed systems into a mutually supportive relationship.

The opportunities that the new law opened up for local initiative, and the entry of new participants into seed production and exchange, can be illustrated by reference to developments in Guangxi Province. The Guangxi Maize Research Institute (GMRI) had formerly exercised a monopoly on maize seed production in the state. Under the new Seed Law, it was able, without reference to any other authority, to sign contracts with a 'seed production base', such as a village or farmers' organization, for the production of new planting seed. The conditions of such contracts are that the seed production base must be ready and able to multiply the seed that the GMRI develops, and to sell the seed harvest back to the GMRI for distribution to other areas. The villagers or farmers benefit by receiving twice the normal price for the new seed in comparison with sales of unimproved seed maize to the government. However, since the incentive price for seed maize remains lower than the market price for maize, new tensions have developed between the GMRI and its suppliers. Meanwhile, since all of the early contracts were issued to 'seed production bases' controlled by men, and to units in the somewhat more favoured areas, at first poor women farmers continued to be excluded.

Participatory Plant Breeding and Varietal Selection in Guangxi

A consortium consisting of researchers and government agencies is trying to resolve the new tensions created as local organizations begin to participate in the formal seed system. It found that the organizations were not fully compensated by the so-called

Table 16.1: Information on PPB/PVS Villages

Items	Wenteng	Zicheng	Niantan	Zhurong	Huaguang
Elevation	52	660	n.d.	580	620
Average annual rainfall (mm)	1860	1734	1800	1820	1860
Predominant soil type	Red soil	Red soil	n.d.	n.d.	n.d.
Agroecology	Open/forest, hilly areas	Prone to drought and waterlogging, rocky, mountainous	Drought-prone	Open, flat valley areas	Prone to drought and waterlogging, rocky, mountainous
Economic situation	Better-off	Very poor	Poor	Better-off	Very poor
Distance from market (km)	2	10	6	3	12
Population	3620	2146	810	4425	2566
Average level of education (years)	7	4	6	7	5
Total labour force	2839	1500	450	2200	1560
Total migrants	519	975	220	570	n.d.
Females among the migrants	140	235	66	120	n.d.
Average per capita income (yuan)*	2216	800	900	1200	7800
% of female-headed households	80	83	70	78	82
Average per capita landholding (ha)	1.62	0.94	0.8	0.79	0.95
Main cropping system (by rank)	Maize, bean, peanut	Maize, sweet potato, bean	Maize, bean, sweet potato	Maize, bean, sweet potato	Maize, sweet potato, bean

Average maize yields (ton/ha)	2.8	1.37	1.5	2.4	1.42
% maize area that is irrigated	62	0	5	20	0
% maize production area using chemical fertilizers	80	15	60	80	15
% households using chemical fertilizer in maize production	100	31	80	98	35
% households using purchased seed (hybrid) in maize production	85	0	15	70	5
Number of varieties used	3	5	5	4	5
% of hybrid growing area	60	0	10	45	3
% of households engaged in maize production for commercial purposes	70	10	40	70	15
Staple food crops (by rank)	Rice, maize	Maize, sweet potato	Rice, maize	Maize, rice	Maize, sweet potato

n.d. = no data

incentive prices for their efforts, and were still confronted by the gender bias that was simply carried over from the old system to the new. The main thrust of the consortium's efforts is to develop technical and institutional capacity in what have come to be called participatory plant breeding (PPB) and participatory varietal selection (PVS). Basically, PPB and PVS are processes for structuring collaboration between scientists and farmers throughout the cycle of maize development (Sperling and Scheidegger 1996; Almekinders and de Boef 2000). The project team is exploring ways to create partnerships in the emerging seed system that cross the private–public divide. The four formal-sector agencies involved are agricultural research and academic institutes located at national or provincial level, and the provincial authority responsible for agriculture.

Maize breeding is carried out together with publicly employed agricultural extension workers (AEWs) based at 'grassroots extension stations' located in the larger villages and rural townships, as well as with village-based farmer technicians (FTs). Although this has moved plant breeding much closer to where poor women farmers live, it has raised new issues. The public extension system itself is experiencing financial and operational difficulties in the transition from a planned to a market economy, especially with respect to the new expectation that the AEWs, who are mainly men, become 'servants of farmers' and not only servants of the state. The male AEWs have found it particularly difficult to adjust their behaviour and expectations in order to work collaboratively and respectfully with farmers who, in their eyes, suffer the double handicap of being women as well as poor. However, women FTs have been recruited who are known expert local maize breeders. They have introduced the male AEWs to other expert women farmers, so that their prejudices are beginning to break down. The advantage is that the AEWs and FTs are becoming enthusiastic about joining participatory networking with other actors in the emerging seed system as a way to develop their own skills and information, and to increase their professional effectiveness.

Participatory networking in the development of the new seed systems

In Guangxi province, five 'farmer plant breeding villages' have been selected in the trial area to represent farmers' seed systems: Wenteng, Zicheng, Niantan, Zhurong, and Huaguang. They have been selected on the basis of Song's previous research and on the analyses of local stakeholders, in order to represent a range of agroecosystems and socio-economic conditions, as well as a range of potential opportunities for institutional collaboration with women farmer groups.

The women farmer groups have welcomed the idea of becoming partners in the emerging network of public–private seed systems. They are proud that their expertise and knowledge have been recognized and valued. There are various kinds of groups, but mostly these turn out to be loosely organized pre-existing networks formed on a voluntary basis for various purposes, such as micro-credit, labour sharing, infor- mation exchange, and sharing (non-farming) knowledge and skills. The idea that they should now collaborate, learn and share for the purposes of maize breeding and seed dissemination thus represents an extension of existing practices, and permits already-existing experience and leadership to be drawn upon. In addition, the collaborating groups in each village have all received training in participatory techniques for collecting, analysing and interpreting their own data, so that they are better able to formalize and systematize their knowledge when in dialogue with the extension workers and scientists.

The process of collaboration

The farmers, extension workers and scientists are collaborating in three types of activities: diagnostic and exploratory studies, experiments in plant breeding and varietal selection, and evaluation of the new planting materials that emerge from the collaboration. Together they have designed eight different forms of collaboration in order to test the most effective ways of ensuring that institutional as well as social goals are met, and that the system delivers maize varieties that meet the technology preferences of both women and men farmers.

It has been something of a surprise to the scientists and extension workers to discover that men and women, the poorer and better-off farmers, or farmers in different farming areas, can make different choices when selecting the varieties and varietal characteristics that they prefer. Today, these actors are together learning, among other things: how to characterize the goals and needs of different types of farmers and of professional plant breeders; the socio-economic environments in which maize is grown; male and female farmers' preferences; indigenous practices and knowledge of plant breeding, seed selection and landrace maintenance; and how to identify the genetic importance of existing landraces and other creolized local varieties. The scientists are also trying to understand how farmers have used the genetic materials introduced by the formal seed system to create creolized local varieties.

In the process, the male extension workers and scientists are beginning to recognize how women's preferences are linked to their roles in the household. For example, women consistently give a higher rating to 'cooking quality', and to their need to ensure food security even if planting seed cannot be purchased from the market. In contrast, men tend to give higher preference to characteristics that match the demands of the market, such as ability to yield well when grown together with other high-value crops such as sweet potato.

The scientists are also realizing that there are marked differences in the number and type of selection criteria that professional plant breeders consider important, compared to those that farmers use. For example, six men and ten women farmers, three men and four women extension workers, and six men and two women formal plant breeders together examined maize trials during a field day in June 2001. The farmers mostly preferred improved varieties of established landraces and creolized populations rather than the 'superior' hybrid preferred by the formal breeders. The formal breeders assessed a variety almost exclusively in terms of yield and its value in the breeding programme, whereas farmers were also interested in a variety's performance during drought, or its ability to perform well even if fertilizer was not used, whether or not seed could be saved for the next year's planting, or the plant's shape, grain

Table 16.2: Comparison of Breeding Approaches and Focus of the Different Field Trials

Comparative items	GMRI Trial (1)	GMRI Trial (2)	Wenteng Trial	Zicheng Trial (1)	Zicheng Trial (2)	Zhurong Trial	Niantan Trial	Huaguang Trial
Breeding approach followed	Conventional scientific breeding	Formal-led PPB	Women-farmer-led PVS	Farmer-led PVS	Farmer-led PPB	Farmer-led PVS	Women-farmer-led PPB	Traditional farmer selection
Organizational form	Centralized top-down system	Decentralized work with some farmers	Decentralized work with women farmers	Decentralized work with farmers	Decentralized work mainly by farmers	Decentralized work with farmers	Decentralized work mainly by women farmers	Decentralized work totally by farmers
Germplasm in trials	Pop 961, 966	Pop 961-966, Tuxpeño 1 Foram and farmer landraces, etc.	Pop 961, 963	Pop 961, 963	F wax, L wax	Pop 961, 963	F white, L white	Pop 961, 963
Technological objectives	Productivity increase	• Productivity increase • Biodiversity enhancement • Local adaptation of germplasm • Increase in farmer-preferred traits	• Local adaptation of germplasm for OPV improvement	• Local adaptation of germplasm for OPV improvement	• Biodiversity enhancement • Crop improvement	• Local adaptation of exotic germpasm for OPV improvement	• Biodiversity enhancement • Crop improvement	• Local adaptation of exotic germplasm

Social/institutional objectives	For trial comparison	• Better understanding of farmers' system • Farmer skill building • Increase farmers' participation	• Farmer skill building • Farmer seed system enhancement • Women's empowerment	• Farmer skill building • Farmer seed system enhancement • Women's empowerment	• Farmer skill building through PPB • PPB testing	• Farmer skill building • Farmer seed system enhancement • Women's empowerment	• Farmer skill building • Farmer seed system enhancement • Women's empowerment	For trial comparison
Seed production and diffusion	Formal	Formal and farmers' system	Farmers' system	Farmers' system	Farmers' system	Farmers' system	Farmers' system	Farmers' system

Table 16.3: Comparison of Selection Criteria between Women and Men Farmers, Guangxi PPB Villages (frequency of selection in %)

Criterion	Women	Men
Drought resistance	100	100
Lodging resistance	90	83
High yielding	80	83
Seed self-saving	80	50
Grain colour	70	50
Cooking quality	50	33
Plant shape/suitability for intercropping	50	83
Low fertilizer rate	40	33
Maturation time	40	33
Market value	30	50
Plant height	30	33
Resistance to rat damage	30	33
Disease resistance	20	33
Insect resistance	20	33
Duration of growth cycle	10	50

colour and cooking quality. In addition to the differences in the selections made by men and women farmers, the farmers from the different villages also made different selections, reflecting the distinct climatic and other conditions of each village.

Empowering farmers' organizations

In all, the partners who work in the formal organizations are recognizing just how heterogeneous farmers' needs and opportunities are, and that a 'one size fits all' approach will not assist China to develop its agriculture as efficiently and productively as the authorities would like. Since the numbers of farmers and the areas to be covered are huge, this in turn is forcing an acceptance of a greater role for local organizations controlled by farmers and villagers themselves, as effective counterparts to the formal plant breeding and seed dissemination system. The process of building a partnership among the various organizations has involved a series of activities designed to help each partner to understand the emerging picture and to deliberate the various roles that each is and should be playing in the new system. The process has drawn in the public seed company managers and officials at the state, provincial and county levels. The current maize seed production and marketing systems, and the contrasting but complementary roles and operation of public seed companies and farmers in seed management, have been jointly investigated. This has led to heated discussions and to the proposal to link the women farmers' activities to the state-sponsored Women's Institutes, which are responsible for guiding women's development throughout China. These discussions and proposals are linked in turn to the major challenges to the authority of the Communist Party as it attempts to maintain centralized government in a vast and tumultuous nation, and the proper balance that should and can be struck between socialist and market forces.

Effects of Collaboration with Women Farmers on the Plant Breeding and Extension Professions

The collaboration is leading to changes in the ways that plant breeders and extension workers think about their work and behave towards women and men farmers. Over time, the knowledge, skills and attitudes of the breeders and extensionists, on the one hand, and of the farmers, on the other, are drawing closer together, which strengthens all participants. Routinely, 70 to 80 per cent of the participants in the collaborative activities are women, with the women professionals taking a lead role in ensuring that their male colleagues 'listen to and learn from' the women farmers.

The relationships forged through this collaboration are bringing about changes in knowledge and in communication. The key element in the strategy is to structure communication so that enduring organizational linkages are created. Procedures for interaction at key points in the breeding cycle are being normalized. One example of the normalization process is the joint design by farmers and formal plant breeders of a trial table that is used to record the preferences of different categories of farmers, by sex as well as by location and other variables.

The communication is centred on action, rather than on sitting around a table together 'just talking'. The 'field days', when farmers are invited to the research station or researchers are invited to farmers' fields, are playing a key role. Here, the slogan 'one family, two strategies,' develops shared meaning. The formal system learns how to meet the diversity of needs of men farmers who sell in state and national markets, as well as the even more diverse domestic and local market needs of women farmers that are related to the niche markets that they are developing for traditional speciality maize products.

Reconciling Conflicts of Interest: Yield Increase and Conservation

This process of linking and sharing among farmers, extensionists and formal plant breeders also reveals conflicts of interest. People working in the formal system in Guangxi are learning that they have to recognize such conflicts explicitly and to deal with them in a non-arbitrary way. Women are playing a central role in reconciling apparently divergent perspectives. For example, the government authorities have an overriding concern to increase yields and thereby promote food security by pushing hybrids into the marginal areas, but this is accompanied by a strong subsidiary anxiety that the maize genetic base is narrowing as the modernization of agriculture proceeds. The women farmers, who have other concerns, nonetheless have perceived that they have an interest in common with the authorities, around the *in situ* conservation of maize diversity within farming systems as a means to achieve food security among farmers who have few resources. The breeders have responded to the newly defined common agenda by prioritizing four types of varieties: exotics; local creolized varieties; and two types of local landraces, those conserved by farmers and those conserved by the research station.

Table 16.4: Decision Making and Division of Labour between Farmers, Formal Breeders and Researchers in Different Trial Models (by Ranking)

Comparative items	GMRI Trial (1)	GMRI Trial (2)	Wenteng Trial	Zhicheng Trial (1)	Zhicheng Trial (2)	Zhurong Trial	Niantan Trial	Huaguang Trial
Breeding approach followed	Conventional scientific breeding	Formal-led PPB	Women-farmer-led PVS	Farmer-led PVS	Farmer-led PPB	Farmer-led PVS	Farmer-led PPB	Traditional farmer selection
Main deciders								
• Setting breeding goals	B, R	B, F, R	F, B, R	F, B, R	F, B, R	F, B, R	F, B, R	F, R
• Defining the plant type for PPB and PVS trials	B	B, F	F, B	F, B	F, B	F, B	F, B	F
• Defining breeding and selection materials	B	B, F	F, B	F, B	F, B	F, B	F, B	F
• Defining breeding and selection methods	B	B, F	F, B	F, B	F, B	F, B	F, B	F
• Setting selection criteria	B	B, F	F, B	F, B	F, B	F, B	F, B	F
• Selecting parent materials and making crosses	B	B, F	F, B	F, B	F, B	F, B	F, B	F
Main implementers								
• Selecting land for the trials	B	B	F	F	F, B	F	F, B	F
• Adaptive testing on-station and in field	B	B, F	F, B	F, B	F, B	F, B	F, B	F
• Evaluating experimental varieties	B	B, F	F, B	F, B	F, B	F, B	F, B	F
• Producing seed	B	B	F	F	F	F	F	F
• Releasing and popularizing new varieties	B	B, F	F	F	F	F	F	F

Key: F = farmers; B = breeders; R = project researchers

As it happens, in two of the five villages the farmers prefer, in all four categories, yellow-grain maize as a good source of Vitamin A, whilst the preference in the remaining three villages is for white grains, for a variety of reasons related to local maize flour products and the relative importance of hog-fattening operations. By opening up the formal system to the diversity of farmers' preferences, while at the same time linking women farmer maize breeders to the wider range of materials held by the research station, biodiversity conservation has been strengthened in two ways: by widening the collection of materials accessible to farmer breeders; and by increasing the range of parental lines used by the formal breeders. In addition, the new genetic technology has given scientists the ability to track over time the impact of formal seed dissemination, the effectiveness of farmer-to-farmer seed exchange, and the efforts of extension, by inserting molecular markers into the seed released by the formal and farmers' seed systems. The impact of seed releases on the maize diversity present in farmers' fields will also be traceable. The information will contribute significantly to debates among experts on the potential for reconciling productivist and conservation goals in agriculture.

Conclusions

The pioneers in Guangxi are the professional plant breeders and extensionists who have reached out to work with women farmers, and the farmer breeders who are collaborating in the development of a major staple crop of national and international importance. They are showing what is possible through collaboration, and why it is important to achieve two interrelated goals – higher production for the market and biodiversity conservation – within the dynamic of a changing agrarian structure. Not without difficulty, they are showing how the barriers that have existed – between public and private, professionals and farmer experts, male extension workers and poor female farmers – can be broken down and a spirit of shared learning created around plant breeding as an activity of mutual interest. They are also forging organizational links that assign new roles and responsibilities among groups that hitherto have been kept apart, as well as dependent on centralized and top-down controls. While the total effort so far is small in relation to China as a whole, the lessons learned offer promise that women farmers' experience, skills and needs will be more respected as agricultural modernization proceeds. As women in the 'seed production base' develop their organizational and leadership capacities, and link up with support agencies on wider networks, they will be positioned to talk directly with decision makers in ways that can help shape the choices made.

References

Almekinders, C. and W. de Boef (eds.) (2000) *Encouraging Diversity. The Conservation and Development of Plant Genetic Resources*, London: Intermediate Technology Publications.

Li Jingxiong (1990) 'Maize growing under stress environment in China', in C. De Leon, G. Granados and M. D. Read (eds.), *Proceedings of the Fourth Asian Regional Maize Workshop*, Pakistan, 21–28 September 1990.

Lin, J. Y. (1998) 'How did China feed itself in the past? How will China feed itself in the future?', CIMMYT Economics Programme, Second Distinguished Economist Lecture, Mexico DF: CIMMYT.

Song, Y. and J. Huang (2001) 'Project annual report', submitted to IDRC and Ford Foundation, February 2001, Beijing: CCAP.

Song, Y. and J. Jiggins (2000) 'Feminisation of agriculture and related issues: two case studies in marginal rural area in China', paper presented at the European Conference on Agricultural and Rural Development in China (ECARDC VI), Leiden, 5-7 January 2000.

Song, Y. (1998) '"New" Seed in "Old" China: Impact Study of CIMMYT's Collaborative Programme on Maize Breeding in Southwest China', PhD dissertation, Wageningen Agricultural University, Wageningen, the Netherlands.

Sperling, L. and U. Scheidegger (1996) 'Results, methods and issues in participatory selection: the case of beans in Rwanda', Gatekeeper Series No. 51, London: IIED.

Botanical Index

General Index

Achuar people 24-5
acorns 197-207, 207n
Aegean islands 183
Africa 10, 12, 16, 101, 119, 239, 243-4; *North* 213; *sub-Saharan* 212, 243; *West* 16
agriculture, *agro-pastoralism* 86; *agro-tourism* 79; *bananas* 165-8, 171, 178, 229, 233-4, 261; *barley* 85, 89-90, 184, 192; *and biodiversity* 4, 17, 30-1, 38, 42n, 51-64, 96, 101, 190, 206, 211-13, 215, 224, 229-30, 239, 241, 243-56, 262-9, 273-87; *cash-crop* 11, 36, 245-6, 250, 254; *cassava* 9-10, 34, 105, 213, 243, 247, 252; *chemical inputs* 4; *in China* 273-87; *commercialization* 243-5, 250; *conuco system* 261-6, 268; *export* 35; *fallow system* 184; *feminization* of 33, 40-1, 274-5; *forager-farmers* 12, 83-96; *industrial* 32; *intercropping* 86; *livestock production* 4, 51, 54, 56-8, 86-7, 89, 92-3, 117, 137, 165, 184, 192, 211, 214, 221, 232-3, 287; *manioc* 24-5, 38, 258-9, 261-6, 269; *maize* 9, 19-20, 59-60, 86, 89-90, 119, 166, 171, 173-4, 193, 243, 245-7, 249-52, 273-87; *millet* 86, 89, 231-2, 243, 247, 249, 252; *modernization* 185, 287; *monoculture* 4; *oats* 192; *organic* 79; *in Papua New Guinea* 165-79; *potato* 9, 20, 86, 89-90, 138, 142, 166-8, 171, 173, 175-6, 184, 188-9, 216, 252; *rice* 105, 213-14, 221, 236, 243, 246, 250-2, 279; *rye* 192; *sorghum* 231-2, 247, 249-50, 252; *soybeans* 86, 89, 93; *subsidies* 185; *subsistence* 11, 21-2, 28, 35, 38-9, 54, 63, 86, 105, 117, 151, 167, 183-5, 195, 211, 230-1, 245-6, 258, 260-1, 263, 265-6; *sugar cane* 165-6, 168, 171, 178, 261; *sweet potato* 166-9, 171, 173, 175-8, 213, 216, 247, 250, 252-3, 261, 279, 281; *swidden/shifting* 38, 43, 83-4, 86, 93-4, 96n, 167, 258, 261, 267, 269; *taro* 165-8, 171, 173-4, 176, 213, 216, 247, 252; *transhumance in* 86, 93; *and urbanization* 232; *wheat* 86, 184, 187, 189-90, 214, 221, 243, 246, 250-2; *and wild plants* 101, 104-6, 112, 183, 190; *and woodland resource scarcity* 116;

yams 12, 87, 107, 165-6, 168, 171, 213, 216, 261
agroforestry 36
aid 35-6
Aksaray Province 183-95
Albania/Albanian people 66-79; *Kosovo* 76
alcohol preparation 88, 90, 95-6, 250
Amazon region 10, 24, 38, 158-9, 258-69
Amazon River 259
Amazonas State 258-69
Anatolia 13, 29, 183-95
Andes region 9, 20, 24, 150-61
Arawak people 38, 258-69
Arbëresh people 11, 29, 66-79
Argentina 3, 157
Arun Valley 85
Asia 16, 101; *South* 213; *South-east* 30, 213

Badala market town 234
Bamako 229
Bamana people 35, 229-41
bamboo 88-9, 91-2, 94, 107, 166, 168, 171, 214
Bangladesh 6, 23, 30, 102, 211-24
Barile village 69–79
Bedouin people 19
biodiversity, *and agriculture/homegardens* 4, 17, 30-1, 38, 42n, 51-64, 96, 101, 190, 206, 211-13, 215, 224, 229-30, 239, 241, 243-56, 262-9, 273-87; *Arawak women and* 262-9; *and beauty* 266, 281; *in Bangladesh* 211-12, 219, 224; *culinary traditions and* 9-11, 13, 32, 36-8, 58-63, 66, 253; *California Indian peoples and* 197-9, 206; *culture and* 3, 32, 36-8, 94, 102, 104, 197, 243, 263-6; *and development* 96, 254, 265-6; *exotic cash crops and* 229-30, 240; *fair and equitable sharing of benefits of* 33, 39, 41; *gender relations and* 35-9, 115, 126, 211-12; *and gendered ethnobotany* 150; *and gendered knowledge* 150, 240-1, 258; *images of* 94; *and indigenous/peasant peoples* 27-8, 94; *intergenerational responsibility for* 2, 51; *of the* jaṅgal 96; *and livestock* 190; *in Mali* 229-41; *Mapuche*

292

Deutsche Gesellschaft für Technische
Zusammenarbeit (GTZ) GmbH
l Dag-Hammarskjöld-Weg 1-5 l 65760 Eschborn
Telefon ++49/(0)6196/79-0l
Telefax ++49/(0)6196/79-1115

GTZ Profile

The Deutsche Gesellschaft für Technische Zusammenarbeit
(GTZ) GmbH is a government-owned corporation for
international cooperation with worldwide operations. GTZ's
aim is to positively shape the political, economic, ecological
and social development in our partner countries, thereby
improving people's living conditions and prospects. Through
the services it provides, GTZ supports complex development
and reform processes and contributes to global sustainable
development.

The GTZ was founded in 1975 as a corporation under
private law. The German Federal Ministry for Economic
Cooperation and Development (BMZ) is its main financing
organization. GTZ also undertakes commissions for other
government departments, for governments of other
countries, for international clients such as the European
Commission, the United Nations or the World Bank, as well
as for private-sector corporations. The GTZ operates on a
public-benefit basis. Any surpluses are exclusively
rechannelled into its own development–cooperation projects.

The organization has more than 10,000 employees in around
130 countries of Africa, Asia, Latin America, in the Eastern
European countries in transition and in the New Independent
States. Around 8,500 are locally contracted nationals
('national personnel'). The GTZ maintains its own field
offices in 63 countries. Some 1,000 people are employed at
Head Office in Eschborn near Frankfurt am Main.

International Development
Research Centre

Centre de recherches pour le
développement international

DPO Box 8500
Ottawa, ON K1G 3H9
Canada
Tel: +1 (613) 236 6163

IDRC Profile

The International Development Research Centre is a public corporation created by the Canadian government in 1970 to help communities in the developing world find solutions to social, economic, and environmental problems through research. IDRC's architects believed that the powers of science and technology could be harnessed to promote economic growth and development in the South. They envisioned an organization that would follow the lead established by Southerners themselves. The result was the first international organization to focus on knowledge gained through research as a means for empowering the people of the South.

IDRC's mandate is to initiate, encourage, support, and conduct research into the problems of the developing regions of the world and into the means for applying and adapting scientific, technical, and other knowledge to the economic and social advancement of those regions. To ensure that the Centre's programmes continue to respond to the needs of the developing world, a 21-member international Board of Governors oversees its operations. It has Regional Offices in six countries: Uruguay, Egypt, Senegal, Kenya, India and Singapore.

The goal of the Sustainable Use of Biodiversity Program Initiative is to promote the conservation and sustainable use of biodiversity. It also aims to develop appropriate technologies, local institutions, and policy frameworks through the application of interdisciplinary and participatory research that incorporates local and indigenous knowledge, as well as gender considerations. Given the changing roles and responsibilities of women and men in natural resource management in many rural areas, the program initiative stresses the importance of rigorous gender/social analysis in projects and programs to insure that the gender-differentiated impacts of these changes are understood.